Generalissimo Chiang K'ai-shek

THE CHINA
OF
CHIANG K'AI-SHEK:

A Political Study

BY

PAUL M. A. LINEBARGER
Duke University

GREENWOOD PRESS, PUBLISHERS
WESTPORT, CONNECTICUT

The Library of Congress has catalogued this publication as follows:

Library of Congress Cataloging in Publication Data

Linebarger, Paul Myron Anthony, 1913-1966.
   The China of Chiang K'ai-shek; a political study.

   Reprint of the 1943 ed. published by World Peace
Foundation, Boston.
   Includes bibliographical references.
   1. China--Politics and government--1912-1949.
2. Chiang, Kai-shek, 1886-   . I. Title.
DS774.L48   1973   320.9'51'042   73-725
ISBN 0-8371-6779-5

Copyright 1942 by World Peace Foundation

Originally published in 1943
by World Peace Foundation, Boston

Reprinted with the permission
of World Peace Foundation

First Greenwood Reprinting 1973

Library of Congress Catalogue Card Number 73-725

ISBN 0-8371-6779-5

Printed in the United States of America

TO MY MOTHER
With Love

ACKNOWLEDGMENTS

ACKNOWLEDGMENTS, for a work of this type, are always insufficient and often ungracious. Today, political and military conditions forbid mention of some of the persons to whom I am most indebted. Furthermore, it is unfeasible to thank those teachers and friends who have prepared me in years past for the present work. Nevertheless, courtesy and candor demand that I indicate the extent of my obligation, and tender these inadequate thanks.

For interviews, hospitality and other kindnesses shown me in Western China I wish to thank Generalissimo and Mme. Chiang K'ai-shek; Their Excellencies, Sun K'ê, Yü Yu-jen, H. H. Kung, Wang Ch'ung-hui, Chang Chia-ngau, T. F. Tsiang, Yeh Ch'u-tsang, Kan Nai-kuang, Ch'ên Kuo-fu, Wang Shih-chieh, Ch'u Chia-hua, Hollington Tong, and Ma Chao-chun; Major Generals J. L. Huang and Ch'u Shih-ming; Bishop Paul Yu-pin; and Messrs. Foo Ping-shêng, Chên Ming-shu, Lo Chia-lun, Edward Bing-shuey Lee, Han Lih-wu, P. C. Kuo, Ch'ên Chih-mai, Kinn-wei Shaw, James Y. C. Yen, Wang Shen-tsu, Shuming T. Liu, Jen Shieh, Li Ch'in-shui, and Ma P'in-ho. Among the foreign community, I wish to thank the American Ambassador, Mr. Nelson Johnson, and Mr. E. F. Drumwright for their kind reception; and to thank Mr. Tillman Durdin, Mr. Theodore White, Mr. George Fitch, Dr. J. B. Tayler, Professor Frank Price, and Professor and Mrs. J. B. Slocum.

I feel myself peculiarly fortunate in having three such good, loyal friends as Drs. Chu Djang, Miao Chung-yi, and Yin Pao-yü, whose kindnesses to me have continued ever since our student days together at the Johns Hopkins.

Dean Shen Ch'un-lu, Mr. Tso T'ao-fên and their associates in the National Salvation movement; Colonel Ch'in Po-k'u of the Communist Party; Mr. Chang Peh-chuen of the Third Party; Dr. Carson Chang of the National Socialist Party, and other spokesmen for minority and unofficial groups were most generous with their time and information.

Messrs. You Shoo-tseng, Yang Chun, Wu Hsüeh-ping, Hawthorne Chen and others translated Chinese materials for or with me. Save for their help, so liberally and painstakingly rendered, this book would have been delayed for months if not years. These gentlemen are not to be held responsible for the selection of materials, nor for the translations in their present form, since I have sought to check and revise this work as far as time and my imperfect command of written Chinese have permitted.

The International Peace Campaign (China Branch), The People's Foreign Relations Association, The Chinese-American Institute for Cultural Relations, and other institutions in Free China were generous with their hospitality and facilities. I owe particular thanks to the Central Bank of China for the high courtesy shown me through the Chief Secretary and the following gentlemen: Mr. T. T. Wang, Chief of the Engineering Division; Mr. Ch'ên Yin-sung, Manager, Kiating Branch; and Mr. Yang Hsia-tz'ŭ, Manager, Chengtu Branch. The officers of the Bank went to enormous pains to ensure my timely, safe return to Chungking when I was ill, hurried, tardy, and in danger of missing my prearranged bookings back to America. Special acknowledgment must also be offered to Mr. C. C. Chi, for his unfailing kindness in providing interviews and trips, and to the China National Aviation Corporation for their unusual courtesies.

In Hong Kong, I was assisted by Dr. Eugene Chen, Dr. Wên Yüan-ning, Dr. Ch'en Han-seng, and Mr. Liu Yu-wan.

In Shanghai, Mr. T. Nakada of the Japanese consulate-general was most helpful.

In Nanking, Messrs. Wên Chung-yao, Kiang Kang-hu, Tsu Min-yi, Lin Pai-shêng, Li Shêng-wu, Hsü Liang, George Wên, P. C. Huang, T'ang Leang-li, K. S. James Woo and L. K. Kentwell were most hospitable. Mr. M. Kimura, of the Japanese Embassy in Nanking, was kind and courteous. I wish to thank these gentlemen for their friendliness to an alien scholar who had just come from the other side of the war.

In Tokyo, Messrs, Yokachiro Suma, Yoji Hirota, Kaneo Tsuchida, and Nobuo Fujimura of the Foreign Office were hospitable and informative.

Mr. Robert Kempton, Mr. George Giffen, and Dr. Louis Wilkinson showed me great kindness on my journey.

In the United States, I am indebted for introductions and advice to Dr. Hu Shih, the Chinese Ambassador; Professor George Taylor, of the University of Washington; and Mr. Frederick V. Field, of the American Council of the Institute of Pacific Relations.

ACKNOWLEDGMENTS

My colleagues and friends at Duke University have been very helpful. Professors Homer Dubs and Paul H. Clyde, my colleagues in the Far Eastern field, read the manuscript and made invaluable suggestions; Professor Dubs' command of Chinese has saved me from many predicaments. Professor Robert R. Wilson has been unfailing in his encouragement, sympathetic interest, and facilitation of my plans.

The Duke University Research Council has assisted me with annual grants for the collections of documentary materials on Chinese politics. Save for this, I have received no financial aid or subsidy from any institution, person, or government whatever.

Mr. J. C. Yang, Mr. and Mrs. R. E. Hosack, Mrs. Freda Townsend, and Mrs. Margaret Linebarger have assisted me with manuscripts and proof.

I wish to thank the Director, Dr. S. Shepard Jones, and the staff of the World Peace Foundation for their patience, and helpfulness during the preparation of this work for the press. Miss Marie J. Carroll has been especially helpful.

All opinions and statements herein expressed are my own, unless clearly indicated as quotation. These acknowledgments are a record of thanks. I assume sole and complete responsibility for the contents of this book.

P. M. A. L.

Durham, North Carolina
March 31, 1941

WORLD PEACE FOUNDATION
40 Mt. Vernon Street, Boston, Massachusetts
Founded in 1910

Board of Trustees
GEORGE H. BLAKESLEE, *President*
FRANK AYDELOTTE
JAMES PHINNEY BAXTER, 3d
HARVEY H. BUNDY
LEONARD W. CRONKHITE
STEPHEN DUGGAN
HARRY A. GARFIELD
CHRISTIAN A. HERTER
BRUCE C. HOPPER
MANLEY O. HUDSON
A. LAWRENCE LOWELL
J. GRAFTON ROGERS
CHARLES SEYMOUR
JOHN H. WILLIAMS
HENRY M. WRISTON

General Staff
S. SHEPARD JONES, *Director*
DENYS P. MYERS, *Research*
MARIE J. CARROLL, *Reference*
MARY J. MACDONALD, *Treasurer*

THE World Peace Foundation is a non-profit organization which was founded in 1910 by Edwin Ginn, the educational publisher, for the purpose of promoting peace, justice and good-will among nations. For many years the Foundation has sought to increase public understanding of international problems by an objective presentation of the facts of international relations. This purpose is accomplished principally through its publications and by the maintenance of a Reference Service which furnishes on request information on current international problems. Recently increased attention has been focused on American foreign relations by study groups organized for the consideration of actual problems of policy.

CONTENTS

Frontispiece—Generalissimo Chiang K'ai-shek

	PAGE
INTRODUCTION	1
The Chinese Political Inheritance: Some Continuing Aspects	1
China at the Outbreak of War	6
The Beginning of Active Hostilities	11
The Hankow Period	15
The Chungking Period	19
I. THE CONSTITUTION	21
The *Yüeh-fa* of 1931	22
The Draft Permanent or Double Five Constitution	25
The Issue of Constitutional Change	31
II. THE POLITICAL ORGANS OF THE NATIONAL GOVERNMENT	41
The Five-Power Constitution	42
The Supreme National Defense Council	46
The President of the National Government	52
The Council of State	53
The Executive *Yüan*	56
The Military Affairs Commission	60
The Judicial, Legislative, Examination and Control *Yüan*	65
III. CONSULTATIVE AND ADMINISTRATIVE ORGANS	69
The People's Political Council	69
The Administrative Pattern	79
The Political Ministries	81
Social and Cultural Agencies	83
The Economic Ministries	85
IV. PROVINCIAL, LOCAL, AND SPECIAL-AREA GOVERNMENT	98
Chart on Provincial and Urban Government	facing 98
The Provinces	99
Local Government	103

	PAGE
The Communist Zone	111
Guerrilla Governments	116

V. THE KUOMINTANG 124
  The Party Constitutional System 125
  Party Organization 129
  The Kuomintang Bid for Leadership 140
  Intra-Kuomintang Politics 142
  The New Life Movement and Other Affiliates 149

VI. THE COMMUNIST AND MINOR PARTIES 159
  The Chinese Communists: Party and Leaders 160
  Communism: Patriotism or Betrayal? 171
  The National Salvation Movement 175
  The Third Party 178
  The Chinese National Socialist Party 179
  Social Democrats and *La Jeunesse* 181

VII. GOVERNING INSTITUTIONS OF THE JAPANESE AND PRO-JAPANESE 183
  The Japanese Army as a Chinese Government 185
  The Problem of Puppet States 188
  The Provisional and Reformed Governments 192
  The Reorganized National Government of Wang Ch'ing-wei 197

VIII. EXTRA-POLITICAL FORCES 211
  The Foundations of Chinese Government 212
  Mass Education 214
  Rural Reconstruction 218
  The Chinese Industrial Cooperatives 223
  Unorganized Pressure 234

IX. SUN YAT-SEN AND CHIANG K'AI-SHEK 239
  Sun Yat-sen 240
  The *San Min Chu I* 250
  Chiang K'ai-shek 254
  Chinese Appraisals of Chiang 266
  The Ideology of Chiang 269

CONCLUSION 273
  The Chief Alternatives in China 274
  The United States in Chinese Politics 277

APPENDICES

	PAGE
APPENDIX I: GOVERNMENT DOCUMENTS	283
A. The Government Draft of the Proposed Constitution	283
B. The System of Organization of the National Congress	300
C. Act of the Legislative *Yüan,* April 31, XXVI (1937) Governing the Election of Representatives to the National Congress	302
D. The Program of Resistance and Reconstruction	309
E. An Outline of War-time Controlment	313
F. A Chart of the Control *Yüan* from July 1937 to June 1940	318
G. Regulations Concerning the Organization of the Various Classifications of *Hsien*	324
H. A Chart of Government Organization facing	330
APPENDIX II: DOCUMENTS ON PARTY POLITICS	331
A. A Chart on Kuomintang Organization facing	331
B. Constitution of the *San Min Chu I* Youth Corps, Year XXVII (1938)	331
C. The Duties and General Activities of the *San Min Chu I* Youth Corps (Ch'ên Ch'êng)	340
D. The *Hsiao-tsu* (Small Group) Training Program	354
E. Party Constitution of the Chinese Communist Party	359
APPENDIX III: MATERIALS ON POLICY	371
A. Reply to Questions (Chiang K'ai-shek)	371
B. What I Mean by Action, or A Philosophy of Action (Chiang K'ai-shek)	373
C. Definition of the Problems Concerning the Organization of the Various Classifications of *Hsien* (Chiang K'ai-shek)	388
Chart on *Hsien* Classifications facing	388
D. A Discussion of Mao Tsê-tung's Comments on the Present State of International Relations (Ch'ên Kuo-hsin)	403
E. China's Long-range Diplomatic Orientation (Wang Ch'ung-hui)	418
GLOSSARY	423
INDEX	435

INTRODUCTION

THE National Government of the Republic of China, located at the auxiliary capital of Chungking, is one of the most important governments in contemporary world affairs. It has provided fairly effective unification for the largest nation on earth, and has fought a great power to a standstill.

The present work is an analysis of this government. Not a biography of Chiang K'ai-shek, it is instead a delineation of the institutions, the parties and movements, and the armies which today determine the Chinese destiny. Free China, mutilated as it is, is still far more populous and complex than the Soviet Union or Germany. Its political institutions cannot be reduced to the terms of one man's caprice, and the personality of Chiang—while brilliantly conspicuous—is not the entire picture of China. Generalissimo Chiang works, perhaps because he wishes to, certainly because he must, within the framework of a triune organization: the National Government, the central armies and the Kuomintang. These institutions have developed to their present efficacy only by means of thirty years of war, preceded by almost thirty years more of conspiracy. They have become the norm of contemporary China and, whatever their particular future, significant determinants of China's eventual development.

The Chinese Political Inheritance: Some Continuing Aspects

Because of cultural and historical differences between China and the West, the application of identical terms to both is probably either wrong or meaningless.

Nevertheless, Westerners can live in China, deal with the Chinese, scrutinize their affairs, and transpose these to such Western descriptions as may suit the purpose. In reading of China, however, one should keep in mind the fact that the words are English, freighted with special meanings, and are used not by scientific choice but for lack of others. Part of this difference can be bridged if one recalls the salient peculiarities of China as against the Western world.

No other society comparable in size, duration and extent has ever existed; the Chinese Empire, from the beginning of the Ch'in (221 B.C.) to the end of the Manchus (A.D. 1911), remains the greatest social edifice mankind has yet brought forth. As such, its modern successor is everywhere stamped with archaic catholic traits which are today both obsolescent and futuristic. To these must be added the characteristics of China as a special area—a cultural zone seeking national form; fragmented economies working their way out of backwardness in technology and helplessness in world economics; a people in quest of government which will give them power without enslaving them. This modern "Chinese Republic," a Western-form state only by diplomatic courtesy in the years succeeding 1912, has been the widest zone of anarchy in the modern world; the Japanese attack on its emergent institutions has helped immeasurably to re-identify the Chinese-speaking people and the officers who presume to govern them.

To understand Chinese government in war time, one might first check the outstanding points of old Chinese development and their modern derivatives.

Pre-eminently, China has been *pro forma* Confucian ever since the tenth century after Christ. This has meant an ordering of classes in society based on the ideal of scholarship and public administration, rather than on ideals of valor, piety or acquisitiveness. By setting the requirements of the examinations, and through concealed but sharp discouragement of heterodoxy or wilful originality, the governing mechanism made of itself a vast machine of scholars which—because its authority rested in tradition, in language, in social usages—was able to ride out domestic revolution and foreign invasion, and was in a position to ensure its own perpetuation despite political or military interruption.

The traditions of scholastic bureaucracy working in a pluralistic society have left the Chinese people largely independent of the routine functioning of government. The Western state becomes the articulation of society. The government of old China was pseudomorphic as a state, having only some of the functions of the Western state, and its governing power was the residual capacity of an organization devoted to the ends of ceremony, exemplarization, education and the cultivation of personality. Administration was confined chiefly to revenue collection, flood control and defense. In the West, the most important purposes of society are framed in law after discussion, and are executed as policy; in China these purposes, defined by the Confucian ideology, were known throughout the society, with scholar-officials as their expositors. Fulfillment was by no means a prerogative of government alone. By contrast with the Confucian standards, the Western states, whether democracies or not, are capricious, despotic and nonmoral; by Western standards, Chinese society was unresponsive, sanctimonious and amorphous.

This political excellence and stability was accompanied by economic phenomena which are, by modern standards, less desirable. Overcrowding and a slow rate of progress have been fairly constant features of Chinese society since the Han. Owen Lattimore has recently appraised the economics behind the dynastic cycle in

China.[1] Each community in old China was cell-like, largely autonomous and autarkic. Hence, the increase of wealth was sought within the cell, and not within a larger framework of economic advance—such as commerce or invention would provide—and the economically predominant class (the landowners) possessed a vested interest in overpopulation (which cheapened agricultural labor and maintained a high, even urgent, demand for food products). Equilibrium was reached, and a cycle of diminishing returns initiated, when population began to outrun the land's subsistence maximum. This drop in returns, in the face of continued population rise, led to peasant rebellion, distributism and a reinauguration of the same type of state—made necessary by the monopoly of managerial expertness (essential to water conservancy, land wealth and the familiar intensive cultivation) in the ideographically literate class. Control of the richest water-conservancy region meant the hegemony of China.

The impact of Western imperialism has struck China in the past century, during the critical or revolutionary phase of this immemorial cycle. Chinese politics took the color of a back-country struggle. The centers of modern power were beyond Chinese administrative reach. The emergent Chinese state, deprived of its foci of power in the metropolises, was promised control thereof only when it had become an effective and complete state—a condition largely unobtainable without control of Shanghai, Tientsin, Hankow, and the British Crown Colony of Hong Kong.

In theory, the Chinese Republic was established January 1, 1912. In practice, the name *Republic* has masked a *mêlée* of governments and power-organizations, ranging from bandit gangs with pretentious political color to

[1] Lattimore, Owen, *Inner Asian Frontiers of China*, New York, 1940, p. 45 and *passim*. The author, a noted geographer, presents significant new analyses of the interconnections of Chinese economics and culture.

authentic regional governments administering large areas. This culminated in the National Government which, beginning as a conspiracy, becoming the leading regional government, is now in the position of *de facto* government for virtually all Free China, the Chinese dominions, and much of the occupied area. None of these governments has ever held an election based on wide suffrage; none has systematically subordinated policy to law; none has possessed a treasury, fleet or air force worthy of a second-class power, until the present war. Out of these unpromising materials the counter-attacking Chinese state has arisen; only by legal formula is it the same Republic as its predecessors; only by courtesy is this the Year XXX (1941) of the Republic.[2]

The governmental developments of the Republican era fall conveniently into four periods: the period of establishment, 1911–1916; the period of *tuchünism*, 1917–1926; the rule of the National Government, 1927–1936; the period of invasion, 1937 to the present. The turning points between these periods are, respectively, the fall of the Manchu Empire of China (1911), the death of the dictator-President Yüan Shih-k'ai (1916), the Great Revolution under Kuomintang-Communist leadership (culminating, 1927), and the Sian affair (December 1936) followed by full-scale invasion (July 1937).

The present governments of China are accordingly the successors of a wide variety of decaying imperial administration, experimental modernism and outright confusion. Any change in China had to be made at the

---

[2] Detailed descriptions of the political history of the period are to be found, *inter alia*, in Holcombe, Arthur N., *The Chinese Revolution*, Cambridge, 1930; MacNair, Harley F., *China in Revolution*, Chicago, 1931; and, most popularly, Escarra, Jean, *China Then and Now*, Peiping, 1940. Descriptions of the government are Wu Chih-fang, *Chinese Government and Politics*, Shanghai, 1934; Lum Kalfred Dip, *Chinese Government*, Shanghai, 1934; and Linebarger, Paul M. A., *Government in Republican China*, New York and London, 1938.

expense of the *haves*—the Western powers and Japan. Japan, in seeking the control of China, is fighting China and the Western powers; China, in fighting back, must fight Japan, and behind Japan the whole structure of imperialism. Most Chinese have abandoned hope of surviving as a people without eventually triumphing as a state. In the past, they absorbed conquerors whose bases were transferred to China; today, they cannot accommodate invaders who come as transients from an overseas base. The Chinese war of resistance is a revolution. It is a continuation of the Nationalist revolution, begun against the Manchus, continued against the imperialist powers, and now directed against the Japanese and their Chinese associates. At the same time, this revolution struggles to incorporate in its dynamics the drive of an endemic peasant rebellion, Communist in its extreme phase. Nationalist in supreme emphasis, the revolution finds its highest expression in the articulation of an effective state—something not known in China for twenty-two centuries.

CHINA AT THE OUTBREAK OF WAR

Sun Yat-sen's legacy of doctrine included a program of revolution by three stages:

(1) the military conquest of power by the Kuomintang;

(2) the tutelary dictatorship of the Kuomintang while democracy was being instilled and adopted from the bottom up; and

(3) constitutionalism, requiring abdication of the Kuomintang in favor of a popularly elected government.[3]

---

[3] This is given in the *Chien Kuo Ta Kang* (Outline of National Reconstruction), of April 12, XIII (1924), particularly points 3, 5, 6, 7, and 23. Translations are to be found in Hsü, Leonard Shihlien, *Sun Yat-sen: His Political and Social Ideals,* Los Angeles, 1933, and Wu Chih-fang, work cited, p. 430 ff.

Upon coming to power in Nanking, the National Government had begun promising a short period of tutelage and had made various gestures in favor of experimental popular government. A Provisional Constitution was adopted by a *Kuo-min Hui-i* (commonly termed, National People's Convention) in 1931, operating under complete government supervision; a transition instrument, self-acknowledged as such, it anticipated a Permanent Constitution upon the accomplishment of constitutional government in a majority of provinces (Articles 86, 87).[4] Although the Kuomintang has ruled parts of China for more than fifteen years, and is by profession the party of democracy, it has not yet relinquished power. The period of tutelage is still legally in force.

In the years immediately preceding the outbreak of war, this monopoly of governmental power by the Kuomintang was not only an important political irritant but also an obstacle to effective Chinese unity. Discontent was aggravated by inelasticity of the Party. Overweighted with petty bureaucracy, it offered too few up-channel opportunities for potential leaders. Since Nationalists were the Ins, Kuomintang membership carried privileges rather than obligations. Many distinguished and active citizens either refused to join, or let their purely nominal membership ride along. The Party was saved from complete decline because it included most of the government personnel, and new recruits to government service gave it some freshness, vigor and inward criticism.

The leading difficulty of both state-building and democratization had been overcome by the creation of a government which was well-designed, functioning *de facto* and able to meet most of the specialized problems of modern administration. The regime was far from being a crude hierarchy of soldiers and taxgatherers,

[4] For the text of this constitution, see Wu Chih-fang, cited, p. 430 *ff.*

but had accrued about its policy-making core the essential staff and line services of modern rule. Inadequacies lay not in absolute lack of species of personnel or structure, but in the relative weakness of many key functions. During the third decade of the Republic the then Nanking Government, under Chiang's leadership, gave China its first modern national government.

Despite this beginning, which—without the invasion—stood a very good chance of evolving into a paternalistic oligarchy in democratic form, such as Brazil, there were enormous difficulties still facing genuine China-wide government. First among these difficulties was the question of regional autonomy—lingering vestiges of *tuchünism,* reinforced by a vigorous provincialism. Whole regions of China were under the merely nominal control of the National Government.

The second difficulty was that of personal politics. Modern China has had ample politics of principle. It is a rare ideological cult, of any kind, anywhere, which does not have its Chinese affiliates. No other nation has known such a wide choice of doctrines, each represented by armed forces and by definite political leadership. At the same time, this ideological struggle was and is paralleled by the politics of individuals and cliques. This made the National Government function as an oligarchy based on three patterns of control:

(1) ideological eminence, orthodoxy, appeal and timeliness;

(2) military or economic control of power in the form of soldiers or cash, the two being for the most part interchangeable; and

(3) governmental incumbency.

A man like Hu Han-min could owe his importance almost altogether to his past associations with the Party and with Dr. Sun, to his authority as an exponent of the *San Min Chu I,* and to his appeal to the sense of prestige, dignity and stability on the part of other people who did not possess such power, which was exercised in the name of the Kuomintang and its ideology. T. V. Soong, in money matters, or Chang Hsüeh-liang, in military matters, were important because they had under their immediate influence so much cash or so many troops, the availability and mobility of which from day to day determined their actual share of power. Lastly, these same men possessed political authority by narrowly lawful means, i.e., by the governmental offices which they held.

Thirdly, the government was deeply out of harmony with an overwhelming majority of college students, much of the professional and intellectual classes, and a broad section of the articulate farmer and labor groups. In the pre-war years of strain, unofficial persons could follow world fashions in ideas associated with Leftism. Although the full Western pattern of Right, Center, and Left was not imposed upon Chinese politics, many of the most active publicists wrote in these terms. There was, accordingly, a traditional China and a Leftist China; the latter faithfully imported European concepts and did much to change the language of Chinese political struggle. The government—itself Left from the point of view of the pre-existent order, yet committed to modes of thought and policy formally little more radical than the American New Deal—was constantly recalled to the most cold-blooded of *realpolitische* considerations.

Fourthly, the student movement—in some phases a part of the general Leftist drive—proved a constant source of difficulty and trouble. Chinese students (both collegiate and secondary) are self-conscious, frequently arrogant inheritors of the Chinese tradition of rule by *literati*. Their influence over the masses is impressive; their patriotism, however unreflective, is ardent; and their interest in international affairs is violent.[5]

[5] In particular, see Freyn, Hubert, *Prelude to War: The Chinese Student Rebellion of 1935-1936*, Shanghai, 1939. Reference to contemporary Left-liberal and Left publications in Europe and America

Fifthly, Chinese society, accustomed to acting independently of government, urged varied foreign policies and sought wars. Almost every kind of organization, from archaic guilds and secret societies to business groups, sought to wage its own attack on Japan. Uncanalized, counter-attacked, dammed up, these efforts might have undone the government. Toward the end, the government raced frenziedly with time, losing power through unpopularity, and increasing power through rearmament and technical preparation. The vigorous extra-governmental pressure of a populace accustomed to spontaneous mass action is a factor which qualifies and will probably continue to qualify Chinese foreign policy. It is often left out of account in Western comment on China.

Sixthly, in the winter and spring of 1936–37, the National Government was under pressure from its own subjects to begin the negotiation of national unity, starting with a Communist armistice and continuing with the incorporation of as many regions as possible into the sphere of the government; but despite such increasing pressure, the government took no effective step in this direction until after the kidnapping of Chiang at Sian.[6]

---

will disclose numerous sympathetic eyewitness accounts of the troubles and the fortitude of the students. Some of these accounts now possess a wry, inadvertent humor in their characterization of Chiang as a willing accomplice of Japan.

[6] For the Generalissimo's own diary of the kidnapping, together with a narrative by his wife, see Chiang, Mme. Mayling Soong, *Sian: A Coup d'Etat*, bound with Chiang K'ai-shek, *A Fortnight in Sian: Extracts from a Diary*, Shanghai, 1938. The Chinese edition of this appeared as Chiang Wei-yüan-chang [Chairman Chiang], *Hsi-an Pan Yüeh-chi* [A Fortnight's Diary from Sian], Shanghai, XXVI (1937). A first-hand Western account is Bertram, James M., *First Act in China*, New York, 1938. Edgar Snow, in *Red Star over China*, New York, 1938, p. 395 ff., gives an account sympathetic to the Left; Harold Isaacs, in *The Tragedy of the Chinese Revolution*, London, 1938, p. 445 ff., presents a penetrating Trotskyist critique. An excellent factual summary of this crucial year, written by a well-known writer who visited the scene at first hand, is to be found in Bisson, T. A., *Japan in China*, New York, 1938.

As a result of this melodramatic affair, however, the National Government revised policies which had become traditions ten years old and agreed to an armistice with the Communists. The Kuomintang—bearing full responsibility for an actual emergent state—found intra-Chinese diplomacy as perplexing as foreign.

Thus, at the outbreak of war, the National Government had reached a higher level of actual political and administrative power than its predecessors, but was faced with grave problems. In any other country the government would presumably have been on the verge of ruin. Controlling only major sections of its internationally recognized territory; faced by autonomous provinces, half-legal military satrapies and outright warlord despotism, all backed by vehement provincialism, great distances, linguistic difficulties and mutual geographical isolation; unpopular with its own student, intellectual and professional elites; ridden by personal politics; just emerging from a ten years' civil war—with these handicaps, a second-rate power undertook to challenge the greatest power of Asia to an irreversibly fateful war. The Chinese went further: they sought in the war not only victory, but unity, democracy and prosperity as well! This background of purpose makes China's internal politics richly meaningful in relation to the world scene.

THE BEGINNING OF ACTIVE HOSTILITIES

After nearly six years of military and political conflict, a full quasi-war [7] broke out with the episode at Lou-

---

[7] "War" used to mean the reciprocal application of violence by public, armed bodies; private and informal homicide was termed "murder" or was otherwise clearly designated. Today these distinctions are less clear. The author must enter a *caveat lector:* no term is employed in other than a general (i.e., literary) meaning, except upon special notice. The Sino-Japanese hostilities differ greatly from war in several interesting but technical respects; they are a very special Japanese invention. Yet it would be cumbersome to refer to Chinese changes in Conflict-time, or to speak meticulously of armies engaged in an Incident.

kouchiao on the night of July 7–8, 1937. It was the evident intention of the Japanese to end an unsatisfactory state of affairs (i.e., Chinese control) in that area once and for all, although they were perfectly willing to express temporary amity and *ad interim* non-aggression toward what was left of China. The National Government, after a few days of uncertainty, began real preparations for war. Since the government's appeasement policy had accustomed many to think of resistance in terms of the Left, there was an enormous inflation of Leftist sentiment, not deflated for about eighteen months.

While new mass organizations were formed, the Chinese military command framed a plan for a three-stage war:

(1) a period of resistance by heavy regular forces fighting positionally;

(2) a period of stalemate wherein enemy forces, immobilized by opposing regular armies, found lines of communication, supplies and business harassed by guerrillas and saboteurs;

(3) a period of counter-attack in which the Chinese, having prepared themselves technologically during the stalemate and having weakened the enemy by a test of endurance, should drive the Japanese back into the sea.

The strategy of this type of war was based upon the plan of retreating in space in order to advance in time— that is, to yield area slowly and purposefully, without too great cost to oneself, in order to outlast the enemy and reach victory. In thus purchasing time by the mile, the Chinese could not afford to yield intact cities, factories, communications, mines, docks, warehouses and the other goods of business; such cessions would only profit Japan: hence *the scorched earth* policy. The strategy was obviously suited to a country rich in territory and population, but poor in *matériel*. It not only made both regulars and guerrillas effective against Japan but made each truly reliant upon the other. Without the Nationalist regular armies, who in attempting to suppress the Communists had done almost everything which the Japanese now had to do—guarding railroads, pacifying disaffected and hostile rural areas, promoting industries and watching agitation—the Japanese forces might disperse enough to enable Japan to patrol and pacify enough of China to pay for the occupation. Chiang had to hold the Japanese together, immobilize large bodies of their troops, keep their war expenses up, and wait for the time to counter-attack. Meanwhile the guerrillas, together with the Communist veterans, were to prevent the Japanese from settling down, to worry them with agitation, to sabotage their economic efforts and to wear them out for Chiang's *révanche*.

One of the first governmental changes in wartime was the re-institution of an effective propaganda service under the Political Department of the Military Affairs Commission. In this Department, many of China's most active controversialists, censored or exiled for years, found officially sanctioned scope for their energies. Formal unity came slowly. Although Shanghai was attacked on August 13, 1937, it was not until September 10 following that a fairly definitive arrangement was reached in regard to the Communist-occupied zone in the Northwest.

The settlement transformed a pre-existing armistice into an intranational alliance; technically it amounted to submission by the Communists and their incorporation into the national government and armies. The area of the Chinese Soviet Republic assumed the name Special Regional Government of the Chinese Republic (*Chunghua Min-kuo T'ê-ch'ü Chêng-fu*), which it had been using informally for months; the Chinese Red Army became the Eighth Route Army (*Pa-lu-chün*); and the Chinese Communist Party accepted the *San Min Chu I* as the constitutional state ideology of China, abandoning immediate measures of class war and expropriation. The settlement was in the form of a Communist reply to Kuomintang terms offered in February 1937 and the reply of the Generalissimo as Chief of the Kuomintang to the Communist declaration.[8]

For the first few months the war kept its quasi-European pattern. The greater part of the fighting was done in the Shanghai area, while Japanese forces proceeded down from North China. The Japanese still had some expectation of localizing the North China and the Shanghai conflicts. At most, they expected the war to be a short one, not extending beyond the capture of Nanking. Occupation of the capital was counted on for the ruin of the central government, the end of Chiang and the reversion of China to a condition of malleable anarchy.

December 1937 was the blackest month of the war for the Chinese. The Japanese advanced toward Nanking, with Chinese resistance crumbling; part of the armies withdrew in good order, but on occasion there were hopeless, panicky routs. To this month the Japanese looked for victory, and were so confident that they formed the pro-Japanese Provisional Government of the Republic of China, in Peking on December 11.[9] Four days later the Japanese forces entered Nanking, and the ensuing fortnight set the record for atrocity in the modern world. The Japanese forces were preoccupied with their own disorder. The National Government

---

[8] See Council of International Affairs, *The Chinese Year Book, 1938-39* [Hong Kong], 1939; article by Chu Chia-hua, "Consolidation of Democracy in China," Chapter IV; "Reconciliation with the Communists," p. 339-40. This Council is an informal and extra-legal offshoot of the Chinese Ministry of Foreign Affairs; accordingly the annual, rich in official materials, provides insufficient data on Communist, guerrilla, and unofficial activities. See also, Epstein, I., *The People's War* [Shanghai], 1939, p. 88 ff., for an excellent, clear account of this period.

[9] See below, p. 193. See also Taylor, George E., *The Struggle for North China*, New York, 1940, in the Inquiry Series of the Institute of Pacific Relations.

escaped up-river to Hankow, where it promptly began to function under the three-headquarters plan: some offices at Hankow, some at Changsha and some at Chungking. The presence of the foreign affairs, propaganda, and military agencies at Hankow made this the practical capital of China, although Nanking was and is the constitutional capital.

The Hankow Period

The greatest part of the year XXVII (1938) was spent in continuation of slow retreat and heavy frontal resistance. Until October communications with the outside world were wide open through the railroad to Canton. Heavy supplies could arrive by the shipload. Hundreds of Japanese air attacks on the railroad disrupted schedules but never led to serious suspension of service. Leftist influence became overwhelming in Hankow. That city had been the capital of the ill-fated Wu-han Kuomintang-Communist government, which fell with the secession of Chiang to Nanking eleven years before; its connotations still lingered. Even conservative Kuomintang leaders, who had gone to lengths of appeasement at which Neville Chamberlain would have blanched, tried to talk like Negrin or Alvarez del Vayo.

In January 1938, two organizations were formed which, along with the Communist zone in the Northwest, were to be among the most active agencies of guerrilla leadership. The first of these was the New Fourth Army (*Hsin-ssŭ-chün*), which emerged in the area just south of the Japanese forces at the Yangtze mouth. It was composed of peasant and student militia, of regular army fragments, and of some Kuomintang volunteers, under the leadership of Communist remnants which had hidden away, banditti-fashion, when the Red Army trekked Northwest. Its emergence was recognized by legal order of the National Military Affairs Commission.[10] The other organization was the Provisional Executive Committee of the Shansi-Chahar-Hopei Border Region (*Chin-ch'a-chi Pien-ch'ü Lin-shih Hsing-chêng Wei-yüan-hui*), established by a conference at Fup'ing, January 8-15, and authorized by central government mandate. This agency also sprang from Leftist organizations—in this case, a bold, determined, student-peasant guerrilla army—which had first developed despite government opposition. It was designed to provide an emergency guerrilla government for those portions of the three provinces which were under occupation by the Japanese. Unoccupied portions of the provinces retained their existing administrations.

In the next month, February 1938, there was established an agency of supreme importance, the Supreme National Defense Council.[11] This replaced the Central Political Council,[12] which had exercised routine functions of the Party's sovereign control over the government; like its predecessor, the Supreme National Defense Council tended to act as the supreme governmental organ, although it was technically a Party organ. The Council provided and provides a unified civilian-military control for the duration of the war; but the Kuomintang shares its power with other groups only in the consultative organs of state, not in the executive.

March 1938 followed with another political step forward—the Emergency Session of the Kuomintang

[10] See Epstein, I., work cited, p. 235 ff. and *The Chinese Year Book 1938-39*, cited, article by the late P. C. Nyi, "Plans for Political and Economic Hegemony in China"; this includes a full administrative description of the Border Region, p. 254 ff. The North China zone is arbitrarily translated "Border Region," to distinguish it from the quondam Chinese Soviet Republic in the Northwest, translated as "Frontier Area."

[11] See below, p. 46.

[12] See chart on p. 47. Descriptions of the pre-war Central Political Council are to be found in the texts cited on p. 5, n. 2, and in the first two issues of *The Chinese Year Book, 1935-36* and *1936-37*, Shanghai, *passim*.

Party Congress. The Party Congress had the functions of a special constituent assembly in part, and in part those of a restricted parliament; in this session two further actions were taken. The first was the adoption of the momentous Program of National Resistance and Reconstruction (*K'ang-chan Chien-kuo Kang-ling*),[13] which provides a plan for the war and commits the Kuomintang and the National Government to a policy of victory, of industrialization, and of economic reform as a means to war.

The second step taken by this important Congress was the provision for a People's Political Council (*Kuo-min Ts'an-chêng Hui*, also translatable as People's Advisory Political Council). This was the first breach in the Kuomintang monopoly of government since the establishment of the Party dictatorship.[14] The government, through the constitutional fiction of appointing members as representative individuals, provided a rough, approximate, but fair representation of the active political forces in China.

While the Emergency Session of the Party Congress took these steps for further national defense, the Japanese were collecting a coterie of ex-politicians, friends of Japan, and old men to serve as the Reformed Government of the Republic of China at Nanking. They disregarded the anomaly of having two "Chinese" national governments—the Provisional Government in Peiping being undisturbed by these measures—and continued to seek the division of China, even on the level of the pro-Japanese States. The Reformed Government was established on March 27, 1938.

The autumn of 1938 brought another phase of discouragement. Relying on the prestige of British power

[13] See Appendix, p. 309.
[14] See below, p. 69. This is to be distinguished from the various constitutional conventions, the proposed national congress (*kuo-min ta-hui*) which exists only in contemplation of the constitutional drafters, and the Kuomintang Party Congress.

and the nearness of Hong Kong, the Chinese were not watchful in the Canton area. The Japanese landed almost unopposed. Chinese negligence, corruption, and a little treachery worked in their favor. The landing forces performed almost superhuman feats of endurance in forced marches overland; on several occasions Japanese advance troops ran so far ahead of schedule that Japanese warplanes, thinking them disguised Chinese, strafed them! [15] Canton fell without a major battle. Hankow, the great radical capital, scene of the 1926–27 Leftist upsurge and of the anti-Fascist enthusiasm of 1938, was entered by the Imperial Japanese army, and the entire Wu-han area was lost to China.

Not only was the Hankow period ended. By breaking the last rail connection of the Chinese government and the outside world, and by driving the Chinese leadership into the remote interior, Japan shut off the ready play of international influence on domestic Chinese politics. Foreign visitors became more rare. The government, moving to the mountain fastnesses of Szechuan, found a home on the great Gibraltar-like promontory of Chungking city, tiered along cliffs above the Yangtze and Kialing rivers. The last withdrawal was a final test of strength. Hankow, six hundred miles up-river, was commercially, architecturally, and politically a coastal city. It was still an outpost of world imperialism and of modern technology. With the next remove the Chinese government found itself beyond tangible Western influence; for the first time since 1860 the capital was out of the military reach of Western

[15] An engrossing first-hand account of this is to be found in Hino, Ashihei, *Sea and Soldiers*, Tokyo, 1940. This, with its three companion volumes, *Mud and Soldiers*, *Flower and Soldiers*, and *Barley and Soldiers*, Tokyo, 1939 and 1940, forms an eloquent, humane, sensitive narrative of a young Japanese writer serving with the Imperial forces in China. The series ranks with the great narratives of the European war of 1914–18, and expresses the Japanolatrist devoutness, the naïveté, and bewildering courage of much of the Japanese infantry, but does so through the medium of a literary craftsmanship rare in any army.

powers, and in a city which had only slight traces of Western influence.

The Chungking Period

The Chungking period began with the transfer of further government offices to the West, to join President Lin Shên, and marks a distinct phase in the process of government-building in China. As the Chungking regime, the National Government took new forms of temper and character. Government, Kuomintang, Communists—all were in the position of an inner-Asiatic state, without convenient access to the sea, seeking to fight an oceanic nation whose trade reached every port in the world. Foreign imperialism could no longer be blamed for the demoralizations of the hour; foreign aid was too tenuous and remote to qualify the inner play of Chinese political growth. Politically, the Chinese had to stand on their own feet.

The second phase of the war had begun. Chinese armies stood front-to-front against the Japanese, and kept hundreds of thousands of invading troops immobilized. The guerrillas got to work. Most of all, the machinery of modernization began functioning; all the programs had been completed, and the task was clear. The international developments of the time—the first American loan, $25,000,000 in 1938; the brief Manchoukuo-Outer Mongol war of 1939, wherein Japan and Russia fought each other through their respective dependencies; even the outbreak of the European war—were remote from this far inland scene. Military events had some effect, but nothing comparable to the Japanese victories at Shanghai, Nanking, Canton, and Hankow recurred. The Japanese invaded Kwangsi in the fall of 1939; they left a year later, when their drive into French Indo-China made it unnecessary to cut those colonies off from China. In South Hunan the Japanese suffered catastrophically when they advanced boldly and contemptuously into non-modern areas and were encircled by the Chinese. Even the flight and treason of Wang Ch'ing-wei at the year's end of 1938, and his open cooperation with Japan in March 1940, did not change the general picture. The emphasis was no longer on sudden changes, on personality, on dramatic shifts of power. It was on construction—on the development of a modern, democratic, technically equipped Chinese state out of the vast resources of China's hinterland. The China which was to win had to be created before it could counter-attack.[16]

[16] The literature of the war and of the struggles of Free China has already reached an enormous extent. The present work makes no attempt to present a step-by-step account of the interplay of personal politics, the progress of the armies, or to provide a first-hand personal account. Observers other than the author have presented these topics exceedingly well. A few of the outstanding works may be mentioned, however; a Shanghai press line usually signifies that the book was reprinted there from a British or North American edition. Epstein, I., *The People's War*, London, 1939, is a spirited, detailed account of development down to the spring of 1939, particularly useful for the New Fourth Army and the Border Region. Among accounts of the war are Bertram, J. M., *Unconquered*, New York, 1939; Oliver, Frank, *Special Undeclared War*, London, 1939, containing interesting accounts, in particular, of Japanese military and political behavior in China. Andersson, J. G., *China Fights for the World* [Shanghai], 1939; Utley, Freda, *China at War* [Shanghai], 1939, a significant personal account with special interest for the Hankow period; Mowrer, Edgar, *Mowrer in China*, Harmondsworth (England), 1938, published in America as *The Dragon Wakes*, New York, 1939; Booker, Edna Lee, *News Is My Job* [Shanghai], 1940, a reminiscent anecdotage; Lady Hosie, *Brave New China*, [Shanghai], n.d., a far more informed work than most of the autobiographical accounts, by the daughter and widow of two British Orientalists, herself a distinguished literary writer on China. On the North China situation, four popular works stand out: Snow, Edgar, *Red Star Over China*, New York, 1938, the great "scoop" on the Communists; and three other books based on first-hand reconnaissance: Bisson, T. A., work cited above; Hanson, Haldore, *"Humane Endeavour"* [Shanghai], n.d.; and Carlson, Evans Fordyce, *Twin Stars of China*, New York, 1940, the work of the U. S. Marine Corps Observer in the guerrilla area, unique in its value as professional military interpretation. Gunther, John, *Inside Asia*, New York, 1939, contains much of great interest. Very special viewpoints are represented in the account of a National-Socialist German observer, Urach, Fürst A., *Ostasien, Kampf um das Kommende Grossreich*, Berlin, 1940; the commentary of two British poets, Auden, W. H., and Isherwood, Christopher, *Journey to a War*, New York, 1939; and the reportage of a distinguished Soviet fellow-traveller, Strong, Anna Louise, *One-Fifth of Mankind*, New York, 1938.

CHAPTER I

THE CONSTITUTION

THE constitutional system, basic in most Western states, plays a peculiar, subordinate role in China. Consideration of the issue of constitutionalism highlights the most practical aspects of the issues of full democracy. Although the purely legal aspects of constitutional development are still unimportant in the internal power politics of China, further constitutional development involves a very real shift in the domestic balance of power. The fullness of national unity, and therefore the effectiveness of resistance against Japan, depend in part on the successful solution or compromise of the problems of constitutionalism.

Ever since the beginnings of political modernization in China, demands for constitutional government have included a written constitution as an imperative prerequisite. The formidable Empress Dowager was troubled in her last days by the Imperial constitution, a rather unimaginative plagiarism of the Japanese Constitution of 1889. Since the Republic began in 1912, China has continued constitutional drafting, amendment, replacement, and suppression; many of these constitutions have gone into legal effect. Law being what it was, practical politics flowed on untroubled.[1]

[1] On the Manchu constitutional programs, see *Columbia University Studies in Political Science*, Vol. XL, No. 1: Yen, Hawkling L., "A Survey of Constitutional Development in China"; Vinacke, Harold Monk, *Modern Constitutional Development in China*, Princeton, 1920; Cameron, Meribeth, *The Reform Movement in China, 1898–1912*, Stanford University, 1931; and Hsieh, Pao Chao, *The Government of China (1644–1911)*, Baltimore, 1925. The earlier constitutional developments under the Republic are summarized in Escarra, Jean, *Le Droit*

Only with the establishment of the National Government at Nanking did constitutional structure and actual government develop similarities.

THE *Yüeh Fa* OF 1931

In 1931, after three years' operation under an Organic Law, the National Government adopted the *Yüeh Fa* (Provisional Constitution),[2] designed to cover the period between the first stage of the revolution, *military conquest,* and the final one of *constitutional government.* This intermediate period was formally labelled the stage of *political tutelage,* although in fact the military unification of the country continued. The Provisional Constitution, designed for five years' use, has continued in force to the present (March 1941). It possesses the merit of attempting to make actual practice and constitutional form correspond. Grandiloquent, unenforceable provisions concerning elections are omitted, and full exercise of the powers of sovereignty are frankly entrusted to the tutelary Party, the Kuomintang. Such a constitution, formally making the Kuomintang different from and higher than any other party in China—and, for all that, in the world, since the Fascist, National Socialist, and Communist parties are not formally the constitutional superiors of their respective governments—and giving the Party unrestricted authority, has provided China with government realistic if not libertarian.

Chinois, Paris and Peiping, 1936, which includes excellent bibliographies; Tsêng Yu-hao, *Modern Chinese Legal and Political Philosophy,* Shanghai, 1934, Ch. VI, "The Law of Modern Chinese Constitutions"; a characteristic proposal for a pre-Kuomintang constitution is Bau, Mingchien Joshua, *Modern Democracy in China,* Shanghai, 1927; and the works of Lum, Wu, and Linebarger, cited above.

[2] The text of the *Yüeh Fa* is to be found in *The China Year Book, 1932,* Shanghai, 1932, and in Lum, work cited, p. 161 ff., and Wu Chihfang, work cited, p. 410 ff. The Chinese texts of all outstanding Chinese constitutions, from the Imperial programs down to the Double Five Draft of the *Hsien Fa* are to be found in Wang Shih-chieh, *Pi-chiao Hsien-fa,* Shanghai, 1937, p. 699–796.

The constitutional basis of the present Party-dictatorship in China is well summarized by the distinguished constitutional commentator, Dr. Wang Shih-chieh:

> According to Sun Chung-shan's [3] *Chien-kuo Ta-kang* [Outlines of National Reconstruction], China should pass through a period of political tutelage under the Chinese Kuomintang, [4] before the stage of constitutional government be reached. The National Government is merely an organization through which a true republic may be formed. Hence, in order to demonstrate the structure of the National Government clearly, we must first understand the meaning of *tang chih* [party government].
>
> "Party government," so-called, signifies that the whole system of government is under the control or dictatorship of one political party only. The only difference between party government and dictatorship is that the former is under the dictatorship of an entire political party, while the latter is under that of a single person. Party government is of course different from democracy, inasmuch as with democracy, all policies are to be decided by the entire body of citizens, while with party government, policies are to be decided by all the members of the particular party only. In other words, the entire party as one man can exercise political dictatorship, without taking into consideration the opinions of those who are not the members of the party. Any resolution passed by that party is considered a law not only in fact, but sometimes even in name; moreover, the party may cancel or change a law by a resolution passed in a meeting.
>
> The above-mentioned points are phenomena common to countries under party governments.
>
> After the Chinese Kuomintang has come into power, the system of party government is not only a fact, but even prescribed in laws. The *Laws Governing the System of Organization of the National Government of the Republic*

---

[3] I.e., Sun Yat-sen; Chung-shan was a revolutionary alias, which became a ceremonial posthumous name.

[4] The term "Chinese Kuomintang" is not a redundancy; the original is *Chung-kuo Kuo-min-tang*, "Central-Realm Realm-people-association," and could be translated as the Chinese Nationalist Populist Party, National Democratic Party, the Nation's People's Party, etc. Several Japanese organizations have had exceedingly similar names; hence the formal style for the Kuomintang is always prefaced by *China*.

of China promulgated for the first time on July 1, Year XIV (1925) were originally formulated by the Political Council of the Chinese Kuomintang. Article I in this code of laws provided: "The National Government discharges all the political affairs of the entire country, under the direction and superintendency of the Chinese Kuomintang." The said code has been constantly amended since its first promulgation, but this article has always remained unchanged. By the summer of Year XVII (1928), when the successful Northern Expedition undertaken by the National Revolutionary Army unified China under one government, the period of political tutelage of the Chinese Kuomintang began with the formulation and promulgation of the *Outlines of Political Tutelage* on October 3, Year XVII (1928). Article I of the said "Outlines" provided: "During the period of political tutelage of the Republic of China, the National Party Congress of the Chinese Kuomintang will take the place of the National Convention to lead the people and enforce all policies." By the beginning of June, in Year XX (1931), when the *Provisional Constitution* for the period of political tutelage was promulgated, the *Outlines of Political Tutelage* were again formed into a part of the *Provisional Constitution,* thereby giving party government a constitutional recognition. Besides the *Outlines of Political Tutelage,* Article 72 ("The National Government [Council of State] has a President and a certain number of state councillors, appointed by the Central Executive Committee of the Chinese Kuomintang."), and Article 58 ("The Central Executive Committee of the Chinese Kuomintang is vested with the power of interpreting this Provisional Constitution.") of the *Provisional Constitution,* and Article 10 ("The National Government has a President, twenty-four to thirty-six state councillors, a President and a Vice-President of every *Yüan,* appointed by the Central Executive Committee of the Chinese Kuomintang."), and Article 15 ("Before the promulgation of the Constitution, the Executive, Legislative, Judicial, Examination and Control *Yüan* will each be responsible to the Central Executive Committee of the Chinese Kuomintang.") of the *Laws Governing the System of Organization of the National Government* (December 30, Year XX [1931]) now being enforced, form the legal basis for party government.[5]

[5] Wang Shih-chieh, work cited, p. 649–50.

THE CONSTITUTION 25

Under Kuomintang trusteeship, demands have been heard within and without the Party, for the promised abdication of the Party and for the initiation of popular government. Since the Kuomintang, unlike European one-party groups, established itself only for the formal purpose of democratic training, and was pledged to tolerate multi-party government as soon as possible, the continued monopoly of power was a frustration of the Party ideology and programs. The frustration was serious; involving much loss of popular sympathy for the government, this and appeasement rather demoralized the Party in the years preceding the invasion.

THE DRAFT PERMANENT OR DOUBLE FIVE CONSTITUTION

The Legislative *Yüan* brought forth on May 5, 1936 (in Chinese chronology, 5/5/XXV, or double-five twenty-five), the celebrated *Hsien-fa Ts'ao-an* (Draft Permanent Constitution), which was promptly dubbed the Double Five Constitution. Ever since its first promulgation, this document has formed the center of all Chinese constitutional debate, and—with very minor modifications—still stands as the official proposal for a permanent constitution, awaiting ratification by the *Kuo-min Ta-hui* (National [Constituent] Congress), when and if that long-postponed body ever convenes.[6] The Draft Constitution is the joint work of many outstanding legal scholars. A product of collective research

[6] The Double Five Draft Constitution is to be found in Chinese in Wang Shih-chieh, work cited, and in English in Council of International Affairs, *Information Bulletin*, Vol. III, No. 10 (April 11, 1937), Nanking; Hsia, C. L., "Background and Features of the Draft Constitution of China"; in Legislative *Yüan*, "Draft of the Constitution of the Republic of China," Nanking, 1937; in *The China Year Book*, Shanghai, and *The Chinese Year Book*, Shanghai and Hong Kong, v.i. and v.d. The latest version of the Draft Constitution is reprinted below, Appendix I (A), p. 283; the latest Chinese annotated version of this is the Legislative *Yüan*, *Chung-hua Min-kuo Hsien-fa Ts'ao-an Shuo-ming-shu* (An Elucidation of the Draft Permanent Constitution of the Chinese Republic), [Chungking], XXIX (1940).

and study, it thereby resembles collective private codification of municipal and international law in the West more than it does the creation of a deliberative assembly. The celebrated Chinese jurist, Dr. John C. H. Wu, prepared the first informal draft,[7] and the 5/5/XXV version represents the fourth draft of the Legislative *Yüan*. The preparation of the various drafts has not, from the scholastic point of view, been secretive or private; but broad popular participation has neither been offered nor solicited.

The Constitution consists of eight Chapters, comprising one hundred and forty-seven articles. Chapter I defines the Chinese state as "a San Min Chu I Republic" (*Art.* 1), declares sovereignty to be "vested in the whole body of its citizens" (*Art.* 2), defines the territories of the republic, specifies racial equality for the "races of the Republic of China," designates the national flag, and declares Nanking to be the capital. Chapter II covers, in nineteen very specific articles, the entire field of private rights and of the civic privileges of individuals. Most specifications carry the qualification, "in accordance with law" or "except in accordance with law." Since law is defined further in the Constitution as "that which has been passed by the Legislative *Yüan* and promulgated by the President," the qualification

---

[7] For a critique and appreciation of the final Draft Constitution, see Wu, John C. H., "Notes on the Final Draft Constitution" in *Tien Hsia Monthly,* Vol. X, No. 5 (May 1940), p. 409–26. (Dr. Wu is one of the most extraordinary personages of the modern world; he has taken all knowledge—East Asiatic and Western—for his province. He writes a spirited, graceful English and is capable of discussing anything from modern politics or abstruse points of Anglo-American law to ancient Chinese hedonism or the philosophical implications of the *Autobiography* of St. Thérèse of Lisieux. Dr. Wu, in a bomb-shelter, possesses much of the moral poise and profound personal assurance for which such Westerners as T. S. Eliot seek in vain.) See also Hsia, C. L., "A Comparative Study of China's Draft Constitution with That of Other Modern States," in *The China Quarterly,* Vol. 2, 1936–7, No. 1 (Summer), p. 89–101 and Hoh Chih-hsiang, "A History of Constitution Making in China," the same, Vol. 1, 1935–6, No. 4 (Summer), p. 105–117.

impresses many persons as sinister rather than encouraging. Except for this point, the specific constitutional guarantees exceed in number and specificity those of almost any other modern constitution.

The *Kuo-min Ta-hui* (either "National Congress" or "People's Congress") is the subject of Chapter III. This body has a function unlike that of any Western agency; the nearest equivalent is the National Assembly of the Third French Republic. This Congress is an electoral and constituent body with fundamental legislative powers. It is not intended to usurp the functions of the Legislative *Yüan* by fulfilling the role of a United States Congress, French Deputies and Senate, or a British Parliament. Meeting once every three years for a one-month session, it will be manifestly unable to act as a routine Western-type legislature.

The Central Government is the topic of the fourth Chapter. The first section of the Chapter describes the Presidency; the remaining five, the five *Yüan*. This applies the five-fold separation of powers. Sun Yat-sen held that a three-fold separation of powers, as known in the West and applied to American government, was efficacious; he also considered that the Imperial Chinese separation of powers (an implicit one only) was also desirable. The West had executive, legislative, judicial; old China combined these three into the governing power, and joined thereto the examinative power and the *chien-ch'a* [8] power. (The *chien-ch'a* power involved the functions of the traditional Chinese censorate; overt and active expressions are found in auditing and in the lodgment of impeachment charges. The term is fundamentally untranslatable, but if the tribunician connotations of *Censor* or the emergency meaning of *Control* be recalled, either of these terms will serve.) Sun Yat-sen

---

[8] For a more extended discussion of this point, see the author's *The Political Doctrines of Sun Yat-sen: An Exposition of the San Min Chu I*, Baltimore, 1937, p. 218 *ff.*, and also p. 96 *ff.*

combined the Western and the old-Chinese separations, developing a theory of the five powers. The Draft Constitution, like its two working predecessors, is a five-power constitution, with five great *Yüan* (Boards, Presidencies, or Courts), each headed by a *Yüan-chang* (*Yüan* President). The fourth Chapter, by including the President and all five *Yüan,* almost covers the full reach of Chinese government.

This Chapter contemplates the creation of a strong President. In the Organic Law of 1928, the five Presidents of the *Yüan* were relatively less strong, and the Chairman of the *Kuo-min Chêng-fu Wei-yüan-hui* (National Government Council; or, Council of State) was the key figure in the government. Most of this time, Chiang himself was Chairman. In the 1931 Provisional Constitution, now in force, the Chairman of the National Government—termed President by courtesy—is an officer comparable to the President of the Third French Republic; the President of the Executive *Yüan* is a more active officer: Chiang K'ai-shek is President of the Executive *Yüan.* The new President, under the Draft Constitution, is one of the world's most powerful officers. Holding office for six years, eligible for reelection, commander of all armed forces, declarer of war, negotiator of peace, treaty-maker, chief appointing and removing officer of the state, holder of an emergency power greater than that conveyed by Article 48 of the German Weimar Constitution, and superior to the executive, legislative, judicial, examinative and control branches of the government—such a President is fully responsible to the triennial People's Congress, and to that only! Since the proposed President may be recalled at any time by the People's Congress, he is in that respect similar to parliamentary chiefs of state.[9]

[9] See Sun Fo [President of the Legislative *Yüan,* and son of Sun Yatsen], "The Spirit of the Draft Permanent Constitution," in *The China Quarterly,* Vol. V, No. 3 (April 1940), Shanghai, p. 377–84.

The President of the Executive *Yüan*, together with his subordinates, is to be appointed and removed by the President of the Republic. The *Yüan* includes Cabinet Ministers—appointed to their posts from among a special group of Executive Members of the *Yüan*, thereby providing a simple, rational equivalent of Cabinet and Privy Council, as in Japan or (less similarly) in Great Britain.

The Legislative *Yüan* is an interesting semi-cameral legislative body, which seeks to embody the better features of legislative research organs and of representative bodies. The Judicial *Yüan* rationalizes the structure and administration of courts and of judicial process.

The Control [or Censor] *Yüan* is, like the Legislative *Yüan*, a quasi-cameral body, with indirect election of members by the People's Congress from territorial electorates. Its functions are audit, inquiry, and impeachment, with such ancillary powers as practice to date has already indicated.[10]

Chapter V of the Draft Permanent Constitution deals with local government. The institutions of provincial government are wittingly minimized, because of recent trouble with provincial satrapies and the dangerously centrifugal effect of provincial autonomism. In contrast to this, government at the district (*hsien*) level is designed in strict accordance with the realities of twenty-odd centuries' experience. It is probable that no other constitution in the world provides for such careful guarantee of district, county, canton, or *Kreis* autonomy. The old Imperial Chinese system was a loose pseudo-centralized federation of two thousand near-autarkic and near-autonomous commonwealths; the Draft Constitution attempts to reinstitute (at the political level) this vigorous cooperative independence of the *hsien*. The *hsien* meeting, extrapolitical, unsystematic, and occasional in the past, is made the foundation for the new

[10] See Appendix I (F), p. 318–24, below.

legal structure. (These proposed reforms are now being anticipated under the Provisional Constitution and current statutory changes.[11])

Chapter VI provides that the economic system shall rest on Sun Yat-sen's principle of *min shêng* (*q.v.*, below). Willing to apply whatever worked best, Sun himself had no theoretical objections to capitalism, communism, state socialism, or any other economic doctrine. Hence, proletarian ownership of the means of production is not guaranteed; yet state ownership is not restricted, and is specifically required in the case of "all public utilities and enterprises of a monopolistic nature" (*Art.* 123). Henry George's influence on Sun is shown by mandatory taxation of unearned increment (*Art.* 119). Room for free future adaptation from corporative economic techniques successful in the outside world is assured (*Art.* 125): "Labor and capital shall, in accordance with the principles of mutual help and co-operation, develop together productive enterprises." It is likely that any imaginable economic system would be constitutional on this basis, provided that it was initiated by due legal procedure and without hardships irresponsibly imposed.

Chapter VII, on Education, opens: "The educational aim of the Republic of China shall be to develop a national spirit, to cultivate a national morality, to train the people for self-government and to increase their ability to earn a livelihood, and thereby to build up a sound and healthy body of citizens" (*Art.* 131), and continues, "Every citizen of the Republic of China shall have an equal opportunity to receive education" (*Art.* 132). State, secular control of educational policy is assured. Articles 134 and 135 provide for tuition-free elementary education for children and free elementary education for previously non-privileged adults. (The constitutional guarantee concerning tuition is indicative

[11] See below, p. 106 ff., and Appendix I (G), p. 324.

THE CONSTITUTION 31

of the scholastic traditions of the Chinese, of the modern educational revolution, and is reminiscent of *Art.* 12 of the 1931 Constitution of the Chinese Soviet Republic: "The Soviet Government in China shall guarantee to all workers, peasants, and the toiling masses the right to education. The Soviet Government will, as far as possible, begin at once to introduce free universal education.") [12]

Chapter VIII deals with the interpretation and enforcement of the Constitution. It was a labor of love by shrewd legal theorists, and defines terms with great clarity. Interpretive power is vested in the Judicial *Yüan*.

The Issue of Constitutional Change

Nowhere in China is there outright denial of a need for constitutional change. The need exists; the Double Five Draft is the government's answer. Yet there are few patent demerits in the existing constitutional system; the present political structure is more realistic, more broadly national, more expressive of effective opinion than any other in modern China. The question arises from commitments (dating back to the Empire) promising to create actual constitutional government. The National Government was established on the basis of this pledge. The democratic ideology, whatever sects it may include, has a clean sweep of the field of doctrine in China. No one seriously advocates monarchy, separatism, or permanent dictatorship. The only question is: how and when?

At the close of the third session of the advisory People's Political Council, Chiang K'ai-shek replied to demands for immediate broadening of popular control

[12] This constitution is available in Yakhontoff, Victor A., *The Chinese Soviets*, New York, 1934, p. 217–21, and in Kun, Bela [prefator], *Fundamental Laws of the Chinese Soviet Republic*, New York, 1934, p. 17–24. The writer has been unable to secure the Chinese text of this document.

over the government by reaffirmation of his adherence to the democratic dogma of Sun Yat-sen, together with the following warnings:

> The democracy which *Tsung-Li* [The Leader, i.e., Sun Yat-sen] wished to establish was of the purest kind without the slightest vestige of make-believe or artificiality. Unfortunately, the Chinese people, having inherited all the evil practices handed down throughout the numerous dynasties of autocratic rule, were then at a low ebb both in intelligence and in vitality. The people were used to disorganization and selfishness. . . .
> We have to wait until our lost territories have been recovered and domestic disorders liquidated before we can have political tutelage and prepare ourselves for constitutionalism. . . .
> People at that time [the inauguration of the Republic in 1912] made the mistake of neglecting the necessary procedures and instead they rivalled each other in talking about democracy. . . . As a result, democracy has remained an ideal. . . .
> We must make it clear to our people that democracy is not a synonym for lack of law and order, or for anarchy.
> The public opinion on which democracy is based must be sound, collective, and representative of the majority of the people's wills. The freedom which democracy endows on people should not conflict with public welfare, nor should it go beyond the sphere as marked by laws of the State. With our nation facing the worst invasion in history, we must teach the people to respect the absolute authority of laws of the State.[18]

The clamor for a constitution continued. The difficulties of introducing mass suffrage to Western China were apparent to everyone, but many leaders felt that the advantages of constitutionalism would outweigh the inescapable loss of efficiency, and would mobilize public opinion behind the war and further democratic progress. The Generalissimo found this view hard to reconcile with his military, direct notions of doing first things

---

[18] China Information Committee, Chungking, *News Release*, No. 351 (February 25, 1939), p. 2269–71.

first, as he saw them, but he yielded in the fourth session of the People's Political Council and accepted the demand. He stated:

> In China . . . [democratization] is a tremendously heavy task which cannot be completed within a few days. I think that the Constitution and laws may as well be promulgated at an earlier date. But, gentlemen, please do not forget the *Tsung-li's* painful consideration . . . [of the necessity of an intermediate stage of real democratic training]. Political tutelage does not end with the training of the citizens by the government. It requires training of the citizens by themselves.
>
> Today we should understand our object: to start the building of a constitutional government. This means laying a permanently sound basis for the nation. We are not concerned with the time of starting constitutional government. Whether to start it early or later does not matter much. What we are really concerned with is, do we have a real intention of forming a constitutional government? If we are truly so minded, we might as well promulgate the Constitution before the labor of political tutelage is completed.[14]

[14] [Chiang K'ai-shek], *Tsung-ts'ai Chien-kuo Yen-lun Hsüan-chi* (The Party Chief's Utterances on Reconstruction), Chungking, 1940, p. 237–43. The Generalissimo concluded his speech with a homiletic touch which is so characteristic that it may be included here; it also explains his relative lack of interest in the Constitution: "Lastly, I have another point to tell you gentlemen. I have already repeated this, again and again, many times. Desiring to complete our revolutionary work and national reconstruction, and to have a constitutional government as seen in many modern states as soon as possible, I often study the causes of the weakness and disorder which exist in our country. . . . [He cites the traditional political vigor and excellence of the centuries before the time of Christ, with the "degeneration" and "departure from order" of the following centuries.] The departure is not simply due to the failures in politics and education and to the deprivation of the popular rights by a few tyrannical kings and lords since the Ch'in and Han periods. It is due to the fact that before the Chou, we had government by law [*fa chih*] as a mere supplement to government by social standards [*li chih*, also translatable as ideological control, or control through moral indoctrination]. We had social organization as the foundation of political organization. Everything was then well-organized and well-trained. Everywhere, in schools, in armies, in families, in society, order and the forms of propriety [i.e., social standards] were regarded as most important. No citizen could evade his duty and obligation."

Chiang thus reconciled the beginning of constitutionalism and the continuance of political tutelage, although implying acquiescence, not recommendation. A theorist holding all men to be driven by "a perpetuall and restlesse desire of Power after power, that ceaseth onely in Death,"[15] might consistently suppose that Chiang merely dissimulated an inward lust for authority; more plausible is the postulation that a man who has for years lived with and for a doctrine, giving his life and future reputation to the fulfilment of a program, would incline to prudence and realism in climaxing that doctrine and program. In Chiang's case this is Sun Yat-sen's *San Min Chu I*. Chiang's reluctance to apply democracy then and there is understandable whatever the inmost motive; so, too, is his yielding to a widespread demand.

The convening of a special *Kuo-min Ta-hui* as a national constituent assembly was set for November 12, 1940; this day was chosen because it was traditionally the seventy-fourth birthday of Sun Yat-sen. Administrative machinery for preparation of a hall, secretariat, publications, and other necessities was established and set in motion. Following the severe fires of August 19–20, and the subsequent large-scale demolition of aboveground downtown Chungking by raids, indefinite postponement of the Congress was announced on September 25—on the grounds that military hazard prevented adequate assembly of delegates, and no reasonably safe place for such a meeting could be found.

Meanwhile, recent years have seen an uproar of constitutional debate. This may be summarized briefly, with the case against the Constitution stated first:

Constitutionalization would lead to the legalization of other parties, instead of a mere condition of nonprosecution; this would disrupt the orderliness required

---

[15] Thomas Hobbes, *Leviathan*, New York and London, 1934 (Everyman's Edition), p. 49.

of a people at war. Why add discord in war time? *Reply:* legitimization of other parties is not a struggle for power but an act of union. It would widen the periphery of cooperation.[16]

Sun Yat-sen required three stages of the revolution: conquest, tutelage, constitution. China is not ready for mass suffrage. The majority of the people are not yet literate. Public opinion is just developing. The nation is, in fact, still in the period of military recapture of national territories. *Reply:* Sun Yat-sen must not be interpreted mechanically. If this is done, tutelage will never end, and Sun's cherished democracy will remain forever in the future. Furthermore, the guerrillas, the Border Region, and other instances have shown that the Chinese masses can and will practice democracy right now. Again, the issue has already been decided; the government has been committed to the immediate inauguration of the Constitution. First it was to be 1939; the elections were held in part, until the war finally stopped them on August 13, 1937. It is too late to raise the issue: is China ready? Everyone—government, Kuomintang, independent groups—has decided that China is.

Why change constitutions? The present one is satisfactory. If a war-time amplification of the *Yüeh Fa* is needed, it can be found in the *Program of Resistance and Reconstruction.*[17] If a convocation of the talents is needed, the People's Political Council is already there. What is the use of a constitutional change in war time? *Reply:* the constitutionalist movement is no new development. The *Program* was a democratic advance. "Besides, formation of the People's Political Council was a step toward democracy. The constitutional move-

---

[16] The writer is indebted for much of the material in this chapter to Dr. Djang Chu, of the New Life Movement Headquarters, Chungking, who supplied it to him in the form of a lecture and other memoranda. Dr. Djang is, of course, not responsible for any reinterpretations here made.

[17] See Appendix I (D), p. 309.

ment was not forced on the government, but was an outgrowth of the war; it has not appeared overnight, but has a clear historical background. As soon as the Sino-Japanese hostilities broke out, it was evident that more democratic rule was necessary. As the war became prolonged, the preliminary steps proved inadequate. A more perfect constitution, whereby the whole people can be mobilized, is imminent. This fact was duly recognized by the people and is the motive power of the present constitutional movement." (This is the comment of an independent writer.) [18]

A pointed question is raised and answered by Tso Tao-fen, one of the Seven Gentlemen (*Ch'i Chüntzu*) who led the National Salvationists:

> Some say that as a matter of fact, the people themselves do not want a constitution. And—to put it more bluntly—that the people do not know what a constitution is. Therefore, the constitutional movement represents the desires of only a minority of the people, not the majority. You have a certain element of truth if you say that most of the people do not know what a constitution is, but it is not true that they do not want a constitution. In the present war period, the burden on the people is enormous. They should not be denied any privileges to which they are entitled. All the proposed constitutional stipulations concerning the duties, rights, economic status, and education of the people have an immediate effect on and relation to the people. Why do they not want a constitution? If you proceed to ask one of the common people, say a peasant, and you talk with him, professorially as though you were in a classroom, about the constitutional movement, he may be at a loss. But if you bother to ask him about his daily life—the work he is doing, his hopes, his bitterness, the cruelties inflicted on him by unscrupulous officials and landlords and gentry—and if he enjoys the freedom of speech, he will give you a good talk! . . . If you say that the people do not know what a

---

[18] Liu Shih, "Chung-kuo Hsien-chêng Yün-tung-ti Chi-ko Chieh-tuan" (Stages of the Chinese Constitutional Movement) in *Li-lun yü Hsien-shih* (Theory and Reality), Vol. 1, No. 3, November 15, 1939, p. 13 ff.

constitution is, you should enlighten them about the close relationship between themselves and the constitution, not discontinue the constitutional movement.[19]

Other questions relate to specific points in the Draft Constitution. In the opinion of some, the phrase "according to law" which follows every guarantee of popular rights is a dangerous phrase, particularly in view of the neat but arbitrary definition of "law" (*Art.* 139). Others, remembering the Weimar Article 48, mistrust the emergency power of the President. The President's sharing of the budgetary, pardoning, and war powers with the Legislative *Yüan* seems illogical to some critics, who feel that these powers should be within reach of a more popular body, not a technically legislative organ.

Further discussion deals with the competence of the *Kuo-min Ta-hui*. Many of the critics, particularly those of the Communist and independent Left group, believe the long-heralded epoch of democracy would open badly if it began with mechanical ratification of a dictated constitution. A Communist leader said, "We want a Constitution, a democratic Constitution—a *real* democratic Constitution!" and pointed out that the first Congress was too large, not truly representative of the common people, and not given enough time to work out a constitution by its own action; its task, as he supposed the government intended, would be to rubber-stamp the Double Five Draft. In his opinion, this Draft had many defects—chief of which was unresponsiveness of the central government to popular control. The proposed Congress could not do much with a mere triennial check; the five-power system as projected was unsatisfactory. Democratic rights were insufficiently assured. He added that the Communist Party of China was for

[19] From Tso Tao-fen, "A Few Questions Regarding the Constitution" in Ch'üan-min K'ang-chan Shê [The United Front Club], *Hsien-chêng Yün-tung Lun-wên Hsüan-chi* (A Symposium on the Constitutional Movement), Chungking, 1940, p. 1 *ff.*

a democracy, but that the Double Five Draft was not "the constitution of a democracy." [20]

Furthermore, the representativeness of the proposed constitution-adopting *Kuo-min Ta-hui* is called into question. The present plan calls for 665 delegates from geographical constituencies, 380 from occupational, 155 "by special methods," 240 by government appointment, and a large number of Kuomintang Party-officers *ex officio* (241 by a recent count).[21] The present administration would obviously have a whip hand over all proceedings. The division into groups has been criticized. A demand, for example, for 120 women members has been made. Under the circumstances, with 1681 members already scheduled, mere additional size could be no handicap.

The question of qualifications has also been raised. About 900 of the representatives had been elected when war broke out. These include men who have since died, or have changed their opinions, or are reported missing, and even a few traitors. Are all the available elected representatives to be gathered together, years later? or is a new election to be held? Whatever occurs, the supreme agency on qualifications is the Election Committee for Representatives to the People's [Constituent] Congress, attached directly to the Council of State.

The constitutional issue in China is no simple problem of reaction versus progressivism. The vast majority of the population is not literate, and is unprepared to deal with a complicated machinery of opinion and election. Wire-pulling, corruption, adherence to form instead of deed—these are all widespread in China. Democracy abruptly established might frustrate further improvement, since sham-democracy would have estab-

---

[20] Statement of Col. Ch'in Po-k'u at the Chungking office of the 18th [Communist] Army Corps Headquarters, on July 29, 1940, to the author.

[21] *China at War*, Vol. IV, No. 5 (June 1940), p. 79 ff.

lished itself. The opponents of sudden action also press the telling point that the common people do not know they want immediate democracy, although believing in the term as a symbol and approving its trial application. The Generalissimo remains clearly mistrustful about creating new organs of opinion, or using new political processes; he would prefer to wait until the nation is unified, better administered, and more literate. Hence his and the Kuomintang's insistence on indirect elections, remoteness of policy-making authorities from the electorate, and self-sufficient government.

China did have, it is argued, an excellent democratic constitution in 1912, many more in the warlord years. All had admirable balances of power, guarantees to the individual, libertarian and progressive provisions. Like Chinese social legislation, they lifted China to the level of the rest of the modern world—*de jure,* and that only! These elevated documents remained elevated; life went on beneath them, and the tragic gap between law and life was so enormous that no one thought of bridging it. The nation would have been humiliated by legislation which limited the working day to fourteen hours, prohibited the mutilation or slavery of children, or required that torture be administered in the presence of a physician. Hence it had eight, ten, or twelve-hour laws, good child legislation, and absolute prohibition of torture for any purpose; these were unenforceable.

To counsels of caution, advocates of immediately responsive institutions reply that the Chinese common people are better democrats than their rulers, citing concrete cases in proof. They mention the general strikes, strong peasant cooperation, the startling phenomena of coordinate mass action—tens and hundreds of thousands strong—in political protest, boycotts, or civic immobility. (In past years many a warlord has been stopped by empty streets and closed houses: no business, no traffic, no talking, no meetings—only the silence, and somewhere, conspicuously inconspicuous, a committee of plenipotentiaries!) They refer to the Frontier Area, the Border Region, the New Fourth Zone, the guerrillas, the industrial cooperatives, and the wealth of leadership called up from the millions by the war. They quote to the Kuomintang its own professions of democracy, and the words of its late Leader. Told that the masses do not understand modern administration, modern economics, modern war, and that the peasantry and workers would proceed to arbitrary class legislation, economic levelling, and social revolution, they reply, "What do you want—democracy?" It is most unlikely that the Communists would sweep the country under free elections, but they and other dissidents, as the political Outs, would be free to criticize the incumbents in a way sure to bring support and involve new alignments of power. Some Kuomintang leaders wish to shut out any group with foreign connections; the Chinese face—despite their definite movement toward constitutionalism—the question of the limits of democratic toleration.

Chapter II

THE POLITICAL ORGANS OF THE NATIONAL GOVERNMENT

BY constitutional stipulation, and by dogma legally established, the National Government of the Chinese Republic is a Kuomintang Party-dictatorship over the Chinese nation. This rule is formally dictatorship by a minority democracy over the absolutely governed majority, since the Party constitution requires intra-Party democracy. No pretense is made of further formal democracy. Actual experience of the past ten years has shown the government to be a broad, loosely organized oligarchy in which the Party, the Government, the Army and regional military, and independent leaders (such as bankers, college professors and presidents, secret society chiefs, community spokesmen) have shared power. The center of gravity has stayed somewhere near Chiang K'ai-shek, who as co-leader and then formal Chief (*Tsung-ts'ai,* "general ruler") of the Party and creator of the central army has combined two of the chief sources of influence. Variety in the sources, nature, and incidence of political power in recent Chinese affairs has, however, not destroyed the constitutional theory: Party-dictatorship pledged to national democracy.

The state machinery—as it has been since promulgation of the Provisional Constitution, 1931—is among the most elaborate in the modern world, but is nevertheless effective. One may justly regard the present government as the most efficacious, generally powerful, and growing Chinese government since the mid-eighteenth century. This government is pre-eminently the creation of the Kuomintang, and of Kuomintang leaders. A war which threatens China's national existence accordingly threatens the leaders as government officers, as Party members, as patriotic citizens, and as members of the Chinese race. At the time that they fight an alien enemy, they must simultaneously increase state power and diffuse it so that a democracy may emerge and survive.

China's leadership is therefore posed a two-fold problem: to perpetuate a regime, successful in one period of relative peace, through years of invasion to a period of even deeper peace; and to permit popular access to policy-forming agencies, allowing freer operation of pressures, without endangering resistance and reconstruction thereby. To the Western political scientist, it is amazing that they have carried into the years of catastrophic war a unique, complex constitutional system, treasuring it like an ark of the covenant. This is the five-power system.

The Five-Power Constitution

The five-power constitution (*wu-ch'üan hsien-fa*) is a legacy of Sun Yat-sen, and is one of the cardinal dogmas of the *San Min Chu I*. Distinctively, two new powers are added to the familiar three: namely, the examinative and the control powers. Westerners might question the importance of segregating the impeaching, auditing and critical powers, unifying them into a new agency of government, along with a glorified, independent civil service system. Yet the five-fold division is to China a key point of governmental development.

The five-power system is based on the notions Sun Yat-sen had of democracy. He anticipated by a generation the need of strengthening democratic machinery to compete with Caesarian techniques. Merely to have qualified the suffrage, or to have narrowed the limits of popular action, would not have sufficed, for it was authentic democracy—government both representative and popular—which he desired, not an empty shell of nominal republicanism. In an effort to solve this dilemma, he employed the concepts *ch'üan* and *nêng*,[1] which may be translated "power" and "capacity," although the rendering would necessarily vary in accordance with the connotations to be encompassed.[2] He felt that it was a major discovery to apply in modern politics a distinction between the power which the people should have over government and the capability they had of operating the machine of state. Abandoning the state to the vagaries of public opinion, allowing the citizens free access to the powerful, complex controls of modern governance, or assuming that anyone and everyone had an expert's qualifications on all political subjects—this would, in Sun Yat-sen's opinion, wreck the government. Nevertheless, the people had to reserve a final power over policies and personnel of government, although they are themselves unqualified to operate the state mechanism. Hence the people were to exercise *the four powers* over the government: initiative, referendum, election, and recall. Compensatingly, the government was to possess the *five rights* over the people, based on the new separation of powers. To Sun, as a Chinese, the state was not the hand of the people; it was a separate institution above other institutions, democratic only in allowing access to itself and in justifying its authority by the ultimate sanction of popular vote. The new government could not be kept clean, prompt, and high-minded by the freak, casual operation of popular censure, nor staffed by whomever a mass fancy threw into

[1] See Sun Yat-sen, *San Min Chu I*, Shanghai, 1927, henceforth cited as "Price translation," p. 296 *ff.;* or d'Elia, Paschal M., S. J., *The Triple Demism of Sun Yat-sen*, Wuchang, 1931, p. 348 *ff.*

[2] An attempt to correlate Sun's democratic theory with Western concepts is made in the present author's *Political Doctrines of Sun Yat-sen*, cited, p. 107–9. The notion is clearly put in *L'Esprit des Lois*, Book 11, ch. 2.

office. It was, instead, to be a traditionally Chinese self-perpetuating bureaucracy, differing from the past only in being controlled and revised by popular instead of imperial will.

Accordingly, the ideal toward which the Chungking government strives may be epitomized as *perfect bureaucracy subject to complete popular control*. The two powers new to the West—examination and control—are to replace public opinion at levels of obscurity, technicality, and persistence where outside criticism could not reach; the plan of Sun Yat-sen provides for as much use of power through voting as is found in any Western state. This attempted solution strikes near the core problems of any modern government, wherever it may operate and whatever its conditions.

The five-power constitution posits a government of educated, expert men, in which qualifying examinations will precede election for administrative posts, and in which the examination and control *yüan* will—professionally, officially—replace the haphazard play of sentiment, anger, fancy, envy upon which Western peoples count to keep their democracy healthy and intact. The United States Government is the most complex and important institution in the United States, possessing inquisitorial powers wider and deeper than those of any private person or institution. Yet the Americans have no unceasing, professional, expert investigation of their government by their government, nor does a merit system extend to offices where it might have the drastic effect of thwarting operation of public opinion locally or temporarily debased.

This function, specializing power to strengthen it, explains the war-time survival of the five-power system as a fundamental theory of state. The Chinese have suffered from weak government for decades. Absence of dictatorship was largely owing to an inability to designate a dictator. The five-power system was preceded by a Nationalist government which employed the soviet form of organization—the one instance outside the Soviet Union of such application.[3] This had been set up for rapid, decisive action; thirteen years' preliminary application of the five-power system has shown this to be no less swift and effectual. Even the Communist leaders in China today are reconciled to the retention of the five-power system, although they would certainly like to modify its present organization.[4]

Reference to the general chart of government organization (see p. 330) shows the intricate pre-democratic system of government now applied. Consideration of the sources of policy in such a structure have, therefore, to appraise not merely two agencies—executive and legislative, with only a glance at the judiciary—as in America, but to examine a whole hierarchy of Party, general governmental, military-governmental, and autonomous policy-making agencies. Were it not for the thousands of miles, the unrelatedness in cultures, the complexities of language, and the inescapable awareness of race, Americans might long since have looked to China as the decisive, fresh political experiment of our times.

One further trait of the Chinese, which in Japan has been carried to the point of a national mania, is the respect for the constitutional (or Imperial) system as a symbol of purity and order. Western governments are like machines in common use; they operate for the general convenience and subject to the criticism of their members. Even dictatorships try to seem practical. The Confucian traditions of government by indoctrination, and particularly that of government indoctrinating

---

[3] See Holcombe, Arthur N., *The Chinese Revolution,* Cambridge (Massachusetts), 1930, *passim,* for the outstanding elaboration of this curious experiment, and for a lucid delineation of the genesis of the National Government.

[4] Statement to the author by Col. Ch'in Po-k'u, interview cited, p. 38, n. 20, above.

through conspicuous example, motivated heavy ceremonialization of state functions. This often led a Chinese Emperor to become more and more majestic and aloof, to strive for archetypal perfection, until he became so much a model that he disappeared from public sight altogether, swilling and carousing himself to death in the gardens of the Forbidden City; his successors, if they came from the people, would seem practical and workable for a few generations, until they too succumbed to their own majesty. Some atrophy through majesty occurs even in the relatively new Chinese National Government, arrested but not eradicated by wartime vigor.

The Supreme National Defense Council

The highest political agency in China is the Supreme National Defense Council (*Kuo-fang Tsui-kao Wei-yüan-hui*).[5] This is not a part of the government, *de jure*, since it is the war-time replacement of the Kuomintang Central Political Council (*Chung-yang Chêng-chih Wei-yüan-hui*), the high Party organ charged with exercise of the Party's sovereign powers in gov-

[5] The names of agencies and offices in the discussion of government and Kuomintang organization are taken from K'ao-shih *Yüan* [Examination Yüan], *Tang Chêng Chien Chih T'u-piao* [Charts of Government and Party Development and Organization], Chungking, XXIX (1940), *passim*. This work has not yet been published, since it is a draft printing, to be revised and re-edited before formal publication. The author was allowed to consult a copy through the courtesy of the Minister of Foreign Affairs, Dr. Wang Ch'ung-hui, and the kind assistance of Mr. C. C. Chi of the Party-Ministry of Publicity. These charts, provisional as they are, are by far the most systematic presentation of modern Chinese government structure which the author has ever seen. For a brief commentary on the Council, see the one-paragraph section, *The Supreme National Defense Council* in Tsiang Ting-fu, "Reorganization of the National Government," *Chinese Year Book 1938–39*, cited, p. 356. Dr. Tsiang, whose other writings on Chinese government have been models of clarity, candor, and concreteness, is obliged to state: "As its major functions are involved in the prosecution of the war, military necessity compels the writer to withhold the details of its organization and work for a later issue."

ernment. The liberalization of the policy-framing agencies in war-time cannot be better illustrated than by the fact that this new Supreme National Defense Council reportedly includes non-Party members, and acts in fact as a central board or council of government, superseding not only the Kuomintang Central Political Council but its governmental counterpart, the Council of State (*Kuo-min Chêng-fu Wei-yüan-hui*) as well. Reference to the chart below will clarify the relationship of these agencies:

The KUOMINTANG, as a Party,
exercises sovereign powers through
[The CENTRAL POLITICAL COUNCIL, superseded in war-time by]
The SUPREME NATIONAL DEFENSE COUNCIL,
which transmits commands
to
The COUNCIL OF STATE, highest governmental agency,
which transforms these commands into government orders applicable
to
NATIONAL, PROVINCIAL, or LOCAL
GOVERNMENT AGENCIES,
in the form of
ORDERS, ORDINANCES, and LAWS

The power of the Kuomintang is exercised by its Chief [*Tsung-ts'ai*] and its Central Executive Committee, Central Committee, and their respective Standing Committees (discussed below, p. 125 *ff.*).

Secretiveness in a nation's highest policy-making organ is somewhat unusual in the modern world. In most states the invisible government of practical acquaintance and association between leaders provides a meeting ground, and traditions require a formal, open exercise of public authority. As a matter of fact, a few generally accepted data concerning the Supreme National Defense Council are readily apparent to the observer in

Chungking. In the first place, it is what its title implies —the highest agency of political control. Its meetings are the constant source of new policy and tangible control. Secondly, one finds a universal belief that the Generalissimo, who attends these meetings in the multiple capacity of Chairman of the Council, Party Chief of the Kuomintang, President of the Executive *Yüan,* Chairman of the People's Political Council, Commander-in-Chief of the Army, Navy, and Air Forces, etc., faithfully employs Council meetings for very real debate and discussion of government and Party policy, and for the conduct of the war. He is not believed to take any important step arbitrarily, without consulting the Council. (In the past, he has been known to act with dramatic and concealed swiftness, opening his mind to no one before the crucial consummation of his plans, but at the present time this has apparently disappeared.[6])

Third, the Council, while extending beyond the men who are primarily Party leaders and including military and political figures who (irrespective of nominal Party membership) are independent, has transformed the arcanum of Party power into a body more representative of the entire nation. Fourth, significant in connection with the Japanese charge of Chungking Bolshevization, the Communists and other Leftists, while fairly represented in advisory and even in military bodies, are presumed to have no representation whatever on the Supreme National Defense Council, nor is such representation regarded as probable in the near future. Chiang K'ai-shek has at hand a counselling and co-governing body whose fundamental purposes are completely one with his own.

[6] For a biased but bitterly graphic portrayal of Chiang's tiger leaps in politics, see Isaacs, Harold, work cited, *passim.* Mr. Isaacs' portrayal of Chiang shows him as ambitious, able, and villainous in his need for power and his hostility to the proletariat. The Trotskyite viewpoint is a usefully different one from that obviously adopted by the present author.

A nice consistency would demand that the Supreme National Defense Council (as a Party agency) should transmit its commands to the Council of State (its government counterpart) for transformation into law. This is actually done, whenever possible, but the frequency of crises and of needs for immediate action have —in the period of hostilities—led to the occasional issuance of commands direct to the Ministry or other governmental organ concerned.[7] To the degree that the Supreme National Defense Council does so, it becomes a directly governing authority, and instead of perpetuating Party authority *over* government, it is itself government.

Since a cloud of military secrecy covers the functions of the Council, some notion of its operation and working authority may be found by analogy with the role of the Central Political Council, which it has displaced. According to the leading Chinese constitutional writer on the subject, the Central Political Council (also called [Central] Political Committee)—for which read Supreme National Defense Council today—acted as follows:

According to Article IV of the *Principles Governing the Organization of the C. E. C.* [of the Kuomintang] passed . . . December 6, XXIV (1935), "the Central Executive Committee organizes a Political Committee, composed of a Chairman, a Vice-Chairman, and nineteen to twenty-five members, appointed by the Central Executive Committee, from among the members of the Central Executive Committee and the Control Committee." . . . "During a session of the Political Committee, the Chairmen and Vice-Chairmen of the Central Standing Committees, the President of the National Government, the Presidents and Vice-Presidents of the Five *Yüan*, and the President and Vice-President of the Military Affairs Commission should be present, while the leading members of the special technical

[7] Statement to the author, August 1, 1940, in Chungking, by Dr. Wang Shih-chieh, Secretary-General of the People's Political Council and Party-Minister of Publicity.

committees under the [control] Political Committee, and other higher officials of the National Government may be notified if necessary to attend the sessions." [The author explains that, on the basis of actual experience, "may be notified" signifies "shall attend if matters relevant to their functions arise."] . . .

It was originally fixed that the Political Committee should meet once every week, but since December XXIV (1935), it holds meetings either weekly or fortnightly. The number of members required to constitute a forum is not fixed, and resolutions have never been put in the form of motions requiring formal vote. Regarding the proposition of a motion, and the discussion of motions proposed *extempore,* the Political Committee has never fixed any rigid regulations; moreover, even if a rule had been established at one time, it has not been followed closely later. Before being put to a decision, a motion is either studied and examined beforehand, or it is not. There is no definite rule as to whether every motion should be so studied or not, but the Committee possesses the power to decide this point *ad hoc.* The entire wording of a motion passed in a meeting is rarely fully read, and is then read in the following session as the minutes of the previous session. *Hence the Chairman and the Secretary-General have a certain liberty in the framing of the wording of resolutions. Judging from above circumstances, important resolutions passed in the Political Committee must actually represent the opinions of the Chairman and a small number of influential members.* . . . [Italics added in translation.] [8]

Many of these features may reasonably be conjectured to have continued in the Supreme National Defense Council, although the regular meetings—whatever others there may be—seem to be considerably less frequent, occurring presumably about once in five weeks.[9] In the matter of authority, again, some continuity may be supposed between the earlier agency and the later. Wang Shih-chieh continues:

[8] Wang Shih-chieh, *Pi-chiao Hsien-fa,* cited above, p. 658 *ff.*

[9] For example, the date of the law given in Appendix I (G), p. 324, below, is given as August 31, 1939, and it is stated to have passed the Council on that date at the *14th* Regular Session; since the Council had been established seventeen months previously, some notion of the frequency or length of sessions may thus be derived.

The authority of the Political Committee (or the Political Council) has undergone very few changes since its establishment. To speak concisely, the Political Committee is the highest directing organ of all governmental policies. Putting it in more detail, we may say that this Committee has the power to decide the basic principles of legislation, of governmental policies and their execution, and has also the power to appoint and dismiss governmental officials . . . [A footnote adds the following detail.] According to the outlines of organization now being enforced, there are still five kinds of affairs that should be discussed and decided by the Political Committee: (1) the basic principles of legislation, (2) the general plans of executing government policies, (3) important plans concerning military affairs, (4) financial plans, (5) the appointment of officials of the Especially Appointed category and of other governmental officials, and (6) [sic] cases submitted for discussion by the Central Executive Committee. The first four may be collectively classified under the two names of execution and legislation.[10]

Only from such description by analogy may the foreigner penetrate to the inmost source of Chinese policy. This ambiguous and all-powerful agency, a Party organ which controls government, a committee constellated about its charismatic Chairman, is the heir both of the Grand Council of the Manchu Empire and of the soviets established by Nationalists during the entente with Soviet Russia. Should the fortune of war remove the Generalissimo from the scene, this Council would become the storm center of power; under his guidance and leadership, this agency above all others distinguishes China from an outright dictatorship. Chiang, unlike many other national leaders, has consistently shrunk from the regalia of arbitrary power. In the highest matters, and at the ultimate control, his action is veiled in

[10] Wang Shih-chieh, *Pi-chiao Hsien-fa*, cited, p. 662. The author adds that though the Central Political Council possesses ample authority to interfere in the specific work of the Judicial, Examination, and Control *Yüan*, such authority was rarely exercised, the Executive and Legislative *Yüan* constituting the prime objects of its attention.

the Supreme National Defense Council. The actual play of personalities and power is hidden from us, his contemporaries. Only the future may discover the exact degrees and *modus operandi* of his authority.

The President of the National Government

The term National Government (*Kuo-min Chêng-fu*) is employed in two senses. In the broad sense, it refers to the entire central government of China. In the narrow sense, it is a synonym for National Government Committee (*Kuo-min Chêng-fu Wei-yüan-hui*), commonly translated as Council of State. The highest governmental officer of China is the *Kuo-min Chêng-fu Chu-hsi*—literally, the Chairman of the National Government. Since this officer is the formal head of the National Government in both senses of the term, his office may with equal appropriateness be described as Chairmanship of the Council of State and as Presidency of the National Government. The latter has been most commonly accepted, although it obscured the clarity of the Chinese governmental pattern. It is essential to note, however, that in the National Government period there has been no *President of the Chinese Republic;* the highest officer has been the *President of the National Government of the Chinese Republic,* and as such the titular head of the Chinese state for international purposes. This officer possesses prestige rather than power, and is roughly analogous to the President of the Third French Republic.

In his official capacity, the President acts as chairman of the meetings of the Council of State, performs the ceremonial functions entailed by his office, and serves as the custodian of the symbols of continuity and legitimacy. Wang Shih-chieh writes: ". . . the Chairman more or less occupies a nominal position. At most, he can give occasional advice, only within certain limits, to the Executive or other *Yüan,* with no power at all to decide or to reject the policies adopted by the *Yüan*. As a matter of fact, from the end of the Year XXI (1932) down to the present, since the man filling the office of Chairman [President] of the National Government is very calm and law-abiding, he has never interfered in the activities or policies of the various *Yüan*." [11] This officer has been the veteran Kuomintang leader, Lin Shên, long a resident of the United States, a key man in overseas affairs of the Party, and a person of much dignity, charm, poise and prestige. With a long beard and a humane, scholarly demeanor, President Lin has fulfilled most admirably the requirements of his office.

Generalissimo Chiang regularly reports on government activities to Lin *Chu-hsi*, addressing him attentively and respectfully. This is no perfunctory sham, but appears to be a very real search for advice and guidance. The two men are close associates and have been such for many years; the Generalissimo gives every indication of regarding his venerable colleague with affectionate esteem. During the Chungking bombings, the President has commonly resided in a secure place outside the city. He is not needed for the daily prosecution of the war, but both the office and its incumbent are strongly stabilizing factors in the National Government. (The Japanophile Wang Ch'ing-wei, establishing his duplicate regime in Nanking, left the Presidency open for many months, pirating Lin Shên's name. Finally Wang gave himself the title, although he patently would have preferred Lin.)

THE COUNCIL OF STATE

The Council of State (*Kuo-min Chêng-fu Wei-yüan-hui*, National Government Committee) is the formal governmental core of the Chinese Republic. Even in peacetime, however, its importance was seriously undermined by the vigorous activity of the Central Political

[11] The same, p. 666.

Council. The members of the State Council are commonly persons who do not hold other important office; hence the Council does not include the most effective leaders. Although its sphere of activity is wide, its role as ratifier of the decisions of the Supreme National Defense Council reduces its plenary powers to a shadow. Amnesties, general appropriation bills, appointments and removals, solemnification of legislation adopted by the Legislative *Yüan,* and inter-*Yüan* problems are all within the scope of the State Council's authority, but except for the power of organizing and supervising the central independent agencies, subordinate only to itself, there has been little practical power for it to exercise.[12]

The independent agencies under the Council of State, together with the latter's relation to the *Yüan* and the Military Affairs Commission, are best shown on the chart on p. 55.[13]

Minor agencies are thus attached directly to the Council of State, which also serves as a link and common formal superior to the five *Yüan* and the Military Affairs Commission. Authority of the Council is directed primarily upon these agencies which, while minor, serve useful needs. The Offices of Military (*Tsan-chün Ch'u*) and of Civil Affairs (*Wên-kuan Ch'u*) are transmission and ceremonial agencies, charged with the

[12] The same, p. 667–68. The following materials on the independent agencies are also adapted in general from Wang Shih-chieh's work, although interviews, other materials, and the practical experience of the author have been taken into account. From 1930 to 1937 the author's father, Judge Paul Linebarger, was Legal Advisor (*Kuo-min Chêng-fu Fa-lü Ku-wên*), directly subordinate to the Council of State, and throughout this period the author served as Private Secretary to the Legal Advisor, being authorized by the Council of State to take charge of the American office of the Advisor during the latter's absences from the United States.

[13] Adapted from the Examination *Yüan, Tang Chêng Chien Chih T'u-piao,* cited; various issues of *The Chinese Year Book,* Shanghai and Hong Kong; and [The China Information Committee] *An Outline of the Organization of the Kuomintang and the Chinese Government,* Chungking, 1940.

POLITICAL ORGANS

THE SUPREME NATIONAL DEFENSE COUNCIL

President of the National Government

THE COUNCIL OF STATE

- Election Committee on Representation in the People's Congress
- Academia Sinica
- Commission for the Disciplinary Punishment of Public Officials
- Planning Committee for the Western Capital
- THE PEOPLE'S POLITICAL COUNCIL

- Office of the Comptroller-General
- Office of Civil Affairs (Transmission)
- Office of Military Affairs (Transmission)

- THE MILITARY AFFAIRS COMMISSION
  - The Chairman
  - The Military Departments
- THE EXECUTIVE *YÜAN*
  - The Executive Ministries ("the cabinet")
- THE LEGISLATIVE *YÜAN*
- THE JUDICIAL *YÜAN*
  - The court system
- THE EXAMINATION *YÜAN*
- THE CONTROL *YÜAN*

formal correctness of state documents and ceremonies; the military office was originally designed to carry on more important functions, including an independent inspectorate of troops, but now seems to be restricted to matters of protocol. Chinese government has for centuries operated on the basis of a two-way current of written materials: memorials, petitions, and other communications come from the provinces and dominions to the metropolis; orders, laws and other commands flow outward in response.[14]

[14] For a description of this function in the T'ang dynasty, see des Rotours, Baron Robert, *La Traite des Examens*, Paris, 1932, *passim;* and see Fairbank, J. K., and Têng, S. Y., "Of the Types and Uses of Ch'ing Documents," *Harvard Journal of Asiatic Studies*, Vol. 5, No. 1 (January 1940), particularly p. 5 ff., for the Manchu empire.

The other four agencies directly dependent on the Council of State are all of important character, but likely to be impaired by a period of crisis. The Academia Sinica (*Kuo-li Chung-yang Yen-chiu Yüan*) serves scientific and educational work through its own research bureaus, through systems of extended aid, and through a program of publications; despite war, it has continued, making heroic efforts to preserve the national cultural vitality and continuity. The three remaining agencies are of less importance, although the Planning Committee for the Western Capital (*Hsi-ching Ch'ou-pei Wei-yüan-hui*) found its work considerably extended when, on October 1, 1940, Chungking was formally denominated an auxiliary capital of the Chinese Republic, and a long-standing anomaly—that of the city's uncertain status—was removed.

The Council of State could be regarded, therefore, as a mere excrescence upon the design of government were it not that ceremonial and formal functions, indispensable to any government but particularly salient in China, can be delegated to it, and the actual policy-making agencies thereby stripped down to maximal utility and efficacy.

The Executive *Yüan*

The Executive *Yüan* is the political organ which includes the ministries, and is therefore roughly analogous to a cabinet, just as the Council of State is in loose parallel to a Privy Council. Together with the Supreme National Defense Council and the Military Affairs Commission, it exercises actual control over the National Government in war time. Its growth involves executive giantism, and atrophy for the remaining *Yüan*. The President (*Yüan-chang*) of the Executive *Yüan* (*Hsing-chêng Yüan*) is the highest executive officer of the government. This post has not always been held by Chiang K'ai-shek. At various times Wang Ch'ing-wei (now in

Nanking) and H. H. K'ung (now Minister of Finance and Vice-President [*Fu-yüan-chang*] of the *Yüan*) have held this office.

The Executive *Yüan* may be compared to a parliamentary cabinet in respect to its relations to the President of the National Government, but it possesses no authority whatever over the Supreme National Defense Council, nor over the Kuomintang C. E. C. and the Kuomintang Congress. It cannot ask for its own dissolution, nor demand the dissolution of the higher policy-making agency whose will it executes.[15] It resembles a cabinet, therefore, in its service as a consultative and unifying agency for the entire executive, but differs in its lack of controlling interdependence with a broad parliament. Again, the *Yüan* is unique among national executive agencies in the modern world with respect to its division of the task of policy-making and policy-supervising. Most cabinets consist of meetings of the heads of executive ministries or departments, with the chief executive officer presiding, but have no elaborate secretarial or administrative machinery interposed between the cabinet and its direct subordinates (departments or ministries). The Executive *Yüan* is peculiar in possessing two elaborate staff agencies which handle as much routine work as possible, act as a clearing house for policy and general administration, and pre-digest a maximum of problems. The outline on p. 58 illustrates the difference.

All matters short of the most critical moment are referred to one or the other of the two staff organs (*Mi-shu Ch'u* or Secretariat, under a Secretary-General; and *Chêng-wu Ch'u*, or Office of Political Affairs,[16] under a Director of Political Affairs), which are nominally separate but actually almost fused, with the Director

[15] Wang Shih-chieh, *Pi-chiao Hsien-fa*, cited, p. 671.
[16] Not to be confused with the Office of Civil Affairs (*Wên-kuan Ch'u*), adjunct to the Council of State, described above.

THE PRESIDENT OR PREMIER
|
THE CABINET
|
Ministry   Ministry   Ministry   etc.
(secretarial and administrative staff
usually concentrated at this level)

THE EXECUTIVE *YÜAN* PRESIDENT
|
THE *YÜAN* MEETING

(composed of officers of ministerial rank
and presided over by the President)

Office of Political Affairs: Sections   Secretariat: Sections

Ministry   Ministry   Ministry   Ministry   etc.

serving as a sort of assistant Secretary-General. All official business (other than crucial matters raised by the members of the Meeting) comes to these agencies, where it is studied, assorted, and usually settled provisionally, pending only formal ratification by the Meeting of the Executive *Yüan*.

The Executive *Yüan* Meeting occurs once weekly, most commonly on Tuesday.[17] Each Meeting is presented with a formidable agenda, prepared by the Secretary-General, and divided into three categories: reports, matters for discussion, and appointments. The membership of the Meeting consists of the *Yüan* President and Vice-President, the Ministers heading the executive Ministries, and the Chairmen of Commissions having the rank of Ministry.[18] The work of the Meeting is car-

[17] A brilliant and informative discussion of the practical work of the Executive *Yüan* is to be found in Tsiang Ting-fu, "Executive *Yüan*," *The Chinese Year Book 1936–37*, cited, p. 241–6.

[18] For these Ministries and Commissions, see the following chapter. These are not to be lumped with the Party-Ministries and Commissions which, if anything, are even more complex in structure, but whose titles follow the same scheme of terminology as that of the government.

ried on in a business-like fashion. The Generalissimo, as incumbent *Yüan* President, takes great interest in the work of the *Yüan,* and makes faithfulness and punctuality in attendance a matter of high importance. Because of the Japanese air raids over the capital, the exact place and hour of the weekly meeting are not announced, nor are the proceedings public.

In giving effect to the decisions reached by the *Yüan* Meeting, the *Yüan* itself issues orders in its own name for matters which are of general interest, or which cannot be handled by any single Ministry or Commission. If the problem is within the province of a particular agency, the *Yüan*—through its Secretariat—addresses the appropriate form of intragovernmental communication, and the decision is then set forth as the order or act of the agency involved. The following subjects are within the jurisdiction of the Executive *Yüan:*

(1) laws or legal problems submitted for promulgation by the Legislative *Yüan;*

(2) the budget, also passed *pro forma* by the Council of State and put into legal form by the Legislative *Yüan;*

(3) declarations of war and peace, on the motion of the Legislative *Yüan;*

(4) appointment and discharge of the higher ranks of officials;

(5) matters which cannot be settled by a single Ministry or Commission;

(6) other matters which the *Yüan* President sees fit to introduce for discussion or decision.

The Executive *Yüan* has far outstripped all other *Yüan* in war-time growth. Its central position, the urgency of most government business, and the need for speed have led to this. Executive exercise of the ordinance-making power has led to the gradual desuetude of the Legislative *Yüan,* which has found ample work in the preparation of the Draft Permanent Constitution and the attempt to systematize legislation in view of rapid territorial and administrative change. The Executive *Yüan*, by controlling personnel, usually short-circuits the functions of the Examination and Control *Yüan;* and the Judicial *Yüan* has never had practical political parity. Hence, the five-power system must be regarded as a system with strong executive, weaker legislative, examinative, and censoral, and dependent judicial divisions. Above the five powers, the Supreme National Defense Council exercises its august authority; within them, the Executive stands forth; and to them, in the course of the war, a new agency, almost comparable to a sixth *yüan*, has sprung forth with an elaborate bureaucracy of its own: the Military Affairs Commission.

THE MILITARY AFFAIRS COMMISSION

Some sense of the perpetual urgencies underlying Chinese government in the past decade may be obtained by consideration of the Military Affairs Commission.[19] A similar agency was one of the political wheels on which the Nationalist-Communist machine rolled victoriously North in the Great Revolution of 1925–27. After the organization of a relatively stable government at Nanking, the separate military commission was due for absorption into the coordinate pattern of government; instead, it has lingered under one form or another for almost twenty years, growing great in recurrent crises, while the Ministry of War (which was to have absorbed it) has become its adjunct. War led to

---

[19] *Chün-shih Wei-yüan-hui. The Chinese Year Book, v. d.*, cited, and most of the official publicity from Chungking translates this term as "National Military Council," which is far from the original, literally "military-affairs-committee." "National Military Council" is also easily confused with the Supreme National Defense Council. Hence the present translation is employed, following Tsang, O. B., *A Supplement to a Complete Chinese-English Dictionary*, Shanghai, 1937, and the original.

sudden distension of the Commission, and the creation of an agency comparable to a sixth *yüan,* if not to a duplicate, shogunal government in the Japanese sense. The Commission had its own head, its own *Pu* (Ministries or Departments), its own staff and field services. Duplicating the regular government on the one side, and the party administration on the other, it flowered into bureaucracy so lavishly that a fourth agency—co-ordinator for the first three—began to be needed.

Simplicity of government structure has not been a part of the Chinese tradition; the quasi-state of the Empire had been as elaborate as its more potent European counterparts; and the foliation of government at war cannot be taken as *prima facie* proof of inefficiency. Personnel is provided by giving each officer two, five, even ten jobs; the work is done—delegation and counter-delegation frequently cancel out—and the creation of new agencies does not inescapably involve confusion.

The Military Affairs Commission consists of a Chairman—the Generalissimo (*Tsung-ssŭ-ling*), who is Chiang K'ai-shek—and seven to nine other members, all appointed by the Council of State upon designation by the Supreme National Defense Council.[20] The key officers of the armed forces are *ex officio* members, and the Commission is charged with the military side of the prosecution of the war. Its power has been liberally interpreted. New agencies have been attached to it as they arose; now it deals with social work, relief, education, agitation, propaganda, espionage, government-

[20] See Ho Yao-tsu, "The National Military Council," in *The Chinese Year Book, 1938-39,* cited, p. 361-3; Carlson, Evans Fordyce, *The Chinese Army: Its Organization and Military Efficiency,* New York, 1940, p. 26 *ff.;* and frequent references in *China At War* and the *News Release* of the China Information Committee, both semiofficial, particularly the issue of the latter for July 15, 1939. A list of the highest military personnel and brief outline of the General Staff may be found in Woodhead, H. G. W., editor, *The China Year Book 1939,* Shanghai, n. d., p. 216-17, and p. 225.

sponsored "social revolution," and many economic matters in addition to its narrowly military affairs.

The work of the Commission falls into two parts. On the one hand, it is the supreme directing agency for all the armies; on the other, the managing agency for a variegated war effort away from the combat lines. The Commission's work in theory covers all armies, but in practice confines its supervisory powers to the forces in Free China and—less clearly—to the major guerrilla units in the occupied areas.

The Commission's governmental structure coordinates military and political functions. The Chief of the General Staff serves as assistant to the Chairman of the Commission. The Main Office serves to smooth interdepartmental affairs and to act as a central clearing point for orders and other transmissions. Beneath the Commission and the main office, there are twelve divisions with the rank of *Pu*. The Department of Military Operations (*Chün-ling-pu*) serves as a military planning and strategic agency. The Department of Military Training (*Chün-hsün-pu*) supervises training facilities, military schools, and in-service training.[21] The Directorate-General of Courts-Martial (*Chün-fa Chih-hsing Tsung-chien-pu*) and Pensions Commission (*Fu-hsüeh Wei-yüan-hui*) are explained by their titles; the pension program is probably behind that of every Western power, and the personal grants made by the Generalissimo under his own extra-governmental arrangements are more effective than governmental pensions. The Military Advisory Council (*Chün-shih Ts'an-i-yüan*) acts as a research and consultative body, in no sense cameral. An Administration of Personnel (*Ch'uan-hsü T'ing*) applies some principles of the merit system. A

---

[21] Descriptions of the subordinate organs of all these agencies but the Pensions Commission and the War-Area Commission will be found in Ho Yao-tsu, cited immediately above. The translations of the titles here given, however, are those of the author.

Service Department (*Hou-fang Ch'in-wu-pu*) is in charge of transportation, supplies, and sanitation. The National Aviation Commission (*Hang-k'ung Wei-yüan-hui*) has won world-wide fame for its spectacular work in procuring a Chinese air arm, and in keeping Chinese air power alive against tremendous odds of finance, transportation, equipment, and personnel; Mme. Chiang's association with and interest in its success has been of material aid. Finally, on the strictly military side, there is the Office of the Naval Commander-in-Chief (*Hai-chün Tsung-ssŭ-ling-pu*), formerly the Naval Ministry, controlling the up-river remnants of the navy. The War Ministry (*Chün-chêng-pu*) occupies an anomalous position in this scheme. Subordinate to the Executive *Yüan*, it is also subordinate to the Commission, so that in effect it is a Ministry twice over, and is even shown as two ministries on occasion.[22] General Ho Ying-chin, as Minister of War, is subordinate to the Generalissimo as *Wei-yüan-chang* (Chairman) of the Commission.

The two remaining agencies of the Commission are of considerable interest. A system of having political commissars in the army, a Soviet device, was adopted by the Kuomintang forces when first organized under Chiang K'ai-shek, and political training accounted for much of that success of the Northward drive (1926–27). After the Nationalist-Communist split, political training as such fell into considerable disuse, and was replaced by ethical training provided by the Officers' Moral Endeavor Corps.[23] With the renewed entente,

[22] As an instance, see *Outline of the Organization of the Kuomintang* . . . , cited above, p. 54, n.[18].

[23] This is a semi-official agency sponsored by the Generalissimo. See below, p. 149. The new war-time change is well illustrated by the following statement: "Special commissioners were assigned to every group army, and political departments in the divisions were augmented. Enough political directors were assigned to every company of troops withdrawn from the front for reorganization, and to Chinese forces behind the enemy lines. In addition, political corps were formed to

and war of national union for defense, a Political Department (*Chêng-chih-pu*) was established. A graceful tribute to Communist skill in combining war and agitation was paid when Chou En-lai, the celebrated Red general, was designated Vice-Minister of this Department. One of the Generalissimo's most orthodox and able subordinates was made Minister. The Political Department extends its function in an enormous sweep across China, and renders aid in military education within the armies, in civilian organization, and in war propaganda. Active and omnipresent, it is an excellent instance of functioning national unity.

The Party and Government War Area Commission (*Chan-ti Tang-chêng Wei-yüan-hui*) is a coordinate agency for propaganda, relief, and social, economic and military counter-attack within the war area (the occupied zone), rather unusual in being a formal amalgamation of Kuomintang and government administration. Through this agency most of the guerrilla aid is extended, and the Nationalists seek to rival the Communists and independents in the number of Japanese

---

organize and train civilians. Because of the lack of personnel, so far there have been no political officers in units engaged in military operations.

"Conscious and hard-working, the political officers have done much to remove irritations which used to occur between the commanding officers and the political men . . .

"Political work in the army formerly consisted in a weekly or fortnightly talk by the officers, whereas now well-planned lessons on political subjects, reading classes, discussion groups, individual conversations and twilight meetings are conducted with clockwise regularity. Singing, theatricals, cartooning, sports, are promoted among the soldiers so long as they do not jeopardize their discipline. Among the civilians, the political officers have also been active. The organization of people's service corps, self-defense units in areas close to the war areas and money contributions to the war chest from people in the rear are a few of their accomplishments." China Information Committee, *News Release*, October 2, 1939.

The comment of Generalissimo Chiang in the interview on p. 371 is, despite its laconicism, relevant to this topic. A further discussion is available in Chên Chêng, "Three Years of Political Training Work," *The China Quarterly*, Vol. 5, No. 4 (Autumn 1940), p. 581–5.

they can destroy, or the amount of damage they can do. The more active branches of this Commission are a part of the Party structure, but the dual function of the Commission enables it to coordinate Party and Army work. The very role of the Commission is indicative of the fact that the Kuomintang is trying to meet rivalry by patriotic competition and not by suppression. Its integration with the military makes it a perfect example of the triune force which Nationalist China is bringing to bear on the enemy—army, government, and Party all seek to reach into the occupied zone, to articulate spontaneous mass resistance, to maintain the authority of the central government pending the *révanche*, and to uphold the existing political system, canalizing social change into evolutionary rather than class-war lines.[24]

The Judicial, Legislative, Examination and Control *Yüan*

The appearance of an actual three-power administration—army, government, Party—has led to the sharp relative decrease in importance of the four further *Yüan*. The Judicial *Yüan* (*Ssŭ-fa Yüan*) was even in peace time the least important of the five divisions of the government, failing to display—as an American might expect—a tendency toward effective judicial independence to counterweight the executive and legislative. The Legislative *Yüan* (*Li-fa Yüan*), while exceedingly active in the years between the Mukden and Loukouchiao incidents, has been reduced in importance by the coming of hostilities. Its work has been confined largely to drafting the Permanent Constitution, and continued codification of administrative law—particularly

---

[24] The official view of this work, silent on the competition of the Communists and independents, is found in Li Chai-sum, "Chinese Government Organization behind the Enemy Lines," last citation above, p. 595–600.

for coordination of central government and war area (occupied China) affairs.[25] The Examination *Yüan* (*K'ao-shih Yüan*) has attempted to continue in the field of civil service reform, and the Control *Yüan* (*Chien-ch'a Yüan*) has maintained war-time efforts.

The Legislative *Yüan*, under the *Yüeh Fa* of 1931, consists of a *Yüan-chang*, a *Fu-yüan-chang*, and forty-nine to ninety-nine members (*Li-fa Wei-yüan*), appointed by the Supreme National Defense Council for a two-year term upon nomination by the *Yüan* President. The term's shortness increases the dependence of members upon the President, and transforms the *Yüan* to a legislative study institute. Furthermore, the newly-developed People's Political Council has assumed the function of representation. The President of the *Yüan* retains sole and arbitrary power over the agenda, the final decision, and the allocation of personnel, although the incumbent, Dr. Sun K'ê, is one of China's leading moderates and an exponent of constitutional process, not likely to exercise arbitrary power.

Apart from its significant constitutional powers, which remain unimpaired, the *Yüan* finds much of its work performed at present through ordinances of the Supreme National Defense Council, administrative action of the Executive *Yüan*, or commands by the Military Affairs Commission. The jurisdiction retained includes:

(1) general legislation;
(2) the budget;
(3) general amnesty;
(4) declaration of war (never exercised);
(5) declaration of peace;

[25] Statement to the author by Sun K'ê (Sun Fo), President of the Legislative *Yüan*, Chungking, July 17, 1940. A summary of the work of the *Yüan* will be found in various issues of *The Chinese Year Book*; in Escarra, Jean, *Le Droit Chinois*, cited above, containing bibliographies; and in Tyau, M. T. Z., "The Work and Organization of the Legislative *Yüan*," *The China Quarterly*, Vol. 2, No. 1 (Christmas Number, 1936), p. 73–88.

(6) "other important matters" (which, in practice, has referred to the more open and solemn aspects of treaty-making, and whatever topic may be assigned the *Yüan* by the highest Party agency).[26]

The Judicial *Yüan* serves as an administrative and budgetary agency for four agencies. The Ministry of Justice (*Ssŭ-fa Hsing-chêng-pu*) is, obviously, the prosecuting agency, attached to the executive in the United States, but made a part of the general judicial system in China. The Administrative Court (*Hsing-chêng Fa-yüan*) is an agency only potentially important; so is the Commission for the Disciplinary Punishment of Public Officers (*Kung-wu-yüan Ch'êng-chieh Wei-yüan-hui*). The *Yüan* President is *ex officio* chief magistrate of the Supreme Court (*Tsui-kao Fa-yüan*). Wang Shih-chieh says of this *Yüan:*

> Because of the fact that the Judicial *Yüan* is itself not an organ of adjudication, and since all affairs concerning prosecution at law are handled by the Ministry of Justice, the actual work to be performed by the Judicial *Yüan* is very simple and light. In addition to framing the budget for the *Yüan* itself and approving the general estimates of the organs under it, the Judicial *Yüan* has only three further duties to perform: (1) to bring before the Legislative *Yüan* legislative measures connected with the Judicial *Yüan* and its sub-organs; (2) to petition the President of the National Government with respect to such cases as special pardon, commutation of sentence, and the restoration of civil rights; and (3) to unify the interpretation of laws and orders, and changes in judicial procedure.[27]

With peace, reconstruction and prosperity, the Judicial *Yüan* might acquire importance through its control of the administrative and technical aspects of the court system. Meanwhile, courts are more closely associated with their respective levels or areas of government than with one another in a unified judicial system.

[26] Wang Shih-chieh, *Pi-chiao Hsien-fa*, cited, p. 676 ff.
[27] The same, p. 691.

The Examination *Yüan,* with a President and Vice-President, is composed of a central *Yüan* office, which supervises two organs: the Ministry of Personnel (*Ch'uan-hsü Pu*), operating a selective promotion system, and the Examinations Commission (*K'ao-hsüan Wei-yüan-hui*). In absolute numbers, few examinations have been held. In practice, standard recruitment technique continues to involve introduction, influence, or family connections. The familiarity of such devices in China at least gives them a high polish, and precludes utter inefficiency. Under the circumstances, the Examination *Yüan* finds scope for valuable, creative work in the preparation of administrative studies and analyses of very considerable importance.

The Control *Yüan* is of interest to Westerners, because of the novelty of its functions. Through the courtesy of the *Yüan* President, a full official memorandum on the structure and procedure was prepared, surveying the work of the *Yüan* during the course of the war. This is reproduced as Appendices I (E) and I (F) below.[28] Some of the unofficial observers, both Western and Chinese, felt that the *Yüan* possessed further enormous possibilities of activity, and that the need for controlment was very great indeed. In general, the *Yüan* resembles its legislative, judicial and examination co-ordinates, in that the war-time executive growth has relegated it to a secondary position.

Decrease in the importance of the *yüan* system during hostilities cannot be taken, by a too simple cause-and-effect argument, as proof of the unwieldy or impractical character of this five-power system. Measured on a scale of other world governments, success is slow; but it is enormous in contrast to other Chinese central political institutions. At present, it is most improbable that the form of government will be changed, save in the event of catastrophe beyond all reckoning.

[28] See p. 313 and p. 318.

Chapter III

CONSULTATIVE AND ADMINISTRATIVE ORGANS

THE outbreak and continuance of war has left the fulcrum of power relatively untouched. The highest organs of state are primarily in Kuomintang hands; the Party Chief of the Kuomintang is, even at law, governmentally more important today than in 1937; and the constitutional monopoly of power remains under the Kuomintang. Even changes in the highest organs—such as establishment of the Supreme National Defense Council and the Military Affairs Commission—have left very little impress on the sources of power. Reforms have altered only the mode of power, not its tenure.

Modifications have, however, been introduced at the level of government just below the apex. These are important in two remarkable ways. The People's Political Council (*Kuo-min Ts'an-chêng Hui*) admixed an ingredient of representation which (save for the Party) had been lacking since the dubious, betrayed, inaugural years of the Republic. Furthermore, sweeping administrative reorganization and reinvigoration made possible the vitalization of the central government in the course of the war, so that despite Japanese pressure and rising Leftist rivalry, the National Government is, on any absolute scale, becoming more powerful year by year.

The People's Political Council

The People's Political Council was established by order of the Emergency Session of the Kuomintang Party Congress held in Hankow, March 1938. Its creation was a compromise measure between the proposal for a European-type United Front government, based on popular elections to a National Convention, and a continuation of the Kuomintang monopoly of government hitherto prevalent. Like many similar compromises in other countries, the institution has proved its viable and useful character. Without exaggeration, it may be stated to be the closest approximation of representative government which China has ever known. Simple, improvised, legally an instrument promising little independence or *élan* in its work, the Council demonstrates the effectiveness of the Chinese when purpose accompanies design. Formally the least representative of the Chinese constitutional parliaments, congresses, or conventions, the Council is the first to get down to business and—almost unexpectedly—to represent!

Membership, originally set at 150, was raised before the First Session to 200, and again in the autumn of 1940 to 240.[1] The number, unlike the 1681 tentatively projected for the People's Congress, is small enough to allow genuine discussion and to avoid unwieldiness. Attendance, considering war-time hazards, has been very good, with between two-thirds and four-fifths of the members usually present.

Although the Council was designed to meet quarterly by its fundamental Statute,[2] it soon changed to semi-annual sessions and has actually met at intervals running from six to eight months. Each session lasted for

[1] China Information Committee, *News Release*, Chungking, September 30, 1940; and the same, December 30, 1940.

[2] Wang Shih-chieh, "The People's Political Council," *The Chinese Year Book 1938–39*, cited, p. 346–55; the same, *The People's Political Council*, [Chungking], [1939?], pamphlet, reprinted from *The China Quarterly*, Vol. 4, No. 1 (Winter 1938–39). Dr. Wang's contributions, brief as they are, worthily supplement his pre-war constitutional studies, and provide the most carefully annotated data on the Council which the present author has found. The list of members given in the first article, above, is one of the most interesting documents of

ten days (legislative, not calendar).[3] As the Council sessions recurred, the Council became more and more free and representative. Despite the narrowness of its legal foundations, the Council has provided invaluable exercise in the arts of democratic discussion.

As a technique of representation, the Council's recruitment system is novel. The membership was, while the Council's total was at 200, divided into the following four categories:

Group A: representatives of the Provinces and Special Municipalities—88;
Group B: four representatives for or from Mongolia and two for or from Tibet—6;
Group C: representatives for or from the overseas Chinese—6;
Group D: representatives of cultural, professional, and economic bodies, or persons who have been active in political leadership—100.

There were no elections. In the case of Group A candidates, nominations were made by municipal or provincial governing bodies in joint session with the Kuomintang Party organ of corresponding location and level. Group B candidates were nominated by the Mongolian and Tibetan Affairs Commission. Group C candidates were nominated by the Overseas Chinese Affairs Commission in the Executive *Yüan*. Group D

---

our time, giving, as it does, the residence, profession, and age of each Councillor. Beside "Former Prime Minister" one finds "Living Buddha attached to the Panchen Lama," "Reserve Member, Executive Committee, the Third International," "Professor, National Peking University" and "Head of the Mêng Clan, Descendants of Mencius."

[3] Woodhead, H. G. W., editor, *The China Year Book, 1939*, Shanghai, n. d., Ch. IX, "The Kuomintang and the Government," contains a detailed summary of the first two sessions of the People's Political Council (p. 231-7). Quigley, Harold S., "Free China," *International Conciliation*, No. 359 (April 1940), includes a judicious appraisal of the work and meaning of the Council in its first two and one-half years (p. 137-8).

candidates, which included the representatives of the Communists and independent Left, were nominated by the Supreme National Defense Council. Two candidates could be presented for each seat on the Council. Subject to a minor detour or two on qualifications or for other reasons,[4] the final selection or election was made by the Central Executive Committee of the Kuomintang.

Thus, an independent or Leftist, whose life had been more or less in danger for years, because of his hostility to the Kuomintang and its policies, might find himself nominated for the Council by the Kuomintang's highest government-supervising agency, and elected by the Kuomintang's highest Party agency. Leaders of the hitherto suppressed, still technically illegal parties and factions—which meant all save the Kuomintang—were designated representatives through the fiction of selection for individual merits. They might take an active share in hammering out policy, and—on the same day—find themselves legally debarred from overt public expression of their own party work. By this device, the Kuomintang provided a safety-valve for opposition without touching the apparatus of its own power.

Had the Kuomintang leaders been obtuse and made the Council something less than a genuine sounding board for public opinion, or had they picked unrepresentative members of the other groups, the whole experiment would have failed. In practice, the compromise worked and gave China a focus for the national concentration of will.

The Council did not elect its own Speaker (*I-chang*) and Deputy-Speaker (*Fu I-chang*); these were elected for it by the Central Executive Committee of the Kuo-

---

[4] Wang Shih-chieh, "The People's Political Council," cited, p. 346 ff. The new system, inaugurated early in 1941, provided for 90 members to be directly elected by Provincial and Municipal People's Political Councils.

CONSULTATIVE AND ADMINISTRATIVE 73

mintang. Down to 1940, the Council elected a Resident Committee of fifteen to twenty-five members from its own membership; under a recent reorganization, this and the Speaker and Vice-Speaker are to be replaced by a Presidium, to be elected by but not necessarily from among the Council, to consist of five members and to hold the authority of designating presiding officers. This would amount to a further step in the independence of the Council. In both cases, the Secretariat (*Mi-shu-ch'u*) of the Council is to be under a Secretary-General (*Mi-shu-chang*) and Deputy Secretary-General (*Fu Mi-shu-chang*) and to include services of correspondence, general affairs, Council affairs, and police.[5]

With respect to competence, the Council is possessed of three powers:

(1) the right to deliberate on all important measures, whether of domestic or foreign policy, before these are enacted into law by the Central Government (but not, however, the right of making such law) ;

(2) the right to submit proposals to the government (but since the Supreme National Defense Council is the highest government-directing agency in China, its concurrence is patently necessary) ;

(3) the right to demand and hear reports from the *Yüan* and the Ministries, and to interpellate the officers of state.

The distinguished Chinese constitutional scholar, Wang Shih-chieh, Secretary-General of the People's Political Council (Generalissimo Chiang himself being the Speaker) writes of its functions:

From the foregoing description, the peculiarities of the People's Political Council may be clearly seen. It is not an advisory body of the Government in the ordinary conception of the term, because the Government is bound, except in emergency cases, to submit to it for consideration

[5] *Tang Chêng Chien Chih T'u-piao*, cited, chart of the *Kuo-min Ts'an-chêng Hui.*

all important measures before they are carried out. The Council possesses not only the power to advise, but also the right to be consulted. Nor is it a legislative organ, as all its resolutions merely embody broad principles of legislation or administration, i.e., lines of policy which, even after being assented to by the Supreme National Defense Council, will still have to go through the ordinary legislative or ordinance-making process in order to become laws or administrative ordinances.

As regards the representative character of the Council, it rests not so much with the method by which the Councillors are chosen, as with the fact that, being composed of men and women most of whom enjoy wide popularity or respect in one way or another, the Council can really speak for almost all the articulate group-interests of the nation. In the less than 30 years of China's experience in republican government, numerous experiments had been attempted at representative government before the convention of the People's Political Council. Few of these were deficient in theoretic grandiloquence, but none of them was found to be serviceable in practical applicability.

Theoretically, the Council is not a popular assembly; but, as I remarked elsewhere,* "it is open to question whether any form of election by popular suffrage can result in so truly representative a body." Even with reference to the limited scope of the Council's powers, I submit that the provision represents a progressive step in that any alternative that is less realistic would impede rather than facilitate the contributive work of the Council.[6]

The author adds that the resolutions have tended to be of an extraordinarily practical character, and that bombast has remained conspicuously absent.

The procedure of the Council has been kept very simple. A quorum requires only a simple majority (101 members), and a simple majority of a quorum (51) is all that is needed to pass a resolution. To ensure the proper spacing of the calendar, all resolutions initiating new business must come within the first four days

* *Chinese Year Book, 1938*, Chap. 17. [Wang Shih-chieh's note.]
[6] Wang Shih-chieh, *The People's Political Council*, cited, p. 5. Obvious misprints have been corrected.

of the ten-day session. Introduction may not be completed by the action of a single member; a petition of 20 members, one proposing and 19 endorsing, is necessary for introduction. Reference may then be either to the plenary session or to the committees. (There are five standing committees—military, foreign, civil, financial and economic, educational and cultural affairs—which provide further facilities through subdivision into subcommittees, or through the addition of special committees.) Reports by the government are introduced during the first three days of each session.[7]

Members cannot waste time over the pork-barrel, log-rolling, riders, or minor fiscal questions. Since they all have the same constituency at law, and that constituency—the C. E. C. of the Kuomintang—asks nothing of them except representation of their moral constituencies—the groups and areas from which they derive, Councillors are untroubled by constituents or appropriations. The budget is submitted by the government to the Council for approval, not enactment. Salaries of the Councillors are nil. Each is given Ch. $350.00 (about U. S. $20.00) per month for expenses, without regard to mileage, and even overseas Chinese representatives receive no further emoluments. Since government officials are excluded from membership, use of a Council seat for purposes of preferment is precluded.

A liberalization of representation and of procedure occurred early in 1941. A new Council—involving the first turnover in membership since 1938—was elected. Educational and other unofficial representatives obtained an additional twenty seats on the Council. The changes were scarcely sufficient to compensate for the further postponement of the promised Constitution, but they indicated a willingness of the government to meet demands for democratization. Procedural changes

[7] The author is indebted for some of these facts to an interview with Dr. Wang Shih-chieh in Chungking on August 1, 1940.

increased the effectiveness of individual members. A minor but characteristic feature was the increase in number and importance of women members.

Partisan organization in the Council, although elementary, has begun to function. Each clique has informal caucuses; careful scrutiny discloses the presence of whips from these caucuses on the floor. The groupings in the Council are so fluid that they can be variously classified by persons with different viewpoints. (Formally, of course, everyone is either Kuomintang or non-Party, even though *The Chinese Year Book,* under informal Chungking government sponsorship, proudly lists the high rank of the Communist members of the Council—"Chen Shao-yu (Wang Ming), [age] 33, [province] Anhwei, [remarks] Member, Presidium, Central Executive Committee, the Third International.") [8] The popular classification of the Council cliques, commonly seen in the press, is based on the Four Parties (*Ssŭ Tang*) and the Four Cliques (*Ssŭ P'ai*). The four parties are the Kuomintang, National Socialist, Communist, and *La Jeunesse*.[9] The Four Cliques, which according to popular credence, formed soon after the first meetings of the Council, are based on intellectual sympathy and the interplay of temperaments, and not on dogma.

The most Leftist clique is believed to be the *Huachung P'ai* (Central China Clique), with the National Salvationists' Seven Gentlemen at their core. Deeply sympathetic with the masses, and violently patriotic, this group helped to bring about the war by opposing appeasement. Like-thinking Council members, however affiliated, are believed to fall under the legislative leadership of the Central China Clique. Near to this, still far to the Left of the government, is the *Tungpei P'ai* (Northeast Clique). The Northeastern Manchurian

[8] *1938–39* issue, p. 351.
[9] Described below, p. 159 ff.

Chinese officers, exiled in the Northwest, were the first bridge between the Communists and the rest of the country. Since their native provinces and kinsfolk have had almost ten years' Japanese domination, the Northeast group is emphatic in demands for national unity. Communists circulate from one group to the other, always cooperative in offering their leadership on the basis of a United Front, which the Comintern still decrees for the Far East after jettisoning the Popular Fronts of Europe.

The two relatively Rightist cliques are the *Ch'ê-yeh Chiao-yü P'ai* (Vocational Educationists' Clique) and the *Chiao-shou P'ai* (Professors' Clique). Composed of men still so far from attaining office that they possess perfect freedom of criticism, they therefore stand Left of the government in daily comment, although they may be Right of it in theory. The former group stresses simple, direct problems: it seeks to attack the opium problem, disease, illiteracy, and so forth, without necessarily fighting the social revolution against the landlords. It derives its name from two distinguished leaders of the vocational education movement who have abstained from active political work until finding a forum in the Council. The Professors' Clique is reputedly led by the group of young professors who were eminent in their fields before the outbreak of war, opposed to the government's appeasement policy, but tactful enough not to rebel. They are considered to stand as far Right as anyone on the Council—that is, to discuss politics in terms of soundness of public policy, budgetary reasonableness, immediate practicality, and other commonsense standards, which appear conservative beside the fervid idealism of their colleagues.

The description of the *Ssŭ P'ai* just given is one which exists in the popular credence. A more authoritative source placed the groups in the Council under the following four headings:

(1) the Kuomintang and non-Party majority;
(2) the *La Jeunesse* Party and the National Socialists;
(3) the Communists;
(4) the "Popular Front" group, including the intellectuals and the National Salvationists.

On this basis, the Kuomintang would retain its working control of the Council, which appears to be the case, in terms of work performed. The unaffiliated majority, selected by their local governments and Kuomintang offices and elected by the Kuomintang C. E. C., would in doubtful cases be inclined to turn to Kuomintang leadership. The *La Jeunesse* Party, despite the fact that it is a Western-returned student organization, is strong in Szechuan; its influence could be expected to run with that of the National Socialists. Both parties, while minute, are decidedly averse to Communist fellow-travelling and not at all disposed to alter the *status quo*, except to carve modest niches for themselves and to advance their programs in an agreeable way. The Communists stand alone, although they offer their cooperation to the independents.

The Popular Front group is a category widely recognized in China—the Left Kuomintang, the discontented idealists, the irrepressible patriots, the minor parties, the indefatigable conspirators of Chinese hopefulness who are always on the scene. For years they have been unforgotten witnesses to the ferocious integrity of ideals which (in individuals scattered at random at all levels of society) call Chinese out of the lethargy of being very practical.

The Popular Front leaders, more than any other in China, have withstood perennial temptation for years and have kept their activities, under whatever name undertaken, intact. They can be distinguished from other Party leaders, both Nationalist and Communist, by the facts that they have never set up a government, with jobs in it for themselves; have never controlled a government, save through lacunae in power politics; and have never preserved a government which they did control. Warm-hearted, philanthropic, patriotic, their shrill zeal has been audible in China for many years. Without formal organization, they have stood behind others who sought real power, and today—between the cold, realistic leaders of the two opposing Parties— are assembled, ever-hopeful, and advocating a Popular Front.

The Secretary-General stated to the author that he regarded three of the Council's contributions as of history-making importance. First, the Council openly expressed a Chinese national unity unprecedented in modern history. Forms apart, never before had a crisis found all Chinese so united; the Council gave a symbol to that unity. Second, the Council raised the probability of successful democratic processes in China. Failures under the Peking parliaments had reduced democratic discussion to a sham. The Council erased this discredit, making many people believe that democracy promises a real value to the country—not merely as an ideal, but as a practicable means of government. This contribution was reinforced by a third: the Council actually served to make definite, serious, concrete improvements in government and Kuomintang structure, through criticism and through the issues aired.

The Administrative Pattern

Central policy-making is complicated by a trifurcation of organs—Party Headquarters, Military Affairs Commission, and Executive *Yüan*. For example, the nation's publicity and broadcasting services, as well as direction of the official news agencies, are under the (Kuomintang) Party-Ministry of Publicity, while the Foreign Office possesses its own publicity organs for the international relations field, and the Political Department of the Military Affairs Commission handles much domestic propaganda and agitation. The strictly governmental, permanent administrative agencies are simplified from their pre-war complexity, as the following list will show:

EXECUTIVE *Yüan*
- Ministry of Foreign Affairs
- Ministry of the Interior
- Ministry of Finance
- Ministry of Economic Affairs (to be reorganized)
- Ministry of Social Affairs (pending)
- Ministry of Education
- Ministry of Communications
- Ministry of Agriculture and Forestry
- Commission on Mongolian and Tibetan Affairs
- Commission on Overseas Chinese Affairs
- National Relief Commission
- Ministry of War (also under the Military Affairs Commission)
- Material and Resources Control and Supervision Ministry (pending; status uncertain)

JUDICIAL *Yüan*
- Ministry of Justice

CONTROL *Yüan*
- Ministry of Audit

EXAMINATION *Yüan*
- Ministry of Personnel
- Examination Commission

The Ministries outside the Executive are well adapted to their respective *Yüan*, although Americans may think the Ministry of Justice misplaced. The Executive Ministries form the heart of the administrative system, immediately below the cabinet (Executive *Yüan* Meeting). The Party scaffolding is to be torn down with constitutionalization; the military scaffolding, with peace. The administrative organs at the center will then bear the real burden of nourishing and protecting the nation which now they help to create.

Despite strong Chinese imprints, the central administrative agencies are organizationally more Westernized than the policy-making agencies. For this reason, and because administrative emphasis is on matters economic (outside the scope of the present work), the reader is referred to other sources for a detailed appraisal of the work of the ministries. Particularly fortunate is it that *China Shall Rise Again,* partly written and partly edited by Madame Chiang K'ai-shek,[10] has been published, including authoritative statements by the leading ministers on the work of their respective ministries.

The Ministries (*pu*) may be classified into three groups, according to the major tenor of their work: political, social and cultural, and economic. Military defense through economic development and social reconstruction remains their common goal, however divergent the approaches.

The Political Ministries

Senior and most famous of all Chinese ministries is that of Foreign Affairs (*Wai-chiao Pu*). It inherits the splendid traditions of Chinese diplomacy, dating back to the redoubtable Pan Ch'ao, who almost single-handed conquered Central Asia in the first century A.D. by unsleeping guile and consistent boldness. Modern Chinese diplomacy has made the best of a hundred years of defeat, successfully exploiting the mutual suspicions of the imperialist powers. The morale and professional

[10] May-ling Soong Chiang (Madame Chiang K'ai-shek), *China Shall Rise Again,* New York, 1941. Chinese economic developments are the subject of careful study by the Institute of Pacific Relations, whose *Far Eastern Survey* follows contemporary developments closely and whose *Inquiry Series* offers a monumental collection of linked works on Pacific affairs, with particular stress on the economic background to politics. The volume in this series on Chinese political development, by Lawrence K. Rosinger, may be expected to fill an important gap in the literature on China today.

cohesion are high. Despite incessant political changes, the foreign office and diplomatic service have preserved their continuity from the Empire to the present. The Chungking government probably possesses a foreign office superior to the Gaimusho of Tokyo.[11]

The effectiveness of Chinese international statesmanship has aroused an almost superstitious dread among the Japanese, publicists, officials, and others. Japan consistently complains that China is superior at propaganda, and sees, behind the world-wide mistrust of Japan, occult forces from the Comintern or vile Chinese guile. After they perpetrated the Nanking horrors, insulted neutral men and women in Tientsin, machine-gunned a British ambassador, sank an American gunboat, and violated all available international law, the Japanese believed that British and American lack of sympathy was mostly due to the machinations of Chinese diplomacy. The recent Minister of Foreign Affairs, Dr. Wang Ch'ung-hui, a former Judge of the Permanent Court of International Justice (World Court), is one of the modern world's greatest legal scholars. Eminent in political leadership ever since the first foundation of the Republic, he has always urged moderation, legality, and intelligence in government.

The Ministry of the Interior (*Nei-chêng Pu*) forms the apex to China's constitutional system of provincial and local governments. In accordance with Sun Yat-sen's teaching, the National Government has consistently sought to reduce the importance of the provinces and to foster direct local-central intergovernmental relationships. The importance of this ministry is reduced somewhat by the fact that other agencies possess their own field services, and are therefore not obliged to

---

[11] For the latest description of the organization of the *Wai-chiao Pu*, see Wang Ch'ung-hui, "China's Foreign Relations during the Sino-Japanese Hostilities 1937–1940," Chapter XIII of Chiang, May-ling Soong, *China Shall Rise Again*, cited, p. 139–40.

route policy through it, but it remains significant because of its control and supervision of China-wide administrative development. The National Health Administration (*Wei-shêng Shu*), formerly separate, is now a department of this Ministry.

Social and Cultural Agencies

The Ministry of Education (*Chiao-yü Pu*) has continued active despite the war. The heroic marches of the Chinese universities to their new homes in the West have become a world-famous epic. Students, faculty, and staffs moved out of the sinister zones of enemy occupation, usually travelling on foot, until they found new homes hundreds or even thousands of miles from their original locations. Some colleges have found homes in old temples or in caves where, with a minimum of equipment and library material, they continue their work. Others, more fortunate, have become guests of West China institutions. West China Union University in Chengtu has four other universities on its campus, all using the same facilities for the duration of the war. Still other institutions have been consolidated.

The Ministry of Education has subsidized education as generously as possible, and fosters progress despite the war and because of it. In spite of all handicaps, institutions of higher learning have risen in number from 91 in 1937–38 to 102 in 1939–40, with a corresponding rise in enrollment of 31,188 to 41,494.[12] The entering class for 1940–41 was about 12,000, indicating a continued rise.[13]

[12] *China at War*, Vol. V, No. 2 (October 1940), p. 37.
[13] The same, Vol. V, No. 4 (November 1940), p. 78. See also Wu Yi-fang and Price, Frank W., *China Rediscovers Her West*, New York, 1940; Chapter VII, "Holding the Educational Front" (p. 69–76) is by Y. G. Chen, President of the University of Nanking. The entire work edited by Messrs. Wu and Price is of value; written from the missionary point of view, it presents first-hand statements of affairs on Western China, and continues with liberal and socially conscious appraisals of the needs of Christian work.

In addition to the accredited institutions, there are innumerable volunteer agencies, some of which are patriotic but educationally elementary schools for saboteurs, agitators, and guerrillas. Education is propaganda, but such is its immediate appeal that Left schools obtain capacity attendance. A few students are disappointed. One wrote, "The most unpleasant thing to me was that, as soon as I entered the Resist-Japan University, I was deprived of my liberty. I was not free in speech; I was not allowed to say anything outside of Marxism-Leninism . . ." and went home.[14] The total attendance remains high; if added to that of the accredited institutions operating according to government standards, it would swell the sum enormously.

In addition to formal aid to institutions of higher learning, and administration of the National Government colleges, the Ministry sponsors the mass literacy movement. In this it has had the benefit of the work of Dr. James Y. C. Yen and his associates.[15] The war, moving vast masses of people and shifting the modernized city-dwellers from the coast to the interior, has proved a stimulus to the rise of literacy and the demand for popular literature.

The Ministry is headed by Ch'ên Li-fu, whose brother, Ch'ên Kuo-fu, is head of the (Kuomintang) Central Political Institute. Together they stand at the Right center of the Kuomintang, exerting enormous influence on the Party and on the country. Both have been very close to the Generalissimo, and took a large share in revitalization of the Kuomintang before and during the war.

The two Commissions serve important needs. The Commission on Overseas Chinese Affairs (*Ch'iao-wu*

[14] Wang Wên-hsiang. "K'ang-jih Ta-hsüeh yü Ch'ing-nien Fan-mên" ("The Sorrows of Youth and the Resist-Japan University") in the symposium entitled *So-wei "Pien-ch'ü"* (The So-called "Frontier Area") , Chungking, XXVIII (1939) , p. 30 *ff.*

[15] See the discussion of the mass education problem, below, p. 218.

Wei-yüan-hui) is the informal Chinese equivalent of a colonial office. The Commission looks after the welfare of the overseas settlements of the Chinese, fostering language schools, hospitals and the like. It acts through Chinese community associations, rarely through official channels. Practices of hyphenated citizenship, so offensive to one Western nationality when undertaken by another, are unobtrusive and necessary in the case of the Chinese. With the outside states putting Chinese in a special economic, legal, and political category—through immigration laws, administrative practice, and extragovernmental pressure including lynching—the individual Chinese who deracinates himself is indeed a lost soul. Few Chinese worry about overseas Chinese *irredentas*. The Commission fosters no *putsches* and mobilizes no fifth columns, but does help to keep Chinese, whatever their nationalities, still Chinese.

The Commission on Mongolian and Tibetan Affairs (*Mêng Tsang Wei-yüan-hui*) is the supreme agency for the dependencies. It has a record of considerable success in fostering a good-neighbor policy toward the half-autonomous dominions of Chinese Turkestan (Sinkiang, also called Chinese Central Asia),[16] Tibet, and Inner Mongolia. Outer Mongolia is under indirect Soviet control, and Eastern Inner Mongolia under the Japanese. The Chinese have utilized every device of courtesy and diplomacy in retaining their precarious grip on these areas. The Commission includes dominion members.

THE ECONOMIC MINISTRIES

The Ministries dealing in economic matters bear the ultimate burden of resistance. Upon their success de-

[16] Among the recent books on Sinkiang, one, unusual because it is by a Chinese author, stands out: Wu, Aitchen K., *Turkistan Tumult*, London, 1940. The travel books of Sven Hedin, Ella Maillart, Peter Fleming, and Sir Eric Teichman also contain material of political interest.

pend China's tools of war. If artillery, aircraft, machineguns, munitions, food, clothing and other necessities are not available to the central armies, the opportunity for counter-attack may come and go, and China be lost—not through the power of her enemy, but through her own weakness. Unless economic mobilization succeeds, the guerrilla warfare in the occupied area will be frustrated, since its purpose is merely to prepare for a *révanche* from Free China; history affords few examples of guerrillas defeating mass armies, fighting positionally, without the intervention of other mass armies.

The Ministry of Finance (*Ts'ai-chêng Pu*) is the leader of the Economic Ministries. Headed by H. H. K'ung, successor to the celebrated T. V. Soong, it has performed fiscal miracles in maintaining the credit of the National Government. Chief among its accomplishments has been the institution, within the past decade, of a managed currency on the gold-exchange standard. Specie had been the immemorial medium of exchange, and Chinese experience with paper money—from the earliest times to the present—had been unfortunate. Starting with the 1860's, China had undergone one paper-money inflation after another. Governmental currency was frequently a receipt for silver on deposit, in which case it amounted to no more than a commodity warehouse certificate, thereby subject to discount for transportation charges, and fluctuating meanwhile with the world price of silver; otherwise it was fiat money, guaranteed by stranglers' cords and long knives. Fractional coins passed by metallic weight; the shifts in the price of copper in New York and London determined the number of pennies which farmers received for their silver dollars, even on the threshold of Tibet.

By putting private bank notes, both Chinese and foreign, out of circulation, systematizing note issuance to four government banks and a limited number of carefully supervised provincial agencies, the National

Government made the change with far less difficulty than anyone, even optimists, dared to hope. Until the outbreak of war subsidiary coinage was copper and aluminum; this has been replaced by fractional paper, circulating decimally without discount for exchange into larger bills. Simple peasants, who used to hide a slug of silver in their fields, now conceal a Bank of China, Bank of Communications, Central Bank of China, or Farmers' Bank of China *fa pi* (legal tender) note in roofs or walls.

Other noteworthy reforms include the standardization of levies in the provinces, now proceeding to some degree, and the imposition of direct taxes, a revolutionary step for China. Income and inheritance taxes, previously thought to be uncollectible in a pre-modern area such as China's hinterland, are yielding substantial sums. War borrowing is done almost entirely through domestic loans. These are issued in the form of patriotic contribution bonds, and are available in denominations as low as Ch. Nat. $5.00 (about 28 U. S. cents). Further support has come in the form of American, British, and Soviet fiscal aid, and—until the outbreak of the European war—additional credits, both private and intergovernmental, from continental Europe. The Ministry has moved with a financial prudence which promises to maintain China's domestic and foreign credit for further years of war.

The Ministry has engaged in direct conflict with the enemy through bank-note rivalry. Throughout the occupied area, National Government currency is in conflict with the issuances of the Japanese army and the pro-Japanese governments. The Chungking policy has been to hold back the invasion currencies, on the assumption that continued circulation of the national currency maintains a continued popular stake in the government. Many guerrilla leaders believe that the occupied areas should use nothing of value to the Japanese, and therefore encourage the issuance of local emergency currency.

Under the Ministry of Finance, numerous efforts have been made to keep foreign trade alive. With war-time pressure on transportation facilities, foreign trade has become a virtual monopoly of the government; few major transactions are made by wholly private interests, since in addition to monopolizing the highways, government-owned corporations also have access to differentials in foreign exchange (which often mark the difference between great profits and none). In the matter of the governmentalized Sino-American trade, correlated with the American credits, the Foo Shing Corporation (export) and the Universal Trading Corporation (import) control the current both ways. The Ministries of Communications and of Economic Affairs also have a share in this state-capitalist business.[17]

Subdivisions in the Ministry of Finance include sections for customs, salt gabelle, internal revenue, general taxation, public loans, currency, national treasury, accounting, and general affairs. Efforts are now in progress to consolidate all intragovernmental fiscal services, so that the budget shall cover the entire government, and separate agencies will no longer be able to make half-controlled collections and disbursements.

The Ministry of Economic Affairs (*Ching-chi Pu*) is in general responsible for the industrialization of an area half the size of Europe with well over two hundred million inhabitants. No non-industrial state can defeat an industrial state unless it has access to the industrial resources of third parties. The Chinese, realizing this, have launched a modernization process unparalleled in modern history. The two greatest migrations of the

[17] *The Far Eastern Survey* keeps effectively up to date with all new developments in this field. An authoritative but understandable explanation of the work of the Ministry is found in H. H. K'ung, "Holding China's Financial Front," Ch. XI, work by Mme. Chiang K'ai-shek, cited above.

twentieth century have occurred, most probably, in China: the first the settlement of Manchuria, and the second the flight to the West. In each case more than twenty million persons have been involved. The Ministry of Economic Affairs has transformed this rout into a pioneering advance. Refugees have been taught to bring their tools with them; when they had no tools their skills have been sought out and utilized. As the national armies and government retreated up the Yangtze and inward, they brought along the personnel of a modern economic system, and set an industrial society down in a world technologically backward.

West-China modernization will probably be the most durable economic consequence of the war. Cities near the edge of Tibet have underground electric power and automatic telephone systems. Primitive salt-drying areas have been modernized; in one instance, steel pipe being lacking, bamboo pipelines, plastered and cemented for reinforcement, run cross-country. Filthy, tax-ridden, vicious little cities which had been the haunts of opium-sotted militarists are now given the double blessing of fair government and a business boom. (The author felt, when he returned to America in September 1940, that he was going from a new country to an old, leaving the hope, zest and high spirits of the Chinese frontier for the comfortable melancholy of American half-prosperity.)

On the government side, the stimulation to technological advance has consisted of broad, experimental use of government personnel, subsidies, and part-ownership, together with some outright state socialism. Four types of encouragement appear with particular frequency: the government-controlled movement of private industries from the endangered areas to the West, government sponsorship of brand new industrial enterprises, official encouragement of cooperatives, and state ownership-management of enterprises.

Many industries were saved for China through compulsory movement. Thousands of tons of industrial equipment were moved up to the West, floated on barges and river-boats, or dragged by hand over macadam highways, dirt roads, and mud footpaths. One single enterprise, the Chung Fu Joint Mining Administration of Honan, successfully transferred one hundred and twenty thousand tons of equipment, now applied to coal mining in the Southwest.[18]

Government sponsorship of new enterprises covers the entire field of modern industry. Investors wait in line before opportune undertakings. Electric light bulbs, safety matches, automobile parts and tools, clothing—everything from machine-shop tools to luxury goods is being produced in the West. Bottlenecks do occur in new industries competing for priorities in imported machinery.

In the field of cooperatives, the C. I. C. (China Industrial Cooperatives) stand out as truly important social and economic pioneering. (See below, p. 223.)

Government ownership has not been niggard or timorous. In most cases it has followed American patterns and appeared in the form of government-owned corporations, but there are also a considerable number of frankly state-operated enterprises, such as municipal food stores, ferries, and heavier industrial undertakings. The munitions and motor fuel trades are, so far as the author could find, entirely a matter of government ownership. In the air communications and airplane production field, government ownership is relaxed to the point of a senior partnership in joint companies with foreign corporations; the latter provide the supplies and trained personnel.

The Ministry of Economic Affairs is under the con-

[18] Wong Wen-hao, Minister of Economic Affairs, "Industrialization of Western China," Ch. XIV, work by Mme. Chiang K'ai-shek, cited above, p. 142.

trol of Wong Wen-hao,[19] whose career was first distinguished in geology and educational administration. His scientific outlook stands him in good stead, since the exploitation of West-China resources requires scientific as well as business application. Subdivisions of his Ministry include those of mining, industry, commerce, water conservancy, and general affairs.

A Ministry of Agriculture and Forestry (*Nung Lin Pu*) was set up in 1940 as the third economic ministry. Industrialization's dependence on farm products makes this an invaluable coordinate to the other two Ministries. The Chinese are in many cases proceeding directly from pre-industrial to the latest chemico-industrial techniques, and skipping the phase of reliance upon subsoil minerals. Gasoline is being mixed with fuel alcohol derived from grain; plastics are appearing.

Agriculture also involved China's greatest social problem—that of encouraging freehold or cooperative farming at the expense of sharecropping. Much of the agricultural reform is undertaken by the new local government and provincial government plans, but the problems of farm prices, general farm planning, and utilization of agricultural products fall on the Ministry. It is headed, not by a farm leader or expert, but by the General Chên Chi-tang, former governor of Kwangtung Province.[20]

A proposed Material and Resources Control and Supervision Ministry (or Ministry of Economic Warfare), based approximately upon the British Ministry of Supplies, is in process of organization.[21] The Ministry may be kept independent of either the Executive *Yüan* or Military Affairs Commission, since it is to coordinate a group of industrial and commercial agencies which

[19] He also spells it Oung Wen-hao; by the Wade transliteration, Wêng Wên-hao.
[20] China Information Committee, *News Release*, Chungking, July 1, 1940.
[21] The same, December 23, 1940.

are now independent. Upon its establishment, the Ministry of Economic Affairs will become one of Industry and Commerce, and a central agency for economic war work will be available.

The National Relief Commission (*Chên-chi Wei-yüan-hui*) supervises the general relief work of the government, which is performed in part by the extragovernmental war and Party agencies and in part by local and provincial authorities. The immensity of the relief problem in China has always been such that organized relief can do no more than stir the misery of the masses. Opportunely for the National Government, the Imperial Japanese Army is securely in possession of the world's greatest relief problem, and unable to relinquish it. Chungking is more fortunate. (The author never dreamed that prosperity such as he saw in West China could exist in Asia. Prices are extremely high, but wages and farm prices tend to follow, and unemployment—always low in China because of the work-sharing role of the family—is almost completely out of sight. Skilled labor commands remuneration fantastic by preexisting scales.)

All these agencies, and much of the rest of the government, depend upon the Ministry of Communications (*Chiao-t'ung Pu*). The invasion struck at existing communications lines; Japanese are now in control of the mouths of all major Chinese rivers, most of China's railway mileage, and the coastal system of modern highways. A glance at the map of China will show that Japanese forces have hugged modern communications lines, whether steamship, railway, or highway. Whenever the Japanese ventured far from these lines, they met with disaster.

The Ministry of Communications has used existing facilities to draw new networks. The short stretches of railway in Free China are still operated; *matériel* from the occupied zone was brought West on them, and they

CONSULTATIVE AND ADMINISTRATIVE 93

are undergoing rapid development. Roadbeds are being constructed in anticipation of future imports of steel rails. Steamship enterprises, under government subsidy, operate extensively, and new reaches of river have been opened to service.

Three lines of reconstruction have proved very fruitful: motor communications, telecommunications, and the rationalization of pre-modern facilities already at hand.

Motor communications, both highway and aerial, have shown enormous progress. Air service is maintained by the China National Aviation Corporation and the Eurasia Company, both owned by the Chinese Government, the former jointly with Pan American Airways and the latter with German interests. Through connections from New York to Berlin are available by the combined services of the two companies.

The highway system can be thought of as spider-like. Three enormous legs reach to the outside: the Chungking-Kunming-Lashio route, famous as the Burma Road; the trans-Sinkiang route, finally connecting with the Soviet Turksib Railroad beyond thousands of miles of desert and mountains; and the due North route, now being developed, reaching the Trans-Siberian Railroad. The body of the system is a tight, well-metalled skein of roads interconnecting the major cities of Free China. Most highways are all-weather, and well-engineered, but niceties of surfacing have been postponed.

Truck and bus service is regular, but very crowded, with inescapable confusion as to priority. The majority of the operating firms are government-owned, either by the central government or the provinces. Complaint has arisen over the restrictions to private enterprise in this field. Since gasoline costs about U. S. $1.00 per gallon and is available only under permit, further official obstructions to highway use seem unnecessary.

Telecommunications have been maintained and extended. Telegraph service has reached into hitherto untapped areas, and wireless is extensively employed. Radio services operate under the Kuomintang, not the government; stations XGOX and XGOY reach North America and Europe with propaganda in the world's leading languages. The telephone has come to be a regular part of Chinese official and business life, and is to be seen, far off the beaten track, as one of the heralds of industrialization.

All these modern services would, however, be grossly insufficient for the needs of the whole nation at war. They have been supplemented through the use of every available type of pre-modern transportation. Most of these rely on man-power, and have had their own elaborate organization for many centuries: boatmen's guilds, unions of transport coolies, carters, muleteers and camel-drivers. It has been possible to ship heavy freight through country consisting of mountains traversable only by stone-flagged footpaths or torrential streams. The Ministry has regimented this complicated pre-modern world, with impromptu modernizations as startling as they are efficacious. Where once couriers trotted, they now speed by on bicycles or motorcycles; the squealing wooden-axled wheelbarrows of the Chinese countryside are yielding to pneumatic-tired carts which resemble American farm trailers. Three to eight men can drag one cart, with half a ton of freight, over any terrain, making up to forty miles a day. Provision can be made, therefore, for moving a quarter-million tons of raw materials across territory lacking even the most elementary roads. The roughness of the country, which bars the Japanese army, is no obstacle to huge coolie gangs, drafted sometimes, but more usually hired.

The Minister of Communications gave the following written answers to questions put by the author: [22]

[22] Communication of August 12, 1940; in the present author's possession.

CONSULTATIVE AND ADMINISTRATIVE 95

1. In view of the political interruptions to commerce through British and French territories south of China, will efforts be maintained to keep communications on the same schedules southward that they had before?

Yes, because commercial and export traffic is still being carried on southward, and there is a large accumulation of important materials to be moved from the frontier inward.

2. Will the restriction of gasoline lead to the abandonment of certain truck and bus routes, and the maintenance of others, or do you expect to restrict all routes evenly?

We expect to restrict all important routes evenly if the motor fuel situation becomes really acute.

3. Is a motor road running through Inner and Outer Mongolia directly north to the Trans-Siberian Railroad a feasible project?

Yes, it is a feasible project.

4. For all practical purposes, is the Soviet route as it exists an adequate although expensive channel for the import of high-class American machinery, such as trucks?

Yes, the Soviet route as it exists is adequate though expensive for the purpose.

5. Is there evidence that mail between the United States and China has been censored or tampered with while in transit past Japan?

No, there is no such evidence so far.

6. How extensive a foreign personnel do you have in the varied agencies under your Ministry?

Postal Service:	28
China National Aviation Corporation:	15
Eurasia Aviation Corporation:	13
Railways:	8

7. What developments of the last three years do you regard with most pride, as evidence of China's power to cope with the emergency?

The timely completion of the Yunnan-Burma Highway may be considered as evidence of China's power to cope with the emergency and as an important development in the field of war-time communications. The Highway is 960 kilometers long from Kunming to Anting on the frontier. Construction began in October 1937. Eleven months later, the road was opened to through traffic. At one time during its construction, as many as 100,000 laborers were employed on the road.

The highest point on the Highway is 2,600 meters above the sea level, yet the road has to pass two deep valleys, the Mekong and the Salween, where the Highway dips a few thousand feet within a distance of several miles in order to reach the river bed, and rises precipitously again in the same manner just beyond the suspension bridges over the two turbulent rivers. The scarcity of local labor, the enervating climate, and the wild and sparsely populated country traversed, all combine to make the construction work difficult. But now, anyone may take a motor car and cover the distance between Chungking and Rangoon in two weeks, as Ambassador Johnson did soon after the Highway was completed.

The Minister Chang Kia-ngau (Chang Chia-ao) is one of the most eminent bankers in China. His Ministry is a model of business-like organization and systematic routines; he has a great reputation for getting things done in the American fashion—quickly, and without ceremony.

In addition to these major ministries, there are the *Pu* of Justice (part of the Judicial *Yüan*, sharing its wartime somnolence), of War (affiliated with the Military Affairs Commission), of Audit, of Personnel, and—in process of establishment—of Social Affairs, supplementing the Party-Ministry of Social Movements (*Shê-hui Yün-tung Pu*) now under the Kuomintang Headquarters.

All Ministries are headed by a Minister (*Pu Chang*), seconded by a Political Vice-Minister (*Chêng-wu Tzŭ chang*) and Administrative Vice-Minister (*Ch'ang-wu Tzŭ-chang*). Since almost all officers are political appointees, and few of the new career men have touched the higher levels of the bureaucracy, this duplication prevents a job famine and keeps personnel levels high; the utility of a large administrative staff depends, obviously, on the nature of the executive. Some of the most crowded ministries seem permanently under-staffed because of the intense activity they maintain; others, with skeleton staff, appear to have far more civil servants than service. The over-all picture of the Ministries, however, leads inescapably to the conclusion that they are really functioning today. Long-transmitted vices of sloth and sinecures are on the wane. The war, highlighting every demerit into treason, has created optimum conditions for administrative progress in China.

CHAPTER IV

PROVINCIAL, LOCAL, AND SPECIAL-AREA GOVERNMENT

CHINA consists of twenty-eight provinces, varying in size about as do the European nations. Of the twenty-eight, fourteen are wholly under Chinese control, or are so slightly touched by invasion that normal governmental processes continue. Ten provinces are under dual or triple government—by the Japanese and pro-Japanese Chinese, by guerrilla and other semi-independent groups, and by the usual constitutional authorities. The remaining four are under firm Japanese domination, under the name *Manchoukuo*.[1] Well over half of China's population is under the National Government, and about one-ninth under unchallengeable Japanese control; the residuum is the subject of sharp political competition. The war is not merely a war between governments: it is a struggle for the creation of government.[2]

This problem would be immense even if there were no war. Under the successive Imperial dynasties of the past millennium, China developed extreme regional

[1] For an excellent definition of Free China, see Quigley, Harold S., "Free China," cited, p. 133–35. The most readable geography of China is Cressey, George B., *China's Geographic Foundations*, New York, 1934.

[2] For further development of this problem, see below, p. 185. The present author considered this question in relation to the Chinese political heritage, in *Government in Republican China*, cited, p. 2–12, 69–74, 188–89. Professor George Taylor, in *The Struggle for North China*, cited, relates this problem to the broad issues of world discussion, in a most acute analysis of "The Problem of China," p. 8–16, and gives a clear answer to the questions thus posed, p. 197–201.

PROVINCIAL AND URBAN GOVERNMENT

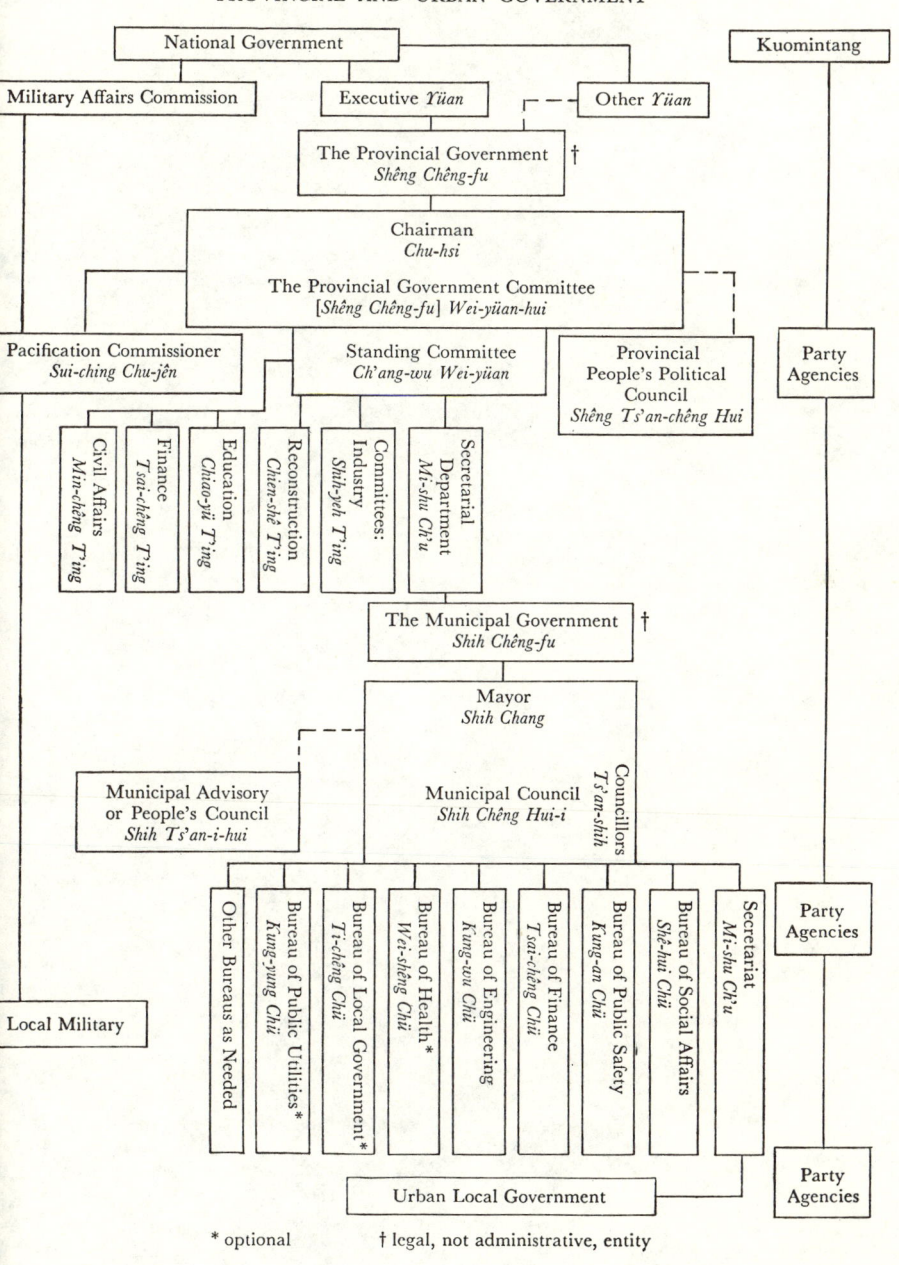

* optional   † legal, not administrative, entity

autonomy. Despite absolutist theory, the provinces under their governors or viceroys were practically as independent as states of the American union in the early nineteenth century. With the advent of war, the position of the provinces has become more precarious, truly new political devices in the form of novel regional governments have appeared, and the concrete problems of reform in the village communities have become as imperative as military measures.

The Provinces

The war-lord period was ushered in by the death of Yüan Shih-k'ai, dictator-President and commander-in-chief, in 1916. He had inherited a tradition of dual government—civil and military—no less sharp than the Japanese distinction, and had continued it by placing his military henchmen in power as provincial satraps. After his death, each province had a military governor (*Tuchün*), who sometimes tolerated a civil governor (*Shêng-chang*) and sometimes held both posts concurrently. The various *tuchün* rivalled one another in a vain turmoil until the rise of the National Government suppressed or incorporated them. Even today some of these men hold remnants of their power, but it is still declining. The power of the National Government has increased almost every year for over fifteen years, and its programs, bequeathed by Sun Yat-sen, call for the constant diminution of provincial authority, until in the end the province shall be little more than a postal link between the central government and the districts (*hsien*).

Continued vitality of the provinces as a form of political life is shown by the chariness with which the government approaches the problem of re-subdividing the nation, by the continued effect of provincialism through the influence of geography, botany, ecology, economics and spoken language, and by the manifest utility of the provinces in the prosecution of the war. It is impossible to discuss any aspect of Chinese affairs for very long without entering into distinctions between provinces.

In mild, modified, and controlled form, the pattern of civil-military contrast in provincial government still prevails. The civil governor, now in almost all cases the weightier official, is legally termed Chairman of the Province (*Shêng Chu-hsi*), but he frequently possesses a military colleague amiably designated Pacification Commissioner (*Sui-ching Chu-jên*).[3] The war has eradicated almost the last vestiges of provincial militarism. No Chinese army is in a position to make peace with Japan through the negotiated treason of its commander, although small groups occasionally change sides both ways.[4] On the other side of the picture, it is not altogether certain how far the National Government could go in replacing local leaders; more has been done than ever before, but the Generalissimo has tried to work

[3] Tsang, O. B., *A Supplement to a Complete Chinese-English Dictionary*, Shanghai, 1937, p. 267. The older, standard dictionaries do not include the term. Lieutenant H. S. Aldrich, in his *Hua Yu Hsü Chih: Practical Chinese*, Peiping, 1934, gives *Sui-ching Ssŭ-ling* as Pacification Commissioner (Vol. II, p. 74).

[4] An apt, grisly story is reported in the semi-official English-language journal of the Nanking regime. The "Peace Movement" is, of course, the Japanophile movement of Mr. Wang Ch'ing-wei. This is the way it was given in *The People's Tribune*, Vol. XXIX, Nos. 7-10 (October-November 1940), p. 305:

"In response to President Wang Ch'ing-Wei's peace appeal to the nation, Mr. Tan Shih-Chang, member of the Chungking Air Force, flew to Hankow by his own plane on June 10 to join the Peace Movement. Upon his arrival in Nanking, Mr. Tan was warmly received by the re-organized National Government. Later, he was sent to Macao on an important mission, but upon his arrival there, he was instantly killed by desperadoes in the employ of the Chungking regime.

"It is learned that the plane he left in Hankow has now been repaired by the Japanese Air Force and brought to the Capital. Following its arrival, the plane was immediately handed over to the Military Commission by the Japanese military authorities."

(This would need further corroboration before it could definitely be accepted.)

honestly with all leaders, provincial or independent, subsuming their power under his and the Government's without destroying it. Four provinces still show traces of autonomy.

Largest of the four is Sinkiang (Chinese Central Asia), under the military leader Shêng Shih-ts'ai; it is subject to very strong Soviet influence, since it is more accessible from the Soviet side of the border, via the Turksib Railroad, than from China. Its trade naturally flows out through the Soviet Union. The provincial authorities have been harsh toward Christian work, and casually cruel to occasional travellers. Since the National Government is exceedingly anxious to maintain good relations with the Soviet Union, and obtains much of its supplies from that country across Sinkiang province, it has made no attempt to interfere. The province has cooperated enthusiastically in war efforts; it is strange to see Central Asiatics with European features marching with Chinese troops. Many of the independent Leftist leaders have been welcomed in the area, although simon-pure Marxians are rare, and the province, with a new university, new air bases, new industries, and a trans-Asia highway, is undergoing rather spectacular development. The British and the Soviets are mutually so suspicious that the Chinese are likely to keep control, but the Chinese central government, taking no chances, cooperates rather than commands.

Yünnan, under General Lung Yün, is the second province with special features. Relatively isolated from the rest of China until the completion of the Kunming-Chungking stretch of the Burma Road, it has never been occupied by large National Government forces. The provincial chairman submitting in form and cooperating in fact has been left unmolested in his position. The province is becoming modernized by a great deal of commerce and development; it is likely that this vestigial autonomy will fade away unnoticed.

Kwangsi province possesses as leader General Pai Chung-hsi, one of the ablest military men in China. A Kuomintang leader of long standing, he followed, in conjunction with the leaders in Kwangtung (Canton), a policy of *de facto* autonomy down to the very outbreak of war. He and his associates even had an independent air force, which was promptly merged into the National air service. During the war, he has fought in central China. The economic ruin of Kwangtung and the occupation of Canton city by the Japanese has quenched Cantonese autonomy, but Kwangsi has been relatively untouched. No whisper of suspicion has imputed separatism to General Pai, but should he desire it, he is one of the few men left in China still to have the means.

In Fukien province, General Ch'ên I serves as Chairman. He studied in Japan and has a Japanese wife. He remains loyal to the National Government, and he has fought the Japanese along the coast. No Chinese observer has criticized him, but Westerners have observed that Fukien is remarkably quiet; the Japanese have done little beyond blockading the coast and seizing the major ports, and the Chinese have launched no counter-attacks. It is possible that some unexpressed sense of understanding between the Governor and the Japanese prevents further conflict, while the Generalissimo—content to leave well enough alone—lets matters stand as they are.

Provincial government, as outlined in the chart at p. 98, is very simple in structure. The Commission plan, similar in many respects to the Galveston plan in American municipal government, reduces the Provincial Chairman to the status of *primus inter pares*. The departments of the provincial government are headed by members of the province's committee. The presence of provincial offices of the Kuomintang, military services, and war agencies makes a provincial capital a place more important than it seems in theory. A valuable innovation in provincial administration has been the inauguration of the Provincial People's Political Councils (*Shêng Ts'an-chêng Hui*). These are being taken seriously by the administrations. Although they occasionally pass visionary, impracticable, or bombastic resolutions, their work has for the most part been concrete. They have aided a great deal in transforming the atmosphere of government, and act as competent outside critical bodies to check the administrative officers.

Provincial government has been significantly transformed by the war. Dr. T. F. Tsiang (Chiang T'ing-fu), a distinguished historian who served on a central inspection commission to the Southwest in 1940, stated [5] that provincial government has improved in two outstanding ways: first, there is a real desire to understand the common people, and to do something for them. This was unheard-of a few years past. Second, all—or almost all—of the officials work very hard. There is far more work than there are men. Money is frequently available but unexpendable because there are not enough experts to go round. Hence, the provincial governments find their need is for men rather than funds, and the war is bringing new levels of actual accomplishment. Although most of the governors have military titles, many of these are like Kentucky colonelcies, courtesy titles from time past. The over-all effect is of hard work and little bombast.

Special Municipalities, most of which are now under Japanese occupation, are directly subject to the National Government and only incidentally a part of the provinces in which they are located. Ordinary Municipalities are under their respective provincial governments, but not under a *hsien* (district or county) administra-

---

[5] In an interview with the author, Chungking, July 31, 1940; the interview was unfortunately terminated by the raid alarm. It might be noted at this point that proposals for the reinstitution of strong provincial executives have been postponed from year to year since 1932. See *The China Year Book 1939*, cited, p. 217 n.

tion; in some cases they include several former *hsien*. The Municipality is headed by a Mayor (*Shih-chang*), advised by a City Council (*Shih-chêng Hui-i*) composed of the chiefs of the administrative sections, several supplementary counsellors, and representatives from the Municipal Advisory Assembly (*Shih Ts'an-i-hui*), if one exists. Below the *Shih* the urban pattern of local government differs somewhat from the rural, but otherwise city government displays no features peculiarly Chinese.

LOCAL GOVERNMENT

Chinese local government has been the ever-fertile soil out of which successive Empires grew. To no other level of government has the Republic reached so poorly. Since China is constituted of about half a million villages, several thousand market towns, and a few hundred major cities, the bulk of the population is rural, but rural in a way foreign to the West. Congestion imposes upon agrarian China many problems and evils known as urban in the West. Corruption in government, extortion in economics, demoralization in social and family life—these start with the village and the *hsien*. Inconspicuous in any single village, each evil summed to its China-wide aggregate becomes tremendous.

Government has not been beloved by the Chinese farmer. Governmental benefits—for the continuance of scholastic culture, the protection of the realm, the creation of grandiose public works—were remote, but taxes were not; government meant the taxgatherer. Fêng Yü-hsiang, one of the great war-lords and now a Kuomintang general, says of his own childhood:

The people, except for paying their taxes, had nothing to do with the government. The government never paid any attention to the conditions under which the people lived, and the people never bothered themselves about what the government was doing. One party collected the taxes; the other paid them. That was all there was to it. Although Paoting city was only about two *li* [less than a mile] away, the inhabitants of Kang-k'ê village showed no interest in city civilization; instead, they rather looked down on that sort of thing. No discussions of politics were heard, and nothing about the encroachments of the foreign powers on China. All the big changes seemed to have taken place in another world, and very seldom affected this place.

When the government was about to collect taxes, the *Li Chêng* [a petty local officer] would ring a gong from one end of the village to the other, shouting:

"Pay your taxes! Four hundred and sixty coins to the *mou* [about one third of an acre] for the first harvest!"

When the people heard the gong, they did not go and pay their taxes immediately. They would walk listlessly to their doorways, only to withdraw after having taken a nonchalant look at the *Li Chêng*—as though they had heard nothing. They would wait until the very last minute, until they could not put it off any more, and then go, group by group, to the city to hand in money they had earned by sweat and blood.

They were industrious and miserable all through the year . . .

This basic level of Chinese society is not easily susceptible to standardization, or the imposition of ready-made bureaucracies. Even in the United States, it would be almost impossible to impose a uniform plan for community organization from Bangor to San Diego and Walla Walla to the Bronx. Sun Yat-sen once said to Judge Linebarger, "China is a land of autonomy from the smallest village upward. Who shall dictate to the sub-governments of China the form and manner in which they shall express their local governmental needs? Of course, we must have a minimum of uniformity for both economy and efficiency in government, but the will of the people must be followed." [7] By seeking to remedy political abuses the National Government ap-

[6] Fêng Yü-hsiang, *Wo-ti Shêng-huo* (My Life), Kweilin, 1940, p. 22.

[7] As reported by Paul M. W. Linebarger in his *Conversations with Sun Yat-sen* [as yet unpublished; in the author's possession]. Book II, Chapter V.

parently hopes that economic inequalities will be ironed out by the people themselves.

The Chinese land problem cannot be understood except at the politico-economic nexus, where low political morale exposes the farmers to the unrestrained power of the gentry, acting in the triple capacity of officials, landlords, and money-lenders. The cycle, familiar in the West, of freehold farmers or yeomen first mortgaging their land, then becoming tenants, and finally ending in utter economic helplessness, has been familiar in China. In China's past, the cycle had another phase: agrarian insurrection sweeping the land with banditry and innumerable rebellions, thereby increasing the fiscal burden on the remaining land, leading to worse exploitation, until the slate was swept clean by dynastic collapse, general civil war, and a new Imperial house, whose administrative decline began another cycle. The peasantry never won completely, and never lost utterly. Today, if one judges by past experience, rebellion or reform seems long overdue.[8]

The detailed legislation adopted by the National Government in war time is given in Appendix I (G), and Chiang K'ai-shek's own explanation of the new system in Appendix III (C).[9] One might explain the general plan quite simply in terms of inter-connection between the central government and the millions of households. The *pao-chia* system is one of mutual aid and mutual responsibility between households and groups of households, under government supervision. It has appeared in China from time to time since the

[8] The author has sought to trace the political and military aspects of this cycle in *Government in Republican China*, cited. There are numerous works on the subject from the economists' point of view. Outstanding are the books by John Lossing Buck, R. H. Tawney, J. B. Condliffe, Karl Wittfogel, Ch'en Han-seng, and the articles by Norman Hanwell (chiefly in *Asia, Amerasia,* and *The Far Eastern Survey*).

[9] Below, p. 324, and p. 388.

PROVINCIAL, LOCAL AND SPECIAL AREAS

Ch'in dynasty (221–203 B.C.). If used for welfare purposes, it amounts to a recognition of the pluralistic character of Chinese society by the government, and the happy utilization of the family pattern. Applied for police purposes, it is well suited to repression and terror. Thus, today the National Government is applying the *pao-chia* system (in relation to its whole scheme of local government) as a measure of progress and reform, while the Japanese encourage the same organizations in occupied China as a device for despotism and exploitation.

Expressed in law, now being applied in fact, the *chia* is a group of six to fifteen families (households), and the *pao,* a group of six to fifteen *chia*. The *hsiang* is formally composed of six to fifteen *pao;* actually it approximates what is loosely termed a community in the United States (*e.g.,* a city ward, a single suburb, part of a rural election district). The *ch'ü* is the rough equivalent of a township. The *hsien* (district; county) is the fundamental unit of the traditional China-wide bureaucracy. Hence the missing steps are not those between the *hsien,* near to two thousand in number, and the central government. The gaps occur between the half-billion Chinese and their two thousand *hsien.* The following chart shows the broad outlines of the system: [10]

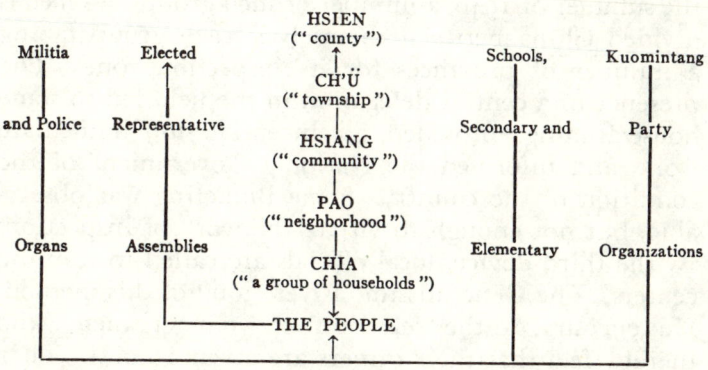

[10] A detailed chart will be found in Appendix III (C), at p. 388.

This is the official government plan. If ever put into complete effect, China will consist of hundreds upon hundreds of thousands of self-governing units, arranged on seven levels (the five local levels; provinces; nation), and the world will wonder at a massive new democracy. In practical politics, what seems to be happening is that the system extends to the National Government areas, involving less than three hundred million people. Much of the application is purely formal, and signifies no more than did the grant of an imaginary suffrage under the first Republic. Elsewhere the new system is installed with telling administrative effect, improving the bureaucracy, strengthening the state, but not arousing much popular participation or enthusiasm. And in the remainder the program is beginning to work as is intended with genuine elections and popular participation in government.

The three chief devices which have been applied to the reform of local government are: instruction, mandate, and other remote controls; inspection systems; and training courses. First are the attempts to change local government by transmission from the capital of voluminous instructions, manuals, etc., supplemented by similar Kuomintang action for Party reform. In the second case, central officials go to the provinces. During the summer of 1940, a number of such groups of officials divided China between themselves, each group taking a number of provinces for its inspection zone. The presence of a central delegation in the field led to some housecleaning, provided an incentive for immediate work, and informed the National Government of the condition of the country. Some junketing was observable, but not enough to vitiate the work of inspection. By the third device, local officials are called to training centers. The Generalissimo is very fond of this method. He encourages the selection of younger men, who thereby feel that their careers are given a boost. They are taught modern governmental practice while living, in most cases, a disciplined but comfortable half-military life. Some training conferences are convened *ad hoc* in a promising area; others continue from year to year under the government or related organizations. Many thousand men and women undergo some form of training. The program has clearly discernible effects in improving local government. The selection of persons who either hold office or are likely to hold office provides a practical self-interest motivation. Further minor devices of local government reform include the grants in aid to the provinces, the establishment of model *hsien*, the military eradication of banditry, the reclamation of farm land and forests, some resettlement, and much planned modernization with small-scale projects. Town after town has received the stimuli of modernization from one of these sources.

Estimates—nothing more could be found—concerning the effectiveness of this program varied considerably. Since two equally skilled observers, considering the same institution at first hand, can differ sharply in their value judgments of efficacy or integrity, this is not surprising. A few Westerners and Leftists have insisted that the program was almost altogether sham. A few formal, optimistic officials have insisted that it has succeeded almost everywhere. One competent foreign observer told the author that he believed the *pao-chia* system to be installed in 90 per cent of Free China, and to be actually working in 50 per cent. Another agreed more or less with these figures, but suggested that there were enormous differences between the provinces, some being genuinely transformed and others remaining unaffected. A Chinese official, himself a social scientist, who had been intimately connected with local reform, stated that 50 per cent application for all Free China would be much too high an estimate, except for the holding of token elections. Only in Kwangsi province was the new self-government structure working over half of the countryside; elsewhere, the ratio was about one-fifth effective as against four-fifths nominal.

Most of all, genuine application consists in making institutions available, and thereupon letting the people help themselves. If local government is of practical use to the common people, they can be counted on to discover its utility promptly. If it is of no practical use, they will know that too. Whatever the present degree of success, obstacles still confront the program. Local extragovernmental institutions possess enormous vitality. If superficial or slipshod reforms are made, the new local governments will be merely operated as screens for secret societies, landlords' unions, or other narrow cliques.

Contrastingly, a tradition of discussion and public action makes it equally possible that the rural masses, familiar with cooperative action, will operate the new institutions successfully. The difference between success and failure is not to be measured in terms of wholly new achievement; it is determined by the choice of existing institutions which, transmuted and fitted, fill the pattern of the rationalized local government system. If narrow, class-bound or unprogressive groups assume the regalia of a novel legality, using their position to obstruct further development, the program will fail. If the town-meeting, cooperative potentialities of the entire adult population are aroused, and if the ordinary farmer or coolie can see that he has the opportunity of bettering his livelihood through political action, the success of democracy will be assured.

Potentialities in the field of local autonomy are enhanced by the fact that the National Government has competitors. The Japanese have an opportunity which, instead of utilizing, they have done their best to destroy: conquest through prosperity. If they and their Chinese associates offered low prices, easy marketing, and fair taxes, in the place of arson, rape, thievery and bluster, their failure would become less certain. As a third side to the triangle of competitive power, the Communists and independent Left, while allied to the National Government, rival it in winning the loyalty of the population. Huge areas in Communist and guerrilla sections are sampling reform of a drastic and immediate kind: the lowering of taxes, the democratization of government, the abolition of usury. With the traitors on its Right and the Communists or guerrillas on its Left, the National Government does not abandon its chief politico-economic weapon by disregarding land and labor reform. None of the three parties has anything to gain by inaction. None has an interest which binds it to self-dooming reaction.

The Communist Zone

Three new governmental areas which are neither provinces nor local governments have come forth out of unification and war. Their relationship to Chungking is strange, perhaps unique. They are not states members of a federal union, since China is a unitary republic. They are not new regional commissions, creatures and extensions of the central government, because —whatever the theory—they were independently initiated. They are not allies, because they profess national unity. They are not rebellions, because they fight a common enemy, only occasionally coming into conflict with government troops. Yet they possess some of the features of each of the following: federal states, regional subgovernments, allied states, and rebellions. They cut across the pattern of the National Government. Two are governments; one is an army. The army and one government are largely Communist; the other government is a genuine United Front of the parties. Two are North Chinese; one is Central Chinese. But all three have this in common: they are Leftist, actively revolutionary; they are objects of patronizing suspicion to the central authorities, who are glad of the help but worry about its post-war cost.

The first and most famous of these areas is the Communist zone in the Northwest. Formally it includes eighteen *hsien;* the Communists claim inclusion of twenty-three. After being termed the Special Administrative District of the Chinese Republic (*Chung-hua Min-kuo T'ê-ch'ü Chêng-fu*), and then Shensi-Kansu-Ninghsia Frontier Area (*Shan-kan-ning Pien-ch'ü Chêng-fu*), the zone assumed the much more modest style of Administrative Area of North Shensi (*Shan-pei Hsing-chêng-ch'ü*).[11] This Frontier Area is in personnel and Party life a direct continuation of the Chinese Soviet Republic. Leftist and Communist circles talk as though it were a wholly autonomous state, resting on its own military power, but cooperating with the National Government for national resistance and reconstruction. This is largely true—at any rate, more realistic than the opposing view, which avers that no change has taken place in the Northern part of Shensi province, and that the Communists are interfering with the proper processes of government. The following is a characteristic statement of the latter position:

> At present the name "Frontier Area" seems to be very common because it is so called in false propaganda about the "independent sovereignty" [*tzŭ-li wei-wang*]. But if we agree that the so-called "Frontier Area" is a part of the territory of the Chinese Republic, the name ought to have been issued in conformity with the decrees of the central government. According to central government decree, it is only a "Supplementary Recruitment Area for the Eighth Route Army," but not an area of civil administration. [The author, in an extended discussion, challenges the re-division of the provinces as a matter not to be under-

---

[11] See above, p. 13. The last term is literally Executive Area (or District) of North Shan (Shensi). In the text, Frontier Area is used throughout as the simplest English equivalent.

taken casually, denies the legal foundation of the term "Frontier Area," and then examines its practical justifications. He finds that the Communists have two: the regime is now a *de facto* system, its existence is a *fait accompli* and further discussion must proceed from this point; also, the regime is founded in popular opinion, and the government should not violate the wishes of the people. He disagrees with both of these and seeks to refute them, insisting on lawful procedure and constitutional government. He concludes with a peroration to the Communists themselves.]
. . . this problem is really quite simple, unlike the Sudeten problem. Was it the Communist Party of China which called the Sudeten Party of Czechoslovakia violators of the unity of their own country and running dogs of Fascism? Therefore, I think that they would never imitate what the reactionary Sudeten party did. And was it the Communists who originated the "United Front"? Hence they must understand very clearly what unification means to China, and must never utter things which they do not really believe. Therefore, with the rising tide of national unity and concentration, I suppose that the odd name "Frontier Area," which is contrary to the real sense of unification, will soon pass away and be a mere historical term.[12]

In practical terms this implies the informal reconciliation of two claims constitutionally and legally incompatible. The Chinese Communist leaders operate under the national law codes as much as they are able. They employ the national currency. They use the nationally standard system for local government. They profess unity. At the same time they maintain, as a hard reality, a separate regime in which the Communist Party is supreme, the Party Line is gospel, and dissidents are dealt with as "pro-Japanese traitors" or otherwise. Transit between National Government territory and Communist territory is not altogether easy. Leftists are reported to have died on their way to the Northwest, and Nationalists are equally well reported to have disappeared after they got there.

[12] Chin Chi-yin, " 'Pien-ch'ü' ti Ming-ch'êng" (The Name "Frontier Area"), in *So-wei "Pien-ch'ü,"* cited above, p. 3–6.

The Area itself is an unpromising piece of land. "From 36° N. Lat. on up, South of the Great Wall and West of the Yellow River, there lies a vast, desolate tract of yellow plateau, inhabited by half a million people. The plateau slopes from North to South; the further South it runs, the lower the land lies, but it is still 1000 meters above sea-level at the lowest place. This is what we have already known as Northern Shensi. In this region, the ground is always covered with a layer of yellow dust . . . Furthermore, rainfall is scarce and no irrigation has been introduced, so that agricultural products are extremely scant. Under such geographical limitations, Northern Shensi has become a region notorious for its poverty." [13] For a Chinese to call an area notoriously poor implies a degree of destitution which the American mind cannot grasp. In such an area, the welcome to Communism is obvious, and the problems of Communism, once settled, are equally obvious. The probability of mineral resources opens up opportunities for development under Red rule, but these are distant.

Interpretation of the achievements of the Communist regime vary with the political standpoint of the observer, just as they do in the case of the Soviet Union. Sympathetic observers, both Western and Chinese, report enormous improvements in agriculture, fair land taxes, new cooperatives, brilliant experimental democracy, bold education, and great enthusiasm.[14] No unsym-

[13] Ts'ui Yün-ch'ang, *Shan-pei Lun Kuo-hua* (A Brief Sketch of Northern Shensi), Kweilin, 1939, p. 4–5. This author concludes that Communist rule worsened the economic status of the area. "Then there occurred the campaigns for 'the extermination of landlordism' and for 'division of the lands.' The result of such proletarian disturbances was an astonishing decrease of population, caused by massacre and emigration, and the devastation of much land." (p. 6.)

[14] See the works cited above, p. 20, n. 16. It is possible to find a contradictory interpretation in Chinese sources for almost every point cited by Western visitors as meritorious. Since the Nationalists are not interested in promoting the international reputation of the Frontier Area, and at the same time are unable to launch any counter-propaganda (for fear of alienating Leftist sentiment in the West, be-

pathetic Western visitors have been reported admitted, and a few neutrals came away enthusiastic; but critical Chinese have found as much to question as one might find in a similar Western situation: terrorism, puppet elections, murder both judicial and plain, sham education, and immorality are charged.

The position of the Frontier Area is clear in a few respects.[15] In the first place, it is not declining. Communist strength is believed to be growing, by persons of almost all forms of political belief; differences arise only over the rate and probable maxima of that growth. The Communist strength in the Northwest is far less than it was in South Central China seven years ago, but much of that loss of power has been compensated for by increased relations with sympathetic guerrillas. Secondly, the Communist area is strategically poorly located. The land itself is poor; the adjacent large cities are completely under Nationalist control; and the general military-political locale is something like northern Arkansas in the United States. This explains the willingness of the Nationalist commanders to avoid friction with the Communists, and the positive zest with which they suggest further consolidation of Communist forces around the one center at Yenan. It soothes the impatience of Communists who wish unrestricted rights

---

cause it would give the Japanese a propaganda advantage, and would disturb the appearance of the United Front), very little criticism—sound or otherwise—of the Chinese Communist area has appeared in the West. Even in a case such as the issuance of paper money, universally regarded as a clever move by the Communists and guerrillas, Chinese writers have charged that the issuance is fiat currency imposed by Communist force (e.g., Wang Ssŭ-ch'êng, *Ju-tz'ŭ Pien-ch'ü* [So this is the Frontier Area!] Chungking, 1938, p. 32 *ff.*) Within China, Communism is just as open to interpretation as the Soviets are in the Western world. Western data now available seems to cover only one side of the case, which is doubtless well-founded; but there must be another. There always is.

[15] Since the author has neither extensive acquaintance with Chinese Communists, nor has visited Yenan, he offers these conclusions more tentatively than he would others, concerning the Kuomintang.

of agitation, organization, and propaganda throughout the country. Although the Communists make little visible headway against the Japanese in the great urban slums of the coast, they are anxious to obtain freer access to city workers. Thirdly, the Communist area displays no structural peculiarities of government. Its profound difference from the rest of Free China is not a difference in institutional forms, but in the forces operating behind and through those forms. The Chinese Communists have achieved very considerable success in working within the legal limits of another state philosophy, and have done it with a minimum of violence; this augurs well for the perpetual continuation of the truce. Their practical accomplishments are extensive and novel; their leadership, brilliant; that their government should be so orthodox in form is all the more significant. By remaining within orthodox limits they challenge the National Government on common ground; the gain is theirs and China's.

Guerrilla Governments

The special area second in importance is the Hopei-Chahar-Shansi Border Region (*Chin-ch'a-chi Pien-ch'ü Lin-shih Hsing-chêng Wei-yüan-hui*). Widely publicized in the Western world as the Hermit Government, this regime functions altogether within the Japanese lines. A number of competent Western observers have visited this area, among them Major Evans Fordyce Carlson, Mr. Haldore Hanson, and Professor George Taylor. All have come away most enthusiastic about the work of the government. The governmental picture which emerges from their and other accounts is one of a highly flexible mechanism, working with great efficacy and superb morale.[16] The driving power behind the

---

[16] Professor George Taylor's *The Struggle for North China* presents a full and clear picture of the Border Region and the Peiping regime in startlingly apposite juxtaposition. He concludes by pointing

regime is social revolution as a means to national resistance, made easy by the flight of many former local bureaucrats, and by the treason of some ultra-conservatives, who affiliated themselves with the Provisional Government established by the Japanese in Peiping. The personnel is as genuinely United Front as may be found anywhere in the world; the position is eased by the circumjacency of the Japanese, and the formal recognition of the area by the Military Affairs Commission and the Executive *Yüan.*

The Border Region, like smaller guerrilla areas elsewhere in occupied China, is scarcely a domestic political problem because it is enfolded by the Japanese armies. Even a United Front area, such as the Border Region, would lead to far greater difficulties in political adjustment if established in Free China. The tension and balance between the Parties is such that this strain might not be borne. Behind the Japanese lines, where the central armies cannot do anything even if they wish, the Border Region finds Chungking's acquiescence to be stimulated by Chungking's impotence. What could or will happen if the Japanese leave the dividing area, and the Border Region has to settle the issue of *status quo* v. *status quo ante bellum* with the central govern-

---

out the significant paradox that the Japanese established a reactionary regime designed to keep China agrarian, backward, and exploitable, but that they had not managed to extend their affiliate beyond the cities. The country, which they had hoped to capture, escaped them through the political resurgence of the Border Region. P. C. Nyi, article cited above, p. 16. n. 10, presents an outline of the regime which supplements the first-hand materials Professor Taylor appends to his work. Major E. F. Carlson's works, which describe this, are *Twin Stars of China* and *The Chinese Army*, both cited above; the latter, a valuable contribution to the *Inquiry Series* of the Institute of Pacific Relations, includes Wang Yu-chuan, "The Organization of a Typical Guerrilla Area in South Shantung" (p. 84–130), a brilliant survey which reveals, sometimes unwittingly, the values and dangers of a Communist-Nationalist-popular union. Mr. Hanson's work is *"Humane Endeavour,"* cited above; as a personal account, it is the most engrossing of the group.

ment, no one knows. The Generalissimo told the present author that he did not fear the encroachments of the guerrilla groups, because he and they were all working for democracy.

Following from this involuntarily protective and insulating role of the Japanese forces is the constitutional theory of the Border Region. Unlike the Frontier Area, where it is exceedingly difficult to gloss over the autonomy of Communist rule, the Border Region is definitely established as a war-time agency, controlling territory beyond the reach of the provincial governments. The provincial governments still function, in unoccupied corners of their provinces, or in exile, and the openly provisional (*lin-shih*) nature of the Border Region makes it palatable even to Kuomintang conservatives.

The pattern of government is one of devolution from an Executive Committee, which was established by a meeting of officials, volunteers, mass organizations, and others at Fup'ing in January 1938. The area is divided into provincial districts which are able to function with economy of personnel. The following outline illustrates the structure of this area: [17]

EXECUTIVE COMMITTEE
Secretariat
Civil Affairs Department
Financial Affairs Department
Education Department
Industry Department
Justice Department

Inspectorates of the Seven Provincial Districts
Hsien Governments or Joint *Hsien* Governments or Sub-*Hsien* Governments
Hsien Districts
Village Committees

[17] P. C. Nyi, article cited in *The Chinese Year Book 1938–39*, p. 255. Reading between the lines will illustrate much of the Chungking attitude.

A very high degree of direct popular government has been achieved. Over wide areas, the average age of the *hsien* magistrates is in the twenties. Recruitment to the Region of numerous professors and students from Peiping has helped to fill the need for trained personnel, and has assisted in maintaining the area as a genuine multi-group affair rather than a Communist front. Communists, although present and highly esteemed, do not hold the highest formal offices. (For further consideration of the United Front problem, see below, p. 123.)

The New Fourth Army (*Hsin-ssŭ-chün*), third of the special zones, was formed by re-consolidation of the small mutually isolated Soviet areas left behind when the main Communist forces made the celebrated Long March. When first assembling under the truce, these Red units faced a certain amount of difficulty from the provincial military who did not grasp the United Front idea, but the Military Affairs Commission recognized them. The Army did not establish a government except through its Political Department, which coordinated political work of the volunteer village committees.[18]

According to available reports, the Army stands far to the Left of the Border Region. Formally United Front, its proportion of Communists is much higher and Communist control more telling. Operating in East Central China—the Anhwei-Kiangsu-Kiangsi-Fukien-Chekiang area—which provided the base of ten years'

[18] On the New Fourth Army, see Epstein, I., *The People's War*, cited above, p. 260 *ff*. Agnes Smedley, the well-known pro-Communist writer, has lived among the New Fourth recently. Another foreign visitor has been Jack Belton, of the Shanghai *Evening Post*. Publicity for the New Fourth Army, reduced to an absolute minimum by Chungking, is handled by an independent agency, the New China Information Committee (not to be confused with the semi-official China Information Committee) in Hong Kong. The China Defense League, in which the moving spirit is Mme. Sun Yat-sen, also in Hong Kong, acts as an agency for receiving gifts, etc., for the Army.

Communist insurrection and was long the home of the Chinese Soviet Republic, the New Fourth Army Zone represents a recrudescence of Soviet activities under different names and with a different military objective. This fact has caused intense dissatisfaction among some Kuomintang generals, who spent half their careers trying to root out Communism in that same area. They do not mind the Communist zone in the Northwest, where an effective informal *cordon sanitaire* can be drawn, but renewed Communist activity in the Yangtze valley impresses them as an evil not much less than pro-Japanese treason.

The New Fourth Zone, the Border Region, and the Frontier Area—together with a wide scattering of guerrilla areas and governments individually of less but collectively of equal importance—are the military stepchildren of the Chinese government. They all receive subsidies for their work, varying in amount. Usually this is calculated on the number of *hsien* actually occupied as bases, so that the sum provides for a far smaller number of villages than those directly affected. In the case of troops, the salary allowances are based on the permitted size of the units, in almost all cases below the actual numbers. The money is paid to the commanders or other leading officials, who then set salary rates incomparably lower than those of the central forces. The money thus saved is applied to the general budget of the forces. Corruption, while occasional and inescapable, seems to be more sharply punished in the guerrilla than in the government areas.

In January 1941, the New Fourth Army was officially abolished, following a clash with regular National Government forces. The clash arose from a fundamental difference between the Generalissimo and the New Fourth leaders concerning the nature of the Chinese government. The Communists and their sympathizers held that the unity of China was a political union between separate groups. When the Generalissimo ordered the New Fourth Army to move North, and oppose the Japanese forces above the Yangtze, the New Fourth countered with a demand for arms and funds. Treating this as military insubordination in war time, the central forces attacked the New Fourth—each side claiming that the other opened hostilities—capturing Yeh Ting, the commander. The rest of the Army was officially abolished, although its main forces were within the occupied zone and outside the Generalissimo's reach. A full Communist-Nationalist clash was avoided, however, and the Red leaders unwillingly acquiesced in the Generalissimo's interpretation of the episode as a military and not a political affair. The conflict brought forth the fundamental Communist question: are the Chinese Communists loyal first to the Chinese government, or first to the Communist Party? No answer was forthcoming, although the Communists failed to rebel elsewhere. The Generalissimo, by military swiftness and political acumen, had triumphed in one more particular instance.

With the parsimonious policy of the central government keeping them in fiscal extremity, the more Leftist guerrilla units make up their lack of funds with direct economic measures. These include suspensions of rents to landlords, regulation of share-cropping, lowering of taxes on the poorer farmers, and creation of cooperatives. The Communists have strained every point to avoid actual class war, and the economic reforms of the guerrilla and special areas are smoothed by the usual absence of the landlords. The political necessity of a bold economic policy remains important, if the special areas are to continue their activity against Japan or—in the Frontier Area case—their independence. Political development thus is inclined to stress the use of popular machinery of government, not for the creation of systematic, modern, responsible bureaucracy, but for pushing vigorous mass action, direct popular government, and socio-economic reconstruction, revolutionary by implication if not by immediate content.

Not all the guerrilla areas fall into the Left pattern. The Kuomintang, so long habituated to control of the state mechanism that its revolutionary background is somewhat dimmed, is bringing Kuomintang guerrilla work into action. The Party and Government War Area Commission is the chief supervisory agency for this work, and an enormous amount of planning has been done. Actual application of mass-movement work seems as yet to lag behind that of the Left. Meanwhile, in most areas except the Communist Northwest, Kuomintang officers, officials, teachers, and volunteers are active. The guerrilla groups all accept the same flag, hail Chiang as their leader, recognize the *San Min Chu I* as the state ideology, and maintain the cherished symbols of unity.

The Government and the Kuomintang were reportedly seeking a settlement of the whole special-area problem, in anticipation of the close of war, by urging the movement of all Communist or Communist-infiltrated forces Northward, so that a more or less continuous Left corridor would run from the Border Region to the Frontier Area. This precipitated the clash with the New Fourth Army; in March 1941 no settlement has been reached. Part of this is owing to the Communist desire to have unrestricted agitational rights, and to official Kuomintang insistence that no Party other than itself is constitutionally legitimate. The special areas meanwhile prepare fighters in the anti-Japanese war, and are helped by a government which is proud of them as Chinese but mistrustful of them as Leftists. And they develop vigorous applications of democratic formulae which challenge the reality and sincerity of everything the National Government does behind the lines.

Despite recurrent clashes, it is likely that the areas and the government will continue their present relations. In part this is owing to the genuineness of the universal hatred of Japan and the devotion to the long-cherished unification now achieved; in even greater part the wrangling, acrimonious, but effective cooperation of the government and the guerrilla Left depends on their equal and great desire for such cooperation. The highest Kuomintang leaders—above all others, Chiang—have pledged themselves to unity and cooperation, and are determined to eschew civil war in the midst of invasion; the higher Communist leaders are equally determined. In three years of collaboration, the highest officers on each side have developed very genuine respect for each other's sincerity. Quarrels are provoked by the men in-between, overbearing Nationalists or the doctrinaire Communists, who cannot forget 1927–37. (The author talked to one Communist leader who had an odd, not unattractive muscular tic in his face: the consequence of Kuomintang torture a few years past. Yet he collaborates, and so do his Kuomintang equivalents, men whose parents lie in unknown graves.) The common people on both sides want peace above all else, internal peace between factions, and peace—after victory, and then only—with Japan. The juxtaposed and competitive forces watch one another, compete in the development of institutions, and engage in an auction of good government: whoever wins the deepest love and esteem of the Chinese people wins China in the end. Few institutional reforms in the West have had such fateful stimuli.

Chapter V

THE KUOMINTANG

THE Kuomintang, a Chinese political party, was formed by federation of old anti-Manchu secret societies, and has become the vehicle for the will of its Leader, Sun Yat-sen: constitutionally and legally it is the superior of the Chinese National Government; administratively, one of the three chief organs of policy execution for the regime; politically, the only legal political party in Free China. It has had undisputed primacy, but not monopoly, in domestic Chinese politics for fourteen years. Despite revolutionary purposes, and idealistic obligations, the Kuomintang is responsible for the welfare of the government which it created. Its interest is therefore superior to and identical with the government's; the party of a one-party state has no business criticizing the government, since the party at all times possesses the means of correction or change.

By its constitution and organization the Party is democratic. In practice it has been a loose oligarchy, similar to the machinery whereby American presidential candidates are nominated. In composition it is by its own statement a cross section of China, composed of persons who qualify as a political elite by their zeal in seeking and obtaining entrance to the Party. Administratively, the Kuomintang possesses a group of Ministries (*pu*), closely similar to the governmental ministries, and executing quasi-governmental policy, plus an additional group of separate or affiliated organizations having common purposes. In power politics, the Kuomintang claims supremacy in all unoccupied

China and legitimate power over the occupied areas; in practice it yields frequently to the demands of dissidents. In function, its highest purpose—bequeathed by Sun Yat-sen—is to destroy its own monopoly of power when the time for democracy shall come; like medicine, it is committed to the eradication of the reason for its own existence.

THE PARTY CONSTITUTIONAL SYSTEM

The Kuomintang adopted a Party-Constitution after thirty-odd years of activity when, at the suggestion of Soviet advisers, it reorganized on January 28, 1924 as a formal party, with membership books, regular dues, etc. Up to then it had operated through techniques intermediate in formality between American major-party looseness and Chinese secret-society formality. In twelve chapters, the Constitution dealt with Membership, Organization, Special Areas, the Leader (Sun Yat-sen, *Tsung-li*), the Highest Party Organs, Provincial Party Organization, *Hsien* Organization, District (*ch'ü*) Organization, and Sub-district (*ch'ü-fên*, roughly equivalent to the *pao* in local government) Organization, Terms of Office, Discipline, and Finance.[1] The actual application of this Constitution is best described in the words of Wang Shih-chieh, who wrote before the current hostilities: [2]

> The system of organization of the Chinese Kuomintang is based upon the *Constitution and Bye-laws of the Chinese Kuomintang* [*Chung-kuo Kuo-min-tang Hsien-chang*] which was passed in the First Party Congress [*Ch'üan-kuo Tai-piao Ta-hui*] on January 28, Year XIII [1924], and amended in the following two Party Congresses on January 16, Year

---

[1] The text of this Constitution is given in Arthur N. Holcombe's invaluable study of the Great Revolution, *The Chinese Revolution: A Phase in the Regeneration of a World Power*, Cambridge, Massachusetts, 1930, p. 356–70.

[2] Wang Shih-chieh, *Pi-chiao Hsien-fa*, Shanghai, XXVI (1937), p. 651–3.

XV [1926] and on March 27, Year XVIII [1929]. No amendment of any sort was made in the Fourth and Fifth Party Congresses held in the Years XX [1931] and XXIV [1935] respectively.

According to the above *Constitution and Bye-Laws*, the Kuomintang has five divisional organizations, *viz.*: one for the whole country, one for each province, one for each *hsien* (or governmental district), one for each district, and one for each district subdivision [*ch'ü-fên-pu*]. The organ possessing the highest authority in the Kuomintang is the Party Congress of the Kuomintang. When this Congress is not in session, the Central Executive Committee is the highest authority. The organization of the Congress and the method of electing the Delegates are fixed by the Central Executive Committee, while the members of the Central Executive Committee are elected by the Party Congress. Moreover the number of these members is also fixed by the Congress. Article I of the "Outlines of the Organization of the Central Executive Committee," passed in the First Session of the Fifth Central Executive Committee Meeting, on December 6, Year XXIV [1935], provides: "The Central Executive Committee appoints nine standing members of the Committee, to form a Standing Committee which shall discharge the duties of the Central Executive Committee when the latter is not in Session. The Standing Committee is provided with a Chairman and a Vice-Chairman, elected from among the nine standing members." Hence it can be said that when the Central Executive Committee is not in session, this Standing Committee represents the highest authority of the Kuomintang. The offices of the Chairman [superseded by the Party Chief, *Tsung-ts'ai*] and the Vice-Chairman have been provided for since December, Year XXIV [1935]. Whether the Chairman can be the representative of the highest authority of the Kuomintang or not, under the tacit consent of the Standing Committee, still depends upon the changes in circumstances. The said "Outlines of the Organization" does not state clearly the rights and duties of the Chairman and the Vice-Chairman. Hence, the highest authorities of the Kuomintang as prescribed by various written laws are (1) the Party Congress, (2) the Central Executive Committee, and (3) the Standing Committee of the Central Executive Committee. When the larger organ is not in session, the next following organ represents the highest authority of the Kuomintang. But this only applies in theory. As a matter of fact, when the lower organs are exercising their power, they can not but be limited by certain restrictions. Whenever important questions arise which may cause fierce disputes among members or among the people, the lower organs which have the authority to decide when the upper organ is not in session usually reserve the questions for discussion in the meeting of the upper organ. The resolutions passed by the upper organs—the Party Congress down to the Central Executive Committee Meeting—are usually elastic so that the lower organs—the Standing Committee up to the Central Executive Committee—do not experience great difficulties or restrictions in facing various troublesome situations.

According to the *Constitution and Bye-Laws of the Chinese Kuomintang,* there is, besides the Central Executive Committee, a Central Control Committee for the Kuomintang. Its organization is similar to that of the Central Executive Committee, though with fewer members. It occupies the same rank as the Central Executive Committee, and its duty is to superintend and inspect the personnel of the Kuomintang.

The names and organizations of the various organs directly controlled by the Central Executive Committee have unavoidably undergone some changes, though in principle their structures have remained the same. According to the "Outlines of the Organization of the Central Executive Committee," the organs under it are divided along three lines: organization, publicity, and popular training, with various committees. These organs are to discharge all affairs of the Kuomintang. Besides these, there is a Political Committee [superseded by the Supreme National Defense Council], to "act as the highest directing organ in all governmental policies and to be responsible to the Central Executive Committee." Although these organs are authorized by the Central Executive Committee and formed in the Plenary Session of the Central Executive Committee, the Standing Committee can still exercise authority over them when the Central Executive Committee is not in session, because in accordance with the *Constitution and Bye-Laws,* the Standing Committee takes the place of the Central Executive Committee. As a matter of fact, since the activities along the lines of organization, publicity, and popular training are the internal activities within the Kuomintang, these organs are usually under the rigid control of the Standing Committee. As the Political Committee discharges various political affairs, its position may be said to be independent. Any resolution passed by this Committee is sent to the government for execution, and the Standing Committee has no power to restrict its activities. Hence under the party government of the Chinese Kuomintang, the Political Committee is in reality the highest directing and supervisory authority in matters concerning governmental policies.

The Emergency Party Congress of the Kuomintang, Hankow, March 29–April 1, 1938, provided for two further amendments to the Party Constitution. It abolished the system of reserve members, and, far more significantly, it created the post of *Tsung-ts'ai,* here translated Party Chief, which was indistinguishable except as a matter of terminology from the post of *Tsung-li,* held in perpetuity by Sun Yat-sen. Chiang K'ai-shek was elected Party Chief, and the powers of his office were stated to be duplicates of those given originally to the *Tsung-li:* a general provision that "all members shall follow the direction of" the *Tsung-li,* which was not implemented; chairmanship of the Party Congress and of the Central Executive Committee (*a fortiori,* of the Standing Committee of the C.E.C.); and a veto over the acts of the Congress and the C.E.C. Furthermore, the Political Committee (Central Political Council) was replaced by the Supreme National Defense Council, of which Chiang was also elected Chairman.

Since Chiang had been Chairman of the Standing Committee, it follows that the change of formal labels did not much alter the constitutional organization of the Kuomintang, nor materially change Chiang's position. Chiang does not help to create machinery of power in order to lurk behind it, thus proclaiming it a mere façade. He, as a public servant reared in the Confucian tradition, possesses sufficient respect for words to let them mean what they are publicly declared to mean. The post of *Tsung-ts'ai* is more than ample in providing Chiang with the power he feels necessary to accomplish national unification, mitigate social injustice, and promote serious representative government. He accepts the full measure of his power; doing so publicly, his subsequent actions appear relatively modest. By Western standards, Chiang is naive enough to be honest.

A point brought out in connection with the National Government (p. 46, above) is worth reiteration. Neither by Party action nor by governmental change has the Kuomintang monopoly of political power been modified by law. There is no United Front, Popular Front, or any other kind of front in the legal system; even in practical administration, the entrance of non-Party men has been at Party direction; and it is only in the Special Areas, the special war services, and the military organization that the Kuomintang has relaxed its control of power. Other groups are sharing in the work of the People's Political Council. The prudence of such a policy may appear open to question; its consistency is not.

Party Organization

Organizationally the Party is bipolar, with the power concentrated in the entire membership at the base, and in the Chief (*Tsung-ts'ai*) at the apex. The highest authority of the Kuomintang is the Party Congress (*Ch'üan-kuo Tai-piao Ta-hui*), which could also be translated as All-Nation Convention of Party Delegates. Party Congresses have been held as follows: I, Canton, 1924; II, Canton, 1926; III, Nanking, 1929; IV, Nanking, 1931; V, Nanking, 1935; and the Emergency Party Congress, Hankow, 1938. Wang Ch'ing-wei organized a rump Kuomintang on the basis of a "Sixth Party Congress" held in 1939; the legitimate Sixth Congress has not yet been called.

The Party Congress is the highest agency of the Kuomintang, and thereby the highest legal authority in China—a position which it now shares with the Party Chief, *ex officio* its Chairman. The Kuomintang Party Constitution provides that the Congress should ordinarily meet every other year (*Art.* 27), but permits the C.E.C. to postpone a Congress for not more than one year. This provision has frequently been violated. In actual effect the Congress is neither an effective governing body, nor, at the other extreme, a completely helpless tool. No Party Congress has led to a drastic shift of actual political power.

The barometer of influence functions outside the Congress, and the Congress ratifies and establishes what has actually occurred. The high authority of the incumbent C.E.C. in matters of accrediting delegates, plus its power to appoint delegates from areas not represented (a feature taken from Soviet practice), gives the political Ins a formidable weapon with which to bludgeon down opposition, but since the value of the Party Congress is that of a legitimizing agency, overt interference with Party functions would destroy the utility of the Congress. Its level of freedom and efficacy may be compared with American party conventions. Unwieldy, improvised agencies are not able to meet the challenges of well-knit executive groups, but their very unmanageability preserves to them a freedom of incalculable action. The Party Congress could not in practice exercise its formal, legal power of overthrowing the entire Party leadership and starting the Party off on a new tack; it could, however, so humiliate the incumbents by subtle but obvious political gestures familiar to all Chinese, that the leadership would retire for reasons of health, or because of a yearning to contemplate the cosmos.

The elaborate structure of the Kuomintang is shown on the chart of organization (p. 331). Abstraction of the most essential features of this chart reveals the following:

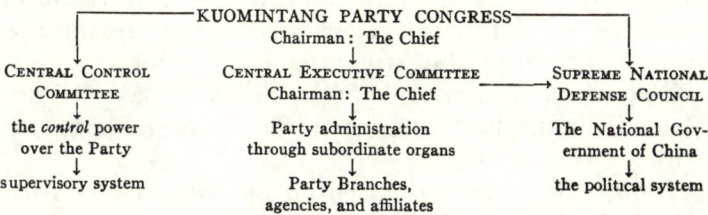

The Central Executive Committee (*Chung-yang Chih-hsing Wei-yüan-hui*) is a relatively large body with one hundred and twenty members. The Party Constitution requires that it meet every six months or less. These sessions, the Plenary Sessions of the C.E.C., are by far the best-established political processes in the Chinese state. Actual shifts in power are here fought out, since the C.E.C. possesses authority ample for almost any emergency. The expulsion of Wang Ch'ing-wei was effected through C.E.C. action, and did not require the work of any higher body.

The Central Control Committee (*Chung-yang Chien-ch'a Wei-yüan-hui*) is an agency which the Chinese adapted from two sources, the Bolshevik pattern of an independent intra-party control system, and the native *chien-ch'a* power. Similar in function to the Commission of Party Control employed by the Communist Party in the Soviet Union rather than to the Organization Bureau, the Central Control Committee (also termed, in another common translation, Central Supervisory Committee) is in charge of an inspective system. Because of the relative laxness of Kuomintang organization, the work of this Committee is far less than one might expect. It has not been adequate to ensure rigidly strict Party efficiency, diligence, or honesty; neither has it become a terrorist agency inflicting an inviolable Party line. Few faults in politics fail to be virtues as well; inefficiency has its minor compensations. In times of secure power, rigid Party discipline might let the Kuomintang grow into a genuine and full-fledged tyranny; nevertheless, in times of stress, such as the present, the Party stands in need of stiffening and control.

The third agency, the Supreme National Defense Council, is the Party's agent in charge of government. (See above, p. 46 *ff.*)

Immediately under the Central Executive Committee there are three agencies of vitality and importance. The first of these is the *San Min Chu I Ch'ing-nien T'uan* (usually translated *San Min Chu I* Youth Corps, or Kuomintang Youth Corps). A war-time addition to the Party, it became politically possible when the abandonment of appeasement re-aligned government and youth. The Communist Youth Corps (*Kung-ch'an Ch'ing-nien T'uan*) provided a model and rival. The Constitution of the Corps, together with an appraisal (from the official point of view) of its work, is given below in Appendices II (B) and II (C). In terms of practical political effect, the Corps is significant, although far less important than its organization scheme would indicate. It combines some of the functions of a military training system with social and propaganda work. Leftists have complained against it bitterly as an agency of espionage and repression within student groups; others have acclaimed it as a meeting of the Kuomintang and the youth, fruitful in terms of national unity. The importance of the Corps lies in its organization of a broad group of young men, one or more steps up from the bottom of the economic scale, and in the fact that the government and Kuomintang—after years of overriding youth opinion—now find it feasible to organize their own affiliate. Few charges of corruption have touched the Corps, which lies particularly within the purview of the Generalissimo. A minor but active element in the political scene, it stands for the Kuomintang's bid for permanence, and, in the event of internal dissension, would be a valuable prop to the *status quo*. The political indecision and laxness of China in general has kept the group from becoming either a *Hitlerjugend* or a frankly democratic C.C.C. (Civilian Conservation Corps) on the American plan; the Corps is at best a laggard bid to young men, and a belated competition with the Left and the Communists.[3]

The Party Affairs Committee (*Tang-wu Wei-yüan-hui*) supplements the work of the Central Control Committee in investigating Party personnel and acting as a supplementary housekeeping agency for intra-Party organization.

The third of these agencies is the [Central] Training Committee (*Hsün-lien Wei-yüan-hui*). To this Committee has fallen the labor of invigorating the Kuomintang under conditions of strain, from war, from the Wang schism, and from new domestic competition. The Generalissimo has put the most vigorous efforts into the work of this agency, and has organized under it a Kuomintang Training Corps (*Hsün-lien T'uan*) which is providing extensive new resources of leadership to the Party. Enterprising or promising young men are gathered together in training meetings, and given intensive work in Party doctrine, propaganda and organization methods, local administration, etc. The Corps has tended to accept youths and some men of middle age from positions of responsibility, and to equip them with the knowledge and the discipline necessary to continuation of pre-democratic government. In the constant race between government activity as a positive force and government apathy combined with outside anti-governmental revolution as negative forces, the training agencies are doing as much as any single enterprise to stabilize the regime.

[3] See *China at War*, Vol. V, No. 3 (October 1940), p. 77-8, for a recent official account of the Corps.

The Central Political Institute (*Chung-yang Chêng-chih Hsüeh-hsiao*) tops the entire program, as a training agency combining features of a university, a camp, and a Party office. Under the personal control and leadership of Dr. Ch'ên Kuo-fu, one of the Generalissimo's intimates and the elder of the celebrated Ch'ên brothers, the Institute stands high for its selection of students, the discipline and instruction it imparts, and its practical political effect. The Kuomintang, pronounced moribund by competent foreign observers ten years ago, today is in a better position for leadership and development than it has been for many years. (The author, who visited the Institute during the summer of 1940, found the student body as well disciplined as any he has seen outside of Germany, the staff highly competent [mostly American-trained], and the physical facilities unsurpassed.) Admission to the Institute is open to graduates of Middle Schools (secondary); students who are married may be admitted, but single students may not marry while in attendance. The courses of study are in general the equivalent of American undergraduate work, although some graduate study is offered. The curriculum includes such subjects as military training, Japanese language and politics, and Marxian thought (in connection with *min shêng chu-i*). The general course is supplemented by two special courses—the Civil Service Training Corps and the Advanced Civil Service Training Corps—which are set up in collaboration with the Examination *Yüan*. Graduates are organized into alumni associations, to which the faculty are admitted as supervisory members. It is a matter of success and distinction to undergo the training of the Institute, which is the equivalent of a West Point for political and governmental work. The Generalissimo visits the Institute and speaks before it as much as possible, frequently as often as bi-weekly, but with occasional gaps of months.[4] In addition to the Central Political Institute, there is a [Kuomintang] Northwest Academy of Youth, which has been even more active in training young men for Party and government service. Proximity to the Red training center at Yenan makes its work urgent; training, according to report, is briefer, cruder, and more vigorous than in the central agency. The sub-surface possibility of renewed class war by the Communists makes the Academy peculiarly necessary.

Apart from the Youth Corps, the training agencies, and the Party Affairs Committee, but also directly underneath the Kuomintang C.E.C., come the coordinated and uncoordinated agencies of Party administration. Their organization is as follows:

[4] Information given the author by Dr. Ch'ên Kuo-fu and members of his staff, at the Central Political Institute, August 18, 1940. Few places are more beautiful than the valley in which the cool, spacious buildings of the Institute are set. Landscaped for centuries, and celebrated as a beauty spot, the area is filled with carved shrines, severely simple monuments, and flagstone walks. A river runs through a forested gorge; waterfalls feed the stream.

Dr. Ch'ên supplemented his hospitality in Western China by transmitting to the author a series of statements in reply to questions which were put to him in writing. Of these, the two most interesting refer, first, to the economic status of the Institute's students, and secondly, to the Kuomintang training plan in the Northwest: "Judged by functions and economic levels, students of the Central Political Institute represent all economic strata of Chinese society. Those of peasant origin are most numerous, forming over 40% of the total number."—"For the purpose of educating young men and women in the border provinces, the Central Political Institute has established a School for the Border Provinces, of which branches were established at Powtow (Suiyuan province), Sinin (Chinghai province), and Kangting (Sikong province) in October 1934. Another branch was established at Shuchow (Kansu province) in August 1935, this being the school sponsored by the Kuomintang in the Northwest. The Powtow branch was suspended in 1940, and those in Sinin and Kangting were handed over to the Provincial Governments concerned at the same time. So the only Kuomintang school in the Northwest at present is the one at Shuchow. It is subdivided into three parts: namely, a Normal School, a Middle School, and a Primary School. Its annual budget is one hundred thousand dollars Chinese national currency." (Letter to the author, March 10, 1941.)

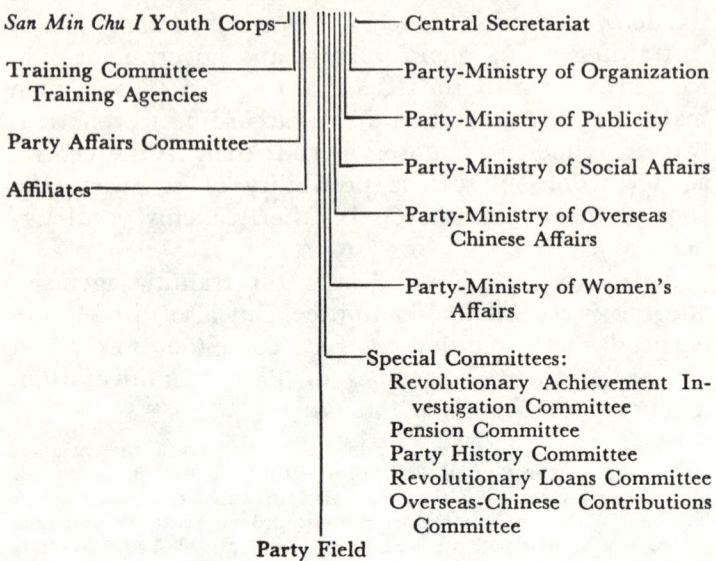

The Party-Ministries [5] constitute a part of the governing machinery of China. The Organization Party-Ministry is important because of its intra-Party work; the Minister, Dr. Ch'u Chia-hua, a German-educated student, is one of the most active Party leaders, and deeply suspect by the Left. His work is the field of Kuomintang Party administration. The Party-Ministries of Social and Overseas Chinese Affairs combine the functions of government with those of the Party; the former is a bureau of protocol, and the latter acts as an extra-governmental colonial office. The Secretariats provide study agencies for the governmental

[5] The term *pu* is usually translated Board, but the *pu-chang* (*pu* chief) is given as Minister. Since the identical terms are rendered Ministry, Minister, Vice-Minister, etc., in the case of the government, the term Party-Ministry is here adopted as both distinct and descriptive.

system. They perform functions which are in the United States both governmental and private (e.g., the work of the Brookings Institution, the Public Administration Clearing House, the various Presidential research and advisory committees, and intra-departmental housekeeping agencies). The system of local government reform is sponsored by the Central Kuomintang Secretariat (*Chung-yang Mi-shu-ch'u*), even more than by the Ministry of the Interior in the government, under whose jurisdiction it falls. The Secretary-General is a benign revolutionary veteran, Yeh-Ch'u-tsang; the Deputy Secretary-General, Dr. K'an Nai-kuang, is a Party official of almost twenty years' standing, who studied in the United States and visited Europe in quest of data on administration. Boundlessly energetic, he is typical of the younger scholars who combine the academic and the political and impart to the Kuomintang a large share of its present energy.

Internationally, the most important Party-Ministry is that of Publicity (*Chung-yang Hsüan-ch'uan Pu*), which carries out most of the Chinese propaganda program. Headed by Dr. Wang Shih-chieh, a very outspoken man, its functions are distributed between Sections of General Affairs, Motion Pictures, Newspapers, Advisory, Consultation, and International Publicity, together with services such as China's leading semi-official news service (the Central News Agency), the Party newspapers, the Central Motion Picture Studios, and the official broadcasting system. Because of the difficulties of language, travel, and passports, the International Department supplies most of the news which reaches the world press from Free China. The function of the Western newspapermen consists largely in editing and supplementing this news from whatever independent source they can find, or, occasionally and at the cost of considerable hardship, to attempt to discover the facts for themselves.

In general, the Chinese follow the policy of giving the favorable side of the news, simply omitting anything that could conceivably be unfavorable. Their publicity services are no more guilty of positive *suggestio falsi* than the services of the British or Americans. Nevertheless, Chinese notions of dignity and public policy differ widely from Americans'; news would be hard to obtain or valueless when obtained, except for the fact that the staff of the International Section is almost entirely American-trained and well-acquainted with American notions of news. The very able and active Hollington Tong, one of China's most successful newspapermen, who was in press work long before he became a Party official, has led in the supply of ample news in the face of great difficulties. He is esteemed by Westerners to be, along with Mme. Chiang, one of the Generalissimo's most effective publicity advisers.

The Party-Ministry of Publicity also attends to the needs and interests of Western newspapermen and other visitors, arranging appointments, schedules, etc., and even boarding many of them at a Press Hostel. These attentions, while from time to time irritatingly restrictive, are in the end almost always appreciated as invaluable. Only the Leftists shun the Publicity Ministry; they do so unsuccessfully, and to their loss. No other Asiatic, and few Western, states can boast as alert and effective a system of propaganda. In the troubled shifts and crises of world politics, the Chinese have managed to retain the sympathy of the most diverse audiences—from American church people to Soviet agitation squads, and from British conservatives to Nazi clubs in Germany. The American traditions of frankness, zest, liveliness in news are transplanted; while they have suffered a sea-change, they still operate with telling effect.[6]

[6] Visitors to Chungking owe much to the Foreign Affairs Section of the International Publicity Department. Its chief, the affable Mr.

THE KUOMINTANG

The Ministry of Women's Affairs, decreed in 1940, is in process of organizing women's work for the Party. Previously, most women's organizations had been knit together in the affiliated New Life Movement. The minor committees of the Party—historical, pensions, etc. —lie outside the scope of war activities. Although they continue, their functions are subordinate to the purposes of resistance and reconstruction.

Formal field organization follows seven patterns:

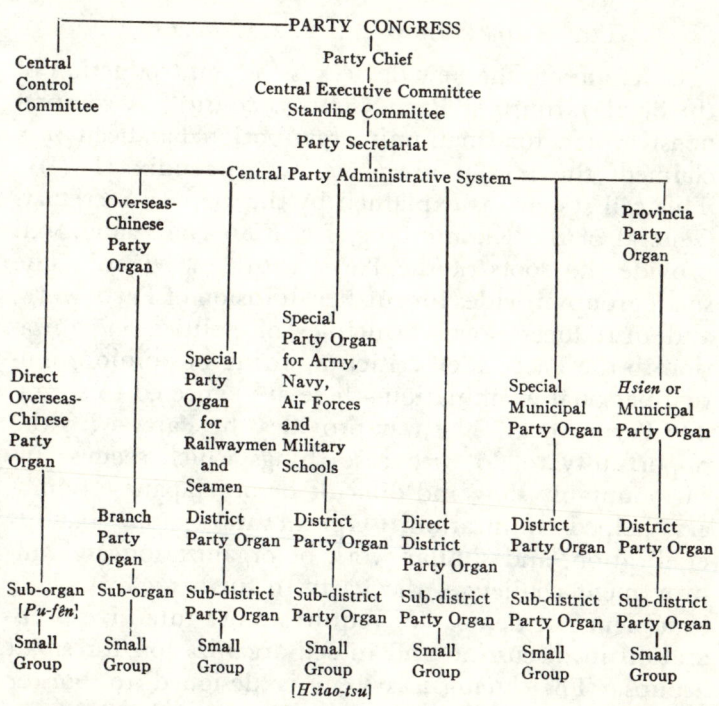

C. C. Chi, a well-known economist from Shanghai, has acted as host to almost every visitor to Hankow or Chungking. He has fulfilled endless requests—many of them irrational—with unfailing patience, good humor, candor, and intelligence. Few books on contemporary China fail to bear the imprint of his help; the present one is no exception.

Much of this exists only on paper. After the break with the Communists in 1927, and the transformation of the Kuomintang from a government-destroying to a governing agency, the functional and agitational groups were allowed to slip into desuetude. Under the pressure of war, and the encouraging political situation, which puts a premium on action, the Kuomintang has adopted a variety of policies designed to maintain its position.

The Kuomintang Bid for Leadership

Chief among the new devices is the reintroduction of the Small Group, or Party Cell (*hsiao-tsu*). A comprehensive plan for small-unit organization has been proclaimed; the text is given below, Appendix II (D). This cell system, as explained by the Deputy Secretary-General of the Kuomintang, Dr. K'an Nai-kuang, will provide the roots of the Party with new vigor.[7] The small group provides for further diffusion of Party work, and introduces novel principles of political organization to the Party. Self-criticism, airing of opinion, mutual personal examination—these are expected to stimulate Party work. The war provides the Party with the opportunity to do with ease things which seemed insurmountably slow and difficult before Japanese bombers helped unification. Opium-suppression, bandit-eradication, and similar work of organization and improvement challenges the Party to further effort. The imminence of democracy requires more intensive preparation in discussion and in self-organization for small groups. The *hsiao-tsu* system is designed to bolster Party morale, improve the Party work, and spread the teaching of Sun Yat-sen.

[7] Statement to the author at Kuomintang Central Headquarters, Chungking, July 16, 1940; Dr. K'an also supplied the facts for the new organizational features of the Party. The following interpretations are the author's alone.

The new governmental pattern of local government is to be reinforced by the corresponding development of Kuomintang agencies. In the government's plan, rural development operates on four levels: the militia; the school system; the agricultural and industrial co-operatives; and the political organization. The same person in each village or hamlet would be responsible for all four. If he is to be a Party man, he must be effective to be of service and a credit to the Party.

In order to eradicate undesirable personnel, the Kuomintang has increased its Party-purging facilities with what is known as the Party Supervisor's Net (*Tang-jên Chien-ch'a Wang*). By action of the C.E.C. on June 13, 1940, the sub-district Party organs are to elect one to three members each to serve, with a six months' term, as Control Members. With a power of report on Party discipline, and responsibility for Party conditions, this change was expected to drive undesirables more effectively out of the Party.

Three years from 1940 was set as the final date for the installation of the new system. While the fractionization of a Party may seem to be of minor importance, it actually is a major factor in the potential development of the Kuomintang. In the period of Party government, the more popular organs of Party members tended to slough off, leaving large *Tangpu* (Party Headquarters) in the *hsien* or cities. These quite often fell into the hands of local machines, with the consequence that they interfered with government, and promoted the usual evils of party machines. The diffusion of Party work, by letting individuals participate more freely as individuals, may help to break the monopoly of these bureaus, and restore the Party effectiveness with less reliance on supervision from above.

The Kuomintang, in addition to these reorganization devices, is meeting competition from the Left by increasing its membership. Membership figures are not available in war time; the total is probably over two million. In some instances the new members are no particular improvement on the pre-existing group, but in the majority of cases the Party broadens its base of popular support.

Intra-Kuomintang Politics

The years which saw the rise of the Kuomintang to power, and its subsequent period of authority, showed a diminution of the disparateness of Party fractions. For a long time the adherents of Wang Ch'ing-wei stood formally Left; those of Hu Han-min, formally Right; while various older Party alignments preserved their outlines more or less clearly (e.g., the Kuomintang Western Hills Group). With the consistent rise of Chiang K'ai-shek to Party and national leadership, and the steady influx of non-Party or merely nominal Party men into the government, Party distinctions lost their cogency in practical affairs.

In terms of influence, patronage, and effective policy-making, the Kuomintang is a conglomeration of innumerable personal leaderships knit together by a common outlook, a common interest in the maintenance of the National Government and formal Party power, and a common loyalty to the Party Chief. The clearest groups are those which are out of the current political stream; most notable among these is the Wang schism, and a few scattered irreconcilables of half-forgotten Party struggles. Within the regime, Kuomintang groups tend to coalesce as the leaders meet, negotiate, and govern together in the councils of state.

So completely in the ascendant that they have lost their general character as groups are the *Erh Ch'ên* (literally "the two Ch'êns"; also termed "C.C. group" by English-speaking Chinese), led by the brothers, Ch'ên Li-fu, Minister of Education, and Ch'ên Kuo-fu, head of the Central Political Institute, and the *Huangpu*

(Whampoa Academy) groups, led by the Generalissimo himself. The Ch'ên brothers have been close adherents of Chiang throughout his career. Brilliant, vigorous, sharp in the retention of power, they have made themselves anathema to the Left. They are effective reorganizers of the Kuomintang, keenly aware of its position as monopoly Party, and their protégés and trainees are omnipresent through government and Party. Their military counterpart is the *Huangpu* group. It includes officers either trained by Chiang himself or under his close supervision. With the passage of each year, the proportion of Whampoa (or daughter-institution) graduates in the national armies rises. The officers include a high proportion of technically qualified men, whose capabilities and interests are chiefly military. Builders of the new army, they look to the Generalissimo and the Party for dicta on social, economic, and political policy; they provide China with the unpolitical army which has been an American ideal, although rejected by Soviet and South American practice. The officers are not encouraged to assume decisive roles in local politics, but to refer such things back to Headquarters. In consequence, although the danger of a new *tuchünism* has almost disappeared, the army staff does not readily adapt itself to a *levée en masse,* or to the problems of a social-revolutionary army. The very factors which make of the army a tool and not a practice-ground of government also make it somewhat rigid in dealing with guerrilla situations.

Both the C. C. and Whampoa groups are instilled with notions of Party and military discipline which trace back in the first place to the instruction given by Russians from the Soviet Union. While they follow Sun and Chiang in accepting the promises of democracy, their notion of democracy is as different from that of the Left as Washington's was from the Jacobins'. They are interested in sound, disciplined, powerful national government, representative, republican, and stable; they see the revolution as largely complete in the power-destroying phase, and are beginning to think in the reconstruction phase. After ten years of strain and terror in fighting the Communists, they look with suspicion on political changes which would open the nation to opportunist Communist agitation, or make Chungking the helpless diplomatic dependency of the Narkomindel. The bitterness of internecine conflict has made them deeply suspicious of sudden or radical reform, although they themselves profess a genuine interest in social welfare. The actual reforms which have been accomplished are, in the scale of political reality, already stupendous: opium eradication, tax collection, diffusion of national authority, communications, industrialization, military advance, etc. To the Kuomintang center, a demand for sharp or shocking change is suspect. They desire to amplify what they have, and to let changes wait on the ability of trained personnel—not entrusting progress to the vagaries of mass movements with incalculable force and direction.

While the National Government was at Nanking, there was a *Fu-hsing Shê* (Regeneration Club), organized by a few hot-headed members of the Kuomintang center. Its activities in support of the Generalissimo and the government, under the further sobriquet of Bluejacket or Blue Shirt group, earned it the reputation of a Chinese *Schutzstaffel*. The comparison was at best fanciful, but any comparison at all was heartily desired by the Europocentric Chinese Left and by the world press. Magnified beyond recognition, the Club was identified with almost every agency in the government and Party, not excluding the New Life Movement. As applied, the name *Blue Shirt* covered a wide scattering of unrelated agencies which had the common features of a Kuomintang-center position, an inclination to effective action (including violence) and some secrecy. Effective political-police work is led by one T'ai Li, whose name is whispered by dissidents; but counter-espionage and supervision of suspects is also performed through Party agents, the regular military, and governmental agencies.

Around the Kuomintang center there are other groups, some closely related to Chiang, some remote. The Political Scientists (*Chêng-hsüeh Hsi*) owe their name to a society which once existed in Nanking. They include many of the administrators, men with American training who are interested in industrial and fiscal development. The clarity of this group has faded by its absorption into the governing center. The Cantonese are represented by two levels of politics: those who based their power on Canton province and those who remained within the government. President Sun K'ê of the Legislative *Yüan* has been outstanding in his willingness to cooperate with the Communists and Left, and is on cordial terms with relatively independent progressives, such as Mme. Sun Yat-sen. Further groups within the Kuomintang are constituted by the loyalist followers of Wang Ch'ing-wei, who now attach themselves to other leaders, and by other personal or regional followings (e.g., the *Tungpei* followers of Chang Hsüeh-liang, ex-*tuchün* of Manchuria and ex-Vice-Commander-in-Chief, still "retired" as a result of the Sian kidnapping). Finally, a number of elder Party leaders remain because of their seniority or connection with Sun Yat-sen; they do not need to attach themselves to any particular clique in order to retain their position. These include such men as the venerable Secretary-General of the Party, Yeh Ch'u-tsang; the President of the National Government, Lin Shên; and the President of the Control *Yüan*, Yü Yu-jên.

What has been said about the groups in the People's Political Council (see p. 76 *ff*.) applies to these. It is possible, as in American congressional or administrative circles, to distinguish blocs of leaders with differing interests or policy; but clarity fades upon scrutiny. The orientation, even by the participants, is subjective. Lacking continuous institutional form, clustering of leaders is transient, shifting with political events.

It is difficult to appraise the role of the Kuomintang without at the same time assessing the position of the government. The two are inescapably connected. Although the Communists profess recognition of the government, and pledge it loyalty, they offer only comradeship—on their own terms—to the Kuomintang. This arrangement may last for a considerable length of time, but the National Government is a Kuomintang creation; short of violent revolution, Party control will scarcely break in war time. Upon the Party, therefore, depends much of the efficacy of the Government.

Many well-known Leftist writers on China—such as Edgar Snow—make the comment that whereas the National Government is deserving as a government, and worthy of support, the Kuomintang is hopelessly corrupt, a creature of landlords and capitalists, or, of even worse, "feudal elements." Such a distinction, based on strong moral urges and a desire to achieve historical parallels, is untenable in practice. Kuomintang power has weathered more than a decade of adversities. The Generalissimo depends upon it. Analysis of the Kuomintang as the party of the Chinese national bourgeoisie, and ascription of a mass character to the Communists alone, is a fallacy, comparable to a consideration of Earl Browder as the real leader of the American working class.

In point of fact, neither the Kuomintang nor the Communist Party in China is a mass party. Neither ever has been, although each sought mass character in the Great Revolution. Still largely apolitical, the Chinese masses are organized socially, culturally, and economically into a village and guild system which functions through most of the country. The Kuomintang includes a very high proportion of shopkeepers, returned overseas-Chinese, Chinese still resident overseas, Christians, landlords, and Western-returned students. The class composition of the Kuomintang is largely incidental to its functional character. Since the Kuomintang was the party of Westernization, it gathered in revolutionary days Chinese of all classes who were sufficiently modernized to be interested. Naturally the poorest peasants and the coastal proletariat did not constitute a large proportion of such membership. The men who entered did so as Christians, as travellers, as temperamental rebels, rather than as representatives of the bourgeoisie. When the Communists, whom a recent writer [8] with unconscious humor calls the party of the Chinese proletariat, came on the scene, the same social elements contributed to its membership. Once the Communist Party abandoned the Trotskyist line of urban revolt for the leadership of endemic peasant rebellions, its composition changed somewhat, although the Communist leaders of today are socially much like their Kuomintang equivalents. The men who are class-conscious are, like Lenin, historically, philosophically, and morally so; it is a matter of literary necessity, not of fact.

The Kuomintang is in power; the Communist and Left parties are not. As the governing group, the Kuomintang naturally attracts those persons who would seek to enter any government. Since it has not and does not promote rural class warfare, pre-existing class rela-

[8] For a Marxian analysis of the Kuomintang, carefully stripped of frank Marxian verbiage, see "Wei-Meng-pu," "The Kuomintang in China: Its Fabric and Future" in *Pacific Affairs*, Vol. XIII, No. 1 (March 1940), p. 30–44. The author *a priori* defines the Kuomintang as the party of the national bourgeoisie in China, in effect exhorting it to fulfill its historic mission of completing the national democratic revolution, whereupon socialism [i.e., Stalinism] may historically follow. Nevertheless, its comment on personalities is informing in terms of practical politics.

tionships continue. The Party and the Government have sought, not always efficiently or faithfully to the nth degree, to carry out the programs of land reform, democratization, etc., to which they have been committed. The Kuomintang has tolerated widespread sharecropping, land destitution, usury, and rural despotism—because it found these in existence, and was preoccupied with building a national government, a modern army, adequate finance, and with eradicating some of the worst evils, such as opium, bandits, and Communists (who, whatever their ideals, nevertheless helped to impoverish a poor nation by merciless civil war).

If the Kuomintang were out, it too could point to existing evils. Whoever controls government bears the responsibility. A class element is to a certain degree inescapable in any government; illiterate, unqualified persons do not assume leadership even in the Soviet Union until they have escaped their handicaps through training. But to make of the Kuomintang the party of the Chinese landlords and merchants alone is as fallacious as to make the Republicans or Democrats solely the instruments of American capitalism. A comment such as this would be unnecessary in the case of the United States; but persons who are not Marxian with respect to the analysis of current American events often assume a Left approach to China because of impatience with evils which they see but cannot understand.

The final appraisal of the Kuomintang must be based on the practical work of the government and the Party. In 1940, their effective control was wider and deeper than ever before. The Chinese state was more nearly in existence. The armies were undefeated. The growth of China in the past ten years, and the stand made by China at war, has been made under the unrelaxed control of the Kuomintang monopoly of constitutional power, together with its clear primacy in more tangible power—schools, finance, armies, and police.

The New Life Movement and Other Affiliates

The important New Life Movement (*Hsin Shêng-huo Yün-tung*) is, strictly speaking, not a Party organization; but Chiang is its Chairman, and in purposes and personnel it interlocks with the Party. Convinced that institutional and economic reform required accompanying moral and ideological reform, the Generalissimo founded an Officers' Moral Endeavor Corps as early as 1927. This organization was placed, soon after its initiation, in the hands of Colonel (now Major-General) J. L. Huang, a graduate of Vanderbilt University and an experienced Y.M.C.A. secretary. The Corps' purposes were comparable to those of a Y.M.C.A. with American armies, but Chinese morality in general, not Christian sectarian teaching, was stressed. With Chiang's encouragement, the Corps came to include a high percentage of the officers. Teaching cleanliness, truthfulness, promptness, kindness, dignity, etc., it helped build morale.

In 1934, after seven years of war against the Communist-led agrarian insurrections in South Central China, the Generalissimo decided to extend to the whole people the type of work done by the Corps. On February 19, 1934, he made his first speech announcing the New Life Movement and on the following March 11, a mass meeting of about one hundred thousand people, representing five hundred organizations, signalized the formal inauguration of the movement.[9] From then on the Movement was continued as a regular phase of anti-Communist reconstruction. It elicited praise for its attempt to reach the roots of China's political demoralization, and its intent to remedy the everyday

[9] The China Information Committee, *News Release*, March 4, 1940. English translations of names such as the New Life Movement, Officers' Moral Endeavor Corps, National Spiritual Mobilization, etc. are often awkward or jejune where the original is not.

life of the people,[10] although there was skepticism as to its effectiveness in removing troubles deeply ingrained in the economic system.

The type of evil against which the New Life Movement struggles is well-illustrated by Mme. Chiang's enumeration of the seven deadly sins: self-seeking, "face," cliquism, defeatism (*mei-yu fa-tzŭ*, the Chinese *nitchevo*), inaccuracy (*ch'a-pu-to*), lack of self-discipline, and evasion of responsibility.[11] In addition to these sins of social and political behavior, there are others such as filthiness, carelessness of infection, indecent or sloppy dress, bad manners, unkindness, etc. The Movement, easily understood in view of the traditional Confucian emphasis on personal conduct, seeks to reach individual behavior. The West European and North American peoples have been disciplined by technology itself: timeliness, cleanliness, regularity, have come to be a part of daily life. Any nation which seeks to shift from an agrarian to an industrial economy discovers that amiable defects become ruinous flaws: machinery cannot wait; a machine society requires a discipline of its own. The New Life Movement is attacking the points of social behavior which strike the newcomer to China most immediately and most unfavorably.

The positive virtues of the New Life Movement were formulated by the Generalissimo. Four in number, they are *li, i, lien,* and *ch'ih*. *Li* is the fundamental Confucian virtue, and is based upon *jên*. *Jên* being

[10] Young, C. W. H., *New Life for Kiangsi*, Shanghai, 1935, is a missionary work which praises the New Life Movement highly. The book includes interesting, first-hand, unfavorable accounts of the rule of the quondam Chinese Soviet Republic, and explains some of the opposition to the Communists. The interconnection between Communist-suppression and the New Life Movement is consciously and clearly demonstrated.

[11] Chiang, May-ling Soong, *China Shall Rise Again*, New York, 1941, p. 38 *ff*. Mme. Chiang's work also includes a full account of the enterprises of the New Life Movement and of its affiliates.

humane self-awareness, or consciousness of membership in society, *li* is the application of this awareness to conduct; it thereby signifies proper behavior, not in the superficial sense of empty formality, but in the sense of behavior which is *human:* the full expression of man's moral and ethical stature. The traditional translation of *li* is *rites, ceremonies,* or *etiquette*—terms which, because of their connotations of an empty ceremonialism, are inadequate as a rendition of the original. The Generalissimo writes of *li:* "It becomes natural law, when applied to nature; it becomes a rule, when applied to social affairs; and signifies discipline, when applied to national affairs. These three phases of one's life are all regulated by reason. Therefore, 'li' can be interpreted as regulated attitude of mind and heart." [12] Chiang thus reconciled, for his own thought, the naturalistic ethics of Confucius, wherein man and nature were parts of an inseparable ethical structure, and the pragmatism of Sun Yat-sen.

I is the element in man which makes him observe *li:* ethics or justice. *Lien* is "clear discrimination (honesty in personal, public, and official life) : Integrity." According to the lexicographer,[13] it is "pure, incorrupt, not avaricious." The fourth principle is *ch'ih,* given by the dictionary as "to feel shame," [14] and rendered by the Generalissimo and Madame Chiang as "real self-consciousness (self-respect) : Honor." [15] From this the Generalissimo evolved his formulation of a theory of action.[16] That he is not unaware of criticisms directed against him for talking about morality when people are

[12] Chiang K'ai-shek, *Outline of the New Life Movement,* Chungking (?) , n.d. p. 8. This is the translation, by Mme. Chiang, of *Hsin Shêng-huo Yün-tung Kang-yao,* Nanking, n.d., originally published in May 1934.
[13] Giles, Herbert, *A Chinese-English Dictionary,* Second Edition, Shanghai and London, 1912; ideograph No. 7128.
[14] The same; ideograph No. 1999.
[15] Chiang K'ai-shek, cited, p. 7.
[16] Reprinted as Appendix III (B) , p. 373, below.

fighting and starving is shown by his spirited counter-attack:

There are two kinds of skeptics:
First, some hold the view that the four virtues are simply rules of good conduct. No matter how good they may be, no benefit to the nation can be derived from them if the knowledge and technique used by that nation are inferior to others.

Those who hold this view do not seem to understand the difference between matters of primary and secondary importance. From the social and national point of view, only those who are virtuous can best use their knowledge and technique for the salvation of the country. Otherwise, ability may be abused for dishonorable purposes. "Li," "i," "lien," and "ch'ih" are the principal rules alike for a community, a group, or the entire nation. Those who do not observe these rules will probably utilize their knowledge and ability to the disadvantage of society. Therefore, these virtues may be considered as matters of primary importance upon which the foundation of a nation can be solidly built.

Secondly, there is another group of people who argue that these virtues are merely refined formalities, which have nothing to do with the actual necessities of daily life. For instance, if one is hungry, can these formalities feed him? This is probably due to some misunderstanding of the famous teachings of Kuan-Tze, who said: "When one does not have to worry about his food and clothing, then he cares for personal honor; when the granary is full, then people learn good manners." The sceptic fails to realize that the four virtues teach one how to be a man. If one does not know these, what is the use of having abundance of food and clothing? Moreover, Kuan-Tze did not intend to make a general statement, merely referring to a particular subject at a particular time. When he was making broad statements, he said: " 'li,' 'i,' 'lien,' and 'ch'ih' are the four pillars of the nation." When these virtues prevail, even if food and clothing are temporarily insufficient, they can be produced by man power: or, if the granary is empty, it can be filled through human effort. On the other hand, when these virtues are not observed, there will be robbery and beggary in time of need: and from a social point of view robbery and beggary can never achieve anything. Social order is based on these virtues. When there is order, then everything can be done properly: but when everything is in confusion, very little can be achieved. Today robbers are usually most numerous in the wealthiest cities of the world. This is an obvious illustration of confusion caused by non-observance of virtues. The fact that our country has traitors as well as corrupt officials shows that we, too, have neglected the cultivation of virtues, and if we are to recover, these virtues must be adopted as the principles of a new life.[17]

Generalissimo and Mme. Chiang both work actively in the Movement, inspecting its branches and enterprises, speaking at its meetings, and supervising its functions. The Movement possesses a small but very active central staff, with Major-General Huang as Secretary-General and Dr. Chu Djang, a Johns Hopkins political scientist, as his assistant. Efforts are made to improve the daily life of the people. Shops are encouraged to join the Movement, on conditions requiring cleanliness, uniform prices, etc. Thus in addition to the work of a Y.M.C.A. for all ages and classes, the Movement attempts the role of a municipal health campaign agency, a better business bureau, and a civic service club. Marriages have traditionally depleted family budgets; many a Chinese farmer or worker has fallen into usurious debt because of the social necessity of extravagant feasting and celebration. The Movement accordingly organized inexpensive mass marriages, collectively celebrated under official auspices; the purpose is not to increase the population, but to circumvent a wasteful custom. Peep-show operators have been given displays which are patriotic instead of mythical, chivalric, or licentious. Story-tellers are taught new, public-spirited stories to tell. The New Life Movement seeks to reinvigorate Chinese society by adapting existing institutions or businesses to new needs.

In addition to attempting change in traditional life, the Movement has introduced innovations. The only

[17] Chiang K'ai-shek, cited, p. 6–7.

cafeteria in Chungking serving cheap but dietetically sound meals is operated by the New Life Headquarters. Chinese foods were hard to preserve and unpleasant to eat in the darkness of air raid shelters; China has had no sandwiches, crackers, or equivalent preparations; the New Life Movement concocted a cheap but tasty and nutritious wheat and soy biscuit, and scattered the recipe broadcast. News is distributed to the illiterates through lantern-slide lectures in market-places. Mass singing, virtually unknown in China until now, is making enormous strides with the war; the New Life Movement is diffusing this, along with calisthenics.[18]

A group of minor New Life agencies are clustered about the Headquarters. These, like the Movement, are not financed by popular subscription, membership fees, or collection drives. All administrative expenses are borne by the Generalissimo and his closest associates, who contribute from their private funds or from available contingent funds of their offices, and from contributions by local governments. Since part of the program is distribution of cash gifts to all wounded soldiers, the budget runs into fairly high figures, but the Generalissimo realizes that in China there is no better way to create mistrust of an enterprise than to collect money for it. The leading agencies affiliated with the New Life are:

(1) the War Area Service Corps, designed for propaganda, instruction, spreading of cooperatives, relief, etc., in the occupied and combat zones;

(2) the Rural Service Corps, designed to perform the same functions behind the lines, and to aid in rural reconstruction;

(3) the New Life Students Rural Summer Service Corps, an organization which organizes students from

---

[18] Most of these and the following facts, but not the interpretations, are based on interviews which the author had with the hospitable Major-General J. L. Huang in Chungking, on July 14, 1940, and subsequently.

the colleges during their summer vacations, and sends them out on the land for service work, along with new agricultural information, hygienic teaching, literacy drives, etc.;

(4) the Wounded Soldiers' League, a self-help organization for disabled veterans, who are assisted and encouraged to set up their own cooperatives; they have done so with particular success in cigarette-making, printing, and shoe-weaving;

(5) the Friends of the Wounded Society, wherein volunteers become friends to veterans who are in hospitals, or who return to civil life as cripples (each Friend contributing money, transmitted direct to the veteran; Friends are also encouraged to write or visit the veterans);

(6) the New Life Secretaries' Camp, virtually a summer undergraduate college, with an academic curriculum, strict discipline, and ample organized recreation; and

(7) the Women's Advisory Council, which in turn tops another pyramid of war-time activity in the hands of women's organizations.[19]

In addition to these major activities, there are innumerable further enterprises, including another industrial cooperative system, a really extensive chain of orphanages for war orphans, schools for girls, training camps for young women, etc. It is no uncommon sight to stand on a city street in West China and see three-fourths of the young people wearing the uniforms of various war activities, most of which—outside the army—are affiliates of the Party or the Movement.

These activities have not received much praise from Leftists or foreign visitors. They begin at a level so far below American requirements of social service that they seem ineffectual. The author once saw, in China's *tuchün* years, old people dying in the streets while

---

[19] For an excellent outline of the role of women in the war, see Chiang, May-ling Soong, *China Shall Rise Again*, cited, p. 287 ff.

pedestrians walked by, uncomfortable but aloof; he saw children with burnt-out eyes whining for alms, to the profit of a beggars' syndicate; he watched soldiers rotting alive on the flagstones of temple courtyards. The Kuomintang, the New Life, and their affiliates cannot relieve the general poverty of China, nor alter the fundamental economic faults and continuing maladjustments of class functions. These agencies do, however, eliminate evils so bad that the ordinary American would not remember them for his schedule of social reform. In the vast reaches of Free China, these organizations—like many others—almost disappear in the perpetual routines of ancient, enduring institutions: the market-place, the hucksters' streets, the tea-house. But their influence is felt. In contrast with the entire American New Deal, they are nothing at all; in contrast with the Y.M.C.A., Komsomol, or similar organizations, they are agents of one of the greatest practical social reforms ever undertaken in Asia, and a step bound to have political repercussions.

Popular non-participation still stultifies them. The leadership of the agencies parallels government personnel. Women leaders are in many instances the wives of officials; an exceptional person, such as Mme. Chiang or her celebrated sisters, may be a leader in her own right, but this is no usual rule. In many agencies, such as intended mass organizations for reform, instruction, health, etc., the mass character is entirely lacking. The masses are the beneficiaries of Kuomintang action, but not often participants in that action. The Communists and the independent Left hold an enormous leverage in popular interest; ignoring class lines, illiteracy, or lack of preparation, they draw the common people into a real share in government and social reconstruction. The Kuomintang has ignored this opportunity—in part because of the Confucian cleavage between scholars and the untutored which made the scholar, however benevo-

THE KUOMINTANG 157

lent or philanthropic, a being apart from the commonalty.

Two further organs—the National Spiritual Mobilization (*Kuo-min Ching-shên Tsung-tung-yüan*) and the Mass Mobilization—are Kuomintang devices for mass participation. The former, developed as an antidote to defeatism engendered by protraction of the war, rising prices, and the treason of Wang, actually consists in a propaganda machine, which holds torchlight vigils, national fealty ceremonies, and similar festivals in the larger cities; it has adapted some of the stagecraft of the German National Socialists, but lacks a broadly popular character. The Mass Mobilization is under the Training Department of the Military Affairs Commission; useful as a military device, its political character is slight in Free China. In the guerrilla and occupied zones, a genuine *levée en masse* has been accomplished; in the free areas, safeguards which hedge Mobilization have robbed it of utility save that which is strictly military. As an adjunct to the army, this is useful; otherwise it has been ineffectual, despite the competitive success obtained by the guerrilla zones in equivalent organizations.

The over-all picture of the Kuomintang and its activities is hard to bring into focus. One general contrast will point some of its strength and weakness clearly: as a governing agency, which created and maintained the government, the Kuomintang has been more effective than any other group in China. The Party has met and overcome obstacles in practical politics, international relations, working administration, internal unification, and national defense. The Party has succeeded well enough to remain in power, which none of its predecessors or competitors have managed to do. As a social and political force, its governing character colors its work. More has been done by the government for the people than in any comparable situation in East

Asia. But Kuomintang rule, however excellent when measured by the standards of authoritary or colonial government, still falls far short of even elementary application of democratic techniques. The flexibility of the Party, and a continued ability to yield power in order to retain power, are the most hopeful factors in the view of the Kuomintang future.

The Kuomintang could not be overthrown by any force—mere force—on earth, unless the Party betrayed itself. Attacked by a major power, it has emerged unscathed. But the Communists or other opponents may find their most useful weapons in the weaknesses of the Kuomintang itself: in the slowness of its change, or in its unadaptability to rapidly changing conditions; or in an extra-Party resentment arising from severe economic dislocation which, though consequent to war rather than to governmental policies, was not swiftly enough controlled by a slowly-moving Kuomintang. By contrast with 1935, however, the Kuomintang has gained much power; the Communists have lost some. Regional and half-separatist regimes, often corrupt, have almost altogether disappeared. Along with the Kuomintang, the independent Leftists have also profited.

No prediction, to be plausible, can assume the early demise or collapse of the Kuomintang. The Party has obtained power; its organization is one of the three policy-executing branches of the new national organization. Ruin of the Kuomintang implies ruin of the emergent Chinese state, so laboriously constructed; though a successor might arise, too much of the work would have to be done over again. Many Chinese, of all classes, realize this. Kuomintang rule is the *status quo;* despite demerits, it is the first stable government modern China has had, and China's chief tool of defense today.

Chapter VI

THE COMMUNIST AND MINOR PARTIES

THE party politics of Republican China fall into two periods: the early period of competitive, pre-parliamentary parties, 1912 to the Great Revolution; and a later period of struggling monopoly-power parties, from the Great Revolution to the present. In the earlier period the Kuomintang and its rivals tolerated one another's existence; each regarded co-existing parties as natural, desirable, and useful. But the sham democracy of the prostituted Republic disheartened the Kuomintang, which thereupon bid for the complete conquest of power, brooking no legitimate competitors; its rivals did likewise. The first coalition (1922–27) of Kuomintang and Communists was therefore not the democratic competition of two parties with different stresses upon a common ideological foundation, but a war-time alliance of basically incompatible forces. After the 1927 break, the Kuomintang became the only legal party in most of the country, while the Communists—with a rebel army, an unrecognized government, and a territory of their own—enjoyed legality within the limits of their own swords. The Kuomintang, embraced by all major groups save the Communists, became the foremost vehicle for Chinese political life. Minor parties enjoyed precarious, ineffectual existences, underground or expatriate.

With the outbreak of war in 1937, Nationalists and Communists adopted a truce, formally a Communist surrender of armed rebellion, subversive ideology, and separate government. In actuality it was an alliance of deadly enemies against the Japan which threatened them both. Today, Chinese party politics revives in the People's Political Council, and to a slight degree in public opinion. The legal prohibition of minor parties, including the Communists, remains in effect. Chinese party politics, in the Western sense of a friendly subdivision of common opinion, remains vestigial. The only guarantee of party rights is an unstable toleration extended by the Kuomintang in the negative form of non-prosecution. The Kuomintang is the Party for most of China. The Communist Party is the party for a separate fraction of China. The minor parties, holding neither territory nor armies in the game of power, maneuver between and about the two, struggling to attain legal existence.

The Chinese Communists: Party and Leaders

Literary Marxism runs back to the Ch'ing dynasty, but the first formal organization of a Chinese Communist Party occurred with the first Congress of the Chinese C.P., in Shanghai, during July of 1921.[1] The Soviet-

[1] Miff, P., *Heroic China,* New York, 1937, p. 14. This valuable pamphlet is by one of the Comintern's leading expounders of Marxism as applied to China. Trotskyist Marxism is represented by a far fuller, more careful work by Harold Isaacs, cited, together with the following, cited on p. 20, n. 16. Edgar Snow, the distinguished American journalist, operates on the basis of an independent, unacknowledged type of Marxism, which shows itself in consistent prejudice against the Kuomintang, and in a soul-hungry search for a dialectical, inner meaning of things with which to supplement common-sense observation; his "Things that Could Happen," *Asia,* Vol. XLI, No. 1 (January 1941), employs Hegelianism at tenth-remove to analyze the future. It leads to a frequent implication of motives and to subjective interpretations which rearrange fact as it ought to be in terms of a rational economic dialectic (i.e., an occult pattern which provides a uniform key to all human experience). Thus, in his *Red Star Over China,* p. 306, he ascribes the massacre of Reds by Kuomintang officers to the fact that the officers were the sons of local landlords, enraged by expropriation of the land. Land-expropriation is a class motive; a moment's reflection would reveal that previous massacre of the officers' families by Communists would be a better common-sense motive for blood-thirstiness. This

Kuomintang entente was, strictly speaking, not a union between the Kuomintang and the Communist parties, although it came to be such in fact; it was collaboration between the Third International, which agreed that Communism was unsuited to China, and the Kuomintang. The development of a Chinese Communist Party, and open Communist debate concerning the assumption of power, made the Kuomintang mistrustful, repressive, and finally hostile. The suppression of the Communists by Chiang in 1927 has become world history; Vincent Sheean and André Malraux have preserved aspects of it in moving literature.[2]

In the period 1927-37 the Chinese Communists operated the Chinese Soviet Republic (*Chung-hua Su-wei-ai Kung-ho-kuo*),[3] primarily in Kiangsi, but also in the Ao-yü-wan (Hupeh, Honan, Anhui) area. In the Long March of 1934-35 the main forces of the Communists, in the most spectacular military move in China since the great Northern raid of the T'aip'ing, marched a distance of some six thousand miles, and established their new area in North Shensi (see above, p. 112 ff.). Not only did the Chinese Red Army remain intact; through great and successful effort, the Communists transplanted schools, banks, and other institutions intact. The Long March was comparable to the celebrated Flight of the Tartars, in that it amounted to the transplanting of an entire people, their worldly goods, and

---

feature of diluted Marxism would not be worth mentioning were it not common to so many books about Communists written by self-proclaimed "non-Communists" habituated to the dialectic. It is found in the writings of Agnes Smedley, Victor Yakhontoff, Anna Louise Strong, and I. Epstein, to mention but a few.

[2] Sheean, Vincent, *Personal History*, New York, 1937; Malraux, André, *Man's Fate*, New York, n.d.

[3] *Kung-ho-kuo* is the Western-type term for Republic; the Kuomintang uses *Min-kuo* or Folk-realm. *Su-wei-ai* is a phonetic representation of "Soviet"; the characters, not intended to have meaning, are unconsciously humorous in that their lexicographical signification is "Revive (and) maintain dust!"

their most highly treasured institutions and traditions.

Despite Kuomintang theory, the Frontier Area is a one-party *imperium in imperio,* and its unchallenged party is the Communist. Under conditions requiring great fortitude, the Chinese Communist leaders have consolidated power, and use their base to spread Marxism through the guerrilla movement. They are thus in the best possible political position; their strategic excellence makes them welcome in precisely those zones wherein their doctrines can best take effect. Their party organization controls the Frontier Area through formal appointment of the leading officials by the National Military Affairs Commission, and through formulae of election for the subordinate officials.

The hierarchy of the Chinese C.P. is much like that of the Kuomintang, which also copied Soviet models: [4]

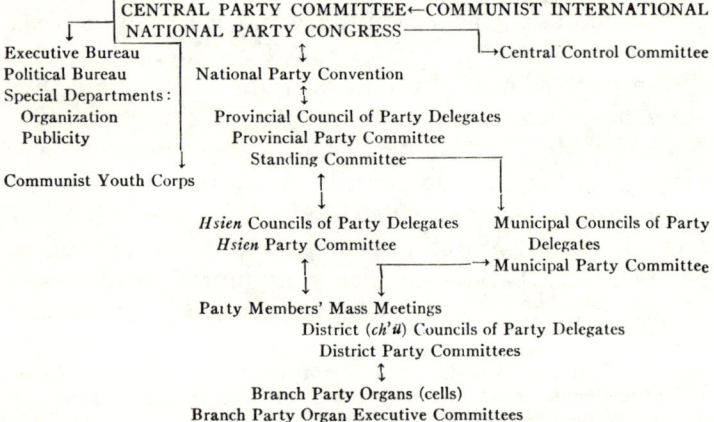

The shibboleth of Democratic Centralism applies to the Chinese as well as to other Communist Parties; in practice this means the high and unqualified concen-

[4] Based on the Party Constitution, *Kung-ch'an-tang Tang-chang* [Party Constitution of the Communist Party], [Chungking?], XXVII (1938), p. 1–21. The entire Constitution is reprinted below as Appendix II (E), p. 359.

tration of power at the top of the hierarchy following action by the democratic, or mass, element of the party through the Party Council or Congress. In effect, nothing is decided at such elections, since the plebiscites, according to the familiar authoritarian pattern, concern questions to which only one answer is reasonably possible: the answer decided by the party rulers. The free use of meaningless elections characterizes Communist activity in governmental as well as party matters. The voting act gives the impression of concurrence, improves morale, and ceremonializes the approval of the majority for the minority. The purpose which elections serve in democracies—that is, of providing a decision to issues not previously ascertained—appears very rarely in Communist elections, where a near unanimity is constructed to indicate popular support, and contested elections, disunity.

In terms of personnel, the Communist hierarchy has been consistently compliant with world Communist policy as made in Moscow. This is a tribute to the high international unity and uniformity of the ecumenical Communist movement, but raises, in China, problems of intra-national Communist policy. Revolutionary veterans of the party, who fought, suffered, studied, and worked for their cause through ten, fifteen, or twenty years of effort, often find themselves displaced, dictated to, or expelled by the clique of younger men who have lived comfortably in Moscow studying the dialectic mystagogy and acquiring an inside track in Stalinist cliquism.[5] The Chinese Communist Party has been shaken by violent schisms, casting off many once highly-valued leaders.

No sooner does a man become suspect to the ulti-

[5] Harold Isaacs, in the work cited, has many passing references to this phenomenon; his caustic indictment of Ch'en Shao-yu (Wang Ming), p. 438 ff., is a case in point. Note Ch'en Tu-hsiu, Li Li-san, Chang Kuo-tao—in China, as in Russia, most of the founders and early leaders of the Communists have been set aside.

mate authorities than his previous record, hitherto praised, is re-examined and captious criticism proves that he was a traitor from the beginning, like Trotsky, Bukharin, Chicherin, and Zinoviev. The profound vitality of the Chinese Communist movement as a quasi-religious, self-sacrificial organization is demonstrated by the fact that it has weathered these storms. The terrible hunger for a guidance in life, an insight into the ethical meanings of things, and an absolute which asks nothing but acceptance and obedience— these factors call for courage, humility, abasement, fortitude. They do not favor imagination, individual integrity of thought, or the examination of fact. There has been no indication whatever, despite the wishful thinking of Western liberals, that the mentality of the Chinese Red leaders is one whit different from that of Western Communists. They talk practical democracy, moderation, collaboration with the Kuomintang; they do so because this is the Comintern's China policy, just as they have fought the National Government in the past when the Soviet authorities disliked Chiang more than they did Japan.

Their all-China collaboration is no doubt sincere; but the sincerity is based not on the wish to collaborate, but on what, in their special phrasing, is termed the "objective" analysis of the situation. If the Soviet Union, the chief "proletarian" force in the world, turned against Chiang, the Communist *ipso facto* would be against collaboration. The war of China against Japan would no longer be a war of "national liberation" but an "inter-imperialist" war in which the true interests of the "working classes" would be against *both* sides. This provides to Marxians, under the name "science," an absolute, infallible guide to ethics in practical politics, because it presumes to reveal the inescapable long-range meaning of human affairs. The supposition that daily affairs may in fact possess none but short-range meaning, outside of slow, general, nearly impalpable changes in ecology, demography, and genetics, etc., is anathema to the Marxians. A humanism trained to deal directly, pragmatically, and simply with events is as far beyond the Chinese Communists as it is beyond other Marxians.

This orthodoxy, so complete that it enthralls the leadership to Moscow and paralyzes Marxian heretics in the very act of dissidence, reaches throughout the upper levels of the party. This fact does not mean that the Chinese Communist movement is in no wise different from other national Communist movements. The historical basis of the Chinese Communism, ever since Chiang smashed the urban unions in 1927, has been that of an exotic faith imposed upon a native *jacquerie,* in which the exoticism is unwittingly traditionalist. Peasant revolts of the Chinese past have operated with the counter-ideocratic leverage of a superstition, normally Taoist in derivation. The heads of the Yellow Turbans (ca. 200 A.D.) and the Boxers (ca. 1900) were all magicians; the T'aip'ing (ca. 1850) leader was a Christian in communication with God Himself. These heresies against the all-pervading order of Confucian common sense disappeared after their high-pitched dynamics died down in social readjustment.

Marxism provides an element of faith, devotion, and irrational submission which has operated in past Chinese history. The frugality, honesty, and integrity of the Chinese Red leaders are celebrated by foreign visitors and even by Nationalist officials; such revolutionary virtues seem new in China, whereas they are the twentieth-century manifestation of a common enough phase of Chinese political activity. However, one cannot herefrom conclude that the Chinese Communist movement is destined to disappear with its predecessors, for it has three things which they did not have: an extra-Chinese application, which not only supports it, but proves its concreteness and relative realizability; a modern system of education, and thereby a class of counter-ideologues to compete with the post-Confucian Nationalists; and leaders with revolutionary experience greater than any in the world, not excepting that of the great Soviet leaders themselves. Ancient peasant uprisings revealed a final cleavage between dervish-type organizers and the peasants, once infuriated, who finally sought normalcy. If the Chinese Communist leaders can, through the example of the Soviet Union, or by education, or by dexterous leadership, make Communism into normalcy, they may retain their hold on such sections of the peasantry as their leadership has captured.

Two men stand forth above all others in Chinese Communism. Both would be remarkable individuals in any historical setting. Their partnership has led them to be described by one hyphenated phrase: *Chu-Mao:* Chu Tê and Mao Tse-tung. Chu Tê, the military genius of Chinese Communism, was born of a gentry family in Szechuan, and attended the Yünnan Military Academy at the time that Chiang was in Japan; he entered the years of his early maturity as an aide to a provincial *tuchün*. According to Edgar Snow, he was at this time sunk in vice, enjoying wealth, opium-smoking, a harem, and the amenities of a war-lord existence.[6] Chu felt an urge within himself to escape this rut. He abandoned his worthless existence, leaving his harem provided for, and went to the coast, where he could become acquainted with the revolutionary movement. On the way he broke himself of the drug habit. He went to Europe, living in France and Germany, and in the latter country joined the Chinese Communist branch established among the students. He returned in 1926 during the Great Revolution, and served as political officer in the Kuomintang forces. Later he

[6] Snow, Edgar, work cited, p. 348 *ff*.

was instrumental in the creation of the Chinese Soviet Republic, and was the prime military leader of the Communist forces in the long civil war. He led the trek to the Northwest, and is esteemed as a military hero of Arthurian proportions. Friendly, candid, interested in specific tasks, he is characteristic of the superb leadership which preserved Communism in China. He is the only Chinese military leader who was not defeated by Chiang, although Chiang pursued him six thousand miles. Major Evans Carlson, the American Marine officer, compares him with Robert E. Lee, U. S. Grant, and Abraham Lincoln—drawing on the best features of each for the purpose.[7]

Mao Tse-tung was born in Hunan in 1893 of a well-to-do farmer family. His autobiography, dictated to Edgar Snow, is a classic of Western literature on China.[8] His history was that of many other restless young Chinese intellectuals, struggling for education amidst turmoil, and adjusting their sense of values to the chaotic early Republic. He was caught up by the Marxism of the literary Renaissance after 1917, served in the Kuomintang during the Great Revolution, and worked as head of the All-China Peasants Union. During the Soviet period, in which he first became a colleague of Chu Tê, he stood forth as the chief political leader. He and Chu between them formed a team to rival Generalissimo Chiang, although Mao shared his political leadership with various others, particularly Chang Kuo-tao. Mao

[7] *Twin Stars of China,* cited, p. 66. Major Carlson adds to this description in his *The Chinese Army,* cited, p. 35 *ff.* Most enthusiastically, he attributes to the Red Leaders honesty, humility, selflessness, truthfulness, incorruptibility, and a desire to do what is right. He praises their superb tactical abilities, their efficiency as organizers, their competence as leaders. He accepts the statements made by the Communist leaders as matters of good faith, and does not question their sincerity. Since he is the only qualified military visitor to put his impressions on record, these appraisals are valuable.

[8] Snow, Edgar, *Red Star Over China,* cited, p. 111–167.

is an expert dialectician, skilled in rationalizing the policies of the Communist International, and keenly critical within the limits of his Marxian orthodoxy. Less genial than Chu Tê, he is nevertheless an inspiring leader. His political skill, in following the lurches and shifts of the Stalin party line while simultaneously leading an enormous Chinese peasant revolt, is monumental. His earlier rivals and colleagues are in most cases dead or forgotten. He survived both ideological and practical ordeals.

A third Communist leader, Chou En-lai, is of importance because he acts as liaison officer between the National Government and the Frontier Area. The Communist quasi-legation in Chungking is maintained as a purchasing and communications office of the Eighteenth Army Corps (formerly Eighth Route Army). Chou, who studied abroad in Japan, France, and Germany, served at the Whampoa academy under Chiang, and in the period of civil war he was one of the chief political officers, twice Chinese Communist delegate to Moscow. He is an old acquaintance of many Kuomintang leaders from Chiang on down, and appears to be one of the most successful diplomats in the world. Despite acrimony from secondary leaders on both sides, Chiang and Mao seek to maintain their alliance against Japan, and Chou is their chief intermediary. At Chungking he is seconded by the alert, brilliant Ch'in Po-k'u, a veteran of Communist political-bureau work.

The difficulties and conditions of Communist collaboration with the National Government are well illustrated in the life of Chang Kuo-tao. One of the founders of the Chinese Communist Party in Shanghai, in 1921, Chang was of the upper classes, like Chu Tê; and like Mao, he was a radical student in Peking. Just before his departure from the party in 1938, he had been chairman of the Northwestern Soviet, taking precedence over Mao himself; but with the coming of national unity, Chang wished to cooperate fully with China's leader, government, and legal Party, the Kuomintang. He adopted subterfuges to get out of the Communist Area. Arriving in Hankow, he announced his desire to form a genuine United Front on the basis of a candid and sincere acceptance of the *San Min Chu I,* which would mean the actual abandonment of Marxian dreams of Communist "proletarian" dictatorship in China, even for the future. He did not renounce Communism, but simply took his colleagues at their words, and announced his intention of cooperating honestly, and not through compulsion of the Moscow dialectic. He wrote:

> According to the views of the Chinese Communists, the present United Front is only a temporary union of many political groups, which are entirely different from one another in nature. These political groups have their own social bases, and they represent the interests of different classes. "The Kuomintang," so they believe, "represents landlords and capitalists, while the Communist Party represents the working class." No [ultimate] compromise can be made between the two parties.
> Now we often hear such slogans of the Chinese Communists as, "Let's lead the people *together,*" "Let's *all* take responsibilities," "Let us *both* be progressive," and "Let's act under the *same* principles." These represent the old ideas of striving for leadership. These show that they do not have the foresight to work unselfishly for the nation and the people. They want to retain their military forces. They want to maintain the Frontier Area and special, privileged positions in certain occupied areas. They keep these in order to await future developments. . . .
> I hope they [the following suggestions] will receive the consideration of the Chinese Communists:
> (1) the Chinese Communists should always remember that the benefits of the nation and the people go before everything. They should support the movement of Resistance and Reconstruction under the leadership of Mr. Chiang K'ai-shek. They should carry out the *San Min Chu I* without hesitation. What they do must agree with what they say;

(2) there should be complete coordination of governmental and military operations, under all conditions. . .
I hope the Chinese Communists will not think that the Eighth Route Army is one privately owned by the Communist Party. . . . The Frontier Area [where Chang Kuo-tao had so recently been leader] should not be made a Communist base, nor made into an isolated place where Communist-made laws are executed and prejudice, together with political persecution, prevails . . .

(3) with a view to working for the nation and the people, the Communists should follow the foreign policies adopted by the central government.[9]

Chang demanded that the Communists react more sincerely, that they accept the full implications of a united China, and abandon their long-range dialectic for power.[10] For this he was denounced, his years of service were reappraised, and he was dropped from the Communist Party.[11] He was accused of hurting the United Front, because he urged a more nearly perfect union. The chief Communist leaders challenged him in open letters, revealing their continued adherence to an ideology which made an eventual struggle for power inescapable.

[9] Chang Kuo-tao, *T'ou-li Kung-ch'an-tang Mien-mien-kuan* [An Impartial Survey of (My) Departure from the Communist Party], Kuangchou [Canton], 1938, p. 27 ff.

[10] The same, p. 10.

[11] The Resolutions of the Enlarged Sixth Plenary Session of the Central Executive Committee of the Communist Party of China comment as follows: "The danger of the 'Right' opportunists lies in the fact that they execute the tactics of an anti-Japanese National United Front at the expense of the independence of the party, politically and organizationally distorting the policy of the proletariat [sic] in building an Anti-Japanese National United Front so that *the working class and the Communist Party become tails of the bourgeoisie rather than the vanguard.*" (Italics inserted in translation.) New China Information Committee, *Resolutions and Telegrams of the Sixth Plenum, Central Committee, Communist Party of China, November 6, 1938,* Hong Kong [1939?], p. 9. The demand for vanguard position from a minority party still technically illegal, and the damning of the Government and Kuomintang as "bourgeois," are continuous features of Communist policy. Their concept of cooperation is, as in Germany, Spain, and elsewhere, cooperation *under* Communist leadership.

The Communists have, therefore, cooperated as far as they are able, without emerging from the infallibilities of their cult. They retain the Marxian rationalization apparatus, and the linkage with Moscow. As such, they are welcome but not completely trustworthy allies. Their presence is undoubtedly the greatest check to the development of democracy in China; the presence of a totalitarian party, respecting no rules but its own, jeopardizes the entire experiment. The Communists want democracy, but they want it quite frankly as a step toward "working-class" (Marxist) power; they accept the *San Min Chu I* on the condition that it be read as elementary Marxism. They do not insist on the term Communism, but employ the terms "working-class" interests for their party, "scientific objectivity" for their ideology, and "a people's movement" for radical, arbitrary reforms to rip Free China open with social revolution. The Kuomintang leaders are fully aware of the support in name plus subversion in fact which the Communists offer, and complain bitterly about the principles of Sun being twisted about to Marxism as in the form of " 'independent' nationalism, 'free' democracy, and 'beneficent' livelihood," the qualifying terms sufficing for the alignment.[12] They understand that the Communists are incapable of sincere extra-class democracy; the Communists are hurt by the Kuomintang's unwillingness to admit that it is not a Party of patriots, but the Party of a transitional, historically doomed middle class.

Communism: Patriotism or Betrayal?

If the Communists were as inflexible, disciplined, ferocious, and intransigeant as they like to appear to

---

[12] Ch'ao Shê [The Morning Club], *Niu-wu Yen-lun Chien-t'ao Kang-yao* [A General Review of Fallacious Utterances], Chungking, XXIX (1940), p. 7. The work is a Kuomintang reply to Communist theses in a debate on the nature of national union.

themselves, China would have had a three-sided war long ago. In practice, however, the Chinese Communists yield amazingly. The Communist International is not goading the Chinese Communists into the sabotage of Chiang and of national resistance. Whether Moscow could do so is a standing question of Chinese politics. The answer cannot be known except by practical test. One might, however, plausibly suppose that an attempt by Stalin to consummate a Moscow-Tokyo pact (possibly in accordance with pressure from Berlin, which would require immediate protection of the proletarian fatherland) would create a deep schism in Communist ranks; but it is unthinkable that all the Chinese Communists would abjure their faith. Moscow would not be naive enough to require the Communists to cease fighting Japan *in form*. Such a Kuomintang-Communist break would probably weaken the National Government; it would not destroy the Chungking regime unless the Generalissimo ignored the chance offered by a Leftward turn, to retain some of the peasant-radical and guerrilla forces in his own ranks. It would, however, enormously strengthen Japan, and be a severe blow to China. The greatest danger of a Kuomintang-Communist break would lie in an American defeat of Japan. By removing the necessity of Soviet support of Chiang, and increasing the power of the National Government, American aid would lessen the opportunities of Communism in China.

At present, however, the Chinese Communists welcome American aid, even though the effect of such aid is to strengthen the China of Chiang as against the China of Chu-Mao. The Communist spokesman, Ch'in Po-k'u, told the author that American aid was not feared in China, but was *welcome,* emphasizing the word. He even stated, in response to a far-fetched hypothetical question, that actual American troops would be welcome at Yenan, and stated that inter-party trouble was to be expected only in case of defeat.[13]

The final picture of the Communist position which emerges in China is about as follows:

(1) the Communists are gaining ground because of their helpfulness and vigorous leadership in organizing the guerrilla areas; wherever the Japanese forces go, the Communists (thus shielded from Chinese National armies) increase their influence;

(2) the Communists are benefiting politically by a genuine popular movement in both Free and occupied China, particularly in the latter, where spontaneous mass action is providing a base either for Sunyatsenist democracy or for Communism in the future;

(3) in view of their belief that time is on their side, because of the present direction of Soviet foreign policy, the Chinese Communists are very cooperative in the alliance against Japan, patiently postponing demands for "democracy" (i.e., unrestricted rights of organization and agitation);

(4) they have superlative leadership, rich in practical experience, which represents the super-orthodox residuum of years of schism and purging; such a leadership is not likely to abandon the fundamentals of Communism, such as the dialectic, the class-outlook on all history and politics, and belief in the inescapable universality of future "proletarian" rule (Communist world conquest); therefore, it is almost unthinkable that they would fail to do Moscow's bidding, if the party line demanded national treason in war time;

(5) the interests of the Soviet Union run parallel with those of non-Communist China for a long time in the future, unless the European balance of power forces the U.S.S.R. to appease Japan; under such circum-

[13] Statement of Col. Ch'in Po-k'u to the author, Chungking, July 29, 1940.

stances, the Soviet Union will be very anxious to maintain the foothold of Communism in China, and will not be likely to ask the Chinese Communists to commit candid treason;

(6) lastly, the Kuomintang possesses the opportunity of rivaling Communism, of overtaking its rate of growth in political power, by a bold policy of freeing speech, constitutionalizing the government, reforming the land tenure system, and pushing cooperative industrialism; the base of Communism has been widespread peasant revolt. If the conditions of peasant revolt are eliminated, Communism will not be much more of a threat to China than it is to the advanced countries of Europe. (Wisely or not, the Kuomintang has not consented to meet the Communists in open ideological competition. If it did so, and won, Kuomintang morale would be strengthened. At present the practical aims of Party policy toward Communists are about as follows: restriction and isolation of the Frontier Area and of the Border Region, so far as agitation is concerned, before ingestion by the constitutional national system; military precautions, balancing Communist forces with Nationalist; standardization of Red military practice by national rules, and the elimination of peculiar political features; eventual dissolution of fellow-travelling organizations, and their absorption into the corresponding officially sponsored movements; supervision of Communists and channels of Communist propaganda; courtesy toward Communist leaders, strictness toward Communist subordinates, and harshness toward the Communist laboring class following. A corresponding policy toward the Kuomintang is pursued by the Communists.)

Finally, the deepest element eludes political analysis: the moderation of the Chinese character, and the heritage of Confucian common sense. The Chinese language and the Confucian inheritance of ideological sophistication lead to clarity, pragmatism, and practicality. The Chinese have long delighted in ingenious formulae with which to meet *de jure* impasses, while proceeding *de facto* in quite another direction. The Chinese are perhaps the only people in the world with enough finesse about "face" to save the Communist face. The Generalissimo is in theory consciously anti-Marxian; but when he was asked whether it is possible that Communists or Leftists might exploit democratic rights for unscrupulous power politics, he answered quietly by writing: "No, because democracy in itself has the ability to work out the solutions for those problems if there are any." A Communist leader said, the Generalissimo would have nothing to fear from the Communists if he won the war. His prestige would be unassailable. Chiang and the Communists both know this.

THE NATIONAL SALVATION MOVEMENT

The National Salvation (*Chiu Kuo*) movement is third in point of size and influence, and has been largely instrumental in assisting national unification and resistance. The movement began in 1935 with the organization of a number of professors, students, and young intellectuals who were influenced by the student anti-appeasement movement in North China. It had a simple, and very clear program: stop civil war; stop appeasement.[14] Unlike the Kuomintang or the Communists, the National Salvationists never developed formal dogma, or a comprehensive ideology. Genuinely a movement, it had no membership books, no formal or systematic organization, no minorities, and no schisms. The movement spread like wildfire, across the length and breadth of China as well as overseas; and, because of its lack of formal hierarchy, was ignored by the Na-

[14] An early statement of National Salvation views is found in Wang Tsao-shih, "A Salvationist's View of the Sino-Japanese Problem," *The China Quarterly*, Vol. II, No. 4 (Special Fall Number, 1937), p. 681–9. The author is one of the Seven Gentlemen.

tional Government. Its loose organization, consciously based on the middle class of clerks, students, business men, professors, etc., followed functional lines familiar to the Chinese.

When the National Salvationists began the creation of a structure, however rudimentary, by forming an inter-professional federation for National Salvation, and when they followed this with the national congress for National Salvation, the government took action, which resulted in the celebrated trial of the Seven Gentlemen (*ch'i chün-tzŭ*). The term (*chün-tzŭ*) is the Confucian word for superior or upright person, without reference to gender, and was applied in affectionate derision by the press. One of the *chün-tzŭ* was a lady. The seven, who included a celebrated and popular law school dean (Shên Chun-lu), a banker, and authors (Tso Tao-fên, the spokesman among them) were tried and imprisoned late in 1936. Demands for their release figured in the Sian kidnapping.

The movement was financed very simply through volunteer contributions. Most of the work was done by volunteers who asked no pay, travelling and working at their own expense. About Ch. $5,000 (then about U. S. $1,000) sufficed to cover the whole expenses of headquarters. Despite the imprisonment of its leaders, the movement gathered momentum. Funds were collected to support guerrillas opposing Japan in transmural China. Most literate persons not already committed to formal Kuomintang or Communist membership fell under the influence of the movement. General Shêng Shih-ts'ai in Sinkiang offered the movement a home, and many of its workers went to the West.

In practical terms, the National Salvationists often work with the Communist Party, although they are strictly Chinese and do not have an elaborate dialectic. A strain of economic determinism runs through their thought, but this is not systematized. The leaders of the movement were released after the outbreak of war, but their organizations continued to be suppressed, and work is largely suspended. The leaders told the author that they had no means of estimating the actual number of their adherents; they had no formal membership roll, and they were still legally suppressed in Chungking areas. The quest for policy and principle instead of power is new to Chinese politics, and the National Salvation leaders are esteemed almost universally and hated by none. Nevertheless the Kuomintang has not admitted the legality of the movement, which continues to exist in non-public fashion. Some of the leaders were recognized to the extent of being put on the People's Political Council. In addition to standing with the Communists in matters of practical domestic reform, the National Salvation leaders demand two fundamental policies: continuation of the war, and unity of the country above all party considerations.

The National Salvation leaders are able, modest, and patriotic. They represent the older non-political sentiment of China, infused with modern Leftist content. Dean Shên of Shanghai, the senior of the movement, is an elderly man of almost dainty gentleness, keenly intelligent demeanor, and serious but charming good humor. Mr. Tso Tao-fên, an author, is a world traveller. Their colleagues are of the student, publisher, author type: intellectual, patriotic, common-sense in outlook.

The National Salvation movement looks forward to constitutionalism. It has become almost universal in the guerrilla areas. The leaders have faith that the Constitution and liberalized public life are developing, although they expected in the summer of 1940 that the Convention would be postponed until 1941, to allow the Communists and Nationalists further opportunity for balancing and adjusting power relationships. The National Salvationists are past masters in the techniques of indirect, almost invisible pressures. Their disinterestedness, high principles, and patriotism put them in an admirable position to act as a determined moderating force between the two major Parties. As such they are the third party of China, although another, smaller group bears this name.

THE THIRD PARTY

The party commonly called The Third Party (*Ti-san Tang*) was organized by dissident Communists and Left Kuomintang members who wished to keep on collaborating after the major parties broke apart in 1927, thus ending the Great Revolution. Led by the indomitable Têng Yen-ta, who was finally shot to death in Shanghai, the party began illustriously with the participation of Mme. Sun Yat-sen (Soong Ching-ling) and the Left ex-Foreign Minister, Eugene Chen. The formal names of the party varied. From 1927 to 1929, and again from 1930 to 1937, it was the Revolutionary Action Commission of the Chinese Kuomintang (*Chung-kuo Kuo-min-tang K'ê-ming Hsing-chêng Wei-yüan-hui*); in 1929–1930, the Chinese Revolutionary Party (*Chung-kuo K'ê-ming Tang*); and after 1937, the Acting Commission for the National Emancipation of China (*Min-ts'u Chieh-fang Hsing-chêng Wei-yüan-hui*).[15] The party is at present led by Dr. Chang Pai-chün, a returned student from Germany and lieutenant to the late Mr. Têng. It suffers from the official ban on minor parties, but retains, by its own statement, a formal organized membership of about 15,000. (This estimate would, in the opinion of independent observers, need to be discounted.)

The Third Party is a *San Min Chu I* party. It accepts the legacies of Dr. Sun, in their Left-most phase as they were at the time of his death. The party is strongly

[15] Statement by the head of The Third Party, Dr. Chang Pai-chün (Chang Peh Chuen), to the author, Chungking, August 2, 1940. The translations were also supplied by Dr. Chang.

anti-imperialist, socialist, and land-reform in its teaching. Its socialism is of an independent kind; the party neither seeks nor wishes collaboration with the Third International, although it is willing to cooperate with the Communists as well as the Kuomintang. It finds its chief political dogma in the last policies of Sun, executed in the period just before his death: (1) a pro-Soviet orientation in international power politics; (2) a Nationalist-Communist entente; and (3) immediate aid for the peasants and workers. It is therefore more like the old Left Kuomintang than the Communists.

At the present time, the party seeks to promote collaboration between the two major parties, thus becoming the second third-party to that friendship, and urges constitutional government. Eventually it would prefer a representative government of the whole people (*p'ing min*), with the executive agencies composed 60 per cent of peasants and workers, 40 per cent of others, chiefly intellectuals. (The proportion is believed to be Mme. Sun's contribution.) In past practical politics, The Third Party took part in the Foochow insurrection of 1933–34, but has on no other occasion obtained power. It is not expected to attain major status.

The Chinese National Socialist Party

The elder brother of Chang Kia-ngau, who is the enterprising Minister of Economic Affairs, has organized a political party after the fashion of the traditional pavilions of learning and patriotism. In China's past, Confucians frequently developed an institution which admixed the features of a perpetual resort camp, a library, a seminar, and a club. Living together amid scenically beautiful and scholastically adequate surroundings, they made their influence felt through their writings and their example, whenever one of their number returned to public life. Dr. Carson Chang (Chang Chia-shêng) has organized an Institute of National Culture at Talifu in Yünnan, in the mountains just below Tibet. There he associates with kindred souls to attempt a restoration of traditional values in the traditional manner.

The confusing and unhappy similarity of the name of his party to Adolf Hitler's party is explained in the following communication:

> To give to the world in a clear and unambiguous way the principles our party stands for and the platform we wish to adopt should we have the chance to serve our country, I have written a book, entitled *What A State Is Built On*. In formulating my political philosophy, though I have drawn freely upon the wisdom of the West, I have kept my eye steadily on the needs of my people and the circumstances of my country as the guiding and controlling principles in shaping my own thought. In view of the possibility of distortions you have suggested in your letter, an extract is now being prepared in English, with the idea to facilitate the understanding of our movement and to present to the intellectual world of the West our principles and policies . . .
>
> The accidental similarity of names between our party and Hitler's is indeed an endless source of misunderstanding, but the similarity is truly "accidental." In Chinese the name of our party runs "Kuo Chia She Hui Tang," which may be literally translated into "Nation (Kuo Chia) Society (She Hui) Party (Tang)," a name we adopted long before Hitler's party became known, embodying principles widely different from what Hitler's party stands for. The suspicion abroad of our connection with Hitler's National Socialist Party may be traced to an incident two years ago at Hankow when Kuomintang first came to recognize the legal status of minor political parties. The foreign correspondents, in reporting my exchange of letters with Generalissimo Chiang with regard to the recognition of our party, referred without a second thought to our party as "Nazi," thus creating all distortions which might have occurred even without such mischief. I shall be more than grateful to you if you would undertake to clear the suspicion on us and pave the way for lasting understanding between us and your people.[16]

[16] Letter to the author, dated October 24, 1940.

Social Democrats and *La Jeunesse*

These two minuscule parties are both expatriate groups organized in Paris. The Social Democratic Party was organized in 1925. It has no connection with the Socialist Party of the pro-Japanese Kiang Kang-hu, but is simply the Chinese affiliate of the Second International. The Social Democratic Party may unite with the Third Party, in view of the close similarity of aims and ideology; its leader, Mr. Yang Kan-tao, has been recognized by being seated in the People's Political Council.

The party called *Kuo-chia Chu-i Pai* (*La Jeunesse,* or *Parti Républicain Nationaliste de la Jeune Chine*) was organized in 1923 in Paris, by a Mr. Tseng Chi, with whom is now associated Mr. Tso Shen-sheng, the most active worker for the party. It survived for years as an expatriate organization, joined by successive generations of Chinese students in France. Its policies are strongly democratic and social-minded. A functional legislature, the cooperative movement and state capitalism have suggested a similarity to Fascism in the minds of some observers; of Trotskyism, to others.[17] The party, through accident and the family connections of its founder, has connections in Szechuan, and the transfer of the National Government to Chungking was a corresponding aid to the slight influence of the party. Long in exile, it is known by one of its French names even in China; all it does is to help diversify opinion. Mr. Tso occupies a seat in the People's Political Council.[18]

The National Salvationists are an operating force

[17] E.g., John Gunther in his *Inside Asia*, New York, 1939, p. 272.
[18] By far the most complete summary of the minor and minuscule parties is to be found in two articles by a young Chinese newspaperman: Shen, James, "Minority Parties in China," *Asia*, Vol. XL, no. 2 (February 1940), p. 81–3; and a second installment, in the same periodical, Vol. XL, no. 3 (March 1940), p. 137–9.

in China, and the Communists, while a minority party, are not a minor party in the American sense. Unhappily, the existence of minuscule parties among both patriots and pro-Japanese elements suggests that multi-party constitutionalism is likely to degenerate into innumerable party fractions, splinter parties, and novel, unstable groups. The Kuomintang and the Communists possess their respective monopolies of power; the National Salvationists have a popular and sincere cause. The other parties exist in part because they obtain recognition. As long as Chinese political processes depend on leadership by personality, individuals will be free to form their own parties, while the geographical, cultural, and economic diversity of the country holds out little hope for the appearance of two or three China-wide democratic parties. Far more likely is it that, with the presumable advent of constitutionalism, the Kuomintang-Communist alignment will continue, while the present minor parties will gain some ground, and innumerable new parties will appear in order to profit by democratic guarantees of minimal representation, or to fulfill functions exercised by fraternal societies in the United States.

CHAPTER VII

GOVERNING INSTITUTIONS OF THE JAPANESE AND PRO-JAPANESE

FACING the National Armies, and encircling the guerrillas, lie the Imperial Japanese forces. Frank agents of Imperial policy, they—unlike the Hitler-Mussolini contingents in Spain—make no pretense of subordination to their Chinese allies. Publicly and legally instruments of the Japanese state, their function is to destroy the Chinese government, to control and bend Chinese society to the Imperial purposes, and to protect Chinese who come forth as allies. The Japanese Empire is accordingly itself militarily extended to China; occasional, half-hearted attempts to deny the ensuing international complications have been sternly rejected by other great powers. The United States is not alone in insisting on full Japanese responsibility for everything that happens within the zone of Japanese control.

The position of the Japanese army as a governing engine, unacknowledged colonial machinery of a vast unassimilable colony, is not one relished by the Japanese people or by their leaders. Even in the case of Manchoukuo, the Japanese played a half-deception on themselves by pretending that they were extending the area of their influence, not the extent of their responsibilities. In part this distaste for overt control is based on the ease, cheapness and irresponsibility of indirect rule, employed in varying degrees by the British in Malaysia, the French in Indo-China, and the Soviets in Outer Mongolia. The Japanese like to think that they are aiding China, and incidentally themselves, to a New Order in East Asia—autarkic, stable, racially independent of the Whites, militarily secure. They do not like to contemplate the slaughter of innocent people for sheer conquest, or to consider the hopeless immensity of trying to overwhelm China. This complicates their position.[1]

For if the status of the Japanese army in China is clear, its purposes are not. The war aims of the Japanese are confused. Japan's goal is defined by overtones of the inexpressible—in economic motivation, once valid, no longer meaningful; in rationalizations so long reiterated that they become genuine; in the toss and push of world affairs, tempting Japan's leaders to this opportunism or that; in sheer sentiments of Japanolatry, Emperor-worship, racialism, archaic resentment against China, fellow-feeling for the Chinese orientals, and plain fear. A few Japanese know exactly what they want. The policy as a whole, the policy of the Imperial state, encompasses ill-assorted economic, political, strategic, racial and purely ideological objectives.

Even at the simple level of institutional control, the Japanese aim in China has been ill-defined. The restoration of the Manchu monarchy in Manchoukuo was an appeal to monarchist legitimism, to the Chinese past, and to common Confucianist values. When the Japanese came further into China, it was at first expected that they might install Mr. Chin P'u-yi as Emperor of all China, and rehabilitate him in the Palace-museum he left when a youth. Instead, they apparently attempted to create a chain of linked, reactionary, agricultural Chinese states, mixed in form—a federation of

[1] An excellent bibliography, providing further references to the Japanese side of the war, is found in Borton, Hugh, *et al.*, *A Selected List of Books and Articles on Japan*, Washington, D. C., 1940. An outstanding short discussion is Colegrove, K. W., *Militarism in Japan*, Boston (World Peace Foundation), 1936.

princes in Inner Mongolia, an Empire in Manchoukuo, republics elsewhere. They began by going as far as to create a dozen or more ephemeral pro-Japanese agencies—for a while one might legitimately have expected that a Nanking government follow a Peking government, a Hankow government, a Canton government, *ad infinitum*. But the trend was reversed when the Autonomous East Hopei Anti-Communist Government of Mr. Yin Ju-kêng was merged with the Peking regime, and—as pressure rose in Japan for a settlement of the China affair—a China-wide Japanophile government was first contemplated, and then established. The establishment of these institutions has not meant the abdication of the Imperial Japanese forces from the government of China. The pro-Japanese governments were and are civil auxiliaries of the Japanese army; their influence has in no case extended beyond the immediately effective reach of the Japanese infantry. Even in planning the long-range permanent settlement of Chinese affairs—on her own terms—Japan does not propose to withdraw all her troops from China.

The Japanese Army as a Chinese Government

The Japanese army is the effective military government of occupied China. The Japanophile Chinese have a few troops, who function in close proximity to Japanese, and are in no sense a military counterweight to the invaders. The Japanese army is a large force, modern by somewhat second-rate standards, which requires the use of an effective communications system, modern economic auxiliaries such as shops, banks, post offices, and a variety of other services including hospitals, shrines, brothels, and crematories. These do not exist in China in forms suited to Japanese needs, nor could Japan afford to trust Chinese with the railways, the air services, the river commerce, the telegraphs, the food warehouses, and other most vital services. Thus, all over occupied China, the Japanese have installed a military government.

This government assumes direct responsibility for administering whatever seems necessary or profitable. Thus, in the city of Nanking, the best buildings are occupied by the Japanese, and the Wang government is profoundly gratified to be allowed to share some of them, obtaining second choice. The Japanese military, through protected corporations, supervises the operation of the railroads and airlines, but it does not even rely on the corporations to provide military transport, which is under direct army control. If a Chinese who has gone over to the Japanese and occupies a high position in their protected governments wishes to ride on a Chinese train between Shanghai and Nanking, he must buy a ticket from a Japanese clerk, show it to a Japanese conductor under the eyes of a Japanese guard, with Japanese detectives standing about, order a Sino-Japanese or pseudo-European meal in a Japanese dining car with Japanese waitresses from a menu printed in Japanese, and must pay, not in his own puppet-bank currency, but in special Japanese currency not acceptable in Japan.

To govern China, the Japanese Army has not developed beyond the usual devices of military rule. There are several reasons for this, primary among them the difficulty of governing Chinese at all. In a pluralistic society, such as China, command is largely superseded by negotiation, and the issuer of a command must be prepared for oblique thwarting. A Japanese who tells a Chinese to do something needs a bayonet with which to gesture; otherwise the Chinese, accustomed to circumventing, avoiding, or mocking authority, will disregard him. The Germans may order the Danes to make a two-way street a one-way street, and the Danes, accustomed to authority, will concur. When the Japanese promulgate a regulation, nothing short of massacre could ensure its absolute, unconditional obedience.

The language difficulty is another obstacle to direct Japanese government. A cultivated Japanese and Chinese may write classical Chinese to one another, and even the barely literate can scribble a few characters, the meanings of which may coincide; but the spoken languages differ from one another almost as much as English differs from either. To govern China directly would involve an enormous feat of language training, or an overnight re-shaping of the Chinese national character. Non-violent resistance, wilful but concealed negligence, lurking impertinence, consistent sloppiness, obsequiousness mingled with hatred—these Chinese tools of resistance, added to the language barrier, prevent any early Japanese hope of direct government. In years to come, if such come, Japanese trained in the Chinese language could supersede every Chinese above the level of foreman. A strong tendency in that direction is observable in Manchoukuo.[2]

The Japanese have abandoned direct government for the present. They would defeat their own purposes by assuming a task for which they have insufficient personnel, which would be very costly, and for which their army is ill-equipped in morale or technical ability. Difficult though it may be to employ pro-Japanese Chinese associates, it would be even more difficult to find Chinese now ready to profess direct loyalty to Japan. The only Chinese thus far Japanized are a number of Taiwanese (Formosans), whose island was ceded to Japan forty-six years ago. Chinese by blood and language, many of them have been reared in the third generation of Japanese rule. Some are fighting with the Chinese forces, but others, loyal to their lawful superiors, betray their fellow-Chinese. The Formosans

[2] Bisson, T. A., *Japan In China*, cited, *passim*, for many instances.

are insufficient in number to govern China, or to provide Japan with even the most elementary foothold. The Japanese have hence turned to the peculiar form of indirect rule identified by the popular appellation, *puppet states.*

The Problem of Puppet States

Lawful, well-established indirect rule is a familiar feature of colonial practice. Constituting an internationally recognized legal relationship between the paramount power and the encompassed state, it has been applied extensively by the European powers in Africa and Asia. The Indian and Malay states, under Britain; Cambodia and Annam-Tonkin, under France; the East Indian sultanates, under the Netherlands—these offer a rich repository of precedent.

Unacknowledged intervention involving no legal relationship is also a known feature of modern politics. The practices of the United States in the Caribbean and Central America, particularly during the 1920's, are familiar, but the leading case of intervention without responsibility occurred in the relationship between the Soviet Union (first the R.S.F.S.R.) and the Outer Mongol People's Republic. Four features of what has since come to be called political puppetry are here made fully manifest: first, the establishment of the subordinate through the military aid of the superior; second, the continued effective control, unacknowledged in law, of the subordinate by the superior, coupled with economic coordination of the two; third, bilateral insistence upon the formal independence of the subordinate state; fourth, the claim of the superior that it *has not* intervened, coupled with international non-recognition of the new relationship. The four features—establishment, coordination, fictitious independence and international nonentity—were clearly defined by Soviet political practice in Outer Mongolia and Tannu-Tuva long before Manchoukuo was created. In addition to this neighborly example, the Japanese had another source, commonly ignored in current Western comment on the Far East, on which to draw: the quasi-familist Confucian international system which prevailed down to the time of men now living. Successive Chinese Empires developed a clear, viable scheme of senior-junior relationships controlling their intercourse with other organized governments. The other, smaller states acknowledged China to be the senior realm, conceding that the Chinese Emperor was lord of the world. They paid formal tribute to China; their envoys were not ambassadors but tributary agents, while Chinese envoys came as high commissioners, superior in rank to the courts to which they were accredited. This relationship (awkwardly termed "dependency," "vassalage," "tributary" status, or subjection to "suzerainty," in Western terms) could not be fitted into the Western state system. Involving the assertion of Chinese power without concurrent admission of Chinese responsibility, it was rejected by the Western states, and lapsed following the French seizure of Indo-China, the British occupation of Burma, and Korean independence under Japanese compulsion. Today, Japan's moral effusions concerning the New Order in East Asia and her digressions from Western patterns of international law in dealing with Manchoukuo and Wang Ch'ing-wei both indicate that the Japanese move freely, sincerely, and unconsciously in a frame of reference which, obvious to them, is invisible to Westerners. The Japan-Manchoukuo or Japan-Wang relationship could be aligned with the relationship which Li Hung-chang wished, sixty years ago, to maintain in Korea, and found significantly similar. The Japanese understood the position of juniority in international relations: to their intense humiliation, they confessed themselves China's junior during the Ashikaga period.[3]

A third meaningful context for Japanese practice is found in the basic, factual scheme of current international relations. No nation in an interdependent world is independent except by legal fiction; none could maintain its present level of civilization without the existence of the others. In these terms, legal independence fades as time passes, and cross-national power becomes more evident. Western imperialism was described by Sun Yat-sen as reducing China to a hypo-colony. More recently, first the Communists and then the Japanese have accused Chiang K'ai-shek of being the puppet of imperialism,[4] while occasional Leftists regard Chiang as even now a puppet of Japan [5] and a few citizens of imperialist states see him as a Communist puppet. The Germans treat Churchill as the puppet of Roosevelt, and Roosevelt as a puppet for international Jewry, while the present Stalinist line attributes puppetry to the entire catalogue of world political institutions save those made quick by its own infallibility. The funda-

[3] It is unfortunate that work on the nature of old Far Eastern international relations has no more than just begun. Descriptions from the viewpoint of Western international law often possess the unreal lucidity of dialectical materialism or of theosophy, since it is necessary to read into Chinese and other Far Eastern political institutions the characteristic features of a European invention—the juridical, omnicompetent, secular, territorially limited state. See Djang Chu, *The Chinese Suzerainty,* unpublished doctoral dissertation, the Johns Hopkins University, 1935; Nelson, Melvin Frederick, *The International Status of Korea, 1876–1910* unpublished doctoral dissertation, Duke University, 1939, particularly Part I, "The International Society of Confucian Monarchies" and Part II, "Korea in Conflicting Societies of Nations"; both attempt to reconstruct the working Asiatic theory in terms comprehensible to the West. Clyde, Paul H., *United States Policy Toward China,* Durham, 1940, Section XXIV, gives a succinct statement and relevant American public documents.
[4] Taylor, George, *The Struggle for North China,* cited, p. 66.
[5] Statements to the author, by persons not in Chungking.

JAPANESE AND PRO-JAPANESE GOVERNMENTS 191

mental point of such appraisal depends upon the *attribution* of power relationships. Dependence is indisputable only if one government functions within the military framework of another, or if the personnel of the subordinate is drawn from the superior, or if clear and immediate causal relationships can be proved between the continued fiscal or military action of the sustaining government and the actual existence of the sustained government—although even this last leads to subjective interpretation.

The term *puppet* is not clear or apt, except in its most concrete sense—that of a person who is almost literally a marionette, whose utterances public and private are not his own, whose actions are supervised, and whose personal choice or opinion is not merely thwarted, but left out of consideration. Not all the Chinese who work with Japan are ventriloquists' dummies. The author talked freely with men who staked their careers on the inescapable success of the Japanese military, and who functioned in absolute conformity to general limits of policy and publicity laid down by the Japanese; these general limits were wide enough to permit a considerable degree of latitude of manners, and to allow variance in power and policy between the various Chinese under Japan. Use of the term *puppet* in such cases is not clear. It implies a higher degree of effective Japanese control, and a greater pliability of Chinese cooperators, than can be shown to exist.

Since, however, the National Government is recognized, both by the majority of the Chinese people and by *all* powers (including Germany and Italy) except Japan, to be the legitimate government of China, representing the Chinese nation, action against that government may properly and strictly be denominated treason; a person so acting may be called, formally, a traitor and, less formally but more descriptively, a Japanophile. Juridically the Chinese Soviet leaders were also traitors, but they were never Japanophile. This term gains by specificity what it loses through awkwardness.

The Provisional and Reformed Governments

The Japanese have determined, assisted and promoted establishment of a number of friendly Chinese governments. Huapeikuo, a North China separatist state, went the way of the Francophile Rhineland Republic; it never got off the drafting board. The East Hopei Autonomous Anti-Communist Government of Mr. Yin Ju-kêng provided, within the North China demilitarized zone, a vast gateway for smuggling; when the National Government withdrew its forces from North China, the Japanese sought more pretentious aids to conquest. The Provisional Government was the first of these, following an Inner Mongol federation (*Mêng-liu Lien-ho Tzŭ-chih Chêng-fu*), affiliated with Manchoukuo; it was soon rivaled by the Reformed Government; and in March 1940, both were incorporated into the Reorganized National Government of Mr. Wang Ch'ing-wei. Other governments, sponsored by various quarreling departments of the Japanese military, or organized by Chinese confidence men, have appeared transiently and then disappeared.

Three points concerning Japanophile governments contribute to assessment of their chances; their origin and structure; their ideological (narrowly, propagandist) position; and their personnel. These points illustrate a significantly ambivalent trend: the Japanese have found their degree of freedom of action less than they had expected in Chinese politics, and to that extent have been defeated; they have also yielded to the damands of the situation, and have won, in part, in that their chances of success appreciate with **realism**.

The Provisional Government of the Republic of China (*Chung-hua Min-kuo Lin-shih Chêng-fu*) was formed at Peking on December 14, 1937, and ended by merger into the Wang Ch'ing-wei government on March 30, 1940, perpetuating a high degree of separatism under the subgovernmental style, North China Political Council. Like its predecessors and successors, it was created by a self-proclaimed committee organized with the consent and knowledge of the Japanese military, if not by the Japanese directly. The members of the Provisional Government were old, weak men, mostly adherents of the Anfu clique which had been Japanophile during and after the War of 1914–18. A few were even brought forth from more archaic strata, lonely adherents to the abandoned monarchy. The youngest were in their fifties and the leading officers were extreme conservatives—men of some intelligence and reputation, but obsolete.

The structure of the *Lin-shih* Government was interesting in that it formed a republic of three committees, as follows:[6]

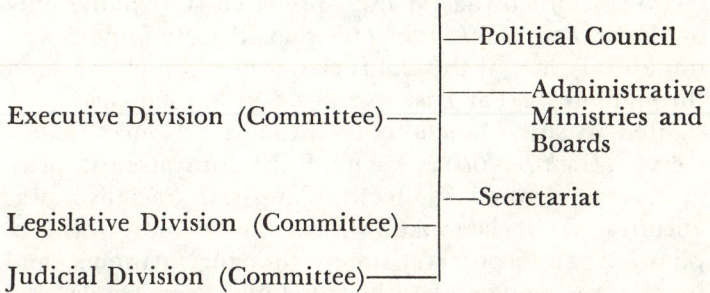

PROVISIONAL GOVERNMENT (Committee)

Executive Division (Committee) —
— Political Council
— Administrative Ministries and Boards
— Secretariat

Legislative Division (Committee) —

Judicial Division (Committee) —

[6] Nyi, P. C., "Plans for Economic and Political Hegemony in China," cited, p. 239. Compare this with the chart in George Taylor, work cited, p. 204. Professor Taylor's study covers the entire history of the Provisional Government, significantly aligned with that of its rival, the guerrilla Border Region.

Structurally important features are: the absence of any method of election, direct or indirect, or of any ultimate source of "sovereign" personnel—the government having borne itself out of chaos, constitutionally a remarkable feat; the elimination of even nominal party control of government, or cameral legislation, or constituent assembly, these being hated vestiges of the Chinese and Western, but not Japanese, notion that popular sovereignty is to receive genuflections if not credence; and, most startlingly, the absence of a head! There was no President, Protector, Chief of State, Leader, or Dictator; the highest officer was the Shanghai banker, Mr. Wang K'ê-min, Chairman of the Executive Division (literally, *yüan,* but not in the Nationalist sense). The scope, succession and competence of this Provisional Government were as much in doubt as its origin.

Under the Provisional Government there flowered a new political philosophy, the *Hsin Min Chu I* ("Principles of the Renewed People," "People-Renewing Principles," or "Principles of the New People"). The similarity of this principle to the *San Min Chu I* is striking, but is no more than verbal. Propaganda under this credo resembled the Japanese-prepared state-philosophy of *Wang Tao,* the *kingly* (as opposed to tyrannous and unnatural) *way* of the Confucian canon, which—revered throughout the Far East, even by Sun Yat-sen—had been slanted to suit Manchoukuo through a Concordia Society (*Hsieh-ho-hui*). Each of the Sunyatsenist principles was refuted in detail, Pan-Asian racialism was encouraged, a class-war *between* the nations was emphasized, and conservatism in thought, manners, and morals recommended. The Peking propaganda machinery was well-financed; the *Hsin-min-hui* became the only tolerated political group. This *hui* was headed by Mr. Miao Ping, a Kuomintang Party veteran whose political-bureau experience dated back to the days of

Borodin. His renegation, never publicly explained, enabled Japan to issue a careful parody of the *San Min Chu I*. His assistant was a Japanese. Business associations, student groups, and educational administration were fitted into the pattern. The principles were not logically or systematically developed, but the key terms sufficed to coordinate opportunist appeals justifying the invasion, and opposing resistance, guerrillas, modernizations, and democracy. The *Hsin Min Chu I* received no credence through conversion, faith, or loyalty. Operating on sound advertising principles, however, they served well even if they failed to command obedience but did unsettle allegiance to the other side, and ubiquitous iteration muddied thought.

The personnel of the Provisional Government included no actively important political leader. Many had been important long before; some were conspicuous in fields other than politics, and had even served on the semi-buffer Hopei-Chahar Political Council which was Chiang's last compromise with Japan. Japan's failure to obtain an effective political leader is important, for this lack eventually led to the acceptance of Wang Ch'ing-wei. The old age, past misfortunes, the motley reputations of the Provisional Government leaders attested a national sentiment sufficient to enforce unity beyond the reach of national law.

The Reformed Government of the Republic of China (*Chung-hua Min-kuo Wei-hsin Chêng-fu*) was established March 28, 1938. It lapsed simultaneously with its rival and colleague, the Provisional Government. There were several suggestive points of difference, although the chief difference was the fact that the Provisional Government operated from Peiping and the Reformed from Nanking. Both were national in form, a difficulty which was solved by the creation of a United Council to speak for all occupied China. This Council had only the power to issue news releases, which it did.

Despite duplication of capitals and national form, the Nanking government revealed a slipping in the Japanese insistence on conformity to their ideas.

In structure, the Reformed Government was a mutilated copy of the National Government. It possessed five *yüan,* thereby continuing the Sunyatsenist constitutional system which Japan first sought to destroy. In doctrine, it took over the North China-Manchoukuo pattern, under the name *Ta Min Chu I* (Principles of the Great People), with a party under the name *Ta-min-hui.* The walls of Nanking were covered with the emblem of the party, a red circular shield with a yellow crescent moon enclosing a white star. Quasi-educational work approximated that of the North; but the Japanese found the Yangtze sympathetic to the National Government and Kuomintang, and hence employed devices reminiscent of Chungking.

For Reformed Government personnel, the Japanese found individuals who were in most instances either as old as their Peiping colleagues, but less famous, or much younger, and relatively unknown. With the city of Shanghai only partially under its control, because local opportunists reached the tax offices first, the Reformed Government provided an outlet for persons who had felt themselves unjustly denied office, or slighted by the Kuomintang, or who had wrecked careers, once promising, by some ghastly misstep or crime and now saw a miraculous chance to return.

These new governments could not on principle claim the allegiance of their own clerks. The personnel, disloyal and of poor morale, was often so corrupt that no government services—needed by Japanese civilians and army alike—could be entrusted to them. Multiple taxes blocked Japanese trade in the area Japan had occupied. The Japanese realized that the United Council and the senescent politicians were not enough. Instead of abandoning interventionist governments, they tried a leader of genuine importance, considerable ability, and some following. His treason was Japan's last chance to govern China without assuming the task herself, risking a premature undertaking. To understand the moves and motives of Wang Ch'ing-wei it is necessary to regard his character and political history.

The Reorganized National Government of Wang Ch'ing-wei

In contrast to Chiang, who receives the obloquy which goes with power, Wang Ch'ing-wei has spent the greater part of his life as a political Out. He began brilliantly. While in his twenties, he became a revolutionary hero by a bold attempt to assassinate the Prince Regent, and after the establishment of the Republic followed the unhappy meanders of the Nationalist movement. His association with Sun in the years before Sun's death was very close, and he has as good a title as anyone to the apostolic succession. (His title is not necessarily much better than that of various other Kuomintang leaders; a score or so of elder statesmen of the Party could claim a longer service of Party leadership and equality or seniority to Wang in Party rank.)

In 1927 Chiang and Wang had different regimes for the first time, and Wang went into exile; he tried again in 1930, and went into exile; and he is trying now. His cooperation with the Japanese must not be regarded as the sudden prostitution of a worthy figure, nor as the culminating criminality of an utter rogue. As in a Greek tragedy, Wang, blinded by self-esteem and goaded by political frustration, has chosen his unsavory course from understandable motives. Several lines of continuity lead up to his establishment of the Reorganized National Government at Nanking, and condition the nature of this government.

Primarily, Wang has been an in-and-out schismatic in Kuomintang ranks. It is quite possible that in terms of a head count, he may have had the immediate support of a greater portion of the membership than did Chiang in the first break in 1927, but his proportion has fairly steadily declined ever since. There have been a large number of men who accepted him as leader, just as in the preceding decade there were men *Wu mi* ("infatuated with Wu [Pei-fu]"). In 1930–31 his organization paralleled the Government-supported Kuomintang in all parts of the world. Today he has some followers who follow even to Nanking. These men are bound to him by ties of long, habitual obedience, by blood kinship, and by generously offered loyalty: the distinguished and vigorous Ch'en Kung-po, now Mayor of Shanghai; by Chou Fu-hai, who—before his proscription—was the most popular commentator on the *San Min Chu I;* Lin Pai-sheng, who had served Wang well as spokesman; and the entertaining T'ang Leang-li, a Javanese-Chinese writer of international fame, who has probably written more books on China in English than any other Chinese.

On the other hand, he has lost office-holding followers by the scores, many of whom hold positions ranging up to Vice-Ministerships in Chungking, and he seems to have lost almost all of his rank and file followers. The chief defection was that of Messrs. Tao Hsi-shêng and Kao Tsung-wu, who fled from Chungking to Shanghai and Nanking, and then fled back again, bringing with them sensational copies of Wang's secret preliminary agreements with the Japanese. Dr. Tao, a historian, served Wang temporarily as Party-Minister of Publicity; Dr. Kao had been in the foreign office while Wang still collaborated with Chiang.[7] His following consisted almost entirely of politicians, ranging from the rank of scholar-bureaucrat down to hooli-

---

[7] *The Japan-Wang Ch'ing-wei Secret Agreements, 1938–1939–1940,* Shanghai, 1940; these also appeared in the *China Weekly Review,* January 27, 1940, p. 318; February 3, 1940, p. 341.

gans. The masses which he led in 1927 have dwindled to hundreds, and the replacements are of distinct unworthiness—persons, already cooperating with the Japanese, whom he must lead for lack of better. He has lost followers with almost every move he has made, whether rebelling, going into exile, accepting government post under Chiang, or working with Japan. The Wang clique may be represented by a consistently declining curve.

In the face of this, it is unexpected to find that Wang has been reasonably honest and consistent, as were Trotsky and Röhm. His consistency may be described as a perfectly regular spiral, which maintains unchanging direction but never goes in a straight line. Wang has always favored not-fighting, peace, civilian and constitutional government, and making friends with any nation which professes friendship for China. The loftiness of his motives might be impugned by pointing out that each is the antithesis of one of Chiang's characteristics; but the ultimate test of Wang's sincerity lies with the psychiatrists rather than with political scientists. Assuming sincerity, how did these consistent standards lead him to Nanking?

In 1927 Chiang broke with the Communists quite a while before Wang did. Wang was willing to yield a doubtful point here, to credit the other side with good motives there, and to keep the Wuhan government going as long as he could. His difficulties were the difficulties of a constitutionalist willing to maintain the constitution at the cost of some appeasement. In the following years of exile, he upbraided Chiang's machine-boss tactics within the Kuomintang; the name "Reorganized Kuomintang" which he selected for his schismatics, is indicative of his desire to promote regularity in party elections and free democratic discussion in party congresses.

A striking instance of repetition may be seen in contrasting the Nanking of 1940 with the Peking of 1930. In 1930 Chiang K'ai-shek had been threatened by military attack and had found a great part of China wrested from him by superior forces, those of the *tuchün* Feng Yü-hsiang and Yen Hsi-shan; but the National Government maintained its position in the capital. In 1940, the capital had moved to Chungking and the armed enemies were Japanese; Hu Han-min (the great Rightist leader) was dead, a new Communist alliance was in effect, and the outside world was in a turmoil more profound than China's. Despite the supervening changes, Wang Ch'ing-wei was found in 1940 in precisely the role of 1930. Again he was the front for a military regime. In 1930 he had been a Left-liberal front for native militarism; in 1940, he was the appeasing, conservative front for the Imperial Japanese army. In 1930 he had his own "Reorganized" Kuomintang; he had his "Orthodox" again in 1940. In 1930 he usurped the National Government offices, titles, and regalia; he did this again in 1940. In 1930 his career ended with military defeat and he went into exile, later bargaining his position back into Chinese politics.

Wang appears to have become the victim of an *idée fixe:* he believes that if he impersonates government devotedly enough, and with careful enough detail, he will become government. Brilliant, sincere, adroit, he is burdened by a pathological self-esteem and is so much the victim of his own past rationalizations that he is no longer inventive. Obviously such a character, in the face of recurrent failure, cannot assume the blame for it. Wang's demon is the Generalissimo.

Another characteristic of Wang appears clearly at this point: the belief of the appeaser that he can outsmart the appeased; he no doubt thought that his *tuchün* colleagues would become victims of the government which they let him create. On his way out of China after Chiang's armies and Chang Hsüeh-liang's intervention had settled this affair, he stopped over in Canton to take part in an even more transitory and less successful rebellion.

The next round of Wang-Chiang rivalry displays the consummate political strategy of the Generalissimo and the ruin of Wang by his own virtues. For three full years, 1932 through 1935, Wang was President of the Executive *Yüan* and second only to Chiang. After a little more than a year out of office—owing in part to a gunshot wound—he returned in the crucial months of 1937 just before the outbreak of general hostilities, and stayed with the National Government through the first year and a half of the war—until December 1938. In fifteen more months he reached terms with the Japanese; eight months after he set up a government with their consent and sponsorship, they recognized that government. Throughout this period Wang advocated peace, non-aggression to the point of non-defense and surrender, and universal conciliation. These attitudes made him very useful to Chiang when Chiang needed him, and made him dispose of himself when he was no longer helpful to Chiang.

Wang was ruined by the long, agonizing appeasement of which Chiang was the leader, in the six years between the Japanese invasion of China's Manchurian provinces and the outbreak of undeclared war in July 1937. Throughout this period the forces of Leftist reform, of Communist pressure (both military and political), of student sentiment, of overseas-Chinese patriotism, and finally of national self-respect itself, fed the opposition to Chiang, who knew that, whatever the cost, China was not militarily or politically ready to fight Japan. Wang Ch'ing-wei, who when out of office had espoused some of the most genuinely popular and necessary reforms, found himself civilian leader of a government following an intensely unpopular policy, and unable to profit by the rise of opposition. The Generalissimo needed someone to replace Hu Han-min, with whom he disagreed and whom he temporarily incarcerated. Wang provided a counter-balance to the Hu Han-min group, undermined his own popularity, and helped shield Chiang from anti-appeasement criticism.

Wang Ch'ing-wei, in this period, feared war and grasped at the conciliation which the Japanese offered between successive invasions. In 1937, Wang worked for the localization of the war at the cost of North China, on the theory that the Japanese could take what they wished. He reiterated his old point that the Chinese could not possibly whip the Japanese on the fields of battle, but that they might outmaneuver them over the tables of diplomacy. The advent of war was a disappointment and source of worry to him.

In the course of the celebrated retreat from Nanking to Hankow, and from Hankow to Chungking, Wang lost no opportunity to work for peace. When the Germans offered themselves as intermediaries in the Hankow period, Wang sought the opening of negotiations. There was a violent uproar in the People's Political Council, not then reported in the press. When the government moved to Chungking, Wang was even more despondent: victory seemed remote, the Communists worried him as much as did the Japanese, and the Generalissimo swept opposition aside with the slogans of resistance. Like other peoples in war time, the Chinese began to confuse peace and treason. Wang and his closest supporters felt that they were being deprived of freedom of speech; their known inclination to surrender and negotiate had supplied Chiang with a weapon which might even prove personally dangerous to them. The death by firing-squad of General Han Fu-ch'u showed that treason, or the charge of it, had become serious. Wang and his followers rationalized their own fearfulness concerning the war into the belief that they were expressing the will of the peace-loving masses.

In December 1938 he got out of China by a surprise flight to Indo-China. His followers had previously been filtering down to Hong Kong. The Konoye statement,[8] just issued, gave him an opening to treat with the Japanese.

Throughout the negotiations, Wang behaved as though he were himself the legitimate Chinese government. He did not accept the minimum Japanese conditions, but held out for an agreement which would preserve the fictions of Chinese independence, allow him to fly the national flag, establish his version of the Kuomintang, and attempt every kind of linkage with the past. One of his followers asked the author in Nanking, "Do you think we were traitors when we spent more than a year getting a fair peace agreement from the Japanese?" This agreement, released by Messrs. Tao and Kao, consisted of the cession of broad military, foreign-relations, and economic rights over China to Japan. The Chinese were to lose no territory *pro forma*, and were to keep a minimum of 35 per cent interest in major economic enterprises.

The regime is sufficiently well known so that there is no need to detail its history: the long dickering with the two Japanophile "governments" already established in Peking and Nanking, since they were the third parties to the Japan-Wang negotiations, the installation of the government in March 1940, and its recognition the following November. The more significant problem is —what part can this Nanking establishment play in the actual contest for power in East Asia?

In the first place, the Reorganized National Government (*Chung-hua Min-kuo Ts'an-chêng Kuo-min Chêng-fu*) of China is not a puppet government in the sense that the Manchoukuoan government is. The

[8] Statement of the Japanese Prime Minister, Prince Fumimaro Konoye, December 22, 1938, Jones and Myers, *Documents on American Foreign Relations, 1939–40*, Boston (World Peace Foundation), p. 299.

Japanese have a very loose surveillance of the officers of state. Interviews with officials indicate pretty conclusively the absence of dictaphones or of Japanese Special Service agents. The leaders in the government at Nanking are not watched or hounded in any intimate way. One of them said: "Why should the Japanese watch us? They know that we cannot do anything to them, and they know that their only chance of success lies in our becoming a real government."

Secondly, the personnel of the Nanking regime is not sufficient to cope with the problems which face it. The Nanking regime has no diplomatic officer who has regularly represented any other Chinese government; only a few consuls, in Japanese territory, joined it.[9] In no single instance can a Nanking officeholder, compared with his Chungking counterpart, be regarded (patriotism apart) as better-qualified or more able than his rival. In an enterprise of this sort, it would seem likely that Nanking should have the better man in some few positions. Diligent and disinterested inquiry fails to reveal a single one. Finally, the personnel is a mixture of Wang cliquists, politically obsolete conservatives, careerist Japanophiles, colorless opportunists, and actual criminals.

A Western newspaper man, well acquainted with the Nanking situation, told the author that he estimated the regime as 5 per cent Japanophiles, 5 per cent upright men who worked with the enemy because of a sense of public duty toward the Chinese people in the occupied areas, 20 per cent opportunists, and 70 per cent low characters interested in thievery. Nanking officials, to whom these estimates were communicated without revelation of the source, felt the latter categories to be much too high. Several of the more intelligent men in

---

[9] Ch'ên Lo died, and the only persons with any diplomatic experience had, in the past, been only casually connected with the Foreign Office.

Nanking offered the argument that if they did not share in the regime, unscrupulous elements would deceive the Japanese and oppress the people; or they stated that the Reorganized Government had brought back the flag, the constitution, the titles, the law codes, and the political doctrines of the National Government, so that occupied and unoccupied China had the same polity. They disregarded the point that this abetted the enemy.

Thirdly, the government has nothing to do. The power of the Nanking regime in no instance reaches beyond the Japanese patrols. No counties are under Nanking control which are not also under Japanese control. The Ministry of Foreign Affairs has no foreign affairs. The Ministry of Finance collects some excises and disburses many salaries, as well as limited amounts for the upkeep of some schools, law courts, minimal public services, and state property, insofar as the Japanese have returned any. (It is interesting to note that the officials at Nanking, deploring the "Communist" tendencies of Chiang, live in commandeered houses, and use the commandeering of private property as a form of patronage for their supporters.) The Central Political Council has so little to do that it draws up a budget and solemnly debates items of less than U. S. $100.[10] The officials cannot ride far from the city limits of Nanking, because of the guerrillas who operate all about. The railroad runs only by daylight. The Nanking police are mostly unarmed, except for clubs—an unprecedented condition for modern China!—and many who carry rifles or pistols seem to have no cartridges.

[10] See *The People's Tribune* (Shanghai), XXIX, p. 130 ff., August 1940. This is the semi-official English organ of the regime; each issue contains a selection of public documents. It is edited by the volatile T'ang Leang-li. The other English-language journal is *The Voice of China*, fortnightly, Nanking, edited by Mr. L. K. Kentwell, a graduate of Oxford and Columbia Universities, Hawaiian-born of British and Cantonese parentage. The journal is spirited, and very anti-British.

Fourthly, the Nanking government is an encouraging indication that the modern Chinese have finally come to the point where five-power republicanism is the norm. It is significant that the Nanking regime practices an extreme purism of organization and nomenclature, conforming precisely to antebellum practice.[11] The regime has changed the theoretical structure of the National Government very little, but added the Party ministries to the government cabinet. One further change has consisted in the logically desirable transference of the Ministry of Justice to the Executive *Yüan* from the Judicial, thus eliminating the anomaly of having both prosecuting and adjudicatory agencies under the same control.[12] The minister, Li Shêng-wu, is a well-known scholar in international law and an educational editor.[13]

Since the Japanese may be expected to foster the kind of Japanophile government which would help them most, it is interesting that their crusade against Sunyatsenism has turned to a quasi-Kuomintang struc-

[11] Such a chart is found in *The People's Tribune*, XXIX (March 1940), p. 214, together with a list of incumbents on the following pages. The issue is headed by an editorial, "The National Government Returns to Its Capital" and "Peace, Struggle, and Save China" by Wang Ching-wei (*sic*). The official outline of the government is to be found in [Reorganized Government], *K'ao-shih Yüan Kung-pao* (Public Gazette of the Examination *Yüan*), Nanking, Vol. I, No. 2 (June 1940), following p. 80.

[12] [Reorganized Government], *Ssŭ-fa Hsing-chêng Kung-pao* (Public Gazette of the Ministry of Justice), Nanking, gives a well-edited résumé of the work of the Ministry and its policy in prosecutions.

[13] [*China Weekly Review;* J. B. Powell, editor], *Who's Who in China, Fifth Edition*, Shanghai, [1937], p. 145. For further information see the supplement on the pro-Japanese leaders in *Who's Who in China, Supplement to Fifth Edition*, Shanghai, [1940]. This presents a hall of notoriety for all the major Chinese leaders affiliated with the enemy. This *Who's Who* is regarded by the present author as one of the most valuable sources on all Far Eastern politics. It is engrossingly good reading and entertainment, the pictures of the subjects being included in most instances. Behind these simple and short biographies, there lies more drama than Hollywood dare produce.

ture for aid. The attempt does not, as yet, seem to be working, but the technique of the deception reveals the depth to which Kuomintang principles and practices have penetrated in the past generation. The Nanking incumbents make every effort to confuse their regime with the National Government at Chungking, even to the extent of copying the names of all minor offices, the forms of the stationery, and the organization of semi-public cultural associations. Chinese fashion, they confuse correct form and legitimacy. Given a long enough period, this technique may succeed. Meanwhile, the failure of the earlier traitor Governments, non-Nationalist in form, is a real indicium of the value of the Sunyatsenist pattern.

Along with the bewildering *Doppelgänger* effect which prevails in all other matters, there are two Kuomintangs. The major, recognized Kuomintang continues from Chungking. At Nanking Wang and his friends have organized the "Orthodox Kuomintang." This can scarcely be thought of as a Party fraction, so much has it dwindled. The overseas branches have been lost, and the populace in its own cities is savagely contemptuous. Wang Ch'ing-wei held a "Sixth Plenary Session of the C.E.C. of the Kuomintang" on August 29, 1939, and the affair seems to have been an uproarious farce, with all of Wang's friends bringing in random acquaintances in order to make up a quorum.[14] Since then, the vestigial party has been equipped with appropriate party organs, and is preparing to share its hypothetical power with an equally *ad hoc* Nanking People's Political Council. The Kuomintang leaders in Nanking, as a part of their application to the Chungking pattern, have even listed a considerable number of minor parties which are on their side of the Japanese army. Persistent, specific inquiry in Nanking failed

[14] For an account of this see, "Wang's Farcical C.E.C. Session," *China At War* (Hong Kong), III, No. 6, p. 57; January 1940.

to elicit the name of a single *bona fide* minor party representative, other than representatives of the *Hsin Min Hui* (ex-Provisional), the *Ta Min Hui* (ex-Reformed), the Republicans (*Kung-ho Tang;* Hankow; merged with the Orthodox Kuomintang), and the Chinese Socialist Party, which consists of the venerable Dr. Kiang Kang-hu. It is perhaps fair to conclude that the Nanking regime is not a Kuomintang regime because a sizable portion of the Kuomintang membership were weary of war, but because some few Kuomintang leaders found no other way to power, and because the Japanese had reluctantly decided that the simulacrum of the Kuomintang was the minimum requirement of any Chinese government.

Lastly, the lack of success of Wang Ch'ing-wei and his government is proof of the emergence of a state in China. This is not the first time that Wang has set up his own government. It is not even the first time that Chinese have accepted foreign aid in such enterprises. Wang thought, and presumably thinks, that he is playing the accepted game of Chinese politics; he is likely to find that he has committed a treason which is disastrously real to him. The non-support of his government is a clear proof of the rising race-national awareness among China's common millions.

Stripped of the confusion and distortion which have surrounded the Wang Ch'ing-wei secession, the rivalry between Wang and Chiang is not so very different from Benedict Arnold's departure from the then dubious American revolution. In this century we have revised our opinion of Benedict Arnold upward—in part—and Wang Ch'ing-wei may, perhaps, justly fit the same category. A gifted but maladroit and unhappy political leader had brought his misfortunes to the Japanese. They, *faute de mieux,* have accepted his aid. So far this has been ineffectual. Most probably, only a very long lapse of time or the truly catastrophic ruin of their opponents could place Wang and his group in a position of autonomous importance and power. On the world scene Wang stands halfway between Quisling and Pétain. A traitor to the emergent Chinese state, he demonstrates the ancient Chinese capacity to surrender, appease, and survive. Had he antagonists less formidable than Chiang and the infuriated masses, his Reorganized Government might secure actual power.

The Japanese finally recognized the Reorganized National Government of Wang Ch'ing-wei on November 30, 1940, after many months of delay. *Art.* I provided for mutual recognition, but added the provision that the two countries should ". . . at the same time take mutually helpful and friendly measures, political, economic, cultural, and otherwise . . ." and in the future prohibit ". . . such measures and causes as are destructive to the amity between the two countries in politics, diplomacy, education, propaganda, trade and commerce, and other spheres." *Art.* II was an anti-Communist agreement leaving Japanese forces in North China indefinitely. *Art.* IV left the problem of Japanese evacuation to separate annexes. *Art.* VI provides "Economic cooperation," with the inescapable implications. By *Art.* VII Japan relinquishes extraterritoriality (in the future), but obtains the opening of all China to Japan.[15] These terms, which not only involve admission of Chinese defeat, but preclude any possible attempt of China to restore military, economic, or political independence, are the best that Japan has to offer. When one considers that even these are merely legal, whittled back to realism by protocols and annexes, and that they are made with Japan's Chinese friends, Japan appears in-

[15] The full text of the treaty is to be found in China Information Committee, *News Release*, December 2, 1940, together with the Generalissimo's comment. For a brief account, clearly interpreted, see Steiger, G. Nye, "Japan Makes Peace—with Wang," *Events*, Vol. 9, No. 49 (January 1941), p. 60-2. The Generalissimo's comment on the Nanking regime will also be found below, Appendix III (A), No. 7.

capable of ending the China incident. The Japanese do not know when to stop. Gauche in power politics, they are undone by greediness and inexperience.

The recognition is important only in that it assists Japan in escaping responsibility for action taken by or through the Chinese affiliates, while at the same time pinning Japan to the Chinese earth and committing the Empire to indefinite continuation of hostilities. If the Japanese achieved complete success in international power politics, there is a possibility that the Reorganized Government might remain as the functioning half-autonomous affiliate of Japan. Otherwise, Nanking can be nothing more than an ornamental, occasionally useful auxiliary to the Imperial Japanese Army, itself an uncomfortable Chinese government *pro tem*. Having ultimate authority, the Army cannot yet escape or delegate final responsibility.

Chapter VIII

EXTRA-POLITICAL FORCES

GOVERNMENT, wherever organized, is distinguished from other social institutions by claims to universality of scope and competence, and paramountcy of authority; the term *political*, on the basis of such a distinction, refers to activities, occasionally individual but more usually collective, involving access to the symbols of government; and the term *governmental* refers to the application of such symbols in governmental sanctions and services. The process of government is accordingly one wherein groups smaller than the totality of society seek ("politically") to obtain action in the name of the totality ("governmental"), for or against other groups according to shifting interests. In the West this politico-governmental process has been further characterized by ceremonial forms ("laws") and reinforced by conceptions of amoral omnicompetence ("sovereignty").

The cellular socio-economic structure of old China, plus the Confucian employment of ideological as opposed to governmental control, kept the entire process of politics and government at a very low level of intensity. Modern China, inheritor of an apolitical past, is still the most pluralistic society in the world, and modern Chinese government—despite recent gigantism —a frail legal superstructure above a flood of extra-political power. Western societies depend upon their states; the Chinese state depends upon a society which could, albeit uncomfortably, dispense with states altogether.

This condition amounts in international politics, to both a strength and a weakness. Chinese society suffers more political ruin with less social disturbance than does any comparable society; the guerrillas, for example, probably find government helpful when available, but regard it as a luxury rather than a necessity. Chinese society is near to an orderly anarchy; uniform conditioning from the past, or uniform present opinion, takes the place of mass organization and totalitarian government. The high death rate of traitors is probably not owing to activity on the part of Chungking, but to the spontaneous action of ordinary men; on one occasion a high pro-Japanese official was shot by his own bodyguard while the two sat in a sedan on a busy street: the bodyguard had experienced a revulsion of conscience. Fu Hsiao-ên, Wang Ch'ing-wei's Mayor of Shanghai, was also killed by a member of his own household. Spontaneous but uniform action applies not only to sensational political matters; it appears in less dramatic but equally important affairs, such as commercial rivalry, landlord-tenant relationships, and the police power of the community and the family. However, in a contest for power, while the Chinese lose little by defeat, their counter-attacks are correspondingly more difficult. The fluid autonomy of innumerable groups slows down the engines of formal power. The political-governmental process is apt to be sluggish in crises.

The Foundations of Chinese Government

The society upon which the National Government of China, its Left associates, and its Japanophile rivals rest is not a settled, stagnant society. An extraordinary ferment has gripped China for more than a century—arising from cadastral, agrarian, technological, economic, fiscal, ideological, political, and governmental change. The Chinese people have endured; they have also acted. Within a single century, three blazing revolutions have swept China: the T'aip'ing Rebellion, put down with Western aid after fifteen years of war; the Boxer uprising, deflected into xenophobia by the Manchus; and the Great Revolution, which succeeded in part. Between these, there have been changes, bloody but of secondary magnitude: the Moslem rebellions; the minor uprisings of Sun Yat-sen; the Republican Revolution; the 1919 movement; the *tuchün* wars; the Communist communes, which failed utterly in Shanghai and Canton; the Communist *jacqueries,* which continued; and the present rip tide of resistance. None of these was effectively mastered by organized government; each was exploited by one government, and opposed by another. Unlike a Western state, wherein government becomes the prime mobilizer during crises, Chinese society shifts its incalculable forces, and governments leap forward to take advantage of them.

This extensive, unorganized residue of opinion and power, outside the reach of government, keeps any modern Chinese government in a peculiar condition. Like a perpetual process of revolution, social changes demand that a government exploit them, deflect them, or employ them—but not launch or stop them. The Kuomintang has failed in its attempts to launch favorable mass movements, and also failed to stop antagonistic ones. The secret of the Chinese Communist power has lain in the skill of the Red leaders, who utilized available movements. Hence the continued development of Chinese government rests upon the wills, fancies, interests, mob action, enthusiasm or dispiritedness of a people who in their own communities do not read newspapers, listen to radios, or pay much attention to the national state. Despite attempts to bring society under the control of government, in order to make it possible to bring government under the control of society (constitutionalism), the decisive forces of modern Chinese life are outside the reach of propaganda or control.

General opinion in China is not ascertainable, except through action. In vital matters this action is apt to be either violent, or the equivalent of violent: sit-down, general, or go-slow strikes; boycotts; universal derision. The National Government possesses unprecedented amounts of power by Chinese standards. By Western standards it is incredibly obliging, casual, and unsystematic. The power which the Government, with Chiang as leader, enjoys, arises from a support which it could not compel, and which it cannot ensure by any means other than the pursuance of support-arousing policies. The Kuomintang, the Communists, the National Salvationists, the independent Left guerrilla leaders—these agencies are not the organization of entire opinion groups, but the spearheads of immeasurable forces. The modernization of government, both administrative and constitutional, awaits the transformation of materials around and under government. Greatest of these is popular mentality. Ancillary are economic, organizational, educational and cultural forces. Progress toward the omnicompetent state is slowed by the fact that few Chinese wish to abandon the freedom of a pluralist society for the efficient universality of legalism. They desire modernization, but haggle at the price.

Three factors in particular are working upon and among the millions of farmers and townsmen: mass education, rural reconstruction, and the cooperative movement. Each not only takes immediate, beneficial effect, but also transforms the political material of China. These forces, not in any strict sense political, possess enormous political importance.

Mass Education

Literacy has risen very rapidly in modern China. Before the impact of the West, becoming literate was in itself a career. By the time one could read at all, one was a scholar, unless one learned the limited quasi-shorthand of the merchants. Educational reforms came about as the result of modern schools, particularly British and American Protestant schools, and the action of the government. The fabric of Chinese society had begun to change even before the downfall of the Ch'ing dynasty. The literary revolution led by Hu Shih after 1915, which popularized *pai-hua* (a written form of the Chinese spoken language) had extensive repercussions, and made possible the rapid diffusion of ideographic literacy. (Phonetization failed then, and later.) Almost every government in China has attempted the diffusion of literacy. The popular demand is intense.

The present status of literacy in China is revealed by official figures from the Ministry of Education, which may err somewhat on the side of optimism. These put the total population of China at 450 million (Manchuria presumably remaining unmentioned), of which 90 million are literate and 360 million illiterate. Such an estimate would give China about the same absolute number of literates as the United States. The remaining 360 million illiterates are broken down as follows: 40.05 million children below the age of six; 45 million aged six to twelve; 29.25 million aged twelve to fifteen; 79.43 million persons over forty-five; and 1.57 million dumb, deaf, cripples, or insane. The adults to be reached by the mass literacy movement amount therefore to 165 million; government estimates state that 46,348,469 illiterates were educated since 1938, of whom 25.2 million were adults between fifteen and forty-five, leaving roughly 140 million to be educated.[1]

The mass education program is supplementary to the education of children, which is far from complete or even adequate. The literacy imparted is of the most elementary kind; but in a civilized society such as China this has immediate effect. The author never knew a

[1] The China Information Committee, *News Release*, April 1, 1940.

Chinese who could read and was not addicted to it; a common sight in Western China is a knot of coolies deciphering a newspaper together. The intense reverence for learning and scholarship makes the training welcome, and the teachers who seek to teach the minimum of one thousand ideographs in six weeks never lack pupils.

The program of the National Government was summarized by Ch'ên Li-fu, the Minister of Education, speaking over the radio after the Mass Education Conference of March 1940:

Accordingly, our first step is to wipe out illiteracy. In this respect we proceed simultaneously with the enlightenment of the masses of adult illiterates, both men and women, and with the education of children in order to put an end to illiteracy that may otherwise arise in the future. At the National Conference on People's Education held from the twelfth day to the sixteenth day of this month in Chungking, the *five-year plan for the people's education,* adopted by the Executive *Yüan,* was further deliberated and promulgated. The proper enforcement of this plan will help to convert at least one hundred and forty million (140,000,000) adult illiterates into intelligent citizens for China within the coming five years.

At present there are already 44 per cent of the entire number of children of school age (from six to twelve) in school; that is, nineteen million and eight hundred thousand (19,800,000). By the enforcement of this plan, there should be, during the first two years, at least one people's school in every three *pao*. And each village should have a nucleus school, according to the plan. In this way there should be at least more than 260,000 people's schools for the 800,000 *pao* of the entire nation at the end of the first two years. Each people's school consists of three divisions or classes, namely, the children's division, the men's division, and the women's division. During the second two years there should be at least one people's school in every two *pao*. In the fifth and last year there should be at least one people's school in each *pao*. That is to say, at the end of the fifth year there should be at least 800,000 people's schools for the 800,000 *pao* of the nation, besides the 80,000 or more nucleus schools and the 200,000 schools of the same grades now already existent which can be improved, to provide education for at least 90 per cent of the entire number of children of school age. As a matter of fact, certain provinces have already succeeded in establishing one or even two people's schools in each *pao*. Kwangsi Province, for instance, has at present one people's school in each *pao*, while Fukien Province even has two people's schools in each *pao*. The fulfillment of this five-year plan needs at least $2,932,000,000 and 1,600,000 properly trained teachers.

Our vocational education aims at building a sound middle cadre for the various professions and industrial enterprises. There are training schools and short-time classes for mechanics, electrical communications, metal work, etc. Also, special classes are opened in more than ten colleges and universities for advanced studies along such lines.

Our attempt to universalize productive education may be evidenced by the incorporation of productive education courses into the middle school curriculum, besides instituting organizations for the same in the various vocational schools in order to facilitate the practice of students along such lines. . . . In 1938, for example, only 53.0 per cent of the entire number of students who took part in the examination studied science and engineering, but in 1939 it jumped to 59.4 per cent.[2]

This statement gives the official view, which is highly optimistic. In terms of practical politics, however, the Generalissimo has given the movement his cordial backing, and sees in it a preliminary to democracy. Although final results might fall far short of the hopeful estimate, the effect would still be considerable. Diffusion of literacy creates a momentary satisfaction with the political system which makes literacy possible, but the after-effect of literacy is to make men of any nationality easier to govern well and harder to govern badly. A government which diffuses literacy without advancing reforms is sharpening weapons against itself. The National Government's American-inspired trust in

[2] The same, April 8, 1940. Minor changes in punctuation have been introduced.

education as a panacea implies that Chiang and his fellow leaders expect to remain popular, and do not contemplate appeasement, reaction, or other unpopular measures.

RURAL RECONSTRUCTION

An even more interesting aspect of the mass-education movement is its connection with rural reconstruction. In this field much is owed to Dr. James Y. C. Yen, a graduate of Yale and Princeton who began his work with the Chinese labor corps in France during the 1914–18 war. The war-time work of the correlated mass education and rural reconstruction movement was summarized by Dr. Yen himself:

The most hopeful factor in the whole China situation is that her greatest and most valuable resource, the three hundred and fifty million farmers, has not yet been tapped for the upbuilding of the nation. The Chinese farmer has had a measure of freedom and responsibility, of dignity and independence. He is thrifty and industrious, intelligent and an expert in intensive farming. A great number of our national leaders are sons and daughters of our farmers. The fathers of Dr. Sun Yat-sen and Generalissimo Chiang Kai-shek were farmers.

These nearly three years of terrible war have proved beyond doubt that our faith in the Chinese farmer has not been misplaced. It has revealed his greatness. Our nation is rediscovering the "forgotten man," the tiller of the soil. Most of our soldiers come from the farm. To a remarkable extent he has also financed the war. He is the real hero of this war.

The Chinese Mass Education Movement was organized in 1923 to explore the potentialities of the rural masses and find a way of drawing out the best in them. Since the first publication of the "thousand character test," it has been estimated that some thirty million illiterate people have been taught to read during the past five years.

Beginning with 1929 the point of emphasis of the Movement shifted from extensive promotion of literacy to intensive study of the life of the farmers in the rural districts. As a living social laboratory in which to do our research and to work out principles and techniques, we selected Tinghsien, a district of four hundred thousand people, one-thousandth of the total population of China, in Hopei Province. This was the first time in our history that an organized group of Chinese intellectuals went deliberately to the country to live among the rural people to study their life and find out how to develop their latent possibilities. The Movement has evolved what is known as the "Tinghsien Four-fold Reconstruction Education" including the cultural, economic, health, and the political.

Several other experimental *hsien,*—Hengshan in Hunan, Central China, and Hsintu in Szechwan, West China, were established in cooperation with the provincial governments. One of our special emphases in these experimental *hsien* has been the reform of the *hsien* government, i.e. the local government.

The Tinghsien Experiment with its "laboratory approach" to social and political problems and with its *correlated* program of rural reconstruction as demonstrated in the district attracted attention from all over China and inspired similar experiments in various parts of the country. As a result the movement for rural reconstruction gained great momentum in China.

Since the outbreak of hostilities the Mass Education Movement has thrown itself unreservedly into the task of assisting the Central and Provincial governments in strengthening the nation's struggle against the enemy. It was most gratifying that at this hour of China's supreme struggle we have been able to help the government to revitalize the *hsien* government, to train civil service personnel and to mobilize the farmers. Extensive application of the new system as developed in the experimental *hsien* was made to an entire province such as we did in Hunan—a rich province with a population of thirty million.

In order to insure that the new political machinery should function effectively a School of Public Administration to train administrative and technical personnel from the magistrate down to the village elders was established with the senior members of our Movement taking full charge. Altogether the School trained about 4,000 higher officials for the local government and some 35,000 of the village elders. Since Generalissimo Chiang Kai-shek assumed concurrently the governorship of Szechwan, a new system of *hsien* government (chiefly modelled after the experimental *hsien* of the country) with the object of releasing the new life of the rural masses has been promulgated. Under his order the same is taking place in neighboring provinces.

Unless serious and painstaking study of rural reconstruction is made by scientists and scholars on the one hand, and administrative and technical personnel are systematically trained and imbued with a spirit of service to the rural masses on the other, the movement for rural reconstruction may dwindle away as so many other movements have done in the past.

It is most heartening to state that Generalissimo Chiang Kai-shek has given his public approval and backing to the new National Institute of Rural Reconstruction which he considers to be of fundamental importance to China's post-war reconstruction. The inspiration of the Institute has already helped to mould the principal rural reconstruction groups in the country into one national force. The rural reconstruction movement has achieved a united front unparalleled in its history. Today it is a great unifying force, an outstanding national platform upon which all Chinese can agree. It will meet the needs of China today and lay the foundation for the China of tomorrow.[3]

This program possesses obvious merit. Lacking a foundation of dogma, it requires no implementation through terrorism. The politically innocuous character of the movement is attested by the frequent demands by provincial officials for personnel from the Mass Education training centers. Since the purpose is to improve the entire community without revolutionizing its class structure, the enlightened landlords are as favorable as the peasants themselves. Unfortunately, enlightened landlords are not always prevalent. Despite the modesty of the program, it finds stumbling blocks in actual corruption, extortion, and illegality. Many *hsien* are under local machines which permit wealthy conservatives to evade tax payments, steal government funds, and repress genuine farmer organization. The consequence has been that the movement succeeds only when it has

[3] The same, May 6, 1940.

the immediate backing of a provincial or central authority; its progress has been slow. Many critics, both Chinese and Western, have become disgusted with the slowness of social reform on the land, and despair of anything save reconstruction through implicit class war.[4]

The present period of resistance and reconstruction opens a very promising period in rural modernization. In the first place, war-time stress puts great power in the Generalissimo's hands. Ubiquitous armies can, on short notice, enforce orders from Chungking. The shift of troops among provinces makes the central government an outside power now physically present in tens of thousands of communities. Devolution of watchfulness by the Commander-in-Chief and his staff results in slow but irreversible accumulation of governmental authority.

Secondly, the proclamation of manifold programs has the effect, obviously, of drawing attention to each of them. The Kuomintang, anxious to retain its paramountcy, promotes new local government changes. These face frustration by mass illiteracy. Mass education is impeded by local economic injustices. The Whampoa and *Erh Ch'ên* groups in the Kuomintang, while they have landlord connections, are interested— even assuming a strong economic-class interest—in the

[4] Research Staff of the Secretariat, Institute of Pacific Relations, *Agrarian China, Selected Source Materials from Chinese Authors*, Shanghai, 1938. A more Leftist and even gloomier view is taken by Chen Han-seng, *Landlord and Peasant in China*, New York, 1936, and the same author's *Industrial Capital and Chinese Peasants, A Study of the Livelihood of Chinese Tobacco Cultivators*, Shanghai, 1939. Two general surveys of the Chinese economy are Condliffe, J. B., *China Today: Economic*, Boston, 1932, and Tawney, R. H., *Land and Labour in China*, New York, 1932. A significant hypothesis of the relations of economics, government, and culture in China is found in Lattimore, Owen, *Inner Asian Frontiers of China*, New York, 1940, Ch. III, esp. p. 39 ff.; this rests in part upon Wittfogel, Karl August, *Wirtschaft und Gesellschaft Chinas*, Leipzig, 1931, the leading Marxian exposition of the subject.

maintenance of government. Action is appearing, slow and haphazard by Western standards, but indisputably present. The minimum of good government in China is a very low minimum, but it is rising in the face of the Communist and Japanese pressure. One may be sure that the National Government will not pass below that minimum if the state's existence is in danger.

Thirdly, there is a very genuine boom condition in Western China. The movement of the government to the West, and lightening of intolerable but long-endured *tuchün* exactions, would in itself have led to sudden prosperity. To this are added more than twenty millions of new population, a growing network of communications, a sharp but controlled inflation. These further stimulate speculation and construction and development. The most important factors in a new prosperity have been, however, the reappearance of handicraft-type industry as a consequence of blockade, and governmental advocacy of every conceivable development. The author beheld, during the summer of 1940, conditions of prosperity in Szechwan which he had not expected to find in China within the space of one lifetime. Narcotics were eradicated. The working population was commanding high wages, but suffering from high prices; the prices were somewhat ahead of the wages, but not so far that social morale was troubled. Skilled labor was in a superb bargaining position; chauffeurs, electricians, good carpenters, etc. were in considerable demand. The salaried classes were suffering at all levels, a factor which was patently wholesome in stimulating working-class morale. The clerical class, which had held itself aloof from manual labor with a persistence which boded ill for China, was placed more nearly on a par with its American equivalent. While poverty was still universal by Western standards, the pathological squalor endemic to the coast was nowhere visible.

The Chinese Industrial Cooperatives

The Chinese Industrial Cooperatives (*Chung-kuo Kung-yeh Ho-tso Hsieh-hui*) are an important and widely publicized outgrowth of the war, and are perhaps the only feature of domestic Chinese affairs—outside of the Communist area and the roads program—which is as well known beyond China as within. The purpose of the cooperatives is to launch an enormous program of decentralized industry throughout Free China, with thirty thousand separate industrial cooperatives for the first major goal. The purpose is to develop an industrial system which will keep China autarkic for resistance and reconstruction; long-range, the purpose is to circumvent impending evils of concentrated industrialism, slums, megalopolitan crowding, extra-legal oppression. China might thus proceed directly from a decentralized half-handicraft economy to the decentralized power economy of the future. Four principles underlie the program: sound technical design, cooperative organization, voluntary self-discipline, and social welfare on the basis of Sun's *min shêng*.[5]

Formally, the C.I.C. Headquarters is a social organization sponsored by the Executive *Yüan*. H. H. K'ung, Minister of Finance and Vice-President of the *Yüan*, is

[5] Publicity release of Indusco, Inc., The American Committee in Aid of Chinese Industrial Cooperatives, New York, January 1940 [1941]. This agency, exceedingly active in publicizing China's cooperative progress, has released a great deal of up-to-date information on the movement. The Western literature on the C.I.C. has appeared mostly in popular sources, to which *The Bulletin of Far Eastern Bibliography* issued by the Committees on Far Eastern Studies of the American Council of Learned Societies, Washington, D. C., serves as a useful guide. The writings of Edgar Snow are of special value and vividness in treating this topic: articles in *Asia*, various dates; "China's Blitzbuilder, Rewi Alley," *The Saturday Evening Post*, Vol. 213, no. 32 (February 8, 1941); and his recent *The Battle for Asia*, New York, 1941, which appeared as this work was completed and sent to press. A convenient handbook is the anonymous *The People Strike Back!* or *The Story of Chinese Industrial Cooperatives*, Shanghai, (1939?).

its Chairman. The Secretary-General and Associate Secretary-General, Messrs. K. P. Liu and Hubert Liang, are both American-returned students; the former once worked in the Ford factories while studying at the University of Cincinnati and later was a banker in Manchuria. The most inspiring force in the movement is Mr. Rewi Alley, a New Zealander strongly interested in cooperatives and in labor welfare, formerly factory inspector in the International Settlement. Familiar, because of his Shanghai experiences and famine-relief work, with the problems of economic organization in China, he presented his plan to Generalissimo and Mme. Chiang through the intervention of that extraordinarily popular British Ambassador, Sir Archibald Clark-Kerr. The Chiangs were impressed with it, and the Generalissimo gave it his support. A headquarters was established at Hankow in August 1938, with the following five departments: *general,* for secretarial and administrative housekeeping; *financial,* administering funds for the headquarters and the cooperative units; *organization,* in charge of planning and inauguration of cooperatives; *technical,* devising simple industrial techniques; and *accounting,* an independent agency of audit.[6] The Executive *Yüan* has continued to make administrative funds available; the central headquarters near Chungking now has a staff of about seven hundred. Professor J. B. Tayler of Yenching University, a noted economic expert, is consultant for staff service.

As projected by Rewi Alley and his fellow-enthusiasts, the C.I.C. had to adjust itself to three zones of China's war-time economy. A guerrilla zone in and around the combat area, as well as behind the Japanese lines, concentrated on the creation of immediate war-time necessities. Some of these were in the form of direct

---

[6] "The Movement in Action," *New Defense, A Journal of the 30,000 Industrial Cooperatives Movement in China* (Chungking) Vol. I, no. 1 (April 1939), p. 5.

medical and military supplies; others, replacements of indispensable articles which otherwise would have been procured from the enemy. The second zone, of light industry, was within easy reach of Japanese air raids and espionage, and consequently given to enterprises having light capital investment, mobile, and readily concealed. The third, or inmost Chinese zone, being best protected, was the proper area for the development of the heavier industries, although even 'here no grandiose or heavily centralized works are planned. The ultimate aim, peace-time as well as military, of the C.I.C. is to distribute industry across the countryside, replacing the once flourishing handicraft industries, and allowing Chinese society to develop naturally and continuously.

The author attended a C.I.C. exhibit in Chungking which presented a startling array of modern goods. Ford tools and auxiliary parts, matches, lamps (electric, kerosene, and an improved wood-oil lamp which equals kerosene), light electric appliances, lathes, machine-shop tools, medical kits, Western shoes, toothpaste, canned foods, paper, printing presses, books, and fountain pens—all were produced in areas which did not even have the spinning wheel in some instances, and which until recently imported all Western or modern goods from the coast or from outside.

The organization and practical accomplishments of the C.I.C. are well summarized in a recent article by K. P. Liu, Secretary-General:

INTRODUCTION: When it became clear that in order to continue economic resistance against Japan China must at all costs develop production in the rear of the fighting line, one of the steps taken was the founding of the Chinese Industrial Cooperatives by Dr. H. H. Kung.

The plan was to construct throughout China chains of small industries which should use local materials to supply the manufactured goods fundamentally necessary to the life of the people.

Industrial cooperative societies are organized around about 60 depots over 16 provinces. An average depot of about 25 cooperatives is supervised and advised by a group of men consisting of depotmaster, accountant, technician, and two or three organizers.

For the coordination of work depots are divided among five regions: the Northwest (NW), the Southeast (SE), the Chuankang (Szechwan and Sikang) region (CK), the Southwest (SW), and Yunnan (Y). Each is headed by regional headquarters, which are responsible to the Central Headquarters at Chungking which represents the C.I.C. on general questions and negotiations, and decides, in consultation with regional chiefs, on broad lines of policy. The Central Headquarters also supplies the services of traveling advisers on engineering, accounting, and organization problems.

The staff of 700 is financed by Government funds, since the C.I.C. has been named a social organization responsible to the Executive Yüan. Further, the C.I.C. was given $5,000,000 by the Central Government to be used as loan capital for cooperatives. More recently, negotiations with various banks have made new large sums available, so that the amount which can now be used for the capitalization of cooperatives is near $30,000,000.

The above two sources of income provide no money for education, research, evacuation of workers from occupied areas, technical training, refugee work relief, medical help, or capital loans in guerrilla regions. Necessary auxiliary activities as these are provided for to a certain extent by gifts from interested men and women in China and abroad . . .

FORMING AN INDUSTRIAL COOPERATIVE: When a depot is first set up, the depotmaster advertises the objectives of the C.I.C. by posters and speeches. But as soon as a few workmen get to know about its activities there is no more need to advertise. There are always plenty of workers who will prefer the security and freedom of a cooperative to unemployment or to working for a master.

The number of men needed to form a cooperative is at least seven, but there is no upper limit. They first come to talk things over with a C.I.C. organizer, present their plan for setting up a factory or workshop, with proof of their qualifications and a tentative budget showing how much loan capital will be needed to start work. The organizer explains to them the cooperative system of self-government,

Chinese cooperative law, and the C.I.C. Model Constitution. Then they take some descriptive literature home, and discuss among themselves whom they want as their officers.

Meanwhile, their plans are talked over by the depotmaster, accountant, organizer, and engineer, and modifications suggested. If, as often happens, it turns out that they are only merchants anxious to get rich quick and not *bona fide* workmen ready to work hard, the plans are rejected.

If all is satisfactory, a meeting is held for the election of officers, determination of share capital, voting of wages, and work begins as soon as the loan is put through. At least one quarter of the subscribed share capital must be paid up immediately, and the total loan—long-term and short—cannot exceed 20 times the subscribed share capital . . . The actual ratio of share to loan capital averages about 1 to 6.

INDUSTRIAL DISTRIBUTION: Distribution of industry is shown in the following condensed table:

Textiles	610 [cooperatives]
Engineering	49
Mining	118
Chemical	206
Pottery	69
Foodstuffs	83
Transport	4
Miscellaneous	395
	1,534

There are no less than 114 types of cooperatives, and almost every daily need of the people can be met.

Before any cooperative is organized, investigations are made to ensure that (I) there are raw materials near at hand, (II) there is skilled workmanship available, and (III) there is a market for the finished product. Where these three do not co-exist at one place, a compromise of the most reasonable kind is effected if possible. Some examples—by no means exhaustive—of the adaptation of types of industry to meet local conditions are described as follows:

Wool . . . In the beginning of 1939 woolspinners of Chentu were still using either the simple old whorl or the handturned wheel. The volume of production was very small. But during 1939 the C.I.C. embarked on a huge program of blanket production for the army, and improved streamlined treadle spinners were introduced, and thousands of men and women taught the technique of using them. Blankets were made at eight centers of west and northern China; everywhere improved woolspinning and woolweaving machines and techniques brought new productive power. During the winter of 1939–40, 400,000 blankets were turned out, and another million and a half will be made during the remainder of 1940.

The wool used by the blanket-making cooperatives comes from the highlands of Chinghai, Kansu, Ningsia, and Shensi, and now instead of being carried raw to Tientsin or Shanghai as in the old days, it is being spun and woven near to the source of supply. Improvements are constantly being made—better machines, finer spinning, use of waterpower, better carding and finishing—so that the whole project works to raise the efficiency and living standard of the local people.

Cotton. Wherever cotton is grown spinning and weaving cooperatives are numerous, for clothing is one of the fundamental needs of life. . . .

Grass Cloth. Linen, or more correctly grass cloth, was introduced into Szechwan from Kwangtung generations ago, and now fine cloth is woven. Production thereof from ramie thread was at its height 20 years ago, but since then the craft has declined until recently, when the partial blockade of the war made the industry profitable again. . . .

Goldwashing. Placer gold exists along every river in West China and in many parts of South China too. Even in Chungking one may see needy coolies scraping up and washing riverside mud for its tiny precious content.

The gold is easily available by simple methods, though certain difficulties have hitherto prevented its extraction on a larger scale. But now every grain is an asset to China in economic warfare, and so many goldwashing cooperatives have been organized. In the whole country there are 66 cooperatives, most of which are in the Han valley. . . . Now the cooperatives . . . are self-supporting and produce 60 to 70 oz. of gold a day.

Coal and Iron. Throughout the hinterland of China new sources of coal and iron are being needed continually by newly transplanted industry. Szechwan has good coal, widespread, but rather thin in seam. . . .

At the same time plans for the construction of blast furnaces have been worked out by C.I.C. engineers, and only wait for adequate financing. It is planned first to set up in South Shensi at a point within easy distance of coal and iron supplies a coke-making and a smelting plant, the total capitalization being $105,000.

Alcohol. A first experimental plant for the production of 96 per cent pure alcohol has been running nearly a year with a maximum output of 350 gallons a day. Since the cost of such a plant is comparatively small, and available supplies of grain make the cost of alcohol much less than that of gasoline, other plants have been set up. There are now six in operation and greater production in the future is envisaged. The sites of alcohol plants are naturally at key positions on the highway, where good supplies of coarse grain meet with the traffic line.

Prime Movers. In many cooperatives one may see a quaint mixture of old and new, where big flywheels are turned by human labor to maintain the spin of lathes, carding machines, and the like. This is a useful temporary expedient, possible where labor is cheap. Animal power is also used.

But C.I.C. engineers are not satisfied with this state of affairs; they are always on the lookout for new sources of power. So charcoal- or gasoline-burning internal combustion engines are commonly employed.

But most popular are waterwheels, and in every part of China will be found old wheels adapted for modern uses —driving textile machinery, turning lathes, grinding flour— undershot or overshot, single or in series. Gradually the wheels are being made of better materials and more efficient. Iron wheels are constructed at present weighing about one ton, at a cost of $3,000, and generating over 30 H.P.

In the plains waterpower is rarely available, but in the foothills of Tibet, the Tsingling Shan, or in the rough country of southern China this cheapest of all forms of power will come more and more into its own as C.I.C. machine shops construct improved waterwheels.

ACCOUNTING: During the past two years the C.I.C. staff has tackled the question of modern accounting wholeheartedly in every depot, and training classes in cost accounting have been given for cooperative accountants who only know old style Chinese bookkeeping. C.I.C. trained accountants have been allocated to cooperatives—for big cooperatives one accountant is employed by each society, for small, one accountant serves two or three. Emphasis has been placed on the presentation of monthly balance sheets and yearly closing of accounts with profit sharing.

Profits are divided among the members once—or in rare cases twice—a year. The usual method of division, all claims including interest on loans and shares having first been paid, is as follows:

Reserves	20 per cent
Emergency Fund	10 per cent
Bonus to Officers of Society	10 per cent
Common Good Fund	10 per cent
Divided among Members	50 per cent

The division accords with Chinese Law. The bonus to officers is usually made to include gifts to apprentices and hired workers such as cooks, and the Common Good Fund is used for education, medical welfare, and other social service. The division among members is made in strict proportion to wage and time worked.

Local conditions and various industries differ so much that no wage-policy has at present been applied. In general it may be said that wages in cooperatives—fixed by the members themselves—are about the same as those in private factories of the district. The products in general sell at prevailing rates, though in some cases the prices have been lowered and profiteering prevented by the action of the cooperatives.

COOPERATIVE FEDERATIONS: Wherever the societies have passed the first short period of infantile dependence on the C.I.C. they have been associated into federations, sometimes according to trade, but more often and more wholesomely, according to districts. The most important immediate function of the federation is to open a supply and marketing agency, which by its centralization, specialization, and greater supply of circulating capital is able to relieve the cooperatives of most of their problems of buying and selling. . . .

TRAINING: Training of organizers is of vital importance, for it is they who will succeed or fail in giving to the workers true conceptions of cooperation, industry, and business, and in inculcating efficient methods and habits. Classes for organizers have consequently been held in every region.

Training of cooperative chairmen in their duties is also

undertaken. They "learn by doing,"—how to conduct meetings, business principles, cooperative law, history of cooperation, scope and significance of industrial cooperation in China. . . . The most usual training is by weekly night classes and meetings. There is also constant informal training by the organizers, who devote about one day a week to each cooperative, and work with the members on the solution of immediate problems by the application of cooperative principles. Popular education of workers will be described later.

Another important aspect of training is technical. In no case is a society organized until the technical ability of the members is adequate for making a successful business. So, with refugees and unskilled peasants it is usually necessary to give preliminary training—mainly in textiles. Wherever there is textile work, training classes have been held in spinning and weaving. . . .

SOCIAL WELFARE WORK: No statistics have been compiled about the social contribution of the C.I.C. to the communities around its depot. The work varies according to local needs and opportunities, and according to available resources in funds and manpower. . . .

OUTLOOK: After the war there will undoubtedly come a period of readjustment, when the renewed influx of machinery and machine-finished goods will demand a shift of emphasis—for instance handspinning cannot survive indefinitely, no matter how essential it is at present. It is to be expected that at that period the C.I.C. will continue to use in some industries methods now employed, but that in others there will be a transition to rationalization and mechanization. With a soundly integrated network of skilled workmen, experienced engineers, and bankers' confidence, the C.I.C. will be able to make this transition without severe dislocation.

The C.I.C. is essentially a non-political organization; its functions are all technical, and its staff is composed of experts in various lines—cooperative methods, accounting, engineering. Success does not depend on political position or power, but on the simple and essential condition that this type of industry produces efficiently the goods that China needs. The C.I.C. objective is just Dr. Sun Yat-sen's Third Principle—People's Livelihood—practically expressed.

The success of cooperative movements in other parts of the world—their ability to weather economic crises and depressions—has been due to the solidarity that comes when the motive force in industry and commerce is not the profit of a few but the livelihood of many. In the same way the C.I.C. can become a permanent force for national stability and strength.[7]

The Model Constitution for an Industrial Cooperative [8] establishes safeguards to keep the cooperatives from becoming profiteering sweatshops. Bankrupts, drug addicts, persons incapable of working, and persons already members of a unit are forbidden to join a unit being formed (*Art.* 7). No member may subscribe more than 20 per cent of the share capital of a single society (*Art.* 9). A general annual meeting, with the quorum set at one-half, and action requiring the majority of a quorum, is the highest authority in a unit (*Art.* 19). This meeting elects a board of directors and a separate board of supervisors (*Arts.* 22 and 23). Sweeping disqualifications keep members from mixing personal or outside interests and cooperative matters (*Art.* 32). The design of the unit constitution is such that each unit is an authentic, autonomous cooperative, governed well or badly in accordance with the abilities and needs of its members, and is not a mere fraction of state capitalism.

The C.I.C. taps a level of Chinese society hitherto largely unused [9]—the family, guild, village, and volunteer-society devices of the peasantry and townsmen who lived beneath the lowest limits of the scholastic bureauc-

[7] The China Information Committee, *News Release,* July 15, 1940. The article and tables have been somewhat abridged. The cooperatives spread so rapidly that figures are often obsolete before they are tabulated.

[8] "Model Constitution for Chinese Cooperative Societies, Revised July 7th, 1940," The China Information Committee, *News Release,* July 15, 1940.

[9] Nevertheless, the rural cooperative movement must be counted in as having made some beginnings, despite the obstacles it has faced. More than seventy thousand credit and marketing cooperatives were in service last year. (The same, April 22, 1940.)

racy. The Communists act as the inheritors to temporarily fanatical peasant rebellions; the National Government and Kuomintang, to ascendant mandarinates; the C.I.C. brings into play the rich experience of the Chinese with collective action. The resources of the social power so mobilized cannot easily be estimated, but general success would reshape much of Chinese society.

In fitting the C.I.C. to the general Chinese scene, however, it is important to compare the movement with some of the New Deal reforms in the United States, such as T.V.A. (Tennessee Valley Authority). Though these are important, neither the American nor the Chinese enterprises proclaim social revolution or charter Utopias. The reforms of President Roosevelt have had incalculable effect; no one knows what would have happened without them. Nevertheless, it is excessive to suggest that the existence of the United States as a political society depends upon these reforms. Similarly, the continuation of the National Government of China does not rest on the C.I.C., or on any other single institution alone.

The C.I.C. extends patterns of cooperation and farm-factory balance already tried in Europe, and also approached by such diverse agencies as the Soviet state and collective farms, and Mr. Henry Ford's worker-garden plans. Hitherto the Chinese cooperative workers have had a closer contact with Dearborn, Michigan, than with Moscow, R.S.F.S.R. The endeavor is a serious and important one. It supplements and develops the facilities—themselves very extensive—which are under full state-capitalist or private control. But Free China's markets, while they contain C.I.C.-made goods, are mostly filled with private or government products. A private Chinese business system which has survived thirty years of domestic war does not obsolesce instantaneously. The cooperative movement is, largely because of the integrity, enthusiasm, and tirelessness of Mr. Alley, the nearest thing to a realization of *min shêng* which China has yet seen; but the Right still plans for a China with vast state-capitalist and state-subsidized private industries, along with an all-pervading flow of *laissez-faire* commerce. The Marxians look on sympathetically but contemptuously.

Unorganized Pressure

The long one-party rule of the Kuomintang, now relaxed but not disestablished, has habituated the Chinese to the use of completely non-political groups—families and their connections; economic associations of various kinds; religious agencies—for political leverage. There are relatively few groups which possess clear public purposes and at the same time maintain unofficial status. Indeed, the stamp of quasi-official approval is so highly prized that many groups which seem to have no affiliation with the government are discovered to seek affiliation or to have acquired it roundabout.

Among the private or quasi-private groups which take most effect may be mentioned, however, the People's Foreign Relations Association, the League of Nations Union, and the China Branch of the International Peace Campaign. The first of these publishes the useful quarterly, *The China Herald*. The Campaign, which was launched as a world-wide center-and-left drive for peace, was under respected European leadership, and was favored by a large labor bloc in England. In the United States it was associated in the minds of some people with the Stalinist fellow-travellers—the elements who sat in the councils of the temporarily-joined forces of anti-Fascism and pro-Stalinism, who organized the American League for Peace and Democracy (a Popular Front movement), the American Friends of the Chinese People, and who dominated groups such as the

American Youth Congress. In China, contrariwise, the International Peace Campaign, fitting in with purposes of government and people, seemed to offer a world-wide sympathy for China's anti-aggression activities. The China Branch was among the most effective organizations in the Campaign. It developed vitality in diffusing peace propaganda—that is, for peace after the war. There was no trace of defeatism, sabotage of national defense, or obstruction to defensive war. With the outbreak of the European war, the I.P.C. disappeared almost altogether from the Western scene, but continues in China. Finally, the China League of Nations Union publishes *The China Forum,* and carries on an educational campaign.

Christian activities have been extended and activized by war. Never before have the missions had as many opportunities for social and national service in China. Their schools are filled; their hospitals, crowded; their cause, related to America, to peace, and to a sane long view, is welcomed. The Chinese Y.M.C.A. has met the shock of war with extensive participation in relief, particularly among students and soldiers. Medical aid, tragically inadequate but infinitely better than nothing at all, is coming into China. The curtailment of mission activities in occupied China makes exploitation of the Christian field in the West even more desirable from the viewpoint of the Western churches. A recent work, by two Christians born in China, one American and the other Chinese, describes this situation clearly and significantly: *China Rediscovers Her West.*[10]

The other side of extra-political pressure comes in the form of class and regional interests. The phenomena of lobbying and special favor are less evident in Chungking than in previous governments of China. Special groups representing industries, areas, or vested interests do appear, but are apt to work through casual,

[10] Wu Yi-fang and Price, Frank W., editors; New York, 1940.

untraceable patterns of personal relationships. There is no Chinese C.I.O., nor A. F. of L., but there is also no National Association of Manufacturers. The politics of economics gains by diffusion and absence of protest what it loses in sensitivity and explicitness. An economic group which feels itself outraged takes a long time to develop group consciousness; hence, it is less apt to feel outraged, and the generality of the people, the public, is often better off. There are undoubtedly scurrilous, politically vile, selfish advantages being taken in West China today; but the net outcome is counterbalanced by concrete improvement in the condition of the people as a whole, and the unquestionable morale of the leading and administrative classes.

Every government, where and however it may operate, has a double set of barriers which form its corridor of further existence: on the left it must meet the minimal needs of the governed, satisfy their physical and moral appetites sufficiently to keep itself from being ignored or overthrown; on the right it must compensate the persons who govern, and do so well enough to retain personnel adequate to government. The Marxians stress the former element; the Paretians, the latter. Both are visible in China. Had the exigencies of reform, social change, and military activity proved too sharp, too violent, too profitless, the personnel trained by experience and fitted by temperament to government might have gone over to Japan. The low caliber of Wang Ch'ing-wei and his clique is testimony to the *élan* of the West Chinese leaders. Chungking has ample reserves of administrative talent, military intelligence, and political acumen upon which to draw.

The last part of the picture is the most important: the *lao-pai-hsing,* the Old Hundred Names, the common people of China. They are the ultimate arbiters of this war, and of all future wars in East Asia: to this degree they are a superlative force in the world. Hundreds of millions strong, adept, flexible, trained in a culture which has flowed under (but not through) literacy for centuries, hard-working, patient, and physiologically sound, they are perhaps the greatest unified human group. Upon their anger against Japan depends the future of that Empire; if the *lao-pai-hsing* are determined to resist, Chiang could go, Chungking fall, the government scatter, the Communists collapse, and there would yet be war—restless, bitter, implacable, with the ferocity of a sane man employing violence as a last defense against violence not sane. Leaders exist aplenty in that sea of men, waiting for circumstance to cast them forth. Intelligence, information, cunning, power, and patience are all at hand.

The difference between a strange half-industrial modern Chinese Republic, striding toward the twenty-first century with seven-league boots of progress, and a Chinese chaos stinking with vice and disease under Japanese rule—this difference lies within the decision of the common people. The war has roused the workers, peasants, and petty townsmen. The Japanese bombers have carried ubiquitous messages of alarm. The Western world gasped when across the dusty plains of North China there rolled the tidal wave of Boxerism; but the *I Ho Ch'üan* of yesteryear is a passing fad in contrast to the bitterness and resolution of today's common people. There is no defeat in most of the faces in Shanghai, no surrender in the eyes of men who live, and must keep on living, surrounded by enemy vainglory. The traitors are marked by their own behavior; they bear the stigmata of a surrender to vice. Yet even they cannot be trusted by Japan. One who has visited the sources and the mouths of the rivers, who has seen the free Yangtze pouring out of Tibet and the captive Yangtze ripple past the grey flanks of Imperial Japanese destroyers, can testify that the Chinese people are not beaten now. If they are ever going to be beaten, it will take a bigger force than Japan to do it—a morally greater, technically surer, politically wiser force.

The Chinese people know they are unconquered. They do not know it with their minds, despite hopeful calculations in terms of years and yen and reserves of oil. They do not even know it with a conscious assumption of faith, a fanatical determination to die for the new state. They know it just as men have always known the simplest things of life—things so simple that they may trouble the psychologist or elude the philosopher, and never even enter the vocabulary of political science. The Chinese sense of victory is like a reminiscent fragrance, a half-heard but poignant sound, a flash of inexpressible but profound meaning out of everyman's irrecoverable past. This omnipresent sense of victory and freedom may be twisted. Weak and cunning men rationalize this sense of victory into self-deceiving subterfuges of boring from within; they accept Japanese salaries while promising themselves sometime, always tomorrow, to subvert Japan; but even they lack no assurance of ultimate Chinese victory.

The winning of that victory lies on the sweating backs of men—in paddy-fields, on flaring highways, on flagstone pathways across a world, or behind the adobe and lattice walls of China's workshops. The war has conjured up an awareness of power. No one asks the *lao-pai-hsing* what they want; no ballots, no polls can reach them. But no people can hold such overt power and be unconscious of their own strength. China has awakened.

Dr. Sun Yat-sen

Chapter IX

SUN YAT-SEN AND CHIANG K'AI-SHEK

THE two highest offices in the Kuomintang are *Tsung-li* (Leader) and *Tsung-ts'ai* (Chief). These are occupied by Sun Yat-sen as Leader and Chiang K'ai-shek as Chief. Sun Yat-sen, though he died on March 12, 1925, holds the higher office in perpetuity. So vast is his legacy to modern China that it exceeds full enumeration: founder of the effective revolutionary movement and Party, first practical republican, political organizer of the modern and overseas Chinese, first President of the Republic, and therefore officially acknowledged State Founder, a drafter of the national plan of modernization, author of the accepted ideology (*San Min Chu I*), initiator of the Nationalist-Communist entente and of the consequent Great Revolution, promulgator of the Outline of National Reconstruction, and posthumous patron of the National Government. Keenly and devotedly an advocate of democracy, Sun Yat-sen established by practical example the principle of charismatic leadership. He most certainly left a mantle. This is now, after years of struggle, draped about the shoulders of Chiang K'ai-shek, although Wang Ch'ing-wei retains a few threads torn from the hem.

Sun Yat-sen was a leader in the sense that the great religious and philosophical figures have been leaders. He is not to be compared to Alexander, Genghis Khan, Napoleon, or Hitler, but to Confucius, Gautama Buddha, or Mohammed. Like the spiritual leaders he blended profound humility and complete assurance.

He knew that he was the savior of China, and knew it long before anyone else did. He did not rely on rising to power within a party, as did Lenin, or within a state, as did Hitler. He created his own Party and his own state. Had he not succeeded, he would have been labelled a maniac; so would most of the other major figures of human history, had they failed. His success, whatever its future fortune, is already so immense that it makes his sense of leadership seem modest. And within the limits of success, he was very modest; throughout life Sun remained more open-minded, ready to consult, deferential to the opinions of others, and more willing to yield power for the sake of harmony than the majority of his compeers. This duality has troubled some of his biographers. As late as 1939 an anonymous Englishman published an attack on Sun, which, missing the history of six decades, failed to note that Sun had lived, had succeeded, and had died objectively justified in his conception of himself.

Sun's example, unconsciously at variance with his teachings, has left a strong Caesarian strain in practical Chinese politics. Without Sun Yat-sen in the background, it is altogether impossible to understand the role played by Chiang, or to resolve the contradiction between a state pledged to democracy and a leader overloaded with power. No group in China, except the officials of Manchoukuo, disavows Sun Yat-sen: the Japanophiles, the Nationalists, and the Communists all claim to execute his will.

Sun Yat-sen

Sun Yat-sen was born in Kwangtung Province, near the Portuguese city of Macao. Although he was uncertain of the date, the National Government has found it to be November 12, 1866. Both his provincial and class background had effect on his later life. The Cantonese are among the most turbulent of Chinese, living at the southern edge of China and speaking a dialect far different from the majority of the country. Active, rebellious, enterprising, the Cantonese were disposed to change. Sun's use of their tongue and knowledge of their customs gave him an audience which both suffered and profited by its distinctness. Sun's family was certainly not of the gentry class, and yet not so utterly poor that it lacked all profitable connections. Otherwise his potentialities might have been thwarted by ruinous poverty, disease, or early death.

In adolescence, Sun felt the stings and urges of resentment driving him to reform and revolution. He had kin who were involved in the T'aip'ing Rebellion (1850–65), the vast peasant uprising which, under Christian collectivist leadership by the Messianic Hung Hsiu-ch'üan, swept North to the Yangtze and drowned in a sea of blood less than two years before Sun's birth. He thus had direct knowledge not merely of Chinese revolt against the alien Manchu empire, but he knew of the revolutionary technique of a religious leader. The effect of this presumptive knowledge has never been explored; it would explain a great deal in Sun's career—much of the sharp enthusiasm, the use of ecstatic slogans, the emphasis on will, his demands for faith in himself—if one could know that he followed the instance of a Chinese Joseph Smith or Brigham Young, not that of a Chinese Mazzini or Marx. The other important feature about his early life was Western education.[1]

[1] *Sun Yat-sen* is the Cantonese pronunciation of *Sun I-hsien*, just as *Chiang K'ai-shek* is that of *Chiang Chieh-shih*. Both men first acquired their world reputations under this pronunciation, which has become standard in English. According to Chinese custom, one's given name is used only by one's elders; consequently Sun Yat-sen has been referred to, by his grateful followers, by his "courtesy name" Wên, which is the name by which one refers to one's elder. In addition, he is referred to by another special name which he took for conspiratorial work, Chung-shan (allusive to an ancient hero), or by his title—as *Tsung-li* or Sun *Tsung-li*, much as we refer to President Wil-

Western training gave him a channel upward which the Confucian system had denied a hundred generations of his predecessors. Patriots, rebels, reformers— these have been sown by temperament and fortune across the centuries of Chinese social existence, but such potential heroes have been ploughed out or crippled by the language and the examinations. No man could command power—save in its transient forms: banditry, conspiracy, commerce—without mastering the Confucian canon. Once the intricate scholarship of the past gripped him, the complex, beautiful, archaic language of the mandarinate stopped up his mouth for plain utterance. He was isolated from the people. Sun escaped this by the use of the English language and the command of Western science. He was par excellence the great counter-ideologue, whose self-confidence and command of men rested upon foundations beyond the ken of his adversaries. Judge Linebarger wrote, on the basis of what Sun told him:

> Like a soldier who after long study and practice has at length mastered the manual of arms so as to have complete confidence in his weapons, Sun now began to feel at last a confidence in his ability to show others the path of his new wisdom, for, while thus enjoying a steady advance under English tutelage in the ways of the foreigner, he was by no means neglecting his study of Chinese politics, even in the pressure of college work. He knew now that he would have to lead out in the Great Reform. At Hong Kong, Macao, and Canton he had college intimates, and these he sought out as often as his college course would permit.[2]

---

son rather than to Woodrow Wilson. Sun was known most widely in life as Sun Wên; Chiang is most commonly mentioned as Chiang Chung-chêng. The question of names is extensively discussed in the biographies of the two leaders, cited below.

[2] Linebarger, Paul [M. W.], *Sun Yat-sen and the Chinese Republic*, New York and London, 1925, p. 176; this is the authorized life of Sun Yat-sen, written much as he wished it. The standard critical biography is Sharman, Lyon, *Sun Yat-sen: His Life and Its Meaning*,

Sun lived with his elder brother in Honolulu on two occasions, and finally, after a period of discontent and rising turbulence at home, went to study medicine in Hong Kong. He was the outstanding student in the school because of his already fluent command of the English language,[3] and was graduated as one of the very first Chinese physicians to be trained in Western medicine. Through their very nature, medical studies impart to the student a sense of responsibility for others, and also incline them toward the expert's indifference to lay opinion. Throughout his life Sun never lost confidence in the powers of his own reason, or in the belief that, although difficult, it was both necessary and possible to know the form and nature of social no less than of biological processes, and to prescribe remedies for an ill civilization as well as for a sick man.

With traditional patriotism, a Cantonese background, the memory of poverty, foreign training, and contact with overseas China, Sun was already a marked man in his twenties. By 1895 he was important enough for the Imperial Chinese Legation in London to kidnap him, preparing to charter a ship to return him to China, where the torturers of the Board of Punishments waited. In a *cause célèbre,* Sun was released; from then on he had an international reputation.

His technique of revolution was little affected by the growing proletarian parties of Europe. He adhered to traditional Chinese methods, working through the con-

---

New York, 1934. Sun Yat-sen also wrote a number of short autobiographies, some of which are deliberately inexact. Western language material on Sun is surveyed in an annotated bibliography appended to the present author's *The Political Doctrines of Sun Yat-sen,* Baltimore, 1937, p. 265 *ff.* A work which has since appeared is "Sagittarius," *The Strange Apotheosis of Sun Yat-sen,* London, 1939.

[3] Statement to the author by Wên Chung-yao, President of the Legislative *Yüan* of the Reorganized National Government of Wang Ch'ing-wei, at Nanking, September 5, 1940. Dr. Wên was a classmate of Dr. Sun at Queen's College.

solidation of pre-existent secret societies, the recruitment of terrorists, the launching of insurrection after insurrection in the hope that one of them would catch the waiting tinder and blaze across China. In Japan, in America, and in Europe, he travelled, gathering funds, carrying on vigorous polemics against his fellow-exiles, the monarchist reformers. His followers were organized under a variety of names, of which Kuomintang is the last and best-known. By 1911 the revolution broke out, flared sporadically across the central and southern provinces, then lapsed into negotiations between the Republicans and the Empire. Sun Yat-sen, in America when the clash was precipitated, returned home to be elected Provisional President of the Chinese Republic, on January 1, 1912. But his revolution had begun to pass into other hands. Opportunists, no rare breed in China, leapt aboard the bandwagon, minimizing the role of the Nationalists and grasping for the materials of power: offices, guns and money, slogans. The new-born Republic was taken over by the formidable Yüan Shih-k'ai and converted into a pyramid of military dictatorships; with Yüan's death the nation fell into *tuchünism* and foreign meddling.

The years following were the saddest in Sun's life. He headed miscellaneous governments in Canton, lived for a while in Shanghai, and died at a fruitless unification conference in Peking. In his last years, obsessed by his clear realization of the evils which beset his country, he was even derided. He saw the vast economic maladjustments which would follow the World War, and wrote a work, *The International Development of China*[4] which in its grandeur anticipated the Five-Year and Four-Year Plans; his idea was to finance a spectacular modernization of China through public works by a scheme of international loans. Not only would the imports of capital goods have benefited the Western

[4] New York, 1922; reissue, 1929.

powers, but the development of a prosperous China would have provided the expansion necessary to support an imperialist capitalism. His argument was that international capitalism needed a market; China, one fourth of humanity, provided a market; international guarantees and supervision would make modernization possible; and modernization, while building state-socialism and the material basis of prosperity in China, would have enriched capitalism throughout the world. There is no evidence that anyone save his followers and friends took his plan seriously.

The next step, in 1922, was a turning from capitalist democracies, which had disappointed him, to a Russia which professed a new justice in the world. Sun negotiated with emissaries of the Third International, accepting Red help on the clear understanding that Communism was recognized, by him and by the Communists, as unsuited to China—a proposition which history calls into question. Only in his last stay in Canton did he escape the ten-year pattern of frustration which had been broken only by his happy second marriage, to Soong Ching-ling. (The author, then a small boy, remembers Sun in Shanghai as a man of gentle kindness and rueful gaiety; Sun was never too busy to speak to him, nor to remember little presents; and in the midst of revolution Sun found time to write a note of encouragement and good cheer.) With the new allies, Sun, a dying man, went South, founded the lineal predecessors of the Chungking government, called his comrades to him, and discovered an effective military helper—his first after Huang Hsing, dead in the years of Yüan. This military aide was Chiang K'ai-shek.

Just before his death Sun made sixteen lectures, out of a scheduled program of eighteen. He did not write them, but they were transcribed and roughly edited. In other years he had drafted monumental political treatises; when the manuscripts were lost he did not reconstruct them. The lectures, improvised, filled with minor inaccuracies, incomplete arguments, and appeals to immediate opinion, rank nevertheless among works of political genius. They are sharp, stirring, pointed, hopeful, concrete. They define China's position in the world, and the goals of the Chinese revolution. They adumbrate the reinforced democracy which was to come and now fights for existence. And they prescribe an economic philosophy humane beyond the dogma of the Russo-German dialecticians and far more self-conscious than the obstinate torpor of Coolidge's capitalism. Sun's lectures are today the foundation of the Chinese state philosophy, taught in all curricula, required in all examinations. As the *San Min Chu I,* they form an ideology with more legal adherents than Marxism and National Socialism and Fascism combined. For democrats, wherever they may be, this is a matter of importance, bearing directly on the confused uncanalized struggles of our time. China possesses a doctrine which indefeasibly associates her independence, her democracy, and her prosperity.

It would be a mistake to consider these lectures and Sun's lesser writings the only source of Sun Yat-sen's dogma. Since the government is in the hands of the Kuomintang, and Kuomintang seniority depends largely on closeness of association with Sun Yat-sen, Sun's personal, casual, unconsidered influence on his friends forms a vital background to state policy. Sun's American biographer wrote,

> Some criticize the *San Min Chu I,* because it seems to them severe and lofty. To this I reply that there are things other than what is written in the *San Min Chu I.* The English and other nations have their laws, written and unwritten. So too do we, the partisans of Sun Yat-sen, have our laws, written and unwritten. And this unwritten law is to us the dearer, is closer to our hearts, and is more moving as the goal of our activity, than even the written com-

mentaries. This unwritten law is for us, who, sitting at his feet, received his teaching, the highest of all laws of truth and fidelity, the law of *bona fides*.⁵

The continuing power of Sun Yat-sen is shown by the prestige and power of his kin. Sun Yat-sen had two families. Early in life, before his medical studies had ended, he was married to a woman of his own class who was devoted, family-loving, characteristically Chinese, untouched by the West, and undisposed to revolution. She bore him three children; the son, Dr. Sun K'ê, was reared largely in the United States and has been an important figure in Chinese politics ever since his return to China from Columbia University. Successively Mayor of Canton, Chairman of Kwangtung Province, Minister of Communications, of Finance, and of Railways, President of the Executive and of the Legislative *Yüan*, he has served with distinction. A practical and moderate man, he has always advocated a moderate, constitutional application of his father's dogma, has espoused full democratic government, stood for Party abdication, and worked for national unity. One of his sisters died young and the other married a gentleman who was later Chinese Minister to Brazil. Mrs. Sun Yat-sen, Sun K'ê's mother, lived to a ripe old age in Macao. Charitable, pious, humane, she was an enthusiastic Christian convert and a terror to sluggard officials in that European outpost of vice. She took no part in politics.

Sun Yat-sen's second family was acquired when he married Miss Soong Ching-ling. After his defeat by Yüan Shih-k'ai and the frustration of the first Republic, Sun Yat-sen felt very much in need of a companion to hearten him, help his work, and share his troubles. He had been on very close terms with C. J. Soong, a

⁵ Linebarger, Paul Myron, *Mes Mémoires Abrégés sur les Révolutions de Sun Yat-sen*, Paris, 1938, p. 194. Paragraphing deleted in translation from the French.

Christian business man, and had asked Mr. Soong's eldest daughter, Ai-ling, to act as his secretary. When Miss Ai-ling Soong left, her sister succeeded her. Sun fell genuinely and deeply in love with the beautiful, vivacious, American-educated girl who understood his work and desired to share his troubles. In all his life, it is likely that Sun met no one more devoted to himself, more understanding of what he sought from life and from his work for China, than Ching-ling Soong. They were married on October 15, 1915, in Japan, Sun Yat-sen having provided for separation from his first wife. The younger wife has since become world-famous as Mme. Sun Yat-sen.

Ching-ling and Ai-ling Soong had a third sister,[6] May-ling, who married Chiang K'ai-shek after Ai-ling had married H. H. K'ung. (Hence Chiang K'ai-shek's closest family connection with Sun Yat-sen consists in being brother-in-law to the second wife.) The three Soong sisters thus married the two outstanding leaders and another who stood just below. The Soong brothers were less successful, although one, T. V. Soong, has been a leading fiscal reformer and financial expert.

The beauty, American education, polished cosmopolitan manners, and sense of publicity of the three sisters have made them sensational news figures. Their eldest brother's success has added distinction to this family. The inescapable consequence has been a great deal of speculation about the "Soong dynasty"; but the surprising feature of the Soongs is not their fame and power through marriage, plus ability, but their slight cohesion as a Chinese family. They have stood together only at times of highest crisis, and not always then. Mme. Sun Yat-sen has continued along the Leftist

[6] In the case of Chinese names which are commonly transliterated in an Americanized form, the Western name-order is preserved. According to standard Sinological practice, the three sisters are Sung Ai-ling, Sung Ch'ing-ling, and Sung Mei-ling; their famous brother (T. V. Soong) is Sung Tzŭ-wên.

tangent which her husband followed just before he died. For years she was the only Leftist in China who did not fear death or a more painful fate. She kept her ideals; from the homes of her family she wrote scathing denunciations of the blood-soaked tyranny of her brother-in-law, her sisters, her stepson, and her brother. Mme. K'ung appears to have worked most steadfastly in the interest of the entire family, although rivalry between her brother and her husband has been a matter of general report. Mme. Chiang K'ai-shek, the youngest of the three sisters, has been a loyal wife first of all, and has contributed enormously to the Generalissimo's international prestige. No other modern leader possesses an able publicity adviser, capable and apt, so near to himself. The family relationships of Sun Yat-sen thus display themselves in his son, constitutional and moderate, who is inclined to favor Mme. Sun, with Sun's sisters-in-law and brothers-in-law following their respective political courses with their own families—all on cordial political terms, but scarcely a monolithic family bloc.

In addition to his doctrine, his Party, his followers, and his family, Sun Yat-sen has bequeathed his name. As Chung Shan, he fills the void in Chinese polity left by the Emperor. Every Monday morning his will is read, throughout every government office in the land. His picture is seen everywhere. His sayings and slogans have become the shibboleths of revolution, union, and reconstruction. The reverence paid to him is a form of secular worship, focussed upon a magnificent mausoleum near the cenotaphs of the Ming Emperors on Purple Mountain, Nanking. All virtues and most knowledge are attributed to him; inescapably, some hard-headed people react against the cult. Dead, he is to the Chinese what the King is to the British, or the assembled forefathers to the Americans, or—save partial eclipse by Stalin—Lenin is to the Soviet Union. Perpetual leader of the Kuomintang, Sun has in death more power than life vouchsafed him. In a world wild with alarm and hungry for leadership, his sense of providential mission and of terrible political urgency no longer seems shrill or vain. His is the greatest of posthumous satisfactions: vindication by history.

The San Min Chu I

Out of the broad body of doctrine embodied in the public and private utterances of Sun Yat-sen, one single integrating philosophy stands forth, which entitles him to rank as a major political thinker. This is the *San Min Chu I*, which may be translated "three principles of the people," "three principles of government for the benefit of the people," "three principles concerning people" and so forth, or may—most accurately—be represented by the neologism, "tridemism."[7] It consists of an affirmation of a body of theory and a scheme of programs to be applied generally to human experience, and particularly to the modern problems of China.

The prime problem faced by Sun Yat-sen was displacement of the Confucian ideology, long refreshed and perpetuated by the mandarinate. (The scholastic bureaucracy rested on the difficulty and character of the language, which removed writing from speaking and, lacking what Westerners commonly consider grammar, depended upon exact, appropriate choice of terms.) Confucius, anticipating semantic controversialists by many centuries, established a doctrine of meaning which made politics the by-product of correct speech and thought, to be performed by conspicuous, informed, and majestic persons. When ideas and ideals were clear,

[7] d'Elia, Paschal M., S. J., *The Triple Demism of Sun Yat-sen*, Wuch'ang, 1931, p. 36–49, gives an exhaustive analysis of possible translations. Stylistically, the term should be given *San Min Chu I* as a classical title; *san-min chu-i* as a noun; and *san-min-chu-i* when used as an adjective. The first form alone is followed because of its wide currency.

moral standards firm and visible, and demeanor correct
—as determined by archaic natural standards—the realm
would prosper. Education was stressed as a means to
public service. In succeeding centuries Confucians first
monopolized education, establishing the Confucian
classics as formal Chinese canons, and then monopolized
the bureaucracy. Providing for elementary circulation
of an academic elite, although economically based on
land-ownership, they gave China a modified sort of
representative government, which operated by the all-
encompassing constitutionalism of common sense itself,
and rested ultimately on the lack of an alternative to
common sense. The Confucians were intellectually in-
different to natural science and economically unfriendly
to technological change; China, unsurpassed for political sophistication and deliberate social order, was
immobilized by an ancient success. Ideological control led to veneration of the scholar, even veneration of
writing. Emperors, officials, people—all were captive to
accomplishment, and so completely indoctrinated that
they presumably enjoyed a very high conscious freedom.
Rigid social and mental uniformity spelled political
laxity; the state became atrophied and vestigial.

Social rigidity made China only very slowly progressive in mechanical terms. Political laxity made the
country weak in the face of invasion, exploitation, and
possible partition. Intellectual traditionalism shut off
stimuli available from the outside. Confucius had said,
"If terms be not correct, language is not in accordance
with the truth of things. If language be not in accordance with the truth of things, affairs cannot be carried on to success." [8] Sun Yat-sen, Confucian in spirit
though not in form, turned to the dynamics of ideological rather than legal control. To stir the immense

[8] *The Analects,* Book XIII, Ch. v; Legge, James, *The Chinese
Classics,* Oxford, 1893 [Peiping, 1939], I, p. 93; the word *terms* has been
substituted for *names* in rendering *ming.*

lethargy of China, he substituted science for archaism; a Party elite for the scholastic system, propaganda to replace doctrinal education, and agitation to supersede incantation and reverence.

He struck at ideas first: "We cannot say in general that ideas, as ideas, are either good or bad. We must judge whether, when put into practice, they prove useful or not. If they are of practical use to us, they are good; if they are impractical, they are bad. If they are useful to the world, they are good; if they are not useful to the world, they are not good." [9] This pragmatic utilitarianism was to be the philosophical foundation of his revolution. The *San Min Chu I* therewith remained alien to Marxism, which is dependent upon the occult mysteries of a topsy-turvy Hegelianism; Sun's thought is kin to the working philosophy of America, a pragmatism tinctured by idealist vestiges.

The first political principle he developed was *Nationalism (min ts'u)*. The theoretical basis for this was a racialism which, scientifically no more tenable than National Socialist Aryanism, is clear in common practice. Very few Chinese have trouble in identifying another Chinese. Sun Yat-sen pointed out that although the European peoples were divided, China was to him both a race and a nation. He thereby established for his followers a foundation for nationality more credible than any mere appeal to state allegiance. Treason against one's government is taken lightly in China: witness the Japanophiles. Treason to the Chinese race is a far more serious matter. In order to preserve the Chinese race-nation, Sun Yat-sen called for ideological reconstruction from three elements: ancient Chinese morality, traditional Chinese social knowledge (e.g., bureaucratic techniques; arbitration instead of adjudication), and Western physical science. He urged a return to cosmopolitanism through nationalism. By

[9] d'Elia translation, cited, p. 130–1.

becoming strong—instead of extinct under alien colonial rule—the Chinese state could lead the world back to the old pacific cosmopolitanism of Eastern Asia.

Programmatically, Sun subsumed under his *min t'su* theory, the necessity of a patriotic elite, formed into the party of his followers, which was to unify China and to cultivate a genuine state-allegiance instead of the veneration of a concretely paramount Emperor or other leader. He also advocated that China maintain independence, make independence a reality in which the entire race-nation should share by fostering actual autonomy (hence, democracy), and by fighting defensively against economic exploitation by the imperialist powers.

The second principle presented was *Democracy* (*min ch'üan*). He pointed out that old China was democratic in allowing considerable social mobility, and much equality within the framework of that mobility, and that popular government was a reality in local affairs, while popular supremacy (corresponding to Western theories of popular sovereignty) followed from the universally admitted Chinese right of rebellion. He justified democracy on the grounds that it was commanded by China's antique sages, was necessarily consequent upon nationalism, was decreed by the *Zeitgeist*, was necessary to good administration, and was a modernizing force. But he modified his democracy by a distinction between *ch'üan* (power) and *nêng* (ability), keeping government and people perpetually dual, and making the problem of democratic personnel one of popular choice plus the control of popular choice. The programs of democracy involved the revolution of three stages, the five-*yüan* government, and emphasis on the *hsien*.[10]

The third principle is based on Sun Yat-sen's own philosophy of history. *Min shêng*, frequently trans-

[10] See above, p. 42.

lated "the principle of the people's livelihood," rested upon Sun Yat-sen's belief that history is not based exclusively on materialism and that it cannot be analyzed merely in terms of the ownership of the means of production. He insisted that history was based on the fundamental fact that man has *jên*—humane self-awareness; human fellow-sympathy; consciousness of being located in society, together with orientation by values social, not individually or materially established; benevolence. *Min shêng* is accordingly an ethical doctrine first, and an economic one afterward. It is the basis of history (*min-shêng wei li-shih-ti chung-hsin*). It presupposes, for China: (1) a national economic revolution against imperialism and for democracy; (2) an industrial revolution for the enrichment of China; and (3) a prophylactic against social revolution. Although showing the influence of Karl Marx, Henry George, and the modern American, Maurice William,[11] the doctrine remained Chinese in spirit, pragmatically collectivist in application. Under the programs of *min shêng* Sun included the bold projects for which he had sought all his life, desiring the independent, socially just prosperity of his country.

These doctrines form the constitutional foundation of government action, as well as being the Party credo of the Kuomintang. Whoever proposes policy in China must first square it with the *San Min Chu I*. In this the Generalissimo has combined adroitness with profound sincerity.

Chiang K'ai-shek

Despite a small shelf of biographies, Chiang K'ai-shek remains a personality above and behind the news,

[11] See William, Maurice, *Sun Yat-sen vs. Communism*, Baltimore, 1932, for an appraisal which stresses the importance and degree of this influence; on the opposite side, see "The Alleged Influence of Maurice William on Sun Yat-sen" by P. C. Huang and W. P. Yuen in *T'ien Hsia Monthly*, V, 4 (November 1937), p. 349-76.

not in it. His former teacher and present publicity adviser, Hollington Tong, has written an authorized life, clear, detailed, and well expurgated. The celebrated Sven Hedin published a study of Chiang; virtues, but not specific personality stood forth. An able American newspaperman had recourse to his files, and some Chinese admirers sketched an incredibly soft, lovely picture: the background was clarified, but not Chiang. Two world-famous reporters, trained to epitomize a life or a nation in a double column or sharp review, failed to grasp Chiang. He eludes everyone.

Part of the trouble comes from the fact that he possesses virtues which, once lauded, are now suspected of being mythical, wheresoever they occur. Frederick the Great, George Washington, Julius Caesar in his careerist years—authentic in history, as contemporaries these leaders would strike the moderns as characters inflated or incredible. Sincerity has become consistency with one's source of income; persons who fail to fit into the accepted moral and intellectual types of Western industrialist society are labelled fakes. One is a gentleman-liberal, an intellectual-liberal, a capitalist, a picturesque *native*, a war-lord sinister, obscene, cruel, and criminal—one fits such a type, and if one doesn't, one does not exist. Yet Chiang exists, and is thereby suspect to a host of commentators. Sun Yat-sen as First President was an acceptable news figure; as Saint of the Great Revolution he became vulnerable. When Chiang seems neither a general nor a reactionary, he bewilders many Westerners.

Within China, Chiang is more readily grasped. In any other age, he would be the founder of a new dynasty. The establishers of Imperial houses have, as a group, combined intense vigor with a flair for the disreputably picturesque, in turn qualified by the highly respectable associates they sought out after success. Several have been bandits; one was an unfrocked Buddhist priest.

For vigor and a timely libertarianism, they compare favorably with the Claudian line. Today the Dragon Throne is irrecoverably remote; the Manchoukuoan Emperor Kang Tê lacks elementary plausibility. Chiang is far too wise, far too modern in his own motivations, to wish or dare dream of Empire. Upon him has descended grace of a new kind, the charismatic halo of Sun Yat-sen. His reputation can be carved in the most enduring of materials: indefeasible history. With a son who is a Bolshevik, a little Eurasian grandchild, and an adopted son of no high merit, Chiang does not face the problem of power-bequeathal. He has power now; it matters little where power goes after his death; the value to him lies in immediate use.

Assuming even an abnormal egocentrism, Chiang—at the apex of state—is above ambition; he has no welfare but that of the state. In fact, Chiang is a man of almost naively insistent morality. Even Westerners act on the stage of today with posterity as an audience; Chinese, state-building, moral, Chiang moves under the glare of his perpetual reputation. As in the case of Sun, his sense of leadership would be maniacal if not grounded on fact; but what assumption would not? A peanut-vendor who thinks he is the King of Egypt is crazy; Farouk is not therefore crazy because King of Egypt. If Chiang were not the leader of China, he would be mad; but he, and he alone, is leader. His humility begins with the assumption of his power.

Twenty-one years the junior of Sun Yat-sen, Chiang was born in 1888 in Chekiang province.[12] His family

[12] Biographies of Chiang are: Chen Tsung-hsi *et al.*, *General Chiang Kai-shek, the Builder of New China*, Shanghai, 1929; Tong, Hollington K. (Tung Hsien-kuang), *Chiang Kai-shek, Soldier and Statesman*, 2 vols., Shanghai, 1937, the authorized biography and a model of its kind; Berkov, Robert, *Strong Man of China*, Boston, 1938; and Hedin, Sven, *Chiang Kai-shek, Marshal of China*, New York, 1940. *Who's Who in China* is, as usual, useful for Chiang and for the members of his family. Almost every book on modern China, or magazine dealing with Asiatic materials, has discussions of Chiang.

was of a class intermediate between the truly eminent landlord-official or merchant families, and the farmers. They had been farmers, but also minor gentry, and had been connected with the salt-revenue system. His grandfather attained considerable renown as a scholar, but Chiang's own father died when Chiang was eight years of age. The child had few special advantages. His family background is one which is of common occurrence among political leaders; his widowed mother, mastering and managing for the family, inculcated a sharp morality, an unrelenting frugality, and a persistent drive of industriousness in her children. To such a person, who rises from poverty and hardship by his own efforts, the failure of others to do likewise becomes a personal problem. By his own case he has proved that opportunities are there. He is impatient with the poor, the stupid, or the shiftless; instead of rearranging society to give them a chance, he expects them to improve themselves to meet existing realities. Chiang has not explicitly stated all these points; many of them are qualified by the fact that the *status quo* in modern China is the *status quo* of perpetual revolution.

Leftist commentators, dubbing Chiang a combined product of landlordism, compradore class, and criminal gangs, explain him through a mystagogic economic determinism. Actually, Western impress on Chiang is of a more special nature: Western religion, and Western warfare. The ideals which animate him, and determine —so far as these are visible—his own sense of values, are concepts and attitudes extraneous to the Chinese scene. Deduct the threaded recurrency of religion, and the sense of technique from military training, and

---

Among the most noteworthy writers on his career and personality are Gustav Amann, whose account remains the most carefully detailed; Edgar Snow and John Gunther, the reporters mentioned above; and Harold Isaacs. The Generalissimo's own diary and speeches, together with Mme. Chiang's writings, are unconsciously rather than deliberately revelatory.

Chiang could be paired with many other modern Chinese leaders—soldiers of turmoil, administrators of the *ad interim,* complacent leaders of hypothetical groups. He and Sun stand out because each had a Western technique so thoroughly mastered that it gave him a clear competence over other men: Sun, the physician; Chiang, the strategist. Each also had a Western moral drive which turned hungrily to the past and justified itself in Chinese antiquity: Sun, the all-around Christian, who professed and denied the churches alternately throughout life, and Chiang, the Bible-quoting Methodist, both cite the Confucian canons; both esteem the Chinese ethics; both discern the forcefulness of Western spirituality.

Leadership, plus technical power, plus alien moral reinforcement, spells preeminence. The Confucians have gone; the serene mandarins are dead. Methodist soldiers, Baptist bankers—such Chinese control China. Marxism, which by combining jargon and act of faith, is both religion and erudition, unites these ideocratic forces; Wang Ming can feel that he is a scientist analyzing society with peculiar objectivity, and he can feel morally gratified at the same time. Chiang and the Nationalist leaders keep such sustenance dual.

The special religious background came to him through his mother. Women have traditionally turned to Buddhism for piety in China, and Mrs. Chiang was one of the exceptional characters who combined intense hard work with great piety. The children grew with the infinite looming over them; every misstep meant thousands upon thousands of years of hopeless, damnable rebirth. Buddhism can match the Christian, "It is a fearfull thing to fall into the hands of the living God . . . ,"[13] with the even more fearful doom of life in a world which does not want to live. Buddhism, so-

---

[13] John Donne, in a sermon of commemoration of the Lady Danvers, late wife of Sir John Danvers; 1627.

cially, goes about in circles; the Mahayana sect provides a qualified kind of salvation, but not the salvation which a determined man can wring bloody-handed out of circumstance itself. The discipline, the austerity, were ready; Christianity, when it came to him, fell on plowed and waiting ground. The other instinct of ascendancy was cultivated by his education: professionalism. His life falls into three stages after childhood: education; wasted years; and the mastery and use of power.

Chiang went to the Imperial Military Academy at Paotingfu. Aloof and ambitious, he was so successful that within a year he was sent to the Shinbo Gokyo (Preparatory Military Academy) in Tokyo; he remained in Japan four years. The Japanese under whom he studied retained no special impression of him, except that he eagerly accepted discipline. As a part of his study, he served with the 13th Field Artillery (Takada) Regiment of the Imperial Army. Chiang therewith acquired not merely military knowledge, but a working insight into Japanese language, mentality, and strength.

His military studies were terminated by the outbreak of the Republican Revolution in 1911. Chiang returned to Shanghai, and began a vigorous military career under the local military commander, pro-Sun in politics. Chiang himself had come into contact with the Republican-Nationalist group while in Japan. There was already no question of where his loyalties lay. He made rapid progress, and saw something of fighting. He took part in the abortive Second Revolution, of 1913, which was the military attempt by Sun Yat-sen and his first military coadjutant, Huang Hsing, to check Yüan Shih-k'ai and to save the newborn Republic by force. In this time, while the enthusiasm of his military studies had not yet worn off, Chiang wrote prodigiously. No Westerner has, so far as the present author knows, taken the trouble to go through Chiang's writings in order to study him. Chinese commentators praise them as full of military acumen, a sense of the novel and important forces in Chinese society, and a vigorous moralism—modern-military in form, but archaic in language—which animated Chiang's youthful desire to improve the world with good, technically apt gunfire. He was at this time twenty-three or twenty-four.

Between this early career and the later years of Chiang's life—the years in which his star rode incessantly ascendant—there is a gap of several years, 1913 to 1918. In this time Chiang lived a life primarily civilian, although he remained under the patronage of his first military leader, General Chen Ch'i-mei, murdered in 1915. Chiang went on a military intelligence trip for the Sun Yat-sen group, travelling through Manchuria in 1915. He opposed Yüan's moves, and stayed in close contact with the patriotic organization. Yet, the total picture of his life in these years lacks the connecting linkage which binds his childhood, his school days, and his mature career. His activity, while considerable, was diffuse.

He went down to Canton in 1918, and fought under the command of Sun Yat-sen, with the inferior troops and hopeless expeditions which the Leader, politically adept but strategically inexpert, kept throwing against the confusion of the *tuchün* wars, with the result that the war-lords, counting him as another element in their balance of power, did not even set up a united front against him. Chiang, a Central Chinese, was unsympathetic to the intense provincialism of the Cantonese, and was hopelessly tactless in criticizing old-type soldiers upon whom Sun then relied. Disillusioned but still loyal, he went back to Shanghai and wrote letters of advice to his friends in the South, including Dr. Sun. Throughout this time he was simply one more among the dozens of bright young military men who were, in the existing crudity of warfare, unneeded in China. (Chu Tê, Chiang's present colleague and rival who heads the Soviet Chinese military system, was at this time besotted in Yünnan—a petty war-lord of landlord family, trapped hopeless on his little island of power amidst ruin.)

The period in the Shanghai years was filled in with business activity. Chiang was acquainted with some of the most influential merchants of the city, among them the crippled Chang Ching-chiang, a Paris merchant whose personal wealth was an informal treasury of Sun's movement. Chiang entered brokerage, and is supposed to have made a great deal of money. He became acquainted with the modernized, Westernized young Chinese of the metropolis, and left many friends behind him among the Chinese business men and industrialists.

Speculative or unfriendly writers asseverate that Chiang joined the Green Gang, an association which combined the features of a protection racket and a benevolent society. (Such a society, common in China during periods of disturbance, is the archetype of the American-Chinese Tong [*tang*] in its more violent phases.) If so, membership gave Chiang the key to an underworld as well organized as François Villon's Paris, wherein beggars, thieves, pickpockets, kidnappers, labor contractors, burial societies, and legitimate associations merged under the extra-legal government of a Masonic-like hierarchy. (The author is acquainted with a Chinese League of Nations official who joined the Gang as a necessary implement of social research, and was afforded genuine courtesy in preparing a report, general but accurate as to prevailing conditions, through the assistance of his fellow-members.)

Chiang's marriage, which had been made Chinese-fashion in his late boyhood, had given him posterity—

a son, now the pro-Communist, Soviet-trained Major-General Chiang Ching-kuo—but little companionship. His wife and son remained most of the time at his native home, whence he returned to see them and his mother, at Fenghua in Chekiang. Social contacts, acquaintance with capitalism, looseness of family connections, spasmodic work for the Revolution, and some military work—this, combined with the making and the losing of a fortune, fill the early maturity of Chiang.

He appeared upon the national and the world scene by his selection in 1923 to go to Moscow under the terms of the Nationalist-Soviet understanding, there to receive military training. He had definitely cast in his lot with Sun Yat-sen, making soldiery his vocation, and the selection implied that Sun began to see in him a military aide, to replace Huang Hsing of the first revolution. Chiang spent four months in the Soviet Union. The Communists, whom he was to fight six years later, showed him their combination of political and military warfare applied in Trotsky's Red Army. Chiang, already the beneficiary of Japanese training, had found Japanese military science dependent upon the framework of a stable constitutional system. In China his earlier training had been superior to its environment and did not have the practical utility of five years' banditry. Chiang, professional by spirit, restless under the drive of conscience and ambition, now found in Moscow the intermediate steps between modern warfare and government-building. He found that an army, from being the tool of pre-existing order, could become the spearhead of an accompanying order. Returning to China via the Trans-Siberian Railroad, he met General Galens (Vassili Bluecher), later his chief Soviet military aide at Canton.

In Canton, the first military creation on Soviet models was the Whampoa (*Huangpu*) Academy. Decreed by Sun Yat-sen, who made Chiang chief, the Academy had

Soviet advisers, eager to instill revolutionary and civil-war techniques. Chiang began the development of a modern army, and the real accretion of his own power. Even before he commanded full armies, Chiang used his cadets to good purpose in actual combat.

From this point on, Chiang's career becomes a part of the military history of the revolution. In his earlier years of power, Chiang emerged to leadership by co-operating with various intra-Kuomintang groups. He stood with the Left and utilized the Communists, although he managed to provoke, suppress, and appease the Communists in a way which no one else managed. He led the victorious Northern Expedition in 1925–27, carrying his forces on the crest of the Great Revolution. He was little known, but seen to be ambitious, zealous, incalculable, and a political strategist of ruthless genius. He soon found himself one of the triumvirate of Sun Yat-sen's successors: Hu Han-min, the Right Kuomintang leader, editor of Sun's works; Chiang; and Wang Ch'ing-wei, the Left Kuomintang leader.

At Shanghai, in 1927, Chiang's troops turned suddenly against the Communists and Left groups, quenching the uprising which had taken the city under his flag. This coup was undertaken because Chiang felt that the Communists were outrunning their promises. The Soviet advisers, who had come to help the Nationalists, had professed their concern for China's national struggle, and for the desirability of a fight against imperialism. They had not told Sun himself that he was a mere precursor to the proletarian revolution, nor informed the Nationalists that they were being given the privilege of fighting a war to advance the historical necessity of Nationalist extinction, as the next step in China's dialectic progression. Trotsky talked openly in Moscow about overthrowing the Chinese revolutionaries, and hijacking the Chinese revolution with the Chinese Communists, while Stalin believed in appeasing the Nationalists longer before discarding them. Of this Chiang was fully aware, and he struck at the sources of Communist power, labor and peasant unions, using a ruthlessness comparable to theirs. He went further, establishing the National Government (in the five-power form) at Nanking, and leaving the Left Kuomintang uneasily in the company of the Communists at Hankow. When the Communists proceeded to debate the question of monopolizing the remnants, even the Left-Kuomintang had had enough. They suppressed the Communists, and dissolved, coming down river to Nanking and joining the new government, while Chiang stepped technically out of the picture to ease the healing of the schism. Chiang's legitimacy in the leadership of the Kuomintang and the Sun Yat-sen revolution is shown by the fact that within two years he had an overwhelming majority of the veteran Kuomintang leaders at his capital.

In the ensuing years Chiang dedicated himself to three tasks: the development of the National Government, the stabilization of his own power, and the modernization of the country, both moral and mechanical. In 1927 he had married Miss May-ling Soong, and brought himself into alliance with the influential Soong family. The success of his efforts is attested by the continued functioning of a National Government at Chungking, the resistance and unification of China, which Chiang has come to symbolize, and the stalemate of Japan. These things would have appeared in some form, even without Chiang, but they would probably not exist with their present clarity and strength. The ten years of armament, modernization, and Japan-appeasement built an area into a nation, changing one more government into an elementary national state.

The Generalissimo has changed in appearance and manner considerably in the past ten years; these changes seem to have immediate bearing on his political role. In 1931 he was unmistakably the first soldier of China—brusque, forthright, sharp-voiced, and dismayingly lacking in the devious but pleasant *k'ê-ch'i* (ceremonial politeness) which is carried to professional heights by Chinese officials. Even then he was a masterful and clear-willed sort of man, who upset political precedents by a directness which would have been naive were it not so obviously both self-conscious and sincere. He possessed a keen awareness of his own historical importance, and a consistent responsibility before history—which still animates him—was the result. When coupled with the regular exercise of authority, this trait may have the consequence of moderating arbitrariness and minimizing opportunism.

With Chiang's self-possession there went an impatience with opposing views, a carelessness of means in the face of ends, and a fanatical insistence on loyalty. He now seems little older in body, despite the injury to his back during the Sian episode, but the years have left a very clear impress on his moral character. To the sharp discipline and authority of the soldier he has added the characteristics of a teacher—reserved kindliness, a daily preoccupation with moral questions, an inclination to harangue his followers on the general meaning of their problems. Ten years ago it was very difficult to find out what Chiang really believed and wanted; his ambition and patriotism were both patent, but beyond them there was little detail to be filled in. He is beginning to have the relationship of, let us say, Lenin to Marx in his treatment of the *San Min Chu I* of Sun Yat-sen, and is beginning to stand forth as an interesting political theorist in his own right. He gives every indication of maturing in office, and of rising in stature in proportion to the responsibilities which are thrust upon him.

Chinese Appraisals of Chiang

Among both official and unofficial circles in Chungking there is a widespread and apparently well-founded belief that the two critical points of China's resistance and continued national independence rest more on Chiang's life, activity, and support than on any other single man or institution. These points are, of course, the domestic armistice and the promotion of resistance and reconstruction. The enormous strains which collaboration imposes on Nationalists and Communists are borne by Chiang. The finesse necessary to keep regions, classes, and groups in line, would probably not be available if the Generalissimo were dead. It is a tribute to his associates and followers of all parties that they work with him and with each other, but at the same time it is the supreme accomplishment of Chiang to have developed so that he can personify unity.

A question which the writer put to almost everyone he met in Western China was, "What do you think of Chiang? And what do you think Chiang thinks of himself?" The answers varied in tone and detail, but showed an interesting unanimity in major stress. One of the National Salvationist leaders,[14] bitter about Chiang's high-handed repression of Left-liberal movements in pre-war years, replied "Impossible!" to the question, "From your point of view, could General Chiang become an outright dictator?" But this leader explained that Chiang differed from President George Washington in that the latter's own conception of his role was in close harmony with public expectation and governmental necessity, whereas Chiang—believing in democracy as a part of his loyalty to his leader, Dr. Sun, and to the *San Min Chu I*—found himself unready to trust democratic processes in really vital issues.

[14] One of the Seven Gentlemen (*Ch'i Chüntzŭ*), whose name is withheld by request, interviewed August 2, 1940, in Chungking.

The critic continued by adding that the difference between Sun and Chiang was to be found in the fact that the former, whatever his impatience, let the Plenary Session of the C.E.C. of the Kuomintang reach its decisions through discussion, whereas Chiang tried to help the committee decide by lecturing at it. He concluded thus: if there were no political group other than the Kuomintang, Chiang might become a dictator in fact while remaining a democratic leader in name. The presence of other parties and groups makes this difficult, if not impossible. For example, the Kuomintang might try to apply the new constitution in such a way as to prevent its being an additional step on the road to democracy; but the other groups, including the Communists, could thwart this move by refusing to take part in any of the constitutional ceremonies, and thereupon [in the traditional Chinese fashion] discredit the whole thing. These opinions are of special interest when one considers that they stem from a group which is still suffering from a very careful police supervision and a state of non-recognition and semi-repression.

Another interesting interpretation of Generalissimo Chiang's role is found among the Communists. One of the Chinese Communist leaders [15] had the question put to him, "On what long-range basis of practical politics can you people and the Generalissimo cooperate? After all, you must be consolidating power which can be used against him and he power which can be turned against you?" He replied that if Chiang made terms with the Japanese, or if he failed to resist, the Communists would need to have nothing to do with him, nor he with them, since he would be ruined in any case. On the other hand, if the war came to a successful end, Chiang would be the supreme hero of modern China; the Communists could not turn against

[15] Communist leader, interviewed in Chungking, whose name is also withheld by request.

him; and Chiang knew this well enough to know that if he defeated Japan he had won China. The commentator did not explore other obvious possibilities, such as a long stalemate in the Japanese war, or a shift in Soviet policies, but what he said indicates the present reality of the common interests between the Communists and the Generalissimo.

From these and other comments, the visitor to China soon learns that although Chiang is the Chief (*Tsung-ts'ai*) of the Kuomintang, his power rests as much on broad national support as it does on Party power. It is significant that although Chiang still has two groups of semi-secret protective police, one Party and the other Army, he has far less occasion to use them than he did five years ago. There is an inadequacy of due process, of course, which would strike the lay American as critically unsatisfactory, but the smoothness, evenness, and relative frankness of government is far greater than at any other time in modern China.

Democracy is obtaining some real beginnings, not because of a sudden lurch in political necessity, nor because of the charm of a theory, but because the firm ground of a common opinion is knitting the country together and affording the limits indispensable to the functioning of democratic techniques; this common opinion, the universal popularity of the war, is based on the resistance-and-reconstruction policy. The same patriotic surge which supports the war supports Chiang, as the hero and chief technician of the war.

The political changes which translated Chiang from the status of a Party leader and a new kind of militarist into a real national leader are mirrored in his writings. His published political works now run to a considerable number of volumes, representing collections of his speeches and essays.[16] It would, perhaps, be interesting

---

[16] Some of the recent volumes are: *Lu-shan Hsün-lien Chi Hsüan-chi* (Collected Papers of the Lu Shan Training Conference), Chung-

to note the main trends of his political philosophy, since it serves as the firm ground of his policy. It is possible that no other leader in the world, except Stalin, has satisfied himself so thoroughly with the connection between his own epistemological and ethical presuppositions and his working conclusions in terms of action as has Chiang.

The Ideology of Chiang

First and foremost, Chiang accepts the *San Min Chu I* of Sun Yat-sen, deviating from the letter of these doctrines by no single brush-stroke. In his spirit of interpretation, he follows in general the Rightist exegeses, as represented by the works of Hu Han-min and T'ai Ch'i-t'ao, although he has developed his own conclusions in great part from his first-hand memory of Dr. Sun, and from his own experience. (Needless to say, he is worlds apart from the interpretations given by such Leftists as the Communists, the Third Party, or Mme. Sun, or such ultra-Rightists as the Japanophiles.)

Secondly, he has found the pragmatic elements of Sun's philosophy highly palatable. Apart from his public life, he has always made a fetish of action, and has stood for getting something done. His orthodox but modified Sunyatsenism and his practicality can best be shown by excerpts from a recent essay of his which states his position.[17] One notes the stress on practicality,

---

king, 1939; *O-mei Hsün-lien Chi Hsüan-chi* (Collected Papers of the Omei Training Conference), Chungking, 1939; *Li-hsing Chê-hsiao* (The Philosophy of Being Practical), Chungking, 1940; *Tsung-ts'ai Chien-kuo Yen-lun Hsüan-chi* (The Tsung-ts'ai's Utterances on Reconstruction), Chungking, 1940; *Tsung-ts'ai Wai-chiao Yen-lun Hsüan-chi* (The Tsung-ts'ai's Utterances on Diplomacy), Chungking, 1940; and *Tsung-ts'ai K'ang-chan Yen-lun Hsüan-chi* (The Tsung-ts'ai's Utterances on Resistance), Chungking, 1940. A collection of the Generalissimo's leading speeches, in English, is in press and is to be issued soon by the China Information Publishing Company, Hong Kong.

[17] [Chiang K'ai-shek], *San-min-chu-i chih T'i-hsi nai ch'i-shih Hsing-ch'êng-hsü* (The *San Min Chu I* System and its Method of Ap-

the Christian influence in the matter of love, and the opinions of Communism, Fascism, and Democracy:

In order to make a scientific study of any subject it is best to use the analytical, deductive and inductive methods. By applying this principle to the study of the *San Min Chu I*, I have made a chart showing its system and working procedure . . . In order to realize his ideas, Sun invented the most complete and the most practical political principles, the *San Min Chu I*. At the present there are mainly three schools of political thought, namely, Democracy socalled, Communism, and Fascism. None of them is perfect. For instance, take Communism. It attaches enough importance to the economic side of life and resembles the Principle of Livelihood, but it ignores the ideas embodied in the Principles of Nationalism and Democracy. Furthermore, it considers the economic interests of only one class of people, and not of all. The Fascist school stresses only those ideas as embodied in the Principle of Nationalism and ignores the other two principles. Besides, it ignores the interests and welfare of other nationalities. So-called Democracy is too much involved with capitalism and can hardly solve the problems of *min shêng*. The Three Principles of Sun are different from these in that they originate from the idea that *the world belongs to the public*. His aim is to bring about the real equality of the people without any distinction of classes, religion, and occupations. After this is realized in China, it is expected that the equality of all nationalities in the whole world can be brought about by means of the spirit of mutual help and sincere cooperation.

Of all the common human feelings, the sentiment of nationality is the most worthy one. The Principle of Nationalism is based on this point. Laws specifically define the popular responsibilities and privileges which underlie the Principle of Democracy. And lastly, in Livelihood, each man's reasoning power is used to advantage in working out the most rational way of distribution, whereby people will be put in an equitable position economically. Thus it can be seen that the Three Principles are very adaptable to China as well as to any other nation.

As I outline above, Sun, starting with the Principle of

---

plication), Chungking, 1939. This booklet is part of a series called *Conclusions of the Party Chief*, published by the Central Headquarters of the Kuomintang Training Corps, Chungking, 1939.

people's livelihood and embodying the idea that *the world belongs to the public,* established the *San Min Chu I.* But just having a Principle won't do; a motive power is needed to fulfill it. That power is revolution . . .

Revolution is not an easy thing. It needs a very strong driving force to carry it out. What are the driving forces in the case of the Chinese revolution? They are wisdom, love, and courage. I wish to point out specially that the second factor is the most important. "Love" means, among other things: Save your country, even at the cost of your life!

Let us define more fully the meanings of these three words. Wisdom means, how to understand Love. It also means: first, wide reading; second, care in your inquiries; third, careful thinking; fourth, the power of distinguishing right and wrong. By Love is meant loyalty, filial piety, faithfulness, and peace. Courage means the determination to do what is right. Besides, what is the most important is the need for persistence, without which nothing can be accomplished.

When you have the virtues of Wisdom, Love and Courage and the persistence required, the next move is to start and work. Sun told us that it is hard to know and easy to do. If you study the *San Min Chu I* carefully and yet don't do what is required of you, it is not because you can't do it, but because you won't do it. If you just won't do it, you are not a faithful disciple of the *San Min Chu I.*

When you are to start the revolutionary work, you must have a Party, because in a Party all the revolutionary forces can be consolidated and all the revolutionary activities can be planned and directed. . . .

The character of Chiang as a political leader which emerges from his military training, his successful marriage and even more successful jockeying for power, his maturity under the influence of that power, and his somewhat crude but austere recognition of responsibility, is quite different from the portraits drawn by the coastal diehards or by Leftists. To the former he is just another Asiatic swashbuckler who conceals murder and extortion behind orotund banality; to the latter he is a sort of Franco, supinely cooperative with Anglo-American imperialism because of his compradore-class mentality, who faces a last chance of dialectical salvation if he yields to the Chinese Communists in their version of democracy and promotes upper-class liquidation in war time. It is likely that he will break the limits of either attempt to define him, and will—if the war succeeds—play a distinctly Chinese part in the construction of a China which, by reason of the speed of technological progress coupled with the rising extent of governmental economics, will break through the ruinous Right-Left pattern of Western politics. Chiang probably has enough awareness of Chinese history to realize that as the founder of an enduring democratic system his prestige would exceed that obtainable by any process of dictatorship. If he becomes a dictator, he will have successors; but as first President of a real democracy, he would be eternally unique, and as *de facto* founder of a great power, a world figure for this century. Against his desire to let democracy grow beneath his military aegis, his conservatism of habit and his anxiety to get things done right continue to militate; but there is thirteen years' evidence to show that he has tried very hard to work within the limits of the constitutional system of the National Government, has avoided arbitrariness as much as he thought possible, and has at worst behaved like a Salazar, Atatürk, or Pilsudski.

CONCLUSION

THE China of Chiang K'ai-shek has withstood the shock of foreign war, and has demonstrated its capacity to grow and survive as a state despite heavy domestic adversity. The constitutional structure nears a condition of realistic operation. The political organs, while still monopolized by the Kuomintang, are highly effective; their unrepresentative character is mitigated by the new experiments with consultative legislation. Administratively, both as to special functions and in developing local government, significant new enterprises are under way. Communist-Nationalist rivalry, while still bitter, has avoided domestic civil war during the invasion; despite the clash of National troops with the New Fourth Army, the postponement may be indefinitely continued. Taken all together, Free China presents a hopeful picture; and it therefore acquires international importance as the presumptive predecessor of a great Asiatic democracy.

Nevertheless, the fact that a Chinese central government has emerged in time for effective action, and has withstood invasion, does not provide proof that Japan is doomed to fail. Japanese progress thus far in China has depended in great part upon Japanese world commerce—on raw materials and finance from her lucrative American trade. China's resistance has depended, but to a lesser degree, on Western aid. In each case, the early history of the conflict was qualified if not determined by the character of third-party relations. If the United States, the Soviet Union, Britain, and Germany continued for the next twenty-odd years to do in the Far East precisely what they have been doing for the past ten, the future might be more or less predictable on the basis of the Far Eastern elements alone. Such a prediction is, however, wholly unsupportable at the present time; it is indeed safe to predict the contrary, and assume that it is impossible for the major outside powers to continue their reciprocal power-relationships unchanged, in the Far East or elsewhere. China's future is therefore bound up with European and American uncertainties. The Three-Power Pact, signed at Berlin, September 27, 1940 between Germany, Italy and Japan, and the American Lease-Lend Bill have already begun to interlock the European and East Asiatic wars.

The Chief Alternatives in China

The Chinese domestic situation will inescapably be bound up with China's international position. The extremes of probability can be readily marked off: on the one hand, it is most improbable that the Chinese resistance should collapse altogether, and leave the way open for an almost effortless Japanese victory, through the consolidation of the Wang regime without guerrilla, volunteer or West-China opposition; on the other hand, an immediate and complete Chinese victory, coupled with solution of Nationalist-Communist rivalry, is not at all in sight. Somewhere between these two extremes there lie a number of more probable alternatives.

Chief among these is a Kuomintang China, winning a slow victory against Japan under the continuation of existent institutions and leadership. Such a country— nationalist, democratic, and economically pragmatist— would, by the fact of victory over Japan, create a nucleus for liberal democracy in Asia.[1] A variant of this solution would be a United Front China, wherein the

---

[1] This discussion includes extracts from the author's "China: Right, Left, or Center?", *The Quarterly Review of the Michigan Alumnus*, Vol. XLVI, No. 14 (Winter 1940).

independents and the Left actually shared power with the Kuomintang under conditions of broad popular suffrage; this would presumably lie between the United States and the Soviet Union in the matter of ideology and foreign policy. Neither of these would afford Japan much opportunity for continued influence on the continent.

A long continuation of the present hostilities might imply the development of a permanently divided China —permanent save in terms of centuries—with Nationalists and Communists landbound in inner Asia, and pro-Japanese governments along the coast. Such a violation of Chinese cultural and economic unity would perpetuate disequilibrium, and imply continuing wars. Differing from this in degree rather than kind would be a reversion of China to *tuchünism* and anarchy. Neither of these possibilities could command acceptance from the awakened, vigorous China of today.

Outside intervention presents a third group of alternatives: the partition of China through a Soviet-Japanese understanding, or the complete Sovietization of China, through the combined efforts of Soviet and Chinese Communists. Soviet-Japanese partition, once almost unthinkable, appears within the range of possibility because of the apparent weakness of the Soviet Union, which calls for unconventional remedies. If Communist dialectic insured the Soviets who shared China with Japan an ultimate victory over Japan as well, the evil might seem transitory to the Soviet Union. Were such a step taken to thwart rising American influence, it might seem the lesser of two evils. Neither this nor a Soviet China (which would swell the Communist frontier and resources immeasurably) appeared probable in the spring of 1941.

The more practical aspects of the China-building problem still concern the immediate, local effectiveness of the Japanese military effort to control the growth of Chinese government.

To create a victorious condition, Japan has sought the collaboration of phantom Japanophile governments. But in the face of the continuing National Government, and guerrilla opposition, these governments are incapable of functioning. When the conquerors of China entered the cities, and took over the government, they were strangers holding mere islands in the greatness of China.

Japan has the seven most important cities of China. She has most of the railroads. The waters around China are closed by the Japanese fleet. But how is Japan to occupy the hundreds of thousands of villages? How is Japan to persuade the Chinese people, who are still overwhelmingly country people, that they are conquered when Japan thinks that they are?

The Japanese have not yet succeeded in making much impression on the Chinese farmers, except to anger them with cruelty and rapine. In Manchuria, where the Japanese have had undisputed sway for ten long years, thousands of bandits, a Chinese version of Minute Men, are still fighting. Ten, five, even three miles from the great fortified centers of the Japanese army in China, Chinese irregulars, peasant volunteers, spring up in the night. In the darkness there is shooting, sudden flames, perhaps an airplane burning or a gasoline storage tank set on fire; when dawn comes there is nothing to be seen except the patient quiet coolies working in their little fields.

At the present time the war has reached its quiescent stage. The Japanese army has done what in most other cases would be called winning a victory. The battle is accordingly a battle between the Chinese government in the West and the Japanese in the East of China, not with guns or ships so much as with words and with price levels—not for strategic territory, but for the support of the Chinese masses.

The Chinese must make it possible for their own people to live successfully and happily. But they have the world's greatest farm problem, a problem of over-indebtedness, sharecropping, soil exhaustion, prices and markets. Japan wanted to prevent the creation of a united China strong enough to take Manchuria back, and to drive the Japanese off the Asiatic continent back to Japan. Japan accordingly took the disastrous and painful step of conquering the world's greatest relief problem—the millions of underfed, undernourished, desperate Chinese farmers. Now she has them.

In this light, the Far Eastern conflict takes on a different appearance from the usual picture of China versus Japan. It is a conflict, not merely of one nation against another but of competing governments within the same territory. China is trying to build one way; Japan, another; but they are both building for the same end, control of the Far East, and on the same foundations, the Chinese people. Both Japan and the independent Chinese government are struggling for the mastery of an area which is in the grip of a tragic farm problem. The key to power is the mastery of the problem, not the mastery of the men. The Chinese farmers would welcome Communism, capitalism, or almost any kind of leadership which could guarantee them a good livelihood in return for their long and patient labor. The basic issues are social, technological, and economic, as well as political and military. The Japanese failure in China is not a failure of the economic resources; Japan could have been a weak but adequate economic partner to China. The failure of Japan now leads China to look elsewhere for help.

The United States in Chinese Politics

The American Lease-Lend Bill, designed primarily to extend effective aid to Britain, also applied to China. The United States executive was clearly aware of the purposes of Japan, and displayed a temper to thwart them. Secretary of State Cordell Hull, presenting a statement in support of the Bill to the House Foreign Affairs Committee on January 15, 1941, stated:

It has been clear throughout that Japan has been actuated from the start by broad and ambitious plans for establishing herself in a dominant position in the entire region of the Western Pacific. Her leaders have openly declared their determination to achieve and maintain that position by force of arms and thus to make themselves master of an area containing almost one-half of the entire population of the world. As a consequence, they would have arbitrary control of the sea and trade routes in that region.

. . . .

It should be manifest to every person that such a program for the subjugation and ruthless exploitation by one country of nearly one-half the population of the world is a matter of immense significance, importance and concern to every nation wherever located.

On March 15, the President's speech to the White House Correspondents' Association included a ringing promise to give help to the Chinese people, who had asked for aid through Chiang K'ai-shek. The United States moved toward a more definite policy in Asia as well as giving more aid to Britain in the North Atlantic area. The lease-lend program might upset the entire balance of power in the Far East even more readily than in Europe; but immediate evidence of such large-scale application was not forthcoming.

In his message to President Roosevelt, March 18, 1941, Chiang K'ai-shek said: [2]

The people of China, whether engaged in fighting the aggressor or toiling in the fields and workshops in the rear in support of the defenders, will be immeasurably heartened by your impressive reaffirmation of the will of the American people to assist them in their struggle for freedom from foreign domination, and in the resumption of their march towards democracy and social justice for all.

[2] Department of State, *Bulletin*, IV, p. 335.

Significantly, the statement of Secretary Hull may apply to future Soviet advance in China as well as to the Japanese invasion. American aid which would weaken Japan and strengthen the Soviet Union thereby, would be welcome to Stalin; but American influence, carried to the point of consolidating the National Government against the Communists, and reducing the probabilities of rising Communist influence, would not be welcome.

Whether the United States Government and the American people are pro-Chinese or not, the National Government of China is pro-American. The only influence to rival the American in modern China is that of the Soviet Union. Soviet and American impress are found in intellectual life, in political ideals, in standards and types of organization, and in ethical creeds. It is no accident that the Kuomintang traces its three principles back to Lincoln, while the Chinese Communists quote Lenin and Stalin. The rivalry is clear, and acute. American aid to China strengthens the pro-American party and weakens the Communists; cessation of the Burma route traffic in the summer of 1940 stimulated discussion of a closer Sino-Soviet rapprochement.

Generalissimo Chiang is a Christian. He is surrounded by American-trained officials. The common secondary language of the Nationalists is English. The Chinese Industrial Cooperatives are based on an American background with New Zealand and British advice. The educational system is patterned after that of the United States in great part; the American impress on the system of higher education, in particular, cannot be overestimated. The interests, appetites, and orientation of the Kuomintang and the National Government are Pacific-centered; much bitterness of an intimate, almost uncomplaining sort, has been aroused by America's continued aid to Japan through business channels.

Adjustments within China are bound to react to the

pressures in the outside world. If the United States abandons Free China, the Japanese will probably not conquer China; but the Soviets will be in an excellent position to try, for themselves or through agreement with the Japanese, to demoralize Chinese resistance so that the Soviet forces could intervene because of a political vacuum and protect the "racially kin working classes," as in Poland. Whether China should go Communist through the triumph of the Chinese Communists, or through military occupation by the Soviet Red Army, would not matter much to the United States. What would matter would be the loss of an incomparable ally, an ally who today is almost embarrassingly cordial toward us, thankful to us, and who admires our institutions and culture.

Once Japan were forced out of the picture as an aggressive power, once the United States and China were to reach an understanding, the Soviet Union—debarred from a warm-water naval base on the Pacific—could be left in the *status quo,* its menace removed, to work out its own destiny if it did not challenge renewed intervention by renewed provocation of co-existing societies. No other challenging power could appear on the Pacific. A group of nations from Buenos Aires to Labrador, from Melbourne to Kashgar, from Lhasa to Boston would cover three and one-half continents. The area thus freed from war and aggression, encompassing the Americas and the Pacific basin, would include every necessary article in the entire schedule of man's appetites. The Chungking government, elementarily and crudely, has broken ground for the culture-political American advance into Asia. Strong without us, Free China is a great power with us, and the one place in the world where construction, liberty, education, and hope still rise day by day. Both cosmopolitan and national, the Chinese are ready to accept their share of responsibility for the new world order.

CONCLUSION

The responsibility for building a democratic world, whether or not the four authoritarian powers go down, lies in great part upon the United States. Generalissimo Chiang, alone among leaders, has stood forth for world government, for world freedom. He has written:[3]

"In as much as cosmopolitanism and world peace are two of the main aims of *San Min Chu I,* China will naturally be disposed to participate in any world federation or confederation based on the equality of nations and for the good of mankind."

[3] See below, p. 371.

APPENDIX I. GOVERNMENT DOCUMENTS

A. THE GOVERNMENT DRAFT OF THE PROPOSED CONSTITUTION [1]

Released April 30, 1937, this differs from the celebrated Double Five Draft (*q.v.* in Text) by the omission of an article providing that the first Kuo-min Ta-hui should exercise full power, and not be confined to the preparation of a constitution. This Draft represents the official viewpoint and was prepared by the Legislative *Yüan* with the help and criticism of private persons; accordingly, it is the outstanding draft constitution.

By virtue of the mandate received from the whole body of citizens and in accordance with the bequeathed teachings of Dr. Sun, Founder of the Republic of China, the People's Congress of the Republic of China hereby ordains and enacts this Constitution and causes it to be promulgated throughout the land for faithful and perpetual observance by all.

CHAPTER I. GENERAL PROVISIONS

ARTICLE 1. The Republic of China is a *SAN MIN CHU I* Republic.

ARTICLE 2. The sovereignty of the Republic of China is vested in the whole body of its citizens.

ARTICLE 3. Persons having acquired the nationality of the Republic of China are citizens of the Republic of China.

ARTICLE 4. The territory of the Republic of China consists of areas originally constituting Kiangsu, Chekiang, Anhwei, Kiangsi, Hupeh, Hunan, Szechwan, Sikang, Hopei, Shantung, Shansi, Honan, Shensi, Kansu, Chinghai, Fukien, Kwangtung, Kwangsi, Yunnan, Kweichow, Liaoning, Kirin, Heilungkiang, Jehol, Chahar, Suiyuan, Ningsia, Sinkiang, Mongolia and Tibet.

The territory of the Republic of China shall not be altered except by resolution of the People's Congress.

[1] *T'ien Hsia Monthly*, v. X, No. 3 (May 1940), p. 493-506. The transliterations have not been altered. *Yüan* therefore appears as "Yuan."

ARTICLE 5. All races of the Republic of China are component parts of the Chinese Nation and shall be equal.

ARTICLE 6. The National Flag of the Republic of China shall have a red background with a blue sky and white sun in the upper left corner.

ARTICLE 7. The National Capital of the Republic of China shall be at Nanking.

Chapter II. Rights and Duties of the Citizens

ARTICLE 8. All citizens of the Republic of China shall be equal before the law.

ARTICLE 9. Every citizen shall enjoy the liberty of the person. Except in accordance with law, no one may be arrested, detained, tried or punished.

When a citizen is arrested or detained on suspicion of having committed a criminal act, the authority responsible for such action shall immediately inform the citizen himself and his relatives of the cause for his arrest or detention and shall, within a period of twenty-four hours, send him to a competent court for trial. The citizen so arrested or detained, or any one else, may also petition the court to demand from the authority responsible for such action the surrender, within twenty-four hours, of his person to the court for trial.

The court shall not reject such a petition; nor shall the responsible authority refuse to execute such a writ as mentioned in the preceding paragraph.

ARTICLE 10. With the exception of those in active military service, no one may be subject to military jurisdiction.

ARTICLE 11. Every citizen shall have the freedom of domicile; no private abode may be forcibly entered, searched or sealed except in accordance with law.

ARTICLE 12. Every citizen shall have the freedom to change his residence; such freedom shall not be restricted except in accordance with law.

ARTICLE 13. Every citizen shall have the freedom of speech, writing and publication; such freedom shall not be restricted except in accordance with law.

ARTICLE 14. Every citizen shall have the freedom of secrecy of correspondence; such freedom shall not be restricted except in accordance with law.

ARTICLE 15. Every citizen shall have the freedom of religious belief; such freedom shall not be restricted except in accordance with law.

ARTICLE 16. Every citizen shall have the freedom of assembly and of forming associations; such freedom shall not be restricted except in accordance with law.

ARTICLE 17. No private property shall be requisitioned, expropriated, sealed or confiscated except in accordance with law.

ARTICLE 18. Every citizen shall have the right to present petitions, lodge complaints and institute legal proceedings in accordance with law.

ARTICLE 19. Every citizen shall have the right to exercise, in accordance with law, the powers of election, recall, initiative and referendum.

ARTICLE 20. Every citizen shall have the right to compete, in accordance with law, in state examinations.

ARTICLE 21. Every citizen shall, in accordance with law, be amenable to the duty of paying taxes.

ARTICLE 22. Every citizen shall, in accordance with law, be amenable to the duty of performing military service.

ARTICLE 23. Every citizen shall, in accordance with law, be amenable to the duty of rendering public service.

ARTICLE 24. All other liberties and rights of the citizens which are not detrimental to public peace and order or public welfare shall be guaranteed by the Constitution.

ARTICLE 25. Only laws imperative for safeguarding national security, averting a national crisis, maintaining public peace and order or promoting public interest may restrict the citizens' liberties and rights.

ARTICLE 26. Any public functionary who illegally infringes upon any private liberty or right, shall, besides being subject to disciplinary punishment, be responsible under criminal and civil law. The injured person may also, in accordance with law, claim indemnity from the State for damages sustained.

CHAPTER III. THE PEOPLE'S CONGRESS

ARTICLE 27. The People's Congress shall be constituted of delegates elected as follows:

1. Each district, municipality or area of an equivalent status shall elect one delegate, but in case its population exceeds 300,000, one additional delegate shall be elected for every additional 500,000 people. The status of areas to be equivalent to a district or municipality shall be defined by law.

2. The number of delegates to be elected from Mongolia and Tibet shall be determined by law.

3. The number of delegates to be elected by Chinese citizens residing abroad shall be determined by law.

ARTICLE 28. Delegates to the People's Congress shall be elected by universal, equal, and direct suffrage and by secret ballots.

ARTICLE 29. Citizens of the Republic of China having attained the age of twenty years shall, in accordance with law, have the right to elect delegates. Citizens having attained the age of twenty-five years shall, in accordance with law, have the right to be elected delegates.

ARTICLE 30. The term of office of Delegates of the People's Congress shall be six years.

When a Delegate is found guilty of violation of a law or neglect of his duty, his constituency shall recall him in accordance with law.

ARTICLE 31. The People's Congress shall be convened by the President once every three years. Its session shall last one month, but may be extended another month when necessary.

Extraordinary sessions of the People's Congress may be convened at the instance of two-fifths or more of its members.

The President may convene extraordinary sessions of the People's Congress.

The People's Congress shall meet at the place where the Central Government is.

ARTICLE 32. The powers and functions of the People's Congress shall be as follows:

1. To elect the President and Vice-President of the Republic, the President of the Legislative Yuan, the President of the Censor Yuan, the Members of the Legislative Yuan and the Members of the Censor Yuan.

2. To recall the President and Vice-President of the Republic, the President of the Legislative Yuan, the President of the Judicial Yuan, the President of the Examination Yuan, the President of the Censor Yuan, the Members of the Legislative Yuan and the Members of the Censor Yuan.

3. To initiate laws.
4. To hold referenda on laws.
5. To amend the Constitution.
6. To exercise such other powers as are conferred by the Constitution.

ARTICLE 33. Delegates to the People's Congress shall not be held responsible outside of Congress for opinions they may express and votes they may cast during the session of Congress.

ARTICLE 34. Without the permission of the People's Congress, no delegate shall be arrested or detained during the session except when apprehended in *flagrante delicto*.

ARTICLE 35. The organization of the People's Congress and the election as well as recall of its Delegates shall be determined by law.

CHAPTER IV. THE CENTRAL GOVERNMENT

Section 1. *The President*

ARTICLE 36. The President is the Head of the State and represents the Republic of China in foreign relations.

ARTICLE 37. The President commands the land, sea and air forces of the whole country.

ARTICLE 38. The President shall, in accordance with law, promulgate laws and issue orders with the counter-signature of the President of the Yuan concerned.

ARTICLE 39. The President shall, in accordance with law, exercise the power of declaring war, negotiating peace and concluding treaties.

ARTICLE 40. The President shall, in accordance with law, declare and terminate a state of emergency.

ARTICLE 41. The President shall, in accordance with law, exercise the power of granting amnesties, special pardons, remission of sentences and restoration of civil rights.

ARTICLE 42. The President shall, in accordance with law, appoint and remove civil and military officials.

ARTICLE 43. The President shall, in accordance with law, confer honors and award decorations.

ARTICLE 44. In case the State is confronted with an emergency, or the economic life of the State meets with a grave danger, which calls for immediate action, the President, following the resolution of the Executive Meeting, may issue orders of emergency and do whatever is necessary to cope with the situation, provided that he shall submit his action to the ratification of the Legislative Yuan within three months after the issuance of the orders.

ARTICLE 45. The President may call meetings of the Presidents of the five Yuan to confer on matters relating to two or more Yuan, or on such matters as the President may bring out for consultation.

ARTICLE 46. The President shall be responsible to the People's Congress.

ARTICLE 47. Citizens of the Republic of China, having attained the age of forty years, may be elected President or Vice-President of the Republic.

ARTICLE 48. The election of the President and Vice-President shall be provided for by law.

ARTICLE 49. The President and Vice-President shall hold office for a term of six years and may be re-elected for a second term.

ARTICLE 50. The President shall, on the day of his inauguration, take the following oath:

"I do solemnly and sincerely swear before the people that I will observe the Constitution, faithfully perform my duties, promote the welfare of the People, safeguard the security of the State and be loyal to the trust of the people. Should I break my oath, I will submit myself to the most severe punishment the law may provide."

ARTICLE 51. When the Presidency is vacant, the Vice-President shall succeed to the office.

When the President is for some reason unable to attend to his duties, the Vice-President shall act for him. If both the President and the Vice-President are incapacitated, the President of the Executive Yuan shall discharge the duties of the President's office.

ARTICLE 52. The President shall retire from office on the day his term expires. If by that time a new President has not been inducted into office, the President of the Executive Yuan shall discharge the duties of the President's office.

ARTICLE 53. The period for the President of the Executive Yuan to discharge the duties of the President's office shall not exceed six months.

ARTICLE 54. Except in case of an offense against the internal or external security of the State, the President shall not be liable to criminal prosecution until he has been recalled or has retired from office.

Section 2. *The Executive Yuan*

ARTICLE 55. The Executive Yuan is the highest organ through which the Central Government exercises its executive powers.

ARTICLE 56. In the Executive Yuan, there shall be a President, a Vice-President and a number of Executive Members, to be appointed and removed by the President.

The Executive Members mentioned in the preceding paragraph who do not take charge of Ministries or Commissions shall not exceed half of those who are in charge of Ministries or Commissions as provided in the first paragraph of Article 58.

ARTICLE 57. In the Executive Yuan, there shall be various Ministries and Commissions which shall separately exercise their respective executive powers.

ARTICLE 58. The Ministers of the various Ministries and the Chairmen of the various Commissions shall be appointed by the President from among the Executive Members.

The President and the Vice-President of the Executive Yuan may act concurrently as Minister or Chairman mentioned in the preceding paragraph.

ARTICLE 59. The President of the Executive Yuan, the Executive Members, the Ministers of the various Ministries and the Chairmen of the various Commissions shall be individually responsible to the President.

ARTICLE 60. In the Executive Yuan there shall be Executive Meetings composed of the President, the President of the Executive Yuan and the Executive Members to be presided over by the President. In case the President is unable to be present, the President of the Executive Yuan shall preside.

ARTICLE 61. The following matters shall be decided at an Executive Meeting:

1. Statutory and budgetary bills to be submitted to the Legislative Yuan.
2. Bills concerning a state of emergency and special pardons to be submitted to the Legislative Yuan.
3. Bills concerning declaration of war, negotiation of peace, conclusion of treaties and other important international affairs to be submitted to the Legislative Yuan.
4. Matters of common concern to the various Ministries and Commissions.
5. Matters submitted by the President.
6. Matters submitted by the President of the Executive Yuan, the Executive Members, the various Ministries and Commissions.

ARTICLE 62. The organization of the Executive Yuan shall be determined by law.

Section 3. *The Legislative Yuan*

ARTICLE 63. The Legislative Yuan is the highest organ through which the Central Government exercises its legislative powers. It shall be responsible to the People's Congress.

ARTICLE 64. The Legislative Yuan shall have the power to decide on measures concerning legislation, budgets, a state of emergency, special pardons, declaration of war, negotiation of peace, conclusion of treaties and other important international affairs.

ARTICLE 65. In the discharge of its duties the Legislative Yuan may interrogate the various Yuan, Ministries and Commissions.

ARTICLE 66. In the Legislative Yuan, there shall be a President who shall hold office for a term of three years and may be eligible for re-election.

ARTICLE 67. In regard to the election of Members of the Legislative Yuan, the Delegates of the various provinces, Mongolia, Tibet and of citizens residing abroad, to the People's Congress shall separately hold a preliminary election to nominate their respective candidates and submit a list of their names to the Congress for election. The candidates are not confined to the Delegates to the People's Congress. The respective number of candidates shall be proportioned as follows:

1. A province with a population of less than 5,000,000 shall nominate four candidates. A province with a population of more than 5,000,000 but less than 10,000,000 shall nominate six candidates. A province with a population of more than 10,000,000 but less than 15,000,000 shall nominate eight candidates. A province with a population of more than 15,000,000 but less than 20,000,000 shall nominate ten candidates. A province with a population of more than 20,000,000 but less than 25,000,000 shall nominate twelve candidates. A province with a population of more than 25,000,000 but less than 30,000,000 shall nominate fourteen candidates. A province with a population of more than 30,000,000 shall nominate sixteen candidates.

2. Mongolia and Tibet shall each nominate eight candidates.

3. Citizens residing abroad shall nominate eight candidates.

ARTICLE 68. Members of the Legislative Yuan shall hold office for a term of three years and may be eligible for re-election.

ARTICLE 69. The Executive Yuan, Judicial Yuan, Examination Yuan, and Censor Yuan may submit to the

Legislative Yuan measures concerning matters within their respective jurisdiction.

ARTICLE 70. The President may, before the promulgation or execution of a legislative measure, request the Legislative Yuan to reconsider it.

If the Legislative Yuan, with regard to the request for consideration, should decide to maintain the original measure by a two-thirds vote of the Members present, the President shall promulgate or execute it without delay; provided that in case of a bill of law or a treaty, the President may submit it to the People's Congress for a referendum.

ARTICLE 71. The President shall promulgate a measure presented by the Legislative Yuan for promulgation within thirty days after its receipt.

ARTICLE 72. Members of the Legislative Yuan shall not be held responsible outside of the said Yuan for opinions they may express and votes they may cast during its session.

ARTICLE 73. Without the permission of the Legislative Yuan, no member may be arrested or detained except when apprehended in *flagrante delicto*.

ARTICLE 74. No Member of the Legislative Yuan may concurrently hold any other public office or engage in any business or profession.

ARTICLE 75. The election of Members of the Legislative Yuan and the organization of the Legislative Yuan shall be determined by law.

Section 4. *The Judicial Yuan*

ARTICLE 76. The Judicial Yuan is the highest organ through which the Central Government exercises its judicial powers. It shall attend to the adjudication of civil, criminal and administrative suits, the discipline and punishment of public functionaries and judicial administration.

ARTICLE 77. In the Judicial Yuan, there shall be a President who shall hold office for a term of three years. He shall be appointed by the President.

The President of the Judicial Yuan shall be responsible to the People's Congress.

ARTICLE 78. Matters concerning special pardons, remission of sentence and restoration of civil rights shall be submitted to the President for action by the President of the Judicial Yuan in accordance with law.

ARTICLE 79. The Judicial Yuan shall have the power to unify the interpretation of statutes and ordinances.

ARTICLE 80. Judicial officials shall, in accordance with law, have perfect independence in the conduct of trials.

ARTICLE 81. No judicial official may be removed from office unless he has been subject to criminal or disciplinary punishment or declared an interdicted person; nor may a judicial official be suspended or transferred, or have his salary reduced except in accordance with law.

ARTICLE 82. The organization of the Judicial Yuan and the various Courts of Justice shall be determined by law.

Section 5. *The Examination Yuan*

ARTICLE 83. The Examination Yuan is the highest organ through which the Central Government exercises its examination powers. It shall attend to the selection of civil service candidates by examination and to the registration of persons qualified for public service.

ARTICLE 84. In the Examination Yuan there shall be a President who shall hold office for a term of three years, to be appointed by the President.

The President of the Examination Yuan shall be responsible to the People's Congress.

ARTICLE 85. The Examination Yuan shall, in accordance with law, by examination and registration determine the following qualifications:

1. For appointment as a public functionary.
2. For candidacy to public office.
3. For practice in specialized professions and as technical experts.

ARTICLE 86. The organization of the Examination Yuan shall be determined by law.

Section 6. *The Censor Yuan*

ARTICLE 87. The Censor Yuan is the highest organ through which the Central Government exercises its censorial powers. It shall attend to impeachment and auditing and be responsible to the People's Congress.

ARTICLE 88. In the discharge of its censorial powers, the Censor Yuan may, in accordance with law, interrogate the various Yuan, Ministries and Commissions.

ARTICLE 89. In the Censor Yuan, there shall be a President who shall hold office for a term of three years and may be eligible for re-election.

ARTICLE 90. Members of the Censor Yuan shall be elected by the People's Congress, from candidates separately nominated by the Delegates of the various provinces, Mongolia, Tibet and Chinese citizens residing abroad. Each group of Delegates shall nominate two candidates. The candidates are not confined to Delegates to the Congress.

ARTICLE 91. Members of the Censor Yuan shall hold office for a term of four years and may be eligible for reelection.

ARTICLE 92. When the Censor Yuan finds a public functionary in the Central or local government guilty of violation of a law or neglect of his duty, an impeachment may be instituted upon the proposal of one or more Members and the indorsement, after due investigation, of five or more Members. Impeachment against the President or Vice-President, the President of the Executive Yuan, Legislative Yuan, Judicial Yuan, Examination Yuan or Censor Yuan may be instituted only upon the proposal of ten or more Members and the indorsement, after due investigation, of one-half or more Members of the entire Yuan.

ARTICLE 93. When an impeachment is instituted against the President or Vice-President or the President of the Executive Yuan, Legislative Yuan, Judicial Yuan, Examination Yuan or Censor Yuan in accordance with the preceding Article, it shall be brought before the People's Congress. During the adjournment of the People's Congress, the Delegates shall be requested to convene in accordance with law an extraordinary session to decide whether the impeached shall be removed from office.

ARTICLE 94. Members of the Censor Yuan shall not be held responsible outside of the said Yuan for opinions they may express and votes they may cast while discharging their duties.

ARTICLE 95. Without the permission of the Censor Yuan, no Member of the Censor Yuan may be arrested or detained except when apprehended in *flagrante delicto*.

ARTICLE 96. No Member of the Censor Yuan may concurrently hold any other public office or engage in any business or profession.

ARTICLE 97. The election of the Members of the Censor Yuan and the organization of the Censor Yuan shall be determined by law.

CHAPTER V. THE LOCAL INSTITUTIONS

Section 1. *The Provinces*

ARTICLE 98. In the Province, there shall be a Provincial Government which shall execute the laws and orders of the Central Government and supervise local self-government.

ARTICLE 99. In the Provincial Government there shall be a Governor who shall hold office for a term of three years. He shall be appointed and removed by the Central Government.

ARTICLE 100. In the province, there shall be a Provincial Assembly which shall be composed of one member from each district or municipality to be elected by the district or municipal council. Members of the Provincial Assembly shall hold office for a term of three years and may be eligible for re-election.

ARTICLE 101. The organization of the Provincial Government and the Provincial Assembly as well as the election and recall of the Members of the Provincial Assembly shall be determined by law.

ARTICLE 102. The government of areas not yet established as provinces shall be determined by law.

Section 2. *The Districts*

ARTICLE 103. The district [*hsien*] is a unit of local self-government.

ARTICLE 104. All matters that are local in nature are within the scope of local self-government.

The scope of local self-government shall be determined by law.

ARTICLE 105. Citizens of the district shall, in accordance with law, exercise the powers of initiative and referendum in matters concerning district self-government as well as the powers of election and recall of the District Magistrate and other elective officials in the service of district self-government.

ARTICLE 106. In the district, there shall be a District Council, the members of which shall be directly elected by the citizens in the District General Meeting. Members of the District Council shall hold office for a term of three years and may be eligible for re-election.

ARTICLE 107. District ordinances and regulations which are in conflict with the laws and ordinances of the Central or Provincial Government shall be null and void.

ARTICLE 108. In the district, there shall be a District Government with a District Magistrate who shall be elected by the citizens in the District General Meeting. The Magistrate shall hold office for a term of three years and may be eligible for re-election.

Only those persons found qualified in the public examinations held by the Central Government or adjudged qualified by the Ministry of Public Service Registration may be candidates for the office of District Magistrate.

ARTICLE 109. The District Magistrate shall administer the affairs of the district in accordance with the principles of self-government and, under the direction of the Provincial Governor, execute matters assigned by the Central and Provincial Governments.

ARTICLE 110. The organization of the District Council and District Government as well as the election and recall of the District Magistrate and the Members of the District Council shall be determined by law.

Section 3. *The Municipalities*

ARTICLE 111. Unless otherwise provided by law, the provisions governing self-government and administration of the district shall apply *mutatis mutandis* to the municipality [*shih*].

ARTICLE 112. In the municipality, there shall be a Municipal Council, the Members of which shall be directly elected by the citizens in the Municipal General Meeting. One-third of the Members shall retire and be replaced by election annually.

ARTICLE 113. In the municipality, there shall be a Municipal Government with a Mayor to be directly elected by the citizens in the Municipal General Meeting. He shall hold office for a term of three years and may be eligible for re-election.

Only those persons found qualified in the public examinations held by the Central Government or adjudged qualified by the Ministry of Public Service Registration may be a candidate for the office of Mayor.

ARTICLE 114. The Mayor shall administer the affairs of the municipality in accordance with the principles of municipal self-government and, under direction of the competent supervising authority, execute matters assigned by the Central or Provincial Government.

ARTICLE 115. The organization of the Municipal Council and Municipal Government as well as the election and recall of the Members of the Municipal Council and the Mayor shall be determined by law.

Chapter VI. National Economic Life

Article 116. The economic system of the Republic of China shall be based upon the Min Shêng Chu I (Principle of Livelihood) and shall aim at national economic sufficiency and equality.

Article 117. The land within the territorial limits of the Republic of China belongs to the people as a whole. Any part thereof the ownership of which has been lawfully acquired by an individual or individuals shall be protected by, and subject to, the restrictions of law.

The State may, in accordance with law, tax or expropriate private land on the basis of the value declared by the owner or assessed by the Government.

Every landowner is amenable to the duty of utilizing his land to the fullest extent.

Article 118. All subterranean minerals and natural forces which are economically utilizable for public benefit, belong to the State and shall not be affected by private ownership of the land.

Article 119. The unearned increment shall be taxed by means of a land-value-increment tax and devoted to public benefit.

Article 120. In readjusting the distribution of land, the State shall be guided by the principle of aiding and protecting the land-owning farmers and the land-utilizing owners.

Article 121. The State may, in accordance with law, regulate private wealth and enterprises when such wealth and enterprises are considered detrimental to the balanced development of national economic life.

Article 122. The State shall encourage, guide and protect the citizens' productive enterprises and the nation's foreign trade.

Article 123. All public utilities and enterprises of a monopolistic nature shall be operated by the State; except in case of necessity when the State may specially permit private operation.

The private enterprises mentioned in the preceding paragraph may, in case of emergency for national defense, be temporarily managed by the State. The State may also, in accordance with law, take them over for permanent operation upon payment of due compensation.

Article 124. In order to improve the workers' living conditions, increase their productive ability and relieve unemployment, the State shall enforce labor protective policies.

Women and children shall be afforded special protection in accordance with their age and physical condition.

ARTICLE 125. Labor and capital shall, in accordance with the principles of mutual help and cooperation, develop together productive enterprises.

ARTICLE 126. In order to promote agricultural development and the welfare of the farming population, the State shall improve rural economic and living conditions and increase farming efficiency by employment of scientific farming.

The State may regulate the production and distribution of agricultural products, in kind and quantity.

ARTICLE 127. The State shall accord due relief or compensation to those who suffer disability or loss of life in the performance of military or public services.

ARTICLE 128. The State shall give suitable relief to the aged, feeble, or disabled who are incapable of earning a living.

ARTICLE 129. While the following powers appertain to the Legislative Yuan in the case of the Central Government, they may be exercised by the legally designated organ if, in accordance with law, such matters may be effected independently by a province, district or municipality:

1. To impose or alter the rate of taxes and levies, fines, penalties, or other imposts of a compulsory nature.
2. To raise public loans, dispose of public property or conclude contracts which increase the burden of the public treasury.
3. To establish or cancel public enterprises, monopolies, franchises or any other profit-making enterprise.
4. To grant or cancel public enterprises, monopolies, franchises or any other special privileges.

Unless specially authorized by law, the government of a province, district or municipality shall not raise foreign loans or directly utilize foreign capital.

ARTICLE 130. Within the territorial limits of the Republic of China all goods shall be permitted to circulate freely. They shall not be seized or detained except in accordance with law.

Customs duty is a Central Government revenue. It shall be collected only once when the goods enter or leave the country.

The various grades of government shall not collect any

dues on goods in transit within the country, with the exception of tolls levied for the purpose of improving the waterways and roads, on vessels and vehicles making use of them.

The right to impose taxes and levies on goods belongs to the Central Government and shall not be exercised except in accordance with law.

Chapter VII. Education

ARTICLE 131. The educational aim of the Republic of China shall be to develop a national spirit, to cultivate a national morality, to train the people for self-government and to increase their ability to earn a livelihood, and thereby to build up a sound and healthy body of citizens.

ARTICLE 132. Every citizen of the Republic of China shall have an equal opportunity to receive education.

ARTICLE 133. All public and private educational institutions in the country shall be subject to State supervision and amenable to the duty of carrying out the educational policies formulated by the State.

ARTICLE 134. Children between six and twelve years of age are of school age and shall receive elementary education free of tuition. Detailed provisions shall be provided by law.

ARTICLE 135. All persons over school age who have not received an elementary education shall receive supplementary education free of tuition. Detailed provisions shall be provided by law.

ARTICLE 136. In establishing universities and technical schools, the State shall give special consideration to the needs of the respective localities so as to afford the people thereof an equal opportunity to receive higher education, thereby hastening a balanced national cultural development.

ARTICLE 137. Educational appropriations shall constitute no less than fifteen per cent of the total amount of the budget of the Central Government and no less than thirty per cent of the total amount of the provincial, district and municipal budgets respectively. Educational endowment funds independently set aside in accordance with law shall be safeguarded.

Educational expenditures in needy provinces shall be subsidized by the central treasury.

ARTICLE 138. The State shall encourage and subsidize the following enterprises or citizens:

1. Private educational institutions with a high record of achievement.
2. Education for Chinese citizens residing abroad.
3. Discoverers or inventors in academic or technical fields.
4. Teachers or administrative officers of educational institutions having good records and long service.
5. Students of high records and good character who are unable to pursue further studies.

CHAPTER VIII. THE ENFORCEMENT AND AMENDMENT OF THE CONSTITUTION

ARTICLE 139. The term "law" as used in the Constitution means that which has been passed by the Legislative Yuan and promulgated by the President.

ARTICLE 140. Laws in conflict with the Constitution are null and void.

The question whether a law is in conflict with the Constitution shall be settled by the Censor Yuan submitting the point to the Judicial Yuan for interpretation within six months after its enforcement.

ARTICLE 141. Administrative orders in conflict with the Constitution or laws are null and void.

ARTICLE 142. The interpretation of the Constitution shall be done by the Judicial Yuan.

ARTICLE 143. Before half or more of the provinces and territories have completed the work of local self-government, the Members of the Legislative Yuan and of the Censor Yuan shall be elected and appointed in accordance with the following provisions:

1. The Members of the Legislative Yuan: The Delegates of the various provinces, Mongolia, Tibet, and of the citizens residing abroad, to the People's Congress shall separately hold a preliminary election to nominate half of the number of the candidates as determined in Article 67 and submit their list to the People's Congress for election. The other half shall be nominated by the President of the Legislative Yuan for appointment by the President.

2. The Members of the Censor Yuan: The Delegates of the various provinces, Mongolia, Tibet, and of the citizens residing abroad, to the People's Congress shall separately hold a preliminary election to nominate half of the number of candidates as determined in Article 90

and submit their list to the People's Congress for election. The other half shall be nominated by the President of the Censor Yuan for appointment by the President.

ARTICLE 144. The Magistrates of districts where the work of self-government is not yet completed shall be appointed and removed by the Central Government.

The preceding paragraph is applicable *mutatis mutandis* to those municipalities where the work of self-government is not yet completed.

ARTICLE 145. The methods and procedure of helping the establishment of local self-government shall be determined by law.

ARTICLE 146. No amendment to the Constitution may be made unless it shall have been proposed by over one-fourth of the delegates to the People's Congress and passed by at least two-thirds of the delegates present at a meeting having a quorum of over three-fourths of the entire Congress.

A proposed amendment to the Constitution shall be made public by the proposer or proposers one year before the assembling of the People's Congress.

ARTICLE 147. In regard to those provisions of the Constitution which require further procedure for their enforcement, such necessary procedure shall be determined by law.

B. THE SYSTEM OF ORGANIZATION OF THE NATIONAL CONGRESS [1]

The following laws were passed by the Legislative *Yüan* April 31, XXVI (1937), in amended form, after the election had been postponed.

ARTICLE 1. The National Congress shall frame the Constitution, and shall determine its date of execution.

ARTICLE 2. *i.* The National Congress shall be organized by the Representatives of the people to the Congress.

ii. The manner of electing these Representatives is fixed in another set of laws.

ARTICLE 3. Members and reserve members of the Central Executive Committee of the Kuomintang, and of the Central Supervisory Committee of the Kuomintang shall be Representatives to the Congress without election; members

[1] "Kuo-min Ta-hui Tsu-chih Fa" in Chung-yang Hsüan-ch'uan Pu (Party-Ministry of Publicity), *Hsien-chêng Chien-shê Fa-kuei*, Chungking, XXVIII (1939), p. 35–8.

of the National Government and its officials may attend the Congress.

ARTICLE 4. The date of convening the Congress is to be fixed by the National Government.

ARTICLE 5. The Congress shall convene in the locality occupied by the National Government.

ARTICLE 6. Representatives to the Congress shall take an oath of allegiance during the opening ceremonies of the Congress, to wit: "I, — — —, do hereby promise with absolute sincerity that as a representative of the Chinese people, I shall receive the instructions of Dr. Sun Yat-sen, the Father of the Republic, and that I shall execute my official power only according to law, and shall obey the discipline of the National Congress."

After taking the oath, the Representatives should thereto sign their names.

ARTICLE 7. Thirty-one members shall be elected from among the Representatives themselves to form the Presidium of the Congress. Their duties shall be:
    i. To fix the manner of discussing motions and to regulate the progress of the discussion.
    ii. To discharge executive affairs of the Congress.
    iii. To perform other duties fixed in this code of laws.

ARTICLE 8. During a meeting of the Congress, the Presidium shall elect the Chairman of the Meeting.

ARTICLE 9. The National Congress shall form special committees to examine the qualifications of the Representatives, to examine motions and proposals and for other matters. These committees shall be organized upon the request of the Presidium and passed by the Meeting.

ARTICLE 10. The period of a session of the Congress is 10 to 20 days; it may be extended whenever necessary.

ARTICLE 11. The duties of the National Congress are fully discharged when its Meeting closes.

ARTICLE 12. A quorum shall consist of at least half of the total number of members. Motion can be passed when more than half of the members present vote for it.

In adopting the Constitution, at least two-thirds of the total number of the members shall be present, and adoption shall require a majority greater than two-thirds of the members present.

ARTICLE 13. The Congress may adopt any of the following methods to put a motion to vote: raising the hands, standing up, or balloting. In case of a tie, the Chairman may cast the deciding vote.

ARTICLE 14. The National Congress shall have a Secretariat and an organization of police guards. Their organization and duties shall be decided by the Presidium.

ARTICLE 15. The National Congress shall have a Secretary General, appointed by the Presidium, and discharging the affairs of the entire Congress.

ARTICLE 16. The Representatives shall not assume any responsibility towards the general public for any opinion expressed by them during the session of the Congress.

ARTICLE 17. Except by approval of the Congress, no Representative of the Congress may be detained or arrested when the Congress is in session.

ARTICLE 18. During the session, a Representative who does not abide by the rules of the Congress may be warned by the Chairman, or may forfeit his privilege to speak. Adequate punishment shall be imposed upon any who may commit serious offenses.

ARTICLE 19. The above mentioned punishment will be decided by the Congress, upon the examination of the Punishment Committee (formed by the Representatives to the Congress).

ARTICLE 20. The date of adoption of this code of laws is to be fixed in an order from the Central Government.

C. ACT OF THE LEGISLATIVE *YÜAN*, APRIL 31, XXVI (1937) GOVERNING THE ELECTION OF REPRESENTATIVES TO THE NATIONAL CONGRESS [1]

[Note particularly the world-wide electoral areas.]

CHAPTER I. GENERAL PRINCIPLES

ARTICLE 1. These laws are formulated in conjunction with what is provided in Section *ii* of Article 2 in the Law concerning the System of Organization of the National Congress.

ARTICLE 2. Besides the Representatives to the National Congress without election, there shall also be provided:

i. 665 Representatives elected through district election.

ii. 380 Representatives elected through professional election.

[1] "Kuo-min Ta-hui Tai-piao Hsüan-chü Fa" in Chung-yang Hsüanch'uan Pu (Party-Ministry of Publicity) *Hsien-chêng Chien-shê Fa-kuei*, Chungking, XXVIII (1939), p. 38–49.

iii. 155 Representatives elected through special election.

iv. 240 Representatives appointed by the National Government.

ARTICLE 3. All citizens of China above 20 years of age have the privilege of voting for Representatives to Congress, upon taking the oath of citizenship.

ARTICLE 4. The following persons have no privilege of voting:

i. Rebels against the National Government, proven or under arrest.

ii. Corrupt officials, proven or under arrest.

iii. Those whose citizenship privileges have been forfeited due to crimes, etc.

iv. Those who are insolvent.

v. Those afflicted with mental diseases.

vi. Those smoking opium or substitutes therefor.

ARTICLE 5. Each voter may have not more than two choices.

Those who may both elect in the district and the professional elections should participate in the professional election. Those who may both elect in the professional election and the special election should elect in the special election. In professional election, an elector eligible in more than two professions should vote only in one of them at his choice.

ARTICLE 6. The Representatives to the National Congress are elected by balloting which does not require signature, and by single entry. The names of candidates for Representative should be printed on the ballot, and the electors are to choose one man out of them.

ARTICLE 7. Candidates for Representative who receive a majority vote are elected as Representatives. In case of tie, the candidates shall draw lots to decide who is the elected Representative.

ARTICLE 8. After the full number of Representatives has been obtained, those candidates who obtain some votes [but less than a majority] will be reserve Representatives. Their rank will be based upon the number of votes. In number the reserve Representatives shall correspond to the elected Representatives.

CHAPTER II. DISTRICT ELECTION

ARTICLE 9. All provinces and cities directly under the Executive Yüan shall elect a number of Representatives corresponding to the attached List No. 1, and according to the laws governing District Elections.

ARTICLE 10. The Representatives from various provinces are elected in various districts. The division of districts and the number of Representatives elected in every district are fixed in the attached List No. 2.

ARTICLE 11. The Heads of the *hsiang* [suburb of a city] and of the *chên* [a village market] of each hsien in the electorate should nominate candidates. The number should be ten times that of the number of Representatives to be elected. If there is a *shih* within the electorate, the Head of the *fang* [a group of houses in a *shih*] should also participate in the nomination. If there is no Head of the *hsiang* or *chên* in a *hsien*, then the corresponding officials of the *hsiang, chên,* or *hsien* shall nominate.

ARTICLE 12. Candidates for Representative should have the following qualifications:

　i. Possess the qualifications of an elector of the Representatives and have taken the citizenship oath in an electorate other than this one.

　ii. Be above twenty-five years of age.

　iii. Be a resident of the respective electoral district.

ARTICLE 13. Representatives to the National Congress in each district are elected in the manner prescribed in Article 6.

ARTICLE 14. The Special Municipalities directly under the Executive Yüan should elect their Representatives according to Articles 11–13 and Article 15.

CHAPTER III. PROFESSIONAL ELECTION

ARTICLE 15. The various professional organs in provinces or Special Municipalities should elect a number of Representatives according to the attached List No. 3.

ARTICLE 16. Organs of the liberal professions shall elect Representatives not according to localities or districts. Their numbers are fixed in attached List No. 4.

ARTICLE 17. The professional organs participating in the election are limited to those who were legally recognized before the adoption of this code of laws.

ARTICLE 18. The officers of the various professional organs shall nominate Representatives for those particular professions. Their number should be three times the number of Representatives to be elected. The officers mentioned above are limited to those who have executive power in that particular professional organ.

ARTICLE 19. Nominated Representatives for professional election should have the following qualifications:
  i. Possess the privileges of an elector.
  ii. Be above twenty-five years of age.
  iii. Have been practicing in that profession for three years or more.
  iv. Be a member of that professional organization.

The period of practicing that profession may be the sum of intermittent periods of practice.

ARTICLE 20. The Representatives of professional organs should be elected by legally recognized electors according to Article 6.

ARTICLE 21. If there are several sub-organs to a professional organization, the nomination of Representatives should be made by the officials of the lowest sub-organ, and elected by the members of the lowest sub-organ.

If the members of the professional organization form groups, then the election of Representatives should be done by the individual members of those groups.

ARTICLE 22. In Special Municipalities directly under the Executive Yüan, the nomination and election of Representatives from professional organizations should be in accordance with Article 24.

ARTICLE 23. For organs of the liberal professions, their manner of nominating and electing is the same as for professional organizations.

CHAPTER IV. SPECIAL ELECTIONS

Section 1. *Elections in the Provinces of Liaoning, Kirin, Heilungkiang and Jehol*

ARTICLE 24. No distinction concerning district or profession is made in the election of Representatives in these four provinces. Their numbers are:
  i. For Liaoning   14
  ii. For Kirin   13
  iii. For Heilungkiang 9
  iv. For Jehol   9

Two of the Representatives from Kirin are elected in the Special Eastern District of that Province.

[Provision is made for the use of polls in exile and for absentee ballots.]

Section 2. *Elections in Mongolia and Tibet*
[This follows the provisions of Section 1.]

Section 3. *Representatives from Overseas*

ARTICLE 32. The numbers of Representatives from overseas are as follows:

1 from Hawaii	1 from Chile
1 from Peru	1 from Cuba
1 from Mexico	1 from Central America
3 from the United States	2 from the Philippines
2 from Canada	4 from Malaya
3 from Annam	2 from Thailand (Siam)
1 from India	2 from Burma
1 from Europe	1 from Japan
1 from Korea	1 from Australia
1 from Tahiti	1 from Africa
4 from The Netherlands East Indies	1 from Hong Kong
1 from Macao	1 from Formosa

ARTICLE 33. The nomination of overseas Representatives is modelled after that of Professional Elections. But the groups nominating the Representatives are to be approved by the Central Committee of Overseas Affairs.

The National Government shall fix twice the number of Representatives electable as nominated Representatives.

ARTICLE 34. The election of Overseas Representatives is modelled after that governing provincial districts.

Section 4. *Elections in the Army, Navy, and Air Forces*

ARTICLE 35. Thirty Representatives shall be elected from the Nation's army, navy, air force, and other military organs.

ARTICLE 36. Nominations of Representatives from the military are as follows:

i. The Army: Two nominations from every division. One from every independent *lü* [brigade] or from special brigades holding more than two *tuan* [regiments]. For the rest of the smaller forces, nomination of Representatives shall be made by combination of the forces.

ii. The Navy: Each fleet may nominate one Representative. All the Marines combined may nominate one Representative. The Department of the Navy will combine the remainder to nominate Representatives.

iii. The Air Force shall nominate one Representative.

iv. Three Representatives shall be nominated by other military organs.

The National Government will appoint ninety Representatives thus nominated as the nominated Representatives.

ARTICLE 37. The nominated Representatives will be elected by the officers and soldiers of the military who have the qualifications of electors. Representatives are elected in the manner prescribed in Article 6.

ARTICLE 38. Representatives nominated should have the following qualifications:

i. Possess the qualifications of an elector.

ii. Be more than twenty-five years of age.

iii. Have served for more than five years in the troops with good record, or be a graduate of good standing from a military school.

CHAPTER V. ELECTION OF THE CHIEF ELECTION OFFICE AND OF THE ELECTION INSPECTORS

ARTICLE 39. The National Government forms the Chief Election Office of the Representatives of the National Congress. The Office is headed by a Commissioner and a Deputy Commissioner. Election Inspectors are also specially appointed to direct and watch all affairs of the election. The appointment of the Chief Election Office is determined by order.

ARTICLE 40. The Election Inspector of every province is the Commissioner of the Bureau of Civil Affairs of the province.

The Provincial Election Inspector is the highest executive official of the province. In case there is no highest official, the Chief Election Office will appoint one of the executive officials to fill the post.

ARTICLE 41. In Special Municipalities directly under the Executive Yüan, the Inspector is the City Mayor.

ARTICLE 42. In elections in Liaoning, Kirin, Heilungkiang, and Jehol, and of liberal professional organizations, the Minister of the Ministry of the Interior will be the Inspector-General. In elections in Mongolia and Tibet, the Chairman of the Mongolian and Tibetan Affairs Commission will be the Inspector-General. In overseas elections, the Chairman of the Overseas Affairs Committee will be the Inspector-General.

ARTICLE 43. Elections in Mongolia, Tibet, and overseas and military elections shall be under the Inspectors appointed by the Chief Election Office.

ARTICLE 44. The qualifications of the electors, the nominated and elected Representatives shall be examined by the Inspectors.

ARTICLE 45. The date and locality of the election are fixed by the Election Inspectors.

ARTICLE 46. The rest of the officials for the election, e.g., ballot administrators and inspectors, etc., are also appointed by the Inspectors-General.

ARTICLE 47. Inspectors and officials for electoral affairs cannot be the Congress Representatives of that district or professional organization.

[ARTICLE 48 omitted in the text.]

CHAPTER VI. ELECTION AND FORFEITED ELECTION

ARTICLE 49. The election is considered null and void if:
 i. It is legally proved that more than one-third of the electorate are cheating in or manipulating the election; or,
 ii. It is legally proved that the election is not conducted according to the laws prescribed.

ARTICLE 50. In case of an election being forfeited, it should be performed again according to law, unless it be too late to repeat under the existing circumstances.

ARTICLE 51. Elected Representatives lose their privilege when:
 i. They die; or,
 ii. It is legally proved that their submitted qualifications are false; or,
 iii. It is legally proved that the number of ballots is incorrect.

ARTICLE 52. When an elected Representative loses his privilege or when he refuses to take his privilege, the reserve Representative will take his place as prescribed in Article 8.

CHAPTER VII. LAW SUITS CONCERNING ELECTION AFFAIRS

ARTICLE 53. Electors or nominated Representatives who are not elected may file suit within ten days of the date of the election against any administrative officer of the election if they hold that he abuses his duty.

ARTICLE 54. If electors or nominated Representatives who are not elected see that the number of ballots cast for the elected Representatives are untrue, or that the qualifications of the elected Representatives are untrue, they may file suit within five days of the date for announcement of successful candidates.

ARTICLE 55. All law suits connected with election affairs will be heard by the Supreme Court. They shall take precedence over all other cases, and sentence will be given after one single hearing. Law suits connected with military elections will be heard before a military tribunal.

ARTICLE 56. Offenses committed during an election are governed by the criminal code.

CHAPTER VIII. SUPPLEMENT

ARTICLE 57. When it is impossible to elect in Special Elections as prescribed in Chapter IV, the National Government may appoint Representatives.

ARTICLE 58. The Chief Election Office for the Election of Representatives to the National Congress is the sole organ empowered to interpret the meaning of this set of laws.

ARTICLE 59. The detailed procedure for enforcing these laws will be fixed by order.

ARTICLE 60. The date of enforcing these laws will be fixed by order.

[The attached lists are omitted.]

D. THE PROGRAM OF RESISTANCE AND RECONSTRUCTION [1]

This quasi-constitutional proclamation of war policy for the nation was adopted by the Kuomintang Party Congress, Emergency Session, at Hankow, March 29, 1938.

A. GENERAL PRINCIPLES:

1. Dr. Sun Yat-sen's revolutionary principles and his other teachings are hereby declared to be the supreme authority, regulating all war-time activities and the work of national reconstruction.

2. All war-time powers and forces are hereby placed un-

[1] Official English text from Ch'u Chia-hua (Party-Minister of Organization of the Kuomintang), "Consolidation of Democracy in China," in Council of International Affairs, *The Chinese Yearbook 1938–39*, [Hong Kong], 1939, p. 337–8.

der the control of the Kuomintang and of General Chiang K'ai-shek.

B. DIPLOMACY:

3. China is prepared to ally herself with all states and nations that sympathize with her cause, and to wage a common struggle for peace and justice.

4. China is prepared to safeguard and strengthen the machinery of peace as well as all treaties and conventions that have the maintenance of peace as their ultimate object.

5. China is prepared to ally herself with all forces that are opposed to Japanese imperialism in order to check Japanese aggression and to safeguard peace in the Far East.

6. China is prepared to improve still further the existing friendly relations with other Powers in order to gain more sympathy for the cause.

7. All bogus political organizations which Japan has created in consequence of her military occupation of Chinese territory, and all their actions, are hereby repudiated and declared null and void.

C. MILITARY AFFAIRS:

8. The army shall receive more political training, so that both officers and men may appreciate the importance of war-time national reconstruction and be ready to lay down their lives for the nation.

9. All able-bodied men shall be trained; the people shall have their military strength increased; the troops at the various fronts shall be supplied with new recruits. Overseas Chinese who have returned home to offer their services at the front shall be given a proper course of training to fit them for their work.

10. All people who have arms of their own shall receive the support and encouragement of the Government and, under the direction of local military authorities, shall cooperate with the regular army to defend the country against foreign invasion. Guerrilla warfare shall be waged in the enemy's rear with the object of smashing and dividing his military forces.

11. Both the wounded and the killed shall be pensioned; the disabled shall be cared for; and the families of soldiers fighting at the front shall be treated with the utmost consideration, so that people will rejoice to fight for their country and the work of national mobilization may proceed with the highest degree of efficiency.

D. POLITICS:

12. A People's Political Council shall be created in order to unify the national strength, to utilize the best minds of the nation, and to facilitate the formulation and execution of national policies.

13. The district [*hsien*] shall be taken as the fundamental unit from which the work of increasing the self-defensive power of the people shall be started. The conditions of local self-government shall be fulfilled as soon as possible, so that the political and social basis of the present war shall have been firmly established and a preparation shall have been made for the eventual promulgation of a constitution.

14. A thorough reform in the central and local governmental machinery shall be instituted with the object of simplifying and making it rational. Only thus can administrative efficiency be obtained to meet the urgent needs of war.

15. The conduct of all officials, both high and low, shall conform to rules of propriety. They shall be faithful to their work, ready to sacrifice themselves for the cause of the nation, observe discipline, and obey orders, so that they may serve as a model for the people. If they prove to be disloyal and obstruct the prosecution of the war, they shall be tried by court martial.

16. Corrupt officials shall be severely punished, and their property shall be confiscated.

E. ECONOMICS:

17. Economic reconstruction shall concern itself mainly with matters of military importance, and incidentally with matters that contribute to the improvement of the livelihood of the people. With these objects in view, a planned economy shall be put into operation, investments by people both at home and abroad shall be encouraged, and large-scale war-time production shall be undertaken.

18. The greatest measure of energy shall be devoted to the development of village economy, the encouragement of cooperative enterprises, the unhampered transportation of foodstuffs, the cultivation of waste land, and the work of irrigation.

19. Mining shall be undertaken; the foundations of heavy industries shall be laid; light industries shall be encouraged; and handicraft industries in the various provinces shall be developed.

20. War-time taxes shall be levied, and thoroughgoing reforms in financial administration shall be instituted.

21. The banking business shall be strictly controlled, so that commercial and industrial activities may be properly adjusted.

22. The legal tender shall be made unassailable; foreign exchange shall be controlled; and imports and exports shall be regulated in order to secure financial stability.

23. Facilities of communication shall be improved; transportation by steamers, automobiles, and aeroplanes shall be undertaken; railroads and highways shall be built; and air lines shall be increased.

24. No profiteering or cornering shall be allowed; and a system of price-fixing shall be instituted.

F. MASS MOVEMENT:

25. The people throughout the country shall be organized into occupational groups such as farmers, laborers, merchants, and students. The principle shall be: From each according to his ability. The rich shall contribute in money, and the able-bodied shall sweat. All classes of people shall be mobilized for war.

26. In the course of the war, the freedom of speech, the freedom of the press, and the freedom of assembly shall be fully guaranteed to the people, provided they do not contravene Dr. Sun Yat-sen's revolutionary principles or the provisions of the law.

27. Refugees from the war areas as well as unemployed people shall receive relief, and shall be given proper training to fit them for war-time work.

28. National consciousness shall be instilled into the people, so that they may assist the Government in detecting and eradicating treasonable acts. Traitors shall be severely punished, and their property shall be confiscated.

G. EDUCATION:

29. The whole educational system shall be reorganized. A course of war-time education shall be instituted and emphasis shall be placed on the cultivation of morals, scientific research, and the expansion of research facilities.

30. Various technical experts shall be trained and assigned to proper posts in order to meet the requirements of war.

31. The youths of the nation shall be properly trained, so that they may offer their services to society and contribute to the cause of the war.

E. AN OUTLINE OF WAR-TIME CONTROLMENT [1]

An official but unpublished statement, this document was presented by the President of the Control *Yüan* to the author for inclusion in the present work.

According to Article 46, Chapter VIII of the Organic Law of the National Government, the Control *Yüan* is "the highest supervisory organ of the government, obliged to exercise the power of impeachment and auditing in accordance with law." Since the beginning of our resistance against the Japanese invasion, the powers of control have been gradually strengthened so as to meet the demands of this critical time. A static control has developed into a dynamic one; that is, more emphasis is laid upon prevention than upon correction. Therefore the duties of the office become heavier and more complicated, as its work becomes more intensified. But the influence which the *Yüan* has exercised over Chinese politics as a whole becomes also wider and wider. In this report, we are going to describe the activities of the *Yüan* under the two headings of the Control *Yüan* and the Ministry of Audit.

THE CONTROL YÜAN:

The function of auditing is performed by the Ministry of Audit, subsidiary to the *Yüan*. What is directly performed by the *Yüan* is impeachment. On the authority of the Impeachment Act, any motion of impeachment, after being proposed by some control Committee or control Commissioner, is to be reviewed by three other control Committees. If the bill is passed by the three, the accused must be punished. Whenever a bill is rejected and its proponent does not agree to the rejection, the bill shall be reviewed once more by five other committees whose determination shall be final. Furthermore, emergency relief measures may be requested, according to the urgency of the occasion; and in order to facilitate the performance of its functions, the *Yüan* is permitted to investigate the documents of other

[1] An unpublished memorandum presented in manuscript by President Yü Yu-jên of the Control *Yüan* to the author in Chungking, September 1940. It consists of nine folios, not numbered, with a chart. It is entitled *Chan Shih Chien-ch'a K'ai-lüeh* (An Outline of War-time Controlment), and is dated August, XXVIII (1939). The present extract is folios 1-A to 4-B.

offices as well as to demand explanations from them. The initiation of a motion of impeachment must be based upon one of the three following conditions:

    a. Article 2, Impeachment Act: "If any illegal action or negligence of duty of an official be discovered, the Control *Yüan* itself is permitted to bring an impeachment against him."

    b. Article 4, Regulations for the Execution of Government Rights; and Article 11, Act for the Punishment of Officials: "Specified officials may be impeached on demand of the superior who has submitted the case of his guilty subordinate to the Control *Yüan*."

    c. "If an official be accused by the people, the case must be investigated. If the accusation prove to be true, the accused shall be impeached."

Although it is very prudent that the legislators have obliged the impeaching officers to take such steps as investigation, motion, and review, yet in this critical time these complicated measures must be considered too slow to keep pace with the development of affairs.

After the outbreak of war, the Central Government published the "Temporary Regulations for the Execution of War-time Controlment," in which the Control *Yüan* was charged with the duties of *censure* and *proposition,* besides what have already been mentioned. By censure it is meant that when emergency measures must be taken against an official whose illegal action or negligence of duty has been discovered, a written notice of censure may be submitted to the officer who directly controls, or is immediately superior to, the official in question. The officer receiving the notice must decide in as short a time as possible to deal with the censured with the administrative power in his hands. If he holds the censured innocent, he must reply, giving sufficient reasons. If he takes no measures, or fails to reply, or replies groundlessly, the control Committee making the censure is obliged to change the motion of censure into one of impeachment, and the impeached is liable to a penalty. Hence the principal significance of censure is that it takes emergency measures against the undesirable conduct of officials, so as to meet the demands of the war-time. This also implies further extension of the controlment to the administrative system, in order to quicken efficiency.

As for *proposition,* this means that when some legally specified obligations of office are administered feebly or inadequately, the Control *Yüan* may make a proposal or express its views to the office involved or to the office immediately superior. The office which receives the proposal must in as short a time as possible take adequate measures to remedy the situation. The duties of *proposition,* therefore, can not only correct administrators, but can also improve agencies. They are preventive, capable of requiring strict improvement of governmental activities. Effective anticipatory control may now be exercised over Chinese government agencies. Since being charged with the two new duties of censure and proposition, the Control *Yüan* has carried them into action with prudence. And the effects are rather remarkable.

When, in 1937, the government was moved to Chungking, a part of the *Yüan* employees were ordered dismissed. But the *Yüan* authorities still prepared copies of "Directions for the Work of Control *Yüan* Employees in Their Native (or Other) Cities (or Provinces)," and "Directions for the Work of Dismissed Control *Yüan* Employees," which were distributed to the dismissed. The former employees have been obliged to make monthly reports upon the local phenomena according to the "Directions." These reports are sent to the *Yüan,* thus helping its understanding of the truth in all corners of China.

In view of the fact that the "Temporary Regulations for the Execution of War-time Controlment" came into force, the Control *Yüan* accordingly prepared "Directions for Inspection and Investigation." From time to time, the control commissioners have been ordered to tour their respective districts. Moreover, control committees have been selected and sent out to different places to perform inspection of administration, national spiritual mobilization, conscription, military confiscation and requisition, the organization and training of the people, hoarding and reserves of supplies, communication and transportation, public support of the war, public security, the utter erasure of traitors, anti-air-raid preparations, ambulance equipment, the management of wounded soldiers and of refugees, taxation and other imposts on the people, production, construction, education, and all other things related to the war. Thus the work of the *Yüan* has become all the more intensified. In order to adapt itself to the circumstances, its organization was readjusted. A "Board of Legislative Study," subordinate to the *Yüan,* was established, with a view to studying Dr. Sun Yat-sen's "Constitution based upon the Principle of the

Separation of Five Powers," the Control system, and anything related to war-time legislation about controlment. Besides, a "Committee on Procedural Technique" was added under the Secretariat, so that it will prepare plans for the improvement of *Yüan* activities, and will help to carry them into action.

In the spring of 1939, a "Plan of War-time Procedure for the Second Stage of War" was passed in the Fifth Plenary Session of the C.E.C. and C.S.C. of the Kuomintang. Both the decision concerning Article VI of Political Report and the lecture delivered by Generalissimo Chiang K'ai-shek in this meeting showed that much was expected from the Control *Yüan*. Abiding by the government's policy and taking into consideration its present needs, the *Yüan*, in addition to the performance of impeachment, censure, proposition and other functions established by law, prepared "An Outline of the Execution of War-time Controlment for the Second Stage" and its "Preliminary Procedure," with the extension of inspection as the chief means to set the machinery in motion.

According to the aforementioned "Outline" and "Procedure," the work of inspection is classified into two kinds. The inspection of the conduct of political officers and administrative officials is termed the *general inspection*. When special agents are sent out to inspect specified cases, this is called the *special inspection*. For the general inspection of the Central Government, the units are the offices, while for that of the local governments, the units are the districts [*hsien*]. In the case of a special inspection, when the agents are sent out solely by the Control *Yüan*, the term used is *exclusive inspection;* the inspection performed cooperatively by agents both of the *Yüan* and of other offices is called *joint inspection*.

The general inspection has, since January 1940, been vigorously put into effect. For instance, the anti-air-raid preparations on the outskirts of Chungking, the relief and management of wounded soldiers, refugees, and suffering children, and the spiritual mobilization of central and local government offices (including problems of efficiency and diligence) have all been carefully examined. Moreover, Control Committees have been sent out to different districts within certain periods, the frequency of which is based upon the importance of the place. Some went to Kweichow and Szechwan to inspect local administration in different districts. Recently, committees have been sent out to Shantung to make a variety of inspections. As for the special inspections, delegates have been incessantly sent out to make exclusive inspections; and joint inspections have also been made, by the joining of many control committees into the Itinerant Inspection Corps for Military Discipline and Morale, and the War-time Economic Inspection Corps. Committees which have thus been delegated to joint work are not only obliged to fulfil duties required by the Corps, but are also permitted independently to impeach or censure illegal or incompetent officials, whether civil or military. The primary functions of the committees remain unaffected.

Since military operations must be in harmony with political administration, wherever the military power reaches, the power of controlment must follow in its wake. The Control *Yüan* recently prepared the "Regulations for the Organization of Control *Yüan* War-time Inspection Corps of War Districts," which were later sanctioned and then promulgated. The number of the corps and of the areas to be inspected are fixed according to the War Districts marked off by the Military Affairs Commission. Each corps consists of three committees, and is organized by the control committees themselves; if there is a control commissioner in the area, he of course joins the committee, and performs all the functions established for him by law. Under each committee there are one secretary, one inspecting agent, three assistants, and one clerk—to assist the committees in routine administration.

Since the work of the control commissioners is stationary, behind the battle lines, the Inspection Corps of War Districts are itinerant, so that their emphasis can be laid upon the front. They are mutually dependent and intimately correlated. The network of national controlment is completed by the mobilization of the control committees to be sent out to make inspections, so that corruption may be eliminated and law and order enforced. And undoubtedly our resistance against the Japanese invasion has been benefited. This work is indeed a great help to the construction of a new China.

F. A CHART OF THE CONTROL *YÜAN* FROM JULY 1937 TO JUNE 1940[1]

THE READJUSTMENT:

Since the outbreak of war, the *Yüan,* together with other offices of the Government, was moved from Nanking to Chungking. In order to adapt itself to the circumstances, its organization was readjusted. A "Board of Legislative Study" was established, while the six sections of General Affairs, Editing, Book-Collection, Printing, Receipt and Transmission,[2] and Archive, all subordinate to the Secretariat, were merged into four departments. Moreover, a "Committee on Administrative Procedure" and two new sections, called the first and the second, were added to the main body of the *Yüan.*

THE FUNCTIONS:

Functions Established by Law
- Impeachment
- Censure
- Proposition
- Supervision of Examinations
- Audit
- Acceptance of Popular Petitions
- Inquiry and Examination
- Emergency Relief Measures
- Interpellation

THE WORK:

1. Acceptance of people's petitions and investigations:
    Number of petitions received in this period ....
    [Number is omitted from original report.]
    Number of cases in which delegates were sent out to investigate ....
    [Number omitted.]
    Number of cases in which other offices were charged to investigate ....
    [Number omitted.]
    (Those petitions which were either outside the function of control or false in the description of facts were remarked upon and preserved by the committees.)

[1] Continuation of Appendix I (E), p. 313; this comprises folios 5-A to 9-A with chart.
[2] A formal agency for the receipt and registry of incoming communications, and of verification and transmission of outgoing ones.

THE PRESENT ORGANIZATION:
The Control *Yüan*

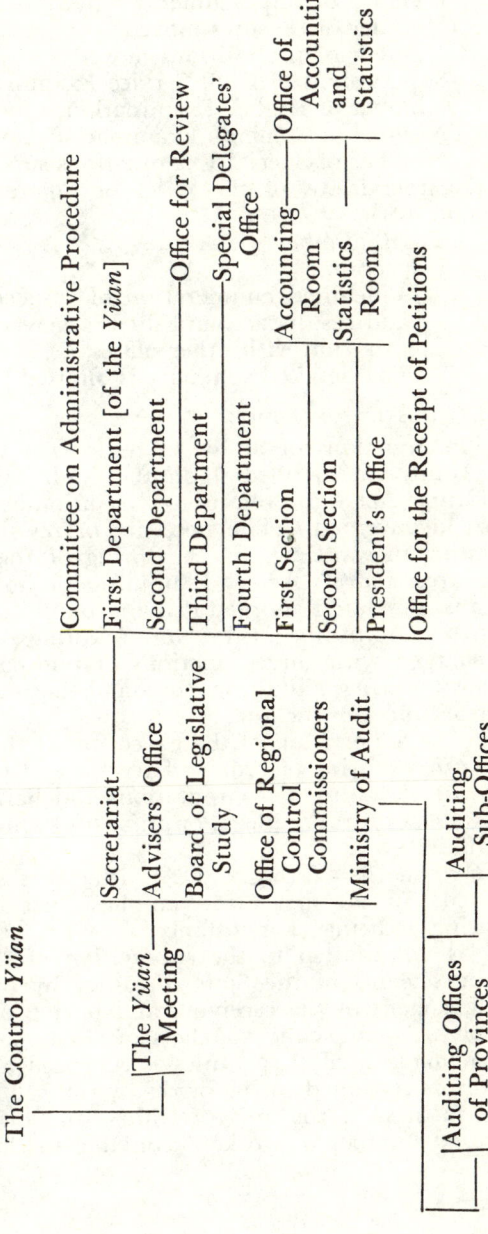

2. Motions:
    Number of impeachments moved 121
    Number of censures moved 149
    Number of propositions moved 234
3. Supervisions of Civil Service Examinations:
    Number of Higher Examinations supervised ...   2
    Number of Common Examinations supervised ..   5
    Number of Special Examinations supervised ... 34
4. Supervisions of the relief of sufferers from natural calamities:
    Total number 5
5. Inspections:
    [A detailed enumeration of inspections performed and results accomplished is here omitted.]
6. Cooperation with other offices:
    [The detailed summary is omitted.]

THE MINISTRY OF AUDIT:

The functions of audit, as performed by the Ministry of Audit, are founded upon the Auditing Act. The old Auditing Act, however, is too tradition-bound and therefore inconvenient. The necessity of revision is especially pressing in war-time. In the spring of 1938, the Ministry prepared a draft Act and submitted it to the Legislative Yüan. The latter adopted this and published a New Auditing Act. According to the New Auditing Act, the Ministry is charged with three functions of internal checking (interior auditing), auditing (post-auditing) and supervision. These functions include:
    i. Supervision of the execution of the budgets;
    ii. Scrutiny of orders of receipt and payment;
    iii. Scrutiny of computations and balance sheets;
    iv. Control of illegal or unfaithful conduct in financial affairs.

Two merits of the New Auditing Act should be mentioned. In the first place, emphasis has been laid upon visiting auditing. For instance, the work of internal checking is not limited to the supervision of the receipts and disbursements of the State Treasury by the scrutiny and indorsement of the receiving and paying orders; but even receiving and paying vouchers of Government offices have been made ineffective, unless scrutinized and indorsed by auditors stationed in the offices by the Ministry. Owing to the vastness of the area of China, and owing also to the limited number of workers available in this line, this system is not universally applicable. Only offices in which the work of receiving and paying is especially heavy find such auditors present. As for auditing, the Government offices were formerly obliged only to submit to the Ministry accounting reports which they themselves had prepared. It is different now. The New Act ordains that auditors should be sent out periodically by the Ministry to visit the Government offices and scrutinize their books and vouchers. Or in each year, some offices should be selected to be thus scrutinized. The duties of supervision were not clearly defined, but they now include the following items: (*a*) the supervision of the revenue and expenditures of the offices; (*b*) the scrutiny of cash, bills, and bonds in the offices; (*c*) the supervision of the construction of buildings and of the purchase or sale of the property attached to the offices; (*d*) the supervision of the drawing and repayment of bonds and the destruction of bonds returned; (*e*) joint-administration with the financial departments of other offices; and (*f*) the scrutiny of other administrative affairs related to finance.

Secondly, the New Auditing Act ordains that the Ministry of Audit is directly responsible for the auditing of financial affairs of the offices of different ranks of the Central Government, while that of the local governments is under the charge of local auditing offices, subordinate to the Ministry.

[A detailed narrative of the war-time work of the ministry is omitted.]

Before the outbreak of war, the Ministry had established auditing offices in the Provinces of Kiangsu, Chekiang, Hupeh, Shensi and Honan and in the city of Shanghai, and one sub-office for the Tientsin-Pukow Railway. The office of Shanghai concurrently took charge of the auditing affairs of the Nanking-Shanghai Railway; and that of Hupeh, the affairs of the Peiping-Hankow Railway. In 1938 the offices of Hunan, Kweichow and Szechwan were established. In July 1939, a conference of auditors was held in Chungking. All auditors sent out now returned to attend it. They reported on their work, assisted the auditors in the Ministry, and discussed with them the directions of war-time auditing. In October, Mr. Lin Yün-kai, the Minister of Audit, visited Szechwan, Shensi, Kansu, and Chinghai to inspect the audit work going on in Shensi and Szechwan and at the same time to examine the local financial conditions as a step toward the extension of the auditing system.

In the spring of 1939, the Ministry prepared "An Outline for the Execution of War-time Audits" which was passed and enacted by the Supreme National Defense Council. There are eleven items, to be carried out in several periods, in this outline. A part of them are required by the New Auditing Act, while the rest are the new work arising from the war. They are as follows:

a. Auditing prefectural [*hsien*] finance: A prefecture, on the authority of Dr. Sun Yat-sen's Constitution, is the unit of self-government; and whenever the self-government is accomplished, China becomes constitutional. This being the case, the prefectural finance actually concerns the future of the country and the people. Therefore, beginning from 1939, the Ministry introduced the auditing of prefectural finance. It ordered the provincial offices to have the prefectures make monthly reports on their revenue and expenditure. The reports should be submitted to the provincial auditing offices which will also send out delegates to scrutinize the accounting records of some selected prefectures as well as to investigate the prefectural financial organizations, the taxation system, and the sorts of taxes. Up to June 1940, there have been 84 prefectures selected for such investigation.

b. The auditing of the Central Government Offices in the provinces and cities where no auditing offices have been established: In such cases, the Ministry has appointed the auditing offices of neighboring localities to take charge. But the Ministry has taken over the auditing affairs of Chungking for the moment. Meantime, plans have been made to establish auditing offices in Kwangsi, Fukien, etc.

c. The auditing of the receipts and disbursements of public treasuries: Since October 1939, when the Public Treasury Act came into force, the Ministry has sent delegates to the State Treasury Bureau to scrutinize and indorse the accounting vouchers, and the provincial offices have sent delegates to Provincial Treasuries as well.

d. The auditing of special funds: As a rule, the institutes in charge of special funds have from time to time submitted their reports on their receipts and disbursements to the Ministry. Since 1939, the Ministry has also sent delegates to examine strictly these funds.

e. Itinerant auditing: The present economic conditions do not permit the Ministry to establish auditing offices in all the government-owned concerns. But itinerant auditing, after the model of circuit courts, has been introduced since 1939. The Suchow-Kunming and Yünnan-Burma Railways have been thus examined. The provincial offices have also applied this system to the business offices.

f. The visiting auditing: The system of visiting auditing has been developed gradually. Delegates have been stationed in Sufferers' Relief Committee, City Government of Chungking, Ministry of Finance, Ministry of Economics, and Ministry of Communications. Other delegates have been sent out to visit some selected offices who have submitted their accounting reports.

g. The supervision of the revenue of government offices: Salt Tax and Commodities Tax have been scrutinized.

h. The supervision of clothing, provisions, and other military supplies: Since the outbreak of war, the amount of clothing, provisions, etc. purchased by the military authorities has greatly increased. The delegates from the Ministry are always present on the occasions of signing contracts, announcing the bids, deciding the winning bidder, and delivering the goods. If the supplies are purchased in the provinces, the provincial offices are in charge of the supervision.

i. The supervision of mass purchase and constructions: The delegates from the Ministry or its provincial offices are always present on the occasions of signing contracts, announcing the bids, deciding the winning bidder, and delivering the goods or completing constructions when there are any mass purchases or sales of government-owned property or any construction work.

j. The financial scrutiny of the war-time provisional organizations: There are huge sums of receipts and disbursements in such organizations as the "Joint Emergency Air Raid Relief Office of Chungking" and the general office of the "National Committee for Soldiers' Comfort," so that their auditing affairs are made the charge of the delegates from the Ministry.

k. The supervision of the payment, preservation, and usage of contributions of all sorts: National Salvation Bonds, Aviation Contribution, and all other contributions donated by the Chinese at home and abroad have been scrutinized by the Ministry delegates.

Many considerable results have been achieved since the execution of the above items from January 1939, to date. The "Auditing Plan for 1941" has already been prepared by the Ministry. When it is passed by the Supreme National Defense Council, it will come into force from January of next year.

G. REGULATIONS CONCERNING THE ORGANIZATION OF THE VARIOUS CLASSIFICATIONS OF *HSIEN* [1]

These laws, a fundamental charter for local self-government, were approved and promulgated by the 14th Regular Meeting of the Supreme National Defense Council, August 31, 1939. For the Generalissimo's lecture on the same subject, see Appendix III (C), p. 388.

A. GENERAL PRINCIPLES

1. Each *hsien* is a self-administrative unit. Its size and area are determined by customs and history but subject to the demarcation of the National Government.
2. There are three to six classes of *hsien*, classified according to area, population, and conditions of economy, culture, and communications. The classifications are to be worked out by the Provincial Government and subject to the approval of the Ministry of Interior.
3. Regulations governing *hsien* administration are to be promulgated by the National Government.
4. Each *hsien* is divided into *hsiang*, and each *hsiang* is further divided into *pao* and *chia*. If a *hsien* is too large, it may be first divided into *ch'ü* to be under the charge of several bureaus. Education institutions, police, public health and tariff offices should be distributed in accordance with above-mentioned divisions.
5. Each *hsien* and each *hsiang* is a legal person.
6. At the age of twenty, a man or woman of Chinese nationality, after living in the *hsien* for six months or more, or having possessed a residence for more than one year, is qualified as a citizen of that *hsien*. He or she has the right of suffrage, recall, initiative, and referendum in this *hsien*. The following persons are disqualified:
   a. Those who are deprived of citizenship by the National Government.

[1] Chung-yang Hsün-lien T'uan [Central (Kuomintang) Training Corps], *Hsien Ko-chi Tzŭ-chih Kang-yao* [Regulations Concerning the Organization of the Various Classifications of *Hsien*], Chungking, XXVIII (1939); these regulations are also found in Chung-yang Hsüan-ch'uan Pu [Central Publicity Board], *Hsien-cheng yü Ti-fang Tzŭ-chih* [Constitutional Government in Relation to Local Self-Government], Chungking, XXVIII (1939), p. 37–44.

    b. Those who owe governmental money.
    c. Those who have been imprisoned for [political] corruption [2] or forgery.
    d. Those who are not allowed to possess personal property.
    e. Those who are opium or other poisonous smokers.

B. THE *Hsien* GOVERNMENT (*hsien chêng-fu*)

    7. There shall be one magistrate (*hsien-chang*) for each *hsien*. His duties are:
    a. To supervise the local administration of the whole *hsien* under the control of the Provincial Government.
    b. To carry out Provincial or Central Government orders under the supervision of the Provincial Government.
    8. The *Hsien* Government consists of the following departments:
    a. Civil Affairs Department.
    b. Financial Department.
    c. Educational Department.
    d. Reconstruction Department.
    e. Land Affairs Department.
    f. Social Affairs Department.
    The number of departments and the distribution of functions are determined by the Provincial Government in accordance with the class and necessities [of the *hsien*], and registered with the Ministry of the Interior.
    9. In the *Hsien* Government there are to be secretaries, department heads, advisors, police officers, clerks and technicians. The number of such staff and their salaries are to be determined by the Provincial Government and subject to the approval of the Ministry of the Interior.
    10. The examination, training, appointing, and discharging of a magistrate or of general staffs are to be done according to the promulgated National law.
    11. There shall be a *Hsien* Council (*hsien chêng hui*) which is to be convened every two weeks. The following matters should be settled in this Council:
    a. Cases brought out by the *Hsien* People's Council.
    b. Other important matters concerning *hsien* policies.
    (The regulations governing the *Hsien* Council are promulgated by the Ministry of the Interior.)
    12. The *Hsien* Council meeting can be held before the establishment of the *Hsien* People's Council.

---

[2] The practice termed *squeeze* on the coast.

13. Regulations concerning a *hsien* shall be drafted by the Provincial Government and submitted to the Executive *Yüan* for its approval through the Ministry of the Interior.

Any organizations which are not mentioned in the regulations should not be established.

14. Regulations governing the *hsien* administration shall be drafted by the Provincial Government and registered in the Ministry of the Interior.

C. THE *Hsien* PEOPLE'S COUNCIL (*hsien ts'ang-chêng hui*)

15. The *Hsien* People's Council is organized by the members of the Council who are elected from People's Representative Committee. Each *hsiang* elects one member. Representatives of public organizations may be recognized as members, but the number of such members should not comprise more than one-third of the whole Council.

16. The chairman of the Council should be elected from its members.

17. The bylaws and the duties of the Council shall be dealt with separately.

D. FINANCES OF A *Hsien*

18. *Hsien* revenue consists of the following items:
    a. Part of the land tax.
    b. Surtax on the land tax.
    c. Thirty per cent of the stamp tax.
    d. Taxes on land after improvement.
    e. Part of the business taxes.
    f. Income from public properties.
    g. Income from public enterprises.
    h. Other legal taxes.

19. Funds required for the execution of Provincial Government orders shall be provided from the National Treasury or the Provincial Treasury. Local collection of such funds is prohibited. *Hsien* which are financially self-sufficient may resort to their own treasuries to meet educational and administrative expenses. *Hsien* with scanty population and most of their area uncultivated may be subsidized by both the Provincial and National Treasuries.

20. Extra expenses for reconstruction shall be collected by a means of floating loans with the approval of the *Hsien* People's Council and the Provincial Government.

21. The incomes and expenses of the *hsien* proper shall be the independent responsibility of the *Hsien* Government.

22. If the *Hsien* People's Council has not been established, the budgets and financial statements shall be examined by the *Hsien* Council and then submitted to the Provincial Government by the Magistrate.

23. After the establishment of the *Hsien* People's Council, the budgets and the financial statements shall be examined by this Council first and then be submitted to the Provincial Government. In case of emergency the Magistrate may submit such documents to the Provincial Government directly.

E. *Ch'ü*

24. Each *ch'ü* is constituted by fifteen to thirty *hsiang*.

25. The *Ch'ü* Bureau, a subsidiary office of *hsien*, represents the *Hsien* Government to perform the educational and administrative work. If the *hsien* is not divided into *ch'ü* then this work is done by the special officers sent by the *Hsien* Government.

26. There shall be one *Ch'ü* Chief (*ch'ü-chang*) and two to five advisers in each *ch'ü*. Their duties are to take charge of civil, reconstruction, educational and military affairs. They shall be trained and examined before appointment.

27. There shall be police stations in each *ch'ü* under the supervision of the *Ch'ü* Chief.

28. A Rural Reconstruction Committee is to be formed in a *ch'ü*. The members of this committee shall be elected from among the popular persons in that *ch'ü*. The *Ch'ü* Chief shall concurrently be Chairman of the Committee.

F. *Hsiang*[3]

29. Each *hsiang* is constituted by six to fifteen *pao*. [See Art. 45 *ff*.]

30. Systems of *hsiang* and *pao chia* are to be worked out by the *Hsien* Government and submitted to the Provincial Government. They must be registered with the Ministry of the Interior.

31. There shall be one *Hsiang* Chief (*hsiang-chang*) and one to two Assistant Chiefs (*fu-hsiang-chang*) in each *hsiang* office. They shall be persons possessing the following qualifications:

   a. Those who have passed the ordinary examinations.

   b. Those who have served in the Delegated Appointment[4] capacity.

---
[3] In some areas termed the *chên*.
[4] A level in the National civil service.

c. Those who have graduated from Middle and Normal schools.

d. Those who have contributed service for the public good.

32. There shall be four sections in each *hsiang* to take charge of the civil, economic, educational affairs and police service. Each section has one chief and several secretaries. One of the secretaries shall take charge of controlment. The *hsiang* staff shall be selected from among the primary school teachers. If the *hsiang's* financial resources are insufficient these sections may be amalgamated into one office.

33. The tenure of *Hsiang* Chiefs shall be two years, with permissible re-election.

34. The offices *Hsiang* Chief, the headmaster of the primary school, and officer of militia [5] may be delegated to one person. If the *hsiang* possesses sufficient financial resources, the headmaster of the primary school shall not be allowed to hold other office.

35. Plans initiated by the *hsiang* itself must be passed by the *Hsiang* Council meeting before they are adopted.

36. The *Hsiang* Chief shall act as the chairman of the *Hsiang* Council Meeting. Every section chief is required to attend the Meeting. The *pao* chiefs must also attend this Meeting.

37. The procedure of training of *Hsiang* Chiefs and other *hsiang* staff shall be dealt with separately.

G. THE *Hsiang* PEOPLE'S COUNCIL

38. The members of the *Hsiang* People's Council shall be elected from the *Pao* People's Council. Each *pao* shall elect two members.

39. The *Hsiang* Chief may act as the chairman of the *Hsiang* People's Council provided that he has been elected by the Council as the Chief.

40. The bylaws and the duties of the *Hsiang* People's Council shall be dealt with separately.

H. FINANCE OF THE *Hsiang*

41. The *hsiang's* revenue consists of the following items:
a. All legal taxes.
b. Income from public properties.
c. Income from public enterprises.

---

[5] The *chuang-ting-tui tui-chang*, heading a local force of able-bodied citizens: the regular rank is not specified.

GOVERNMENT DOCUMENTS

d. Subsidiary funds.

e. Special incomes to be collected with the approval of the *Hsien* Government.

42. The procedure of purchasing properties shall be dealt with separately.

43. The bylaws of the *Hsiang Treasury* Committee shall be dealt with separately.

44. The financial report prepared by the *hsiang* office shall be submitted to the *Hsien* Government. The expenses of the *hsiang* shall be included in the *hsien's* financial report after audit.

I. Pao AND Chia

45. Each *pao* is constituted of six to fifteen *chia*.

46. Public primary schools, cooperatives, and warehouses [6] shall be established within two or three *pao* where the population is dense. The *Pao* Chief shall be in charge of these institutions. Reserves of each *pao* shall be trained separately.

47. There shall be one *Pao* Chief (*pao-chang*) and one assistant *Pao* Chief (*fu-pao-chang*) in each *pao*. They are elected by the *Pao* People's Council. And they must be chosen from among persons with the following qualifications:

a. Those who have graduated from middle schools.

b. Persons who have worked more than one year in Government.

c. Those who have been specially trained.

d. Those who are active in social work.

Before the time of election, the *Pao* Chief may be recommended by the *hsiang* office to the *Hsien* Government for appointment.

48. The tenure of the *Pao* Chief shall be two years; he may be re-elected.

49. The offices of *Pao* Chief, headmaster of the *pao* primary school, and militia officer may be delegated to one person. When the *pao's* financial resources are sufficient the headmaster is not allowed to hold other office.

50. There shall be two to four secretaries in each *pao* to take charge of the political, educational, cultural affairs, and police service. The *pao* staff shall be elected from among the primary school teachers. If the *pao's* financial resources are not sufficient, there shall be only one person to take care of all these activities.

[6] In Far Eastern English parlance, *godown*.

51. The procedure of training of the *pao* office staff shall be dealt with separately.

52. One representative of each family is required to be present at the *Pao* People's Council (*pao-min ta-hui*) meeting. The bylaws and the duties of this council shall be dealt with separately.

53. Each *chia* consists of six to fifteen families.

54. There shall be one *Chia* Chief (*chia-chang*) in each *chia*. He is elected by the Family Chiefs Council and is registered with the *hsiang* office through the *pao*.

55. There shall be established a Family Chiefs Council and *Chia* People's Council in each *chia*.

56. The old names of the streets may be used as the names of *pao*.

57. The bylaws of *pao* and *chia* shall be dealt with separately.

58. The controlment procedure for *pao* and *chia* shall be dealt with separately.

59. The present bylaws shall become effective after the date of promulgation.

60. If any item in these regulations conflicts with the National laws, it shall be null.

H. A CHART OF GOVERNMENT ORGANIZATION

The chart facing this page is a composite of various official charts to which the author was allowed access in Chungking. Revisions cover changes down to the opening of 1941.

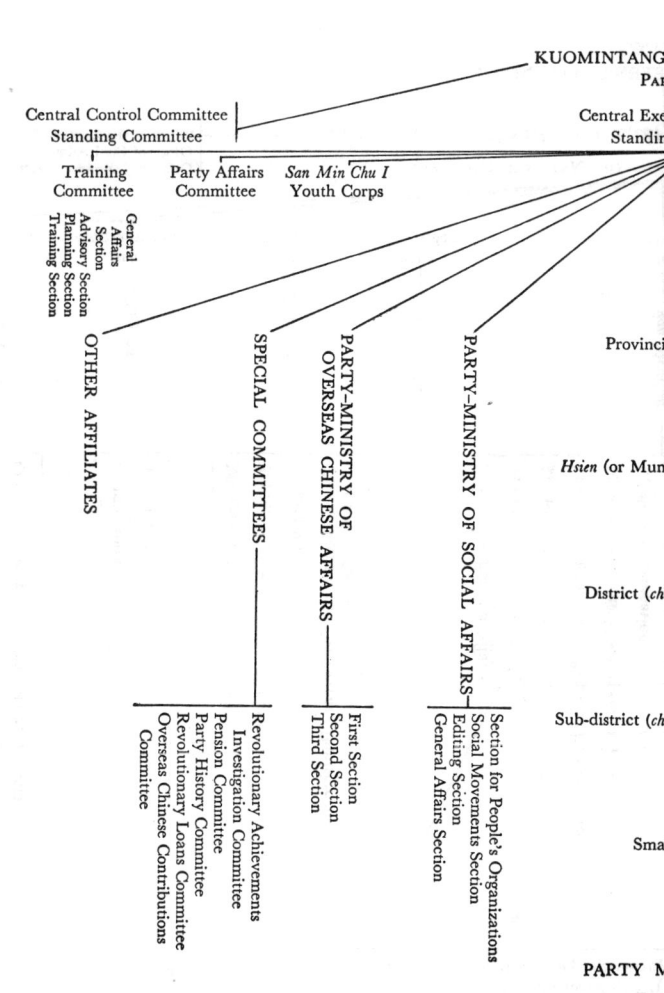

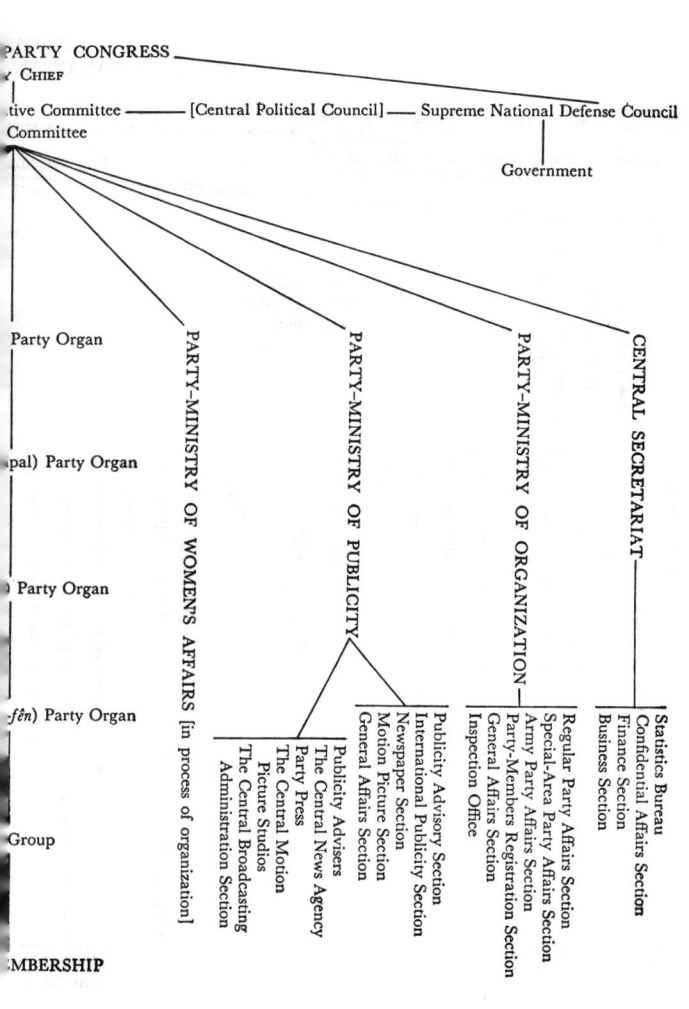

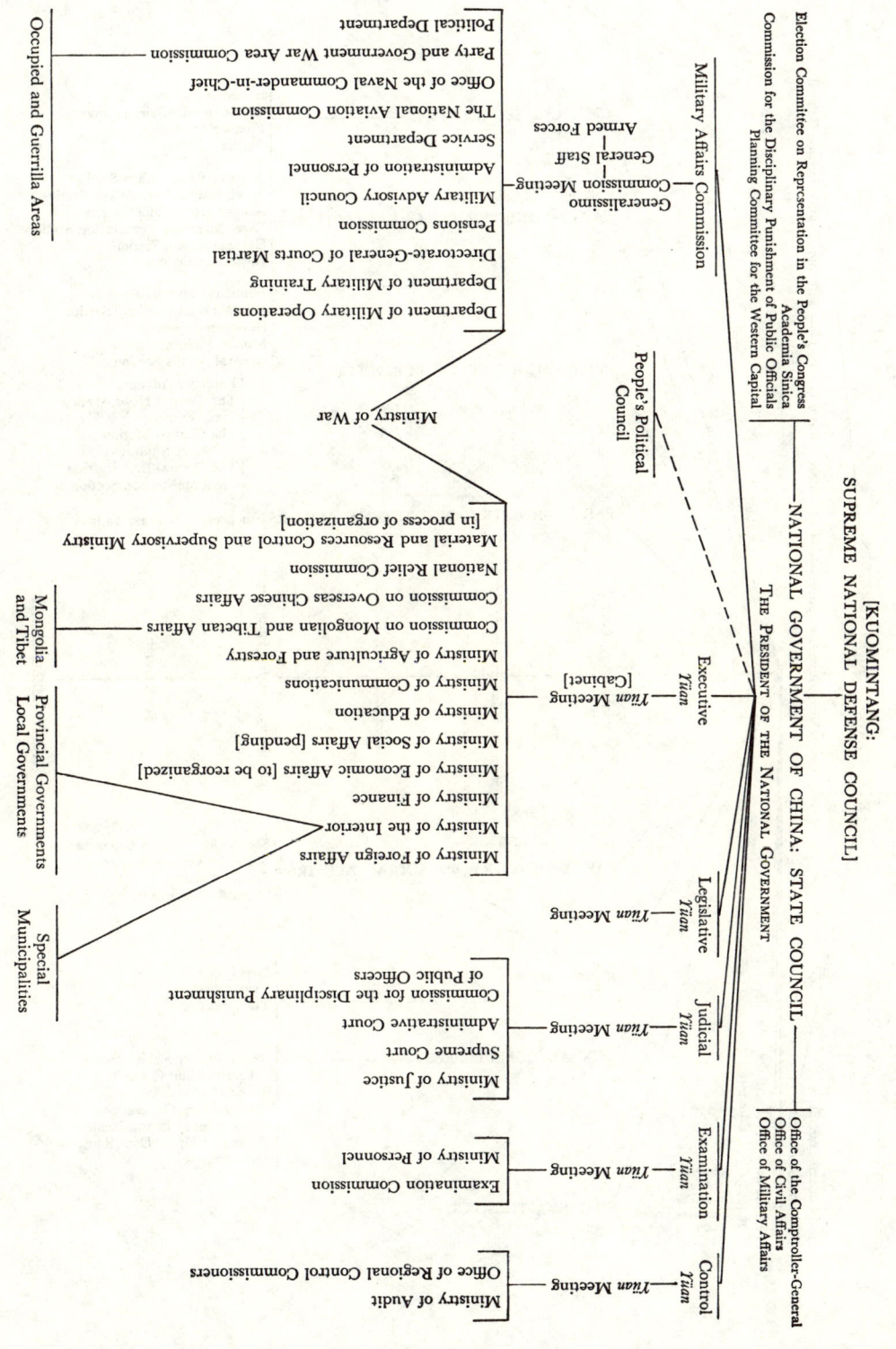

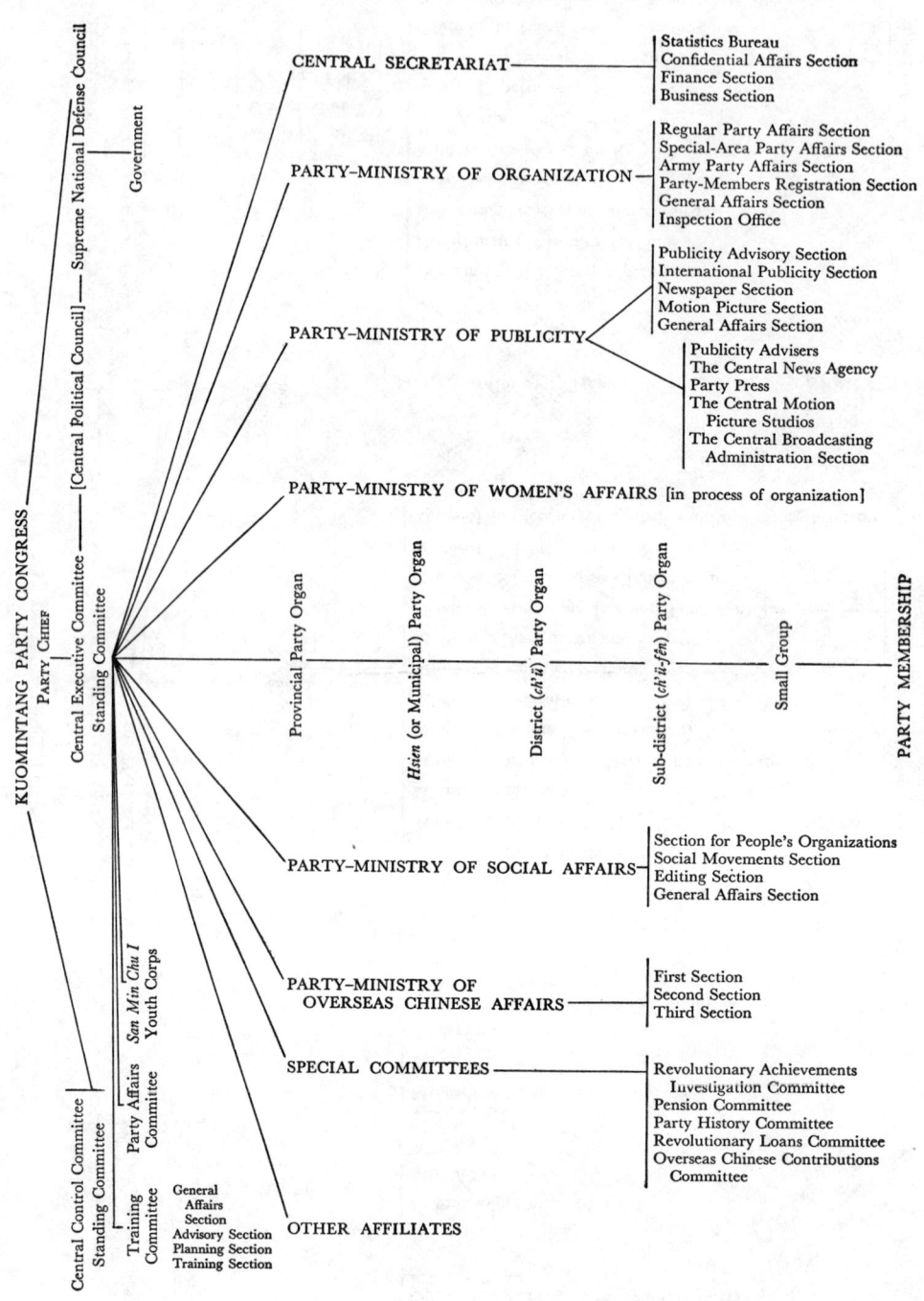

APPENDIX II. DOCUMENTS ON PARTY POLITICS

A. A CHART OF KUOMINTANG ORGANIZATION

The chart facing this page is a composite of various official charts to which the author was allowed access in July and August 1940.

B. CONSTITUTION OF THE SAN MIN CHU I YOUTH CORPS, YEAR XXVII (1938) [1]

Proclaimed June 16, 1938, amended by the Fourth Meeting of the Corps' Provisional Central Managing Board, July 17, 1939, this is the fundamental charter of the most significant Kuomintang auxiliary to appear in many years.

CHAPTER I. GENERAL PRINCIPLES

1. The name of the organization is the San Min Chu I Youth Corps.
2. The object of the Corps is to unite and train young people, to enforce the San Min Chu I, to defend the nation, and to bring national rebirth.

CHAPTER II. MEMBERSHIP

3. All Chinese youths, male or female, aged between 16 to 25, vowing to abide by the Corps constitution, can become members of the Corps upon the payment of the membership fee.

Members of the Managing Boards of various subordinate Corps agencies and other Headquarters officials specially admitted are not restricted by the above rule. Members who pass 25 years of age can still retain their membership in the Corps.

---

[1] San-min-chu-i Ch'ing-nien T'uan Chung-yang T'uan-pu [*San Min Chu I* Youth Corps Central Corps Headquarters], *San-min-chu-i Ch'ing-nien T'uan T'uan-chang* [Corps Constitution of the *San Min Chu I* Youth Corps], Chungking, n.d.

4. Two members of the Corps must propose and second a member before the latter can become eligible. The new member must also be approved by the Sectional Corps and Troop and his name registered in the Central Corps Headquarters.

5. New members must take an oath before admittance, as follows:

"I hereby swear that I promise to abide by the principles of San Min Chu I, to obey the order of the Corps Leader, to abide by the constitution of the corps, to act according to the principles of the New Life Movement, to be ever loyal to the Principles, to work for all other people, to stand firm against all hardships, and to be prepared to sacrifice my all. I promise that if I fail to perform the above duties, I will be willing to receive the severest punishments."

6. The private life of the members should be in conformity with the regulations fixed by the Corps.

7. Members of the Corps who die in service or who lose their profession because of service in the Corps will receive pensions or other relief. The detailed procedure will be fixed later.

8. Members, upon a change of profession or job, or upon removal to other localities, must register with their identification cards at the local Corps Headquarters.

Chapter III. System of Organization

9. The system of organization of the Corps is as follows: the Central Corps Headquarters, the Branch Corps, the Divisional Corps, the Sectional Corps, the Divisional Troop, the Sectional Troop.

10. Besides the above, the Corps may organize other sub-organizations according to the nature of the locality, the profession of the members, etc. The details will be further fixed.

Chapter IV. The Corps Leader

11. The Corps Leader is the highest executive of the Corps, and is concurrently the Party Chief of the Kuomintang [Chiang K'ai-shek].

12. The Corps Leader is the chairman in the All-Corps Representative Assembly, and has the power to veto a resolution already passed by the Assembly; he also has the power to finally sanction all resolutions passed by the Central Managing Board and the Central Controlment Board.

CHAPTER V. THE ALL-CORPS REPRESENTATIVE ASSEMBLY AND OTHER MEETINGS OF REPRESENTATIVES

13. The All-Corps Representative Assembly may be held every two years. At the discretion of the Corps Leader or the Central Managing Board, however, it may be postponed or a temporary meeting be held instead.

14. The works of the All-Corps Representative Assembly are:

a. to discuss and examine the report submitted by the Central Managing Board and the Central Controlment Board.

b. to fix plans for the Corps activities.

c. to discuss motions proposed by the Corps Leader.

15. The Meeting of Representatives of the Branch Corps may be held once a year. At the discretion of the Central Managing Board, however, the Meeting may be postponed or a temporary Meeting be held instead.

16. The duties of the Meeting of Representatives of the Branch Corps are:

a. to examine and discuss the reports submitted by the Managing Board and the Controlment Board of the Branch Corps.

b. to fix plans for the Branch Corps activities.

17. The Meeting of Members of the Sectional Corps is held every six months. At the discretion of the Managing Board of the Branch Corps, it may be postponed or a temporary meeting be held instead. If the number of members of the Section is too big or if the communication system is unfavorable, a Meeting of the Representatives of the Sectional Corps may be held.

18. The duties of the Meeting of the Members of the Sectional Corps are:

a. to examine and discuss the reports submitted by the Managing Board and the Controlment Board of the Sectional Corps.

b. to fix plans for the Sectional Corps Activities.

19. The Meeting of Members of the Divisional Troop is to take place every three months. At the discretion of its Managing Board, it may be postponed, or a temporary meeting be called.

20. The duties of the Meeting of Members of the Divisional Troop are:

a. to examine the reports submitted by the Leader of the Divisional Troop.

b. to fix the plans for the Divisional Troop activities.

21. Meetings for the Members of the Sectional Troop will be held every week, to be presided over by the Leaders of the Sectional Troop. Unless specially permitted, these meetings must not be postponed. During these meetings, reports concerning politics, the Troop activities, discussions, etc., will be read. New members are admitted through these meetings too, and plans for the Sectional Troop activities will be fixed.

22. The system of organization for the various Meetings of Members or Meetings of Representatives will be fixed later.

Chapter VI. The Central Headquarters

23. The Central Managing Board of the Central Corps Headquarters is formed by twenty-five to thirty-five managing directors, in addition to the nine to fifteen reserve members of the Managing Board.

24. The Central Managing Board has the following powers:

a. to execute the orders of the Corps Leader [Chiang K'ai-shek] and to execute the resolutions passed in the All-Corps Representative Assembly.

b. to fix the plans for activities.

c. to form various corps of lower rank, and to command or inspect their activities.

d. to execute all resolutions submitted by the Central Controlment Board.

e. to form a budget to regulate various financial questions of the Corps.

25. The Central Managing Board forms a Standing Managing Board consisting of nine Standing Managing Directors, appointed by the Corps Leader from among the twenty-five to thirty-five Managing Directors. This Standing Managing Board fulfills the duties of the Central Managing Board Meeting when the latter is not in session.

26. The Corps Leader appoints a Secretary-General to the Central Managing Board from among the Standing Managing Directors, to direct all the affairs of the Board.

27. The various sub-organs of the Central Managing Board will be formulated later, together with their system of organization.

28. There are a Manager and a Vice-Manager in the

Office of the Secretary-General. They are nominated by the Secretary and appointed by the Corps Leader.

29. In every Department of the Central Managing Board there is a Commissioner and one or two Deputy Commissioners. They are appointed by the Corps Leader upon the nomination of the Secretary-General.

30. The Central Corps Headquarters has a Central Controlment Board of twenty-five to thirty-five members and nine to fifteen reserve members.

31. The duties of the Central Controlment Board are:
   a. to inspect the progress of the Corps activities.
   b. to raise and examine all statements concerning any member who does not fulfill his duties.
   c. to audit all incomes and expenditures of the Corps.
   d. to direct Controlment Boards of lower rank in their work of inspection.

32. The Central Controlment Board forms a Standing Controlment Board consisting of five members of the Controlment Board, appointed by the Corps Leader. This Standing Controlment Board shall function when the Controlment Board is not in session.

33. The Central Controlment Board has also a Secretary-General, appointed by the Corps Leader from among the Standing Controlment Board members. He shall direct the affairs of the Central Controlment Board.

34. The Central Controlment Board has various sub-organs, of which the system of organization will be fixed later.

35. Both the Central Managing Board and the Central Controlment Board will hold meetings every three months, to be presided over by the Corps Leader. Under special circumstances there may be temporary meetings or combined meetings for the two Boards.

Chapter VII. The Branch Corps

36. The Branch Corps has a Managing Board consisting of seven to eleven members, besides the three to five reserve members.

37. The duties of the Branch Corps Managing Board are:
   a. to execute the orders from the Central Corps Headquarters and the resolutions passed in the Meeting of the Representatives of the Branch Corps.
   b. to fix the plans for the activities of the Branch Corps.

c. to command and inspect the works of the lower organs.

d. to execute all resolutions submitted by the Branch Corps Controlment Board.

e. to form a budget regulating the financial state of the Branch Corps.

38. The Managing Board has a Secretary, appointed by the Corps Leader, from among the members of the Managing Board. He is to direct all affairs of the Managing Board.

39. The Managing Board has various sub-organs, the system of organization of which will be fixed later.

40. The Branch Corps has a Controlment Board consisting of three to five members with three reserve members.

41. The Controlment Board has a Secretary, appointed by the Corps Leader from among the Controlment Board members, to discharge all affairs of the Board.

42. The system of organization of the various sub-organs of the Controlment Board will be fixed later.

43. The duties of the Controlment Board are:

a. to inspect the progress of the activities done by the lower organs.

b. to raise and examine statements concerning any member who rebels against the discipline of the Corps.

c. to audit the budget and all financial statements of the Branch Corps.

d. to direct the Controlment Boards of lower rank in their work of inspection.

44. The Managing Board of the Branch Corps should hold meetings every half-month. The Controlment Board should meet once every month. The meetings are to be presided over by the Secretaries. Under special circumstances, temporary sessions or combined meetings may be held.

45. The Branch Corps has also one to five Directors, appointed by the Corps Leader, to direct the affairs of the Branch Corps.

CHAPTER VIII. THE DIVISIONAL CORPS

46. The Divisional Corps has three to five Managing Directors, who have power to command, direct, inspect, and examine the work done by the Divisional Corps, in accordance to the will of the higher Corps Headquarters.

47. There is a Secretary of the Divisional Corps, appointed by the Corps Leader from among the Managing Directors, whose duty it is to discharge all the affairs of the Divisional Corps.

48. The Managing Directors should perform their duties in various localities at various periods.

49. Whenever necessary, the Secretary of the Divisional Corps can call a Managing Directors' meeting.

50. A Divisional Corps will be formed when there are more than five Sectional Corps under it. But this may not take place if the Managing Board of the Branch Corps sees no necessity for such action.

Chapter IX. The Sectional Corps

51. The Sectional Corps has a Managing Board formed by three to five members and one to three reserve members, elected in the General Meeting of the Members of the Sectional Corps or in the Meeting of the Representatives of the Sectional Corps.

52. The duties of the Managing Board are:
a. to execute the orders of the higher Corps Headquarters and the resolutions passed in the Meeting of the Members of the Sectional Corps or the Meeting of the Representatives of the Sectional Corps.
b. to fix the plans for activities.
c. to direct and watch the activities of the lower organs.
d. to form a budget and other financial statements.
e. to execute the resolutions passed in the Meeting of the Controlment Board.
f. to examine the work done by the Divisional Troops and Sectional Troops.

53. The Managing Board has a Secretary, appointed by the Corps Leader from among the members of the Managing Board, to discharge all the affairs of the Managing Board.

54. The system of organization of the various sub-organs of the Managing Board will be formulated later.

55. The Sectional Corps has a Controlment Board formed by three members and one reserve member. Under special circumstances, there is sometimes only one Controller without any Controlment Board.

56. The Controlment Board has one Secretary, appointed by the Corps Leader from among the members of the Controlment Board, who is to discharge all affairs of the Board.

57. The duties of the Controlment Board are:

a. to inspect the works done by the Sectional Corps, and by the Divisional and Sectional Troops under the Sectional Corps.

b. to raise and examine statements concerning members who rebel against the Corps discipline.

c. to audit financial statements of the Sectional Corps and those of the Divisional and Sectional Troops under it.

58. The Managing Board and the Controlment Board of the Sectional Corps will hold separate meetings once every half-month. The respective Secretaries shall preside. Under special conditions they can call for temporary sessions.

Chapter X. The Divisional Troop

59. The Divisional Troop has a Leader and an Assistant Leader, elected from among the Leaders and Assistant Leaders of the Sectional Troop and by themselves.

60. The Divisional Troop executes the orders of the superior organs and the resolutions passed in the All-Corps Representative Assembly. The Divisional Troop also directs and examines the work of the members.

Chapter XI. The Sectional Troop

61. The Sectional Troop is the basic organization of the San Min Chu I Youth Corps. It is formed by eight to fifteen members, with a Leader and an Assistant Leader elected by the members themselves.

62. The chief duties of the Sectional Troop are:

a. to execute the orders of all superior organs and all resolutions passed in the Sectional Troop Meeting.

b. to call for new members and to collect the fees.

c. to train and examine every member.

d. to read books, to propagate San Min Chu I and its policies, to distribute publicity literature.

e. to participate in all social activities.

f. to investigate political and social conditions.

63. All extra-Corps organs holding more than three members may form special Groups, upon the sanction of the Sectional Troop. Their duty is to execute the principles of the Corps and to watch the work of the members. Whenever necessary, the chief of the Group may attend the Sectional Corps Meetings.

Chapter XII. The Election of Officers and Their Term of Service

64. Unless already specified, the members of the Managing Boards of the various Corps and Troops are elected in the General Meeting or the Meeting of Representatives of the respective Corps and Troops. Before the General Meeting or the Meeting of Representatives, the members of the Managing Boards are appointed by the Corps Leader.

65. The duration of service of members of the Managing and Controlment Boards of the Central Corps Headquarters is two years. That of members of the corresponding Boards of the other Corps is one year. That of the Leaders and Assistant Leaders of the two Corps is six months. All of them can be re-elected.

Chapter XIII. Discipline

66. All members should obey the following commandments:

a. All questions may be freely discussed. But no dispute is allowed, once the final resolution is passed.

b. It is not allowed to rebel against the principles of the New Life Movement.

c. It is prohibited to reveal the secrets of the Corps.

d. It is prohibited for members to join other organizations.

e. It is prohibited to criticize unfavorably the Kuomintang and the Corps, or to plot against other members.

f. It is prohibited to express one's ideas too freely upon current events, especially those that are against the resolved plans or policies of the Kuomintang or the Corps.

g. It is prohibited to form other organizations within the Corps.

67. Those who are proved to act against the above rules will be punished in the following ways:

a. warning
b. demerit
c. cross-questioning
d. expulsion
e. other appropriate punishments.

Chapter XIV. Fees

68. Every member must pay a membership fee of ten cents on entering the Corps.

69. A monthly contribution of ten cents is required of every member. Under special circumstances other contributions may be called for.

Chapter XV. Amendments, etc.

70. This Constitution may be amended, with the approval of the Corps Leader, in the All-Corps Representative Assembly or in the Meeting of the Central Managing Board.

71. The Constitution is enforced upon the day of announcement, having been approved by the Corps Leader.

C. THE DUTIES AND GENERAL ACTIVITIES OF THE SAN MIN CHU I YOUTH CORPS (CH'ÊN CH'ÊNG) [1]

A lecture delivered May 9, 1940, before a Kuomintang training class: note the somewhat pedagogical outline. General Ch'ên Ch'êng, until recently Secretary-General of the Corps, is one of the closest military associates of the Generalissimo.

Outline

A. THE DUTIES AND NATURE OF THE CORPS:

1. *Duties:* to organize and train the nation's youth with a view to enforcing the San Min Chu I; to lead and unify the ideals, opinions and activities of the nation's youth; to centralize and cultivate special talents, forming a nucleus to serve as a model.

2. *Activities:* to urge youths to join the practical work connected with the war of national defense; to enforce military and political training; to encourage civil progress, labor and skill in production.

3. *Nature:* the Corps is an organization composed of young people and included within the Kuomintang. The Kuomintang and the Corps are one and indivisible.

[1] Ch'ên Ch'êng, *K'ang-chan Chien-kuo Yü Ch'ing-nien Tsê-jen* [Resistance and Reconstruction in Relation to the Duties of Youth], Chungking XXIX (1940), p. 43–68. The book was published by the Political Department of the Military Affairs Commission (*Chün-shih Wei-yüan-hui Chêng-chih-pu*) of the National Government.

B. THE GROWTH AND THE PLAN CONCERNING THE INTENSIFICATION OF THE WORK OF THE CORPS:

1. *Growth:* Period of formation, July 9, 1938 to September 1939; full establishment since September 1939, when the Central Managing Board and the Central Controlment Board were formed.

2. *Plan concerning the intensification of activities:* Amendment of the Corps Constitution; issuing of general procedures for the carrying out of the activities to various sections; general principles governing the future activities of the Corps.

C. GENERAL ACTIVITIES OF THE CORPS:

1. *Organization:* general development of the organization in various localities; calling for new members; regulating the inner structures of the organization; the formation of a selected central nucleus.

2. *Training:* entrance training and normal training; young men's summer camp; training of talented gliders.

3. *Publicity:* periodicals at fixed intervals; the compilation of various collective works; the formation of a committee for publicity.

4. *Social works:* the establishment of a Young Men's Labor Service Camp; the distribution of Young Men's Entertaining Offices in various localities; the work of Youths' Service Associations and Corps in various localities.

5. *Financial assistance:* compilation of Dr. Sun's works on economics; aid given to young men's work for material productivity; planning of business organizations under group management.

D. GENERAL DISCUSSION OF THE TWO YEARS' ACTIVITIES OF THE CORPS AND THE PRINCIPLES GUIDING THE NATION'S YOUTH:

1. *General discussion of the two years' activities:* its good as well as its bad points.

2. *Principles guiding the nation's youth:* conclusion.

A. THE DUTIES AND NATURE OF THE CORPS

1. The Duties

It is two years since the establishment of the San Min Chu I Youth Corps was declared at Hankow on July 7, 1938. From the name, we know that the purpose of its creation is to employ the unified efforts of the nation's youth in the work of carrying out the San Min Chu I. As youth is the vital element in a nation's life and the foundation for all future social and political progress, the Kuomintang has, in the second and present stage of national salvation, especially organized a Youth Corps to reinforce the powers of the Kuomintang by shouldering the following epochal duties:

First, to unite and train the nation's youth for the promulgation of San Min Chu I, the defense of the nation and the salvation of its people.

Secondly, to lead the nation's youth to a unity of thought and activities so that they can justly perform the great task of national salvation, thus completing the second phase of the achievements of the People's Revolution.[2]

Thirdly, to collect youth of especial talents for the central nucleus as a model for all, thereby giving new and ever-confirming life to the Kuomintang, and enabling it to carry out its future work.

2. The Activities

The Corps Leader [Chiang K'ai-shek] has clearly stated in his open letter to the nation's youth that the chief activities of the Corps are six in number:

1. To mobilize the activities of youth according to the National General Mobilization Act.
2. To give thorough military training to develop the skill in defending the nation.
3. To heighten political training, giving every youth the required political knowledge for a citizen of a republic.
4. To encourage civil progress, thus raising the general intellectual standard of the nation.
5. To encourage labor and service, according to the motto: Life is to serve.
6. To develop the skill in material productivity according to scientific principles, thus hastening the work of national construction.

The first two of the above are collectively the fundamental works of military reconstruction, the third and fourth are those of education, and the last two those of economic reconstruction. The Corps has classified the various aspects of the above works of national construction as

[2] *Kuo-min kê-ming*, i.e., the revolution (*kê-ming*) as planned by Sun Yat-sen.

the works of the youth. Besides, we should clearly understand that they are the fundamental requisites of a complete system of national defense, and form the first stage towards the completion of a republic based upon the San Min Chu I.

3. The Nature

The Corps is a Youth association included within the organization of the Kuomintang, under one principle, one leader, one command, and is willing to struggle for the sake of the People's Revolution. The Kuomintang and the Corps are one and indivisible. It is "The Kuomintang's [own] Corps." If a distinction is necessary, then we may say that the members of the Corps have a special duty to organize and train the nation's youth so that it may be able to shoulder the responsibilities and work concerning social welfare and national salvation. Thus the Corps may be said to be the younger and newer life of the Kuomintang. Besides, it may also serve the Kuomintang in various aspects; for example, if, as in case of overseas localities, Kuomintang work is difficult to execute, the Corps may be established instead, or also, if people are not willing to join the Kuomintang, they may join the Corps. With the formation of the Corps, therefore, the Kuomintang may be enlarged and strengthened.

The relation between the Kuomintang members and the Corps members is clearly stated. According to the amended Constitution of the Corps, the age of members has been changed from eighteen to thirty-eight years, to sixteen to twenty-five years. Also according to the resolution of the Central Regular Meeting of the Kuomintang, the relation between the two is as follows:

1. Members joining the Kuomintang should be above twenty-five years of age.
2. Corps members reaching the age of 25 will become Kuomintang members.
3. Students staying in schools, irrespective of their age, are considered Corps members. Those who previously joined the Kuomintang should also become members of the Corps, reserving their membership in the Kuomintang.

We can see that Kuomintang members and Corps members differ chiefly in their ages. Except for this, the two are in fact one.

With a view to the system of organization, the Kuomintang and the Corps each has its own structure. The Kuomintang leads the Corps, but this does not mean that the Corps is under the Kuomintang in authority. In the speech, "The Relation between the Kuomintang and the Corps," made by the Corps Leader [Chiang K'ai-shek], we are told that under the same general system of organization, the aim of the Kuomintang's leadership of the Corps is to unite all our efforts under the same banner. Leading does not mean in the least commanding or ordering. To lead is to help. Hence a Corps member may also lead a Kuomintang member. The idea is to make both members combine their energy towards helping our leader. The strength of the Corps depends upon the well-being of the Kuomintang, while the future of the Kuomintang depends upon the growth of the Corps. There should be mutual help between the two in order to reach the same final goal. Hence the activities of the two organizations should be everywhere combined into one, employing division of labor and cooperation wherever and whenever possible.

B. The Growth and the Plan concerning the Intensification of the Works of the Corps

1. The Growth

In April 1938, the Representatives of the Kuomintang gathered together for a Meeting (Congress) to amend the Constitution of the Kuomintang and to form the San Min Chu I Youth Corps in order to gather the nation's youth for the great task of national reconstruction. It was also resolved that the Party Chief (Generalissimo Chiang K'ai-shek) is at the same time the Corps Leader. On June 16, the Corps Leader issued his Letter to the Nation's Youth, and announced the constitution of the Corps. On July 9, a Central Managing Board was temporarily formed as the Corps' central organization. The growth of the Corps activities can be divided into two periods:

1. *Period of formation:* July 1938 to September 1939. During this period, the Central Managing Board was formed. While the other work of organizing was done according to a principle of simplicity, as advised by the Corps Leader, all other internal organs were formed according to their necessity. The various subsections in different provinces and districts were also formed during this period.

2. *Period of full establishment:* September 1939 to the present. In accordance with general opinions, the Central Managing Board temporarily formed was dissolved after

its fourth general meeting, and on September 1, 1939 a permanent Central Managing Board and a Central Controlment Board were formed. The Corps Leader has on various occasions appointed thirty-five members for the Central Managing Board with fifteen more as reserve members, and thirty-five members for the Central Controlment Board with fifteen reserve members also. Besides, there are five standing members of the Central Managing Board and five standing members of the Central Controlment Board. The rest of the officials are also appointed. The system of organization is as follows:

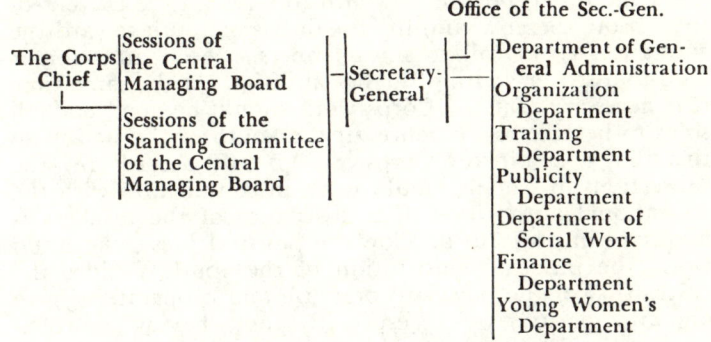

2. Plan concerning the Intensification of Activities

The aim of having a permanent Central Managing Board is to conclude the work of the formative period and start the work of calling for the nation's youth in the task of national reconstruction. The plans concerning the intensification of activities are all based upon the orders of the Corps Leader, the past experiences of the Corps members, and the present situation; the chief plans are:

1. *Amendment of the Constitution*—to increase the training of the Corps members and to fix the system of organization for the All-Corps Representative Assembly in accordance with the idea of democracy. The chief points are (*a*) the change in age limit from eighteen to thirty-eight years to sixteen to twenty-five years, and (*b*) to fix the system of organization for the General Meetings of the Corps members and their Representatives; the fixing of rules concerning the election into office of the members and their period of service.

2. *Issuing of general procedures for the carrying out of the activities of various sections:* (*a*) to make all members and all youth understand that the Corps is a youth organization to train and unite all youth in the principles of San Min Chu I, with the aim of strengthening the nation's defense; (*b*) to lead the nation's youth in the cultivation of good national characteristics, to exemplify their deeds and actions, and to correct all fallacious beliefs, and childish actions. These are the ways of training good useful youth for the national service; (*c*) the subsections of the Corps should work for all the members of the Corps, while the members should work for all the youth of the country. They should encourage all youth to serve all the citizens of the nation, thereby fulfilling the duties of youth toward the country; (*d*) in calling for members, special attention is paid to discover youth of higher abilities. At the same time it is necessary that the Corps work should be good enough so as to be able to influence all the youth of the nation so that they will join the Corps of their own accord; (*e*) the subsections in schools should work in conjunction with the educational authorities. The assistance of the teachers is necessary in order to develop the political ideas, the mind work, the physical constitution of the youth, besides the cultivation of the power to organize and cooperate; (*f*) to organize society's youth, especially those having a profession or those who are capable of material productivity, so that they may be joined to the youth in schools in forming a combined strength necessary to the establishment of a revolutionary nation; (*g*) to point out to the youth the activities done in the war of national defense, the international relations, and the intrigues of the traitors and enemies, thus making every youth able to distinguish the right from the wrong. At the same time, they should be encouraged under favorable conditions to work for national defense; (*h*) to help every youth solve the problem of his livelihood. For example, the choice of a profession, the question of education, etc. The members should therefore look upon their Corps as their family, not as a mere institution for work.

3. *General principles governing the future activities of the Corps:* (*a*) in obedience to the ideas expressed by the Corps Leader, and based upon the experience obtained during the period of two years, it has been resolved that the chief aim of the activities of the Corps is to solidify the union of the members, so that it may become the central

motivating force for all the youth of the nation; (*b*) the activities of the Corps will also be directed to benefit youths, especially those in school, to help them solve all questions and troubles that usually confront young men. Besides, the Corps also aims at mobilizing the youth in war districts, and behind the enemy front, to increase the force of national defense; (*c*) the principles regarding the admittance of new members will be: 1, that quality as well as quantity will be considered; 2, that youths in schools will be especially fitted for membership, although youths having professions will not be neglected; 3, that women members will be especially welcome; (*d*) in establishing the various subdivisions of the Corps in various localities, importance will be especially given to provinces of Szechwan, Kweichow, Shensi, and Kansu. Except these, attention is also given to overseas districts (the Malay Archipelago) and behind the enemy lines. All subdivisions formerly established will be unified under one status, and be turned into regular subdivisions; (*e*) a date for the All-Corps Representative Assembly will be fixed, as well as the dates for the General Meetings of Members; (*f*) the training of the members will be chiefly military and political, emphasizing the skill to produce, with plenty of practice in various actual fields, so that the works of the Corps and those of society will be interrelated; (*g*) the training of the members is divided into primary, middle, and senior parts, with special attention upon the lower two. Different training courses are given according to the abilities, talents, and inclinations of the members; (*h*) the training of the central nucleus is based upon the general training for groups, laying special emphasis upon mental and physical training so that the central nucleus may be the model for other members.

(*i*) The central aim of publicity is to lead the nation's youth to recognize the history and national character of the Chinese nation, to fight for national unity and salvation, to find the way of becoming a "Chinese," and to abolish all fallacious beliefs that are detrimental to the growth of the nation; (*j*) to intensify the movement to all classes of people, attention is drawn to the fact that: 1, every member is a publicity member; 2, actions and not words should be the basis of publicity; 3, care should be given to the difference in locality, time, or people, when the members are helping to do social work; 4, members' actions and thoughts should be earnest, devoted, intelligent, ingenuous, and truthful; (*k*) to increase the cooperation between youths, the amount of publicity literature should be increased. Encouragement should also be given to the study of science and to development of the physical constitution; (*l*) social service is especially aimed at relieving the poor and the sick, paying attention to the wounded soldiers, their families, refugees, and other helpless people; (*m*) the calling in and training of students who have no chance to study should be emphasized. Help should be given them to find work or continue studies. Attention should also be given to those behind the enemy's lines so that they may not turn out to be traitors.

(*n*) The work of the Young Men's Labor Service Camp, the Young Men's Service Association and Corps should be intensified, aiming at the increase of necessary public services during wartime, and the hastening of social advancement; (*o*) concerning the financial help given to the members, attention is given to group works like cooperative stores, etc. Encouragement is given for thrift, saving, etc.; (*p*) members should be encouraged to produce more, to heighten the skill in production; (*q*) members should spread the new economic thought expressed in the San Min Chu I. They should also study the various books on economics; (*r*) encouragement is given to young women, especially those in war districts and students who want to join the Corps. Training will be given to them. Their work is chiefly to spread the spirit of the Corps among women, to render war-time assistance and educational help; (*s*) rigid inspection of the Corps personnel is to be enforced: 1, not only may a lower officer be reprimanded by a senior officer, but vice versa; 2, in every subdivision of the Corps an organization to inspect the personnel is formed; 3, attention is given to the reserve list of the Corps personnel; 4, rigid censure of careless and corrupt officials, and also of those who recommended them.

(*t*) A system of inspecting the various activities of the Corps is to be formed; 1, the inspectors are given the authority to watch and to lead; 2, the various subdivisions should elect officials who shall constantly make inspection tours; 3, close cooperation with the Central Controlment Board should be established; (*u*) a competition of activities among various subdivisions should be encouraged, whether it be interdivisional, personal, etc. Competitions are based upon research statistics, exchange of views, grading of work, etc.

C. THE GENERAL ACTIVITIES OF THE CORPS

1. Organization

With the formation of the Central Managing Board of the Corps, organizing work has been pushed ahead to hasten the mutual movements of the nation's youth, especially those in the provinces of Szechwan, Shensi, Kansu, and Kweichow. The chief points concerning the organizaing movement are as follows:

1. *General development of the organization in various localities.* The subdivisions originally planned have all been formed. In Szechwan, subdivisions are formed in every city (*hsien*). In the rest of the provinces, subdivisions are formed in different districts. Subdivisions have also been formed in the chief universities and middle schools in the country. Owing to special circumstances, overseas and war districts are under the investigation of special officials sent there to inspect the local surroundings before the subdivisions be formed.

2. *Membership enrollment:* Members are chiefly youthful students and youths with some ability. According to the report made in April 1940, there are 126,111 members in the Corps. Members will be called according to the basic plan in the future, and especially women members and other young men will be encouraged to join.

3. *Regulation of the inner structures of the organization and the formation of a central nucleus:* to insure perfect harmony in carrying out various activities, those temporary subdivisions which have been doing good work and which have an efficient central nucleus are to be made into regular subdivisions. The selection of the central executive nucleus will be based upon the talent of the members. The method of selection is by means of questioning, recommendation, or other ways.

2. The Training

Training of the Corps members is to organize an efficient executive organization for the sake of practical national reconstruction according to the principles of San Min Chu I. Besides military and political training, attention is given to the development of skill in production. At present, the chief training work of the Corps is as follows: (*a*) Entrance training and normal training: there are usually three stages of training, *viz.:* entrance training,

normal training, and special training for nucleus members. Except the last mentioned, all members of the Corps must undergo the first two trainings. The period of entrance training is two weeks, during which the training of the mind is emphasized. Normal training is divided into reading, discussion, and recommended readings. Weekly gatherings are held for all members of a division to attend. The recommended readings are based upon the Corps Leader's "Recommended Readings and Methods of Discussion." Every member must read a number of required books, according to the systematic plan given.
(b) Young Men's Summer Camp—this is aimed at collectively training all members who are attending schools. During July and August 1938, a tentative camp has been formed at Chungking and Chengtu, with mostly university and middle school students as attending members. It is planned to start similar camps at Chengtu, Chungking, Sian, and Changsha this year. (c) Training of gliders: this is aimed at heightening the interest in aviation shown by youths. The Corps has arranged with the Aviation Committee to form a class of amateur gliders, who will become pilots in the future.

3. Publicity

Besides the normal work concerning publicity, special attention is given to:
1. Fixed periodicals, such as the "Chinese Youth Monthly," the "News of the Corps Activities," the "Civil News," the "Materials for Publicity," etc. They aim at teaching the various subdivisions the work of publicity and at supplying materials for publicity. Besides these, there are many local publications of the Corps.
2. The compilation of collected works, such as the "Young Men's Books concerning National Defense," the "Young Men's Books of History and Geography," the "San Min Chu I Series for Youth," etc. Among pamphlets for publicity are "Dr. Sun's teachings for the Young Men," "The Way of Leading Youth's Career," "The May 4 Movement and Modern Young Men's Movements," etc. Besides these, the Corps has other publicity organs, such as the Central Publicity Corps, the Youth's Dramatic Associations of various subdivisions, etc. Publicity literature is distributed in various localities by the China Civil Supply Association, or its branches, or sometimes by specially chartered book companies.

4. Social Work

At present the Social Work of the Corps is aimed at cultivating youths' ability to serve, especially in the present stage of warfare: (a) the formation of Young Men's Labor Service Camps—this is to develop the skill of production so as to help the country materially. This camp was tentatively formed at Chengtu and Chungking where young men were gathered to receive the required training; (b) various local Young Men's Entertaining Offices—these are established in eleven places among which are Chungking, Sian, Changsha, Kweilin, Kinhwa. There is a monthly accommodation capacity of about three thousand men. Many of them are to be sent later to the Young Men's Labor Service Camp for training; (c) various local Young Men's Service Associations and Corps—their aim is to serve in the war zone, and to help the productivity of society. The Service Associations under the various subdivisions of the Corps are formed at Chengtu, Sian, Lanchow, Changsha, Kweilin, Ch'ü-chiang, etc., numbering forty-two in all. The Service Corps are formed in twenty-three places, such as Hungyang, Neichuan, Wanling, Kingshan, etc.

5. Financial Assistance

The aim of this branch of work is to spread Dr. Sun's economic thoughts as shown in the San Min Chu I, besides helping the members financially by means of cooperative movements. At present, the works emphasized are:

1. Compilation of Dr. Sun's economic works—they are based upon the San Min Chu I, the various manifestos issued, and a study of comparative economy of other countries. There are twelve series of books thus published, *e.g.*, "The Economic Theories and System of the San Min Chu I," "The Population Policy of China," "The Labor Policy of China," "The Policy of Land Tenure in China," etc.

2. Aid given to youth along material productivity—the Corps pays special attention to the theory and practice of material productivity. It has arranged with the Board of Economy a plan to establish cooperative organizations with the Board, and the Central Office for Agricultural Research, so that the Corps members can have practical work in economic reconstruction.

3. Planning of business organizations under group management—temporarily, the activities along this line will be the establishment of cooperative stores. These are now the

"Young Men's Dressing Stores," the "Haosen Cooperative Store," and other local Young Men's Cooperative Stores.

D. GENERAL DISCUSSION OF THE TWO YEARS' ACTIVITIES OF THE CORPS AND THE PRINCIPLES GOVERNING THE NATION'S YOUTH

1. Discussion of the Corps' Past Work

Due to lack of experience, there were some unavoidable points which await reformation. According to the reports submitted by the touring inspectors, the work for 1939 and that of the first three months of 1940 can be described in a list:

1. *Bad Points:* 1, Due to the short period of time, activities of the Corps have failed to cope with the original plan and schedule; 2, The development of the Corps activities has not yet been made known to the mass of youth. Thus the foundation of the Corps is not yet strong enough; 3, Publicity and service have not yet been adequately mixed. The ideal "service is publicity" has not yet been reached. At the same time, owing to traffic interruption, publicity literature has not been widely distributed; 4, Members are deficient in their conception of the central activities of the Corps. The subdivisions in schools are especially lacking in this conception. They require further training; 5, The officers lack adequate force. Many of them occupy other positions so that their whole attention cannot be concentrated upon the Corps activities.

2. *Good Points:* 1, On the whole, officers and members of the central nucleus are persevering, and possess the will to sacrifice. The remuneration of the Corps officers is very low. Those working in the front receive a monthly maintenance fee of only fifteen to twenty dollars. They are living a soldier's life; 2, Due to the care of the Corps bestowed upon social services, many social activities were first started by the Corps to be followed later by the people; 3, As a rule, the youths trained by the Corps have good discipline; example may be taken from the fact that all the university students of Chungking behaved very well in their schools after the training; 4, As a rule, members are influenced by the spiritual loftiness of the Corps Leader [Generalissimo Chiang]. They have the will to sacrifice, as shown by the fact that many have willingly taken up work behind the enemy's lines.

2. Principles Guiding the Nation's Youth

Since the Corps has for its mission the training of youth, the officers must shoulder the responsibility of leading youth to be good, to avoid all past errors, corruption, etc., that harms the mind of youth instead of benefiting it.

We must lead the youth according to the following principles:

1. As ones who have joined the People's Revolution, we should lead the youth in accordance with the principles of San Min Chu I, in order that we may conclude the work of the People's Revolution. We must use every possible method to love and train all youth so as to make them strong figures in the work of national defense and reconstruction.

2. In order to lead youth, we must know the youthful mind. The few young men who went the wrong way are not bad in themselves, but merely influenced by untrue and selfish ideas. To correct this we must first correct ourselves, and be their example. We must love them as we do our own children. In this way they shall certainly be happy to come to us.

3. It is necessary to know that the only real danger against our People's Revolution is Japanese imperialism. The rest of the political factions will be easily dealt with by political action in the future. We must not be irritated at their existence.

4. In leading the youths to fight against imperialism and other reactionary ideas, we must first of all conquer our own worst selves before we can expect to be their leaders.

5. In leading the youths, we must induce them to shoulder all future responsibilities. Let them understand that what they suffered in youth should not be suffered by posterity. Do unto others what you expect others to do unto you. The generations must progress, not go backward.

The future activities of the Corps will be chiefly to unite and train youth in productive work. On the one hand, we should call for all good youths to be members of the Corps. On the other, we should select specially qualified ones to form a central nucleus to shoulder jointly the activities of the Corps. In this respect, the Corps shall and must be able to accomplish the task that has been ever hoped for by the Corps Leader.

D. THE *HSIAO-TSU* (SMALL GROUP) TRAINING PROGRAM [1]

A formal statement of Party policy, this was passed by the 117th session of the Fifth Central Standing Committee of the Kuomintang on March 23, 1939 and amended by its 123rd session on June 15, 1939. This typifies the Kuomintang drive to establish closer contact with broad reaches of the population.

INTRODUCTION

The Sub-District Party Organ (*ch'ü-fen-pu*) is the fundamental unit of the Kuomintang. Due to its large membership, it has been found extremely difficult to give the members proper training. As a measure of remedy, the Central Party Headquarters has promulgated a set of regulations governing the small-group conference. However, due to the fact that the position and nature of such an institution as well as its relations with the Kuomintang have not been adequately defined, this plan has not been successfully carried out. Recently, the Chairman of the Central Executive Committee of the Kuomintang [The Party Chief, Chiang K'ai-shek] has repeatedly instructed that the small-group conference be put into practice in order to improve the Party affairs. Hence, the regulations were promulgated to be enforced by the various Party organs.

The Kuomintang aims to have a Party organ established in every organization.[2] In order to realize this aim, the following points must be observed:

1. The small-group conference is just for training the Party members. It is different from the Sub-District Party Organ which is the lowest administrative authority. Consequently, only matters concerning the Party principles are to be discussed in the small-group conference while other important issues are left to the Sub-District Party Organ.

2. The Sub-District Party Organ may have unlimited membership. Its members may be organized into more than two small-group conferences. If the members are not more than ten in number, one small-group conference may be formed.

---

[1] Mimeographed memoranda from the Central Party Headquarters of the Kuomintang; presented to the author on July 17, 1940, by Dr. K'an Nei-kuang, Deputy Secretary-General of the Kuomintang. The original title is *Hsiao-tsu Hsün-lien Kang-ling;* undated, unpublished.

[2] I.e., factory, cooperative, school, etc.

3. As the small-group conference is to be organized from the Sub-District Party Organs, a distinction between the District Party and the Sub-District Party Organ must be made. The fundamental principle is that there will be one Party organ for one single [extra-Party] organization. If a Sub-District Party has too many members, several Sub-District Party Organs may be formed under the charge of a District Party Organ. It is not permissible for several parallel Party Organs to exist in one single organization nor may the members of several organizations go into one Party organ. However, if the number of Party members of one organization is too small to form a Sub-District Party Organ, they may join the neighbor Sub-District Party Organ. It is to be remembered that the best policy is to have enough Party members in each organization to form its own Sub-District Party Organ.

4. Small-group conferences may be named in numerical order such as, First and Second Small-Group Conference, or the First and Second Small-Group Conference of a certain *hsien* or Sub-District Party Organ. If there is only one small-group conference, it will not necessarily be named as such.

5. When such small-group conference is organized in every institution down to the *pao-chia*, then the people will be better enlightened concerning the Government and Party policies. Thus it will help the Government in having its orders fully enforced.

6. The small-group conference and the Sub-District Party meeting should take place every two weeks alternately.

All the Party organs upon receipt of this memorandum should make a careful study of the local conditions and submit to the Provincial Kuomintang in ten days' time their working plan. Approval should be given not later than ten days, and within a month all such small-group conferences should be organized. However, if there should be any difficulty encountered or any comments to be made they may be submitted to the proper Party authority for their consideration.

A. ORGANIZATION

1. A small-group conference is established for training the Party members of the Sub-District Kuomintang Organ.

2. A small-group conference may have three to ten members. If a Sub-District Party Organ has more than ten members, two or more small-group conferences may be organized

and members distributed according to their intellectual standing, interests and occupations. It is the best policy that the members of higher education should be evenly distributed among the small-group conferences.

3. In the border districts, if the number of Party members is less than five, and consequently a Sub-District Party Organ cannot be formed, a small-group conference may be organized first to be under the direct charge of some other higher Party authorities.

4. A small-group conference may be reorganized every six months. If there are too many shiftings of members and any other difficulties, it may be reorganized before that time.

5. Every small-group conference has one Chief who is responsible for calling conferences, reading reports and giving guidance regarding the thoughts and activities of his members. He is to be elected by the members and may be re-elected after six-months' service.

6. If the intellectual standing of the members of a small-group conference is equivalent to that of a primary school student, the Chief may be appointed by the Executive Committee of the Sub-District Party.

B. Conferences

7. Small-group conferences are to be held every two weeks. The conference is to last not more than two hours. Members are to be notified by the Chief of the time and place of the conference. It is important that conferences should be planned so as not to interfere with the work of the members.

8. In the conferences each member may be the Chairman by turn. Minutes are to be recorded by any member appointed at the conference. The minutes are to be read by the Chief in the Sub-District Party meetings.

9. Agenda of the small-group conference includes:
   a. The Chief announces the opening of the conference.
   b. The Chief reads Dr. Sun's will.
   c. The Chief reports communications from the Sub-District Party Organ, important current problems, publications of the Chairman of the Executive Committee of the Central Kuomintang Headquarters, and any other topics.
   d. Discussions.
   e. Comments.
   f. The Chief reads regulations governing Party members.
   g. The Chief announces the adjournment of the conference.

10. The discussions include:
   a. Party principles,
   b. current issues,
   c. working abilities,
   d. book reviews.

11. Materials for discussion may be given by the Central Party Headquarters or prepared by the *Hsien* Party Organ, if necessary.

12. Members are required to read certain books. In the case of those who cannot read by themselves, assistance may be given by the fellow members or by an instructor especially appointed for this purpose. Encouragement should be given to those who can do good written work.

13. Small-group conferences are responsible for the education of the illiterate members.

14. Every member should take part in the discussion.

15. If the members of the small-group conference cannot reach an agreement regarding any one of the four topics enumerated in the Item No. 10, they may refer to Central Party Headquarters or the *Hsien* Party Headquarters through the Sub-District Party Organ.

16. If it is found that all the small-group conferences cannot reach an agreement regarding certain topics discussed or if the Secretary of the Sub-District Party Organ considers it necessary, a Sub-District mass meeting may be called to discuss these topics. The agenda for the small-group conference can also be used for the Sub-District Party meetings.

17. When the small-group Chief considers it necessary, he may decide whether to have the Item "Comment" only on the agenda.

18. In commenting, the members may do:
   a. Self-comment: Members may tell in the conference their own thoughts, activities and past experiences, as well as plans for the future.
   b. Mutual comment: Members may make comments upon each other's thoughts, activities, etc., in the most sincere and friendly manner.

19. All the comments should be recorded in the minutes for future reference. After the conference members should not broadcast each other's secrets.

20. At every fourth meeting, the conference may be held in the form of a tea party or a picnic. In such meetings, members may express their ideas freely regarding Party, politics, economics, and any other social problems. It is not

necessary to reach a conclusion, but the discussions should be recorded.

21. Regulations governing leave of absence for the Sub-District Party Organ are applicable to the small-group conference.

C. Guidance and Examination

22. Small-group conference is the major work of all the Party organs. The Sub-District Party Organ may appoint a person to attend and supervise the small-group conferences.

23. The Sub-District Party Organ will see to it that the small-group conferences are held according to schedule. It will submit monthly to its superior organ the results of such small-group conferences and in every three months to the Central Party Headquarters.

24. The small-group conference Chiefs may attend the Sub-District Party meeting to discuss matters concerning small-group training.

25. The District Party Organ may send out inspectors at any time to supervise the small-group conferences. Every six months it may call a meeting which all the Secretaries of the Sub-District Party Organs, small-group conference Chiefs, will attend to discuss matters concerning small-group conferences. The Secretary of the Sub-District Party Organ will take the chair in the meeting and the minutes will be submitted to the *Hsien* Party.

26. The *Hsien* Party Organ may also send out inspectors to supervise the small-group conferences. Every six months, after the meeting as stated in Item 25 has taken place, a *Hsien* Party meeting is to be called to discuss the small-group conferences in the whole *hsien*. The Secretary of the *Hsien* Party Organ will preside in such meetings. Minutes are to be submitted to the Provincial Party Headquarters.

27. If necessary, the *Hsien* Party Organ may hold different competitions in such fields as sports, speeches, Party principles, etc., in order to make the small-group conferences more interesting.

28. The Provincial Party Organ, besides sending out inspectors to make inspections of the small-group conferences, may obtain at any time the minutes of a certain small-group conference of a certain *hsien* for examination.

29. The Provincial Party Organ may have a general examination of the small-group conferences that have taken

place, taking the *hsien* as a unit. Encouragement and punishment should be given according to merit.

30. The Central Party Headquarters, besides sending out inspectors, may obtain any number of minutes of the small-group conferences for examination.

31. Those Party organs below the *Hsien* Party Organ should pay especial attention to the character, morals and intellectual ability of the members. The names of those members who have made special contributions to the Party work should be filed with the Central Party Headquarters for appointment.

D. Appendix

32. All the *Hsien* Parties upon receipt of this Program should make a study of local conditions and make out a plan for carrying them out.

33. For the border districts and war areas strict observance of these items may be dispensed with, upon the request of the local Party organ to the Central Party Headquarters.

34. The items contained in this memorandum are applicable to Special Municipal Party Organs, Seamen's Party Organs, Overseas Party Organs, and agencies under the charge of the Central Party Headquarters.

35. The above is effective after the approval of the Central Executive Committee of the Kuomintang.

E. PARTY CONSTITUTION OF THE CHINESE COMMUNIST PARTY [1]

Despite the many changes in the governmental form of the Communist-controlled areas, the Chinese Communist Party has retained the same Party Constitution for many years. The following constitution was adopted in 1928 by the Sixth Party Congress.

Chapter I. Title

Article 1. *The Title:* The Communist Party of China is a branch of the Communist International. Therefore the title is "The Chinese Communist Party."

[1] *Kung-ch'an-tang Tang-chang* [Party Constitution of the Communist Party], [Chungking?], XXVII (1938), p. 1–21.

Chapter II. The Members

ARTICLE 2. *Qualifications of Party Members:* The Party members should accept the regulations and constitution of the Communist International and of the Chinese Communist Party. They should join one of the Party Organs and abide by the resolutions which have been passed by the Communist International and the Chinese Communist Party. They are required to pay the Party dues regularly.

ARTICLE 3. *Procedure to Join the Party:* The candidates of the following qualifications can be recognized as Party members with the approval of the *hsien* Party Councillor and the sanction of the Branch Organs:

a. Factory Laborers: recommended by one Party member and approved by one Branch of Production Party Organ.

b. Farmers, handicraft men, intellectuals and public functionaries of the lower grades: recommended by two Party members.

c. High public functionaries: recommended by three Party members.

Note:

1. The sponsor must take full responsibility for the candidate. In case qualifications are false, the sponsor shall receive punishment according to the regulations. He may be expelled in a serious case.

2. The candidate shall be asked to do some Party work for trial before he can be recognized as a member, in order that his qualifications and understanding of party principles can be examined.

d. A candidate who is an ex-member of other Parties shall become a Communist Party member by the recommendation of three Party members of more than three years' standing. If he was an ordinary Party member of the other Party, his membership in the Communist Party shall be sanctioned by the Provincial Party Committee; if he was a special member of another Party, then his membership shall be sanctioned by the Central Party Organ.

ARTICLE 4. *The Adherence of Organized Groups:* In case other political groups or branches of other parties want to join the Communist Party, their organization systems must be studied and amended according to the ideas of the Communist Central Party Organ.

ARTICLE 5. *The Transfer of Members:* The Party members may be transferred from one Organ to another if they move from one place to another. The transfer, however, must be approved by the Central Party Organ.

ARTICLE 6. *The Expulsion of Members:* The expulsion of members must be first passed by the general meeting of that particular Branch Organ and then be approved by the higher Organ. Until the approval is obtained, it is necessary to stop the work of the member involved. In case the member is not satisfied with the discharge, he is allowed to send a petition to the highest Party Organ for final judgment. Every Party committee has the power to expel a member who is discovered as an anti-Communist. The resolution must be communicated to the Organ to which that member belonged.

CHAPTER III. THE ORGANIZATION

ARTICLE 7. *The Principle of Organization:* Like other Communist International Branch Parties, the essential of organization of the Chinese Communist Party is Democratic Centralism. By Democratic Centralism is meant:

a. Both superior and subordinate Party Organs shall be formed according to resolutions which have been passed in the Councils of Party Delegates and the National Communist Party Congress.

b. Each Party Organ is required to make a report of its newly elected members.

c. Subordinate Party Organs must accept orders issued by the higher Organs. They shall strictly obey the regulations of the Party. They shall effectively carry out the resolutions and plans which have been determined by the Communist International Central Committee and its supervisory Party Organs. The Party members may discuss and argue on certain points which are not yet passed by the Party Organ. In other words, they must obey unconditionally the resolutions which have been already determined by the Communist International or their superior Organs, whether they agree with these resolutions or not.

ARTICLE 8. *The Supervisory Party Organs:* Under certain circumstances, subordinate Party Organs are allowed to appoint new supervisory Committees to join the Party with the sanction of its superior Organs.

ARTICLE 9. *The Distribution of Party Organs:* The distribution of Party Organs is according to geographic units. The Administrative Party Organ in a certain place is the supervisory Organ of that place. People of different nationalities may all join the Communist Party. However, they must first join a Chinese District Party Organ before they can become members of the Chinese Communist Party.

ARTICLE 10. *Duties of the District Organs:* The District Organs have the power to settle their local affairs within the scope of resolutions passed by the Communist International and the Chinese Communist Party.

ARTICLE 11. *The Supreme Party Organs:* The supreme Party Organs are the Party Members' Mass Meeting and the Councils of Party Delegates.

ARTICLE 12. *The Party Committee:* Different classes of Party committees shall be elected from among the Party Members' Mass Meeting and the Councils of Party Delegates [2] and the National Communist Party Congress.[3] The committees shall supervise the routine procedures of their subordinate Organs.

ARTICLE 13. *Problems of Criticism:* In the case of *hsien* Branch Party Delegates, it is necessary for them to undergo criticism by the (subordinate) officers of higher Party Organs.

ARTICLE 14. *The Organization System of the Communist Party Organs:*

a. Different Branch Party Organs shall be established in every factory, workshop, shop, street, village, and army unit.

b. There shall be a District Party Council and District Council of Party Delegates in every city or country district, under the supervision of a District Party Committee.

c. There shall be a Hsien or Municipal Council of Party Delegates in each *hsien* or municipality, under the supervision of a Municipal Party Committee.

d. A special Council of Party Delegates which is constituted by several *hsien* or parts of a province shall be established when necessary. The establishment must be approved by the Provincial Committee.

e. There shall be a Provincial Council of Party Delegates in every province, to be supervised by a Provincial Party Committee.

f. There shall be a National Communist Congress in the nation, supervised by the Central Committee.

[2] The term *Tai-piao Ta-hui* rendered "Council of Party Delegates," may also be put as "Party Conference." Cf. "The Rules of the Communist Party of the Soviet Union" in Rappard, William E., *et al., Source Book on European Governments,* New York, 1937, p. v34–v52.

[3] *Ch'üan-kuo Ta-hui* is given as "National Party Congress"; the term *Ch'üan-kuo* has been translated as "All-China" elsewhere.

g. For the convenience in training Party members, a special Central Executive Bureau shall be established and special central officers shall be sent to different places. This Bureau and the officers shall be appointed and supervised by the Central Committee.

ARTICLE 15. Further departments and subordinate committees shall be established to deal with special Party functions, such as the Organization Department, Publicity Department, Labor Movement Committee and Women's Movement Committee. These departments and committees shall be under the supervision of their respective Party Committees.

Note: To improve understanding of differences in custom and language among Party members of different nationalities, several Nationality Movement Departments shall be formed.

CHAPTER IV. BRANCH PARTY ORGANS

ARTICLE 16. *Fundamental Organizations:* Branch Party Organs of the factories, mines, workshops, shops, streets, villages, and armies are the fundamental organization of the Communist Party. Members working in the above-mentioned places shall join the Branch Party Organs. New Branch Party Organs can be organized when there are at least three or more members. But they must be under the control of the *Hsien* Committee.

ARTICLE 17. *Special Organizations of the Branch Party Organs:* Members of certain businesses can join the Production Branch Organ of the same occupation in their neighboring city. Special Branch Organs shall be organized according to the localities and the nature of their work, such as handicraft laborers, free laborers, family laborers, or intellectuals.

ARTICLE 18. *Duties of the Branch Party Organs:* The Branch Party Organ unites the strength of the farmers and laborers. Its duties are:

a. To use its systematic and effective agitation and slogans to absorb farmers and laborers into the Communist party.

b. To use its power of organization to join the political and economic struggles of the farmers and laborers. To encourage the people's revolutionary spirit. To teach the meaning of class-struggles. To supervise the farmers' and laborers' revolutions. To lead proletarians to the Communist International and the Chinese Communist Party.

c. To enlist and train new members. To distribute Party periodicals among members and non-members in order to encourage political and educational work.

ARTICLE 19. *Branch Organ Executive Committee:* Each Branch shall have three to five executive committeemen to manage the routine Party work. They shall take charge of the division of labor, such as the publicity work, distribution of printed materials, organization of farmer and labor parties, women's movements, and youth movements. There shall be one secretary; he shall carry out resolutions and orders.

CHAPTER V. CITY AND COUNTRY DISTRICT PARTY ORGANS

ARTICLE 20. *The District Council of Party Delegates:* In the sphere of the city or country districts the supreme Party Organs are the Party Members' Mass Meeting and the District Councils of Party Delegates. The Party Members' Mass Meeting and the Councils of Party Delegates shall receive and approve the reports of the District Party Committee; shall elect the Delegates to District, *Hsien,* Municipal, or Provincial Councils of the Party Delegates Meeting.

ARTICLE 21. *District Party Committee:* The District Party Committee shall take charge of the supervision of affairs within that district before and after the Party Members' Mass Meeting or the District Council of Party Delegates' Meeting. Regular meetings of the city or rural District Party Committee shall be directed by the Standing Committee, elected by the Party Committee itself.

CHAPTER VI. *Hsien* AND MUNICIPAL PARTY ORGANS

ARTICLE 22. *The Hsien Council of Party Delegates:* The supreme Party Organ in the *hsien* is the *Hsien* Council of Party Delegates. The special meeting of the Council shall be called once in three months. It shall be called by the demand of a majority of other organizations in the *hsien;* by determination of the Provincial Party Committee or Special District Party Committee. The *Hsien* Council of Party Delegates which is called by the *Hsien* Party Committee shall read reports issued by the *Hsien* Party Committee or the *Hsien* Control Committee. It shall elect Delegates of the *Hsien* Party Committee, *Hsien* Control Committee, Provincial Party Committee, and Special District Party Committee.

ARTICLE 23. *Hsien Party Committee:* The *Hsien* Party Committee is elected by the *Hsien* Council of Party Delegates. Before and after the meetings of *Hsien* Council of Party Delegates this Committee is the supreme Party Organ in the *hsien*. The Committee shall be constituted by *Hsien* Delegates and delegates from important villages. The meeting of the Committee shall be called at least once a month, and its date shall be determined by the *Hsien* Committee itself. A Standing Committee shall be elected to take care of routine Party affairs. There shall be one secretary of the Standing Committee, to be elected from among the Committee members.

ARTICLE 24. A *Hsien* Party Committee shall put into effect previously passed resolutions of the *Hsien* Council of Party Delegates, the Provincial Party Committee, and the Central Party Committee. Whenever possible, different committees, such as the Organization Committee, Publicity Committee, Women's Movement Committee, and Farmers' Movement Committee, shall be established. The *Hsien* Party Committee shall also appoint the editors of *Hsien* Party newspapers. It shall take dual responsibilities to obey the orders of its superior Organ and to report its own merits to its superior Organs.

ARTICLE 25. No Municipal Party Committee shall be formed in a city where a *Hsien* Party Committee has already been established. In such a case the Party affairs of the city shall be in charge of the *Hsien* Party Committee. A City District Party Committee under it may be formed to take an active part in the City Party affairs.

ARTICLE 26. *The Municipal Party Committee:* The organization of the Municipal Party Committee is the same as that of the *Hsien* Party Committee. A City District Party Committee is subordinate to it. This Committee shall administer its Branch Party Organs and Branch Organs of its neighbors. No Municipal Party Committee shall be established in a place where the Provincial Party Committee or Special District Party Committee has already been established.

ARTICLE 27. The organization and functions of the Special District Party Committee shall be the same as the *Hsien* Party Committee. In the place where there is no Provincial Party Committee provided then the Special District Party Committee shall be directed by the Central Party Committee. In such a case the functions and organization of the Special Party Committee shall be the same as the Provincial Party Committee.

Chapter VII. Provincial Party Organs

ARTICLE 28. *The Provincial Council of Party Delegates:* The Provincial Council of Party Delegates is the supreme Party Organ in the province. The regular meeting of the Council shall be called to meet once semi-annually. Special meetings shall be called according to the demand of a majority of other organizations of the province, or by the determination of the Central Party Committee. The regular meeting of the Provincial Council of Party Delegates, which is called by the Provincial Party Committee, shall have the responsibility of hearing reports issued by the Provincial Party Committee, and by the Provincial Control Committee. It shall discuss the social work and Party affairs problems of the province; and elect delegates to Provincial Party Committee, Provincial Control Committee, and National Party Congress.

ARTICLE 29. *Provincial Party Committee:* Before and after the meeting of the Provincial Council of Party delegates, the Provincial Party Committee is the supreme Party Organ in each province. Delegates of the central Provincial organizations or other district Party Organs are required to join the Provincial Party Committee. The meeting of the Provincial Party Committee shall be called at least once in two months; the date of the meeting shall be determined by the Committee itself. A Standing Committee under it shall be authorized to take charge of Party affairs before and after the meeting of the Provincial Party Committee. Secretaries are to be appointed accordingly.

ARTICLE 30. *The Duties and Organization of Provincial Party Committees:* The duties of the Provincial Party Committee are: to put into effect the passed resolutions of the Provincial Council of Party Delegates or Central Party Committee; to organize the subsidiary Party Organs; to appoint editors for the Party newspapers; to distribute the Party funds; to control the accounting department; to supervise the Party work among non-Communists; to draft regular reports to the Central Party Committee; to announce the Party Movement to its subordinate Organs. For the furtherance of important work different departments and committees shall be provided, such as the Provincial

Organization Department, Publicity Department, Labor Movement Department, etc. The department heads who act concurrently in the Provincial Party Committee shall supervise Party affairs under the control of the Provincial Standing Committee.

ARTICLE 31. The Provincial Party Committee shall help the District Party Committee to carry out the Party activities. Therefore the *Hsien* Party Committee in that particular city should only take care of the Party work within its own sphere.

CHAPTER VIII. THE NATIONAL PARTY CONVENTION [4]

ARTICLE 32. The National Party Convention shall be called to meet twice annually. The numbers of candidates and Delegates to be elected by different organs are to be determined by the Central Party Committee.

ARTICLE 33. The previously passed resolutions of the Convention shall be put into effect after the approval of the Central Party Committee.

ARTICLE 34. In case the Convention meeting is held before the meeting of the Communist International then several Delegates can be elected to attend the meeting of the latter. However, they must get the consent of the International Communist Committee.

CHAPTER IX. THE NATIONAL PARTY CONGRESS

ARTICLE 35. The National Party Congress is the supreme Party Organ in the country. The meeting shall be called once annually by the Central Party Committee and the Communist International. Special meetings can be called by the Central Party Committee or initiated by the Communist International. It may also be called by request of a majority of the Delegates who attended the last meeting. The call of the special meeting, however, must be approved by the Central Party Committee first. Resolutions which have been passed by the majority of the Delegates shall become effective. The number of Delegates and percentage in each Party Organ shall be determined by the Communist International, the Central Party Committee, or the preliminary session of the Party Convention.

ARTICLE 36. The duties of the National Party Congress are:

a. To receive and examine reports issued by the Central Party Committee.

[4] *Ch'üan-kuo Hui-i.*

b. To determine Party regulations.
c. To determine the important political or organization plans.
d. To elect the Central Party Committee.

ARTICLE 37. Delegates to the Party Congress are to be elected by the Provincial Councils of Party Delegates. In special cases requiring secret action, they may be appointed by the Provincial Party Committee with the approval of the Communist International Committee. A provisional Congress can be substituted for the regular Congress with only the consent of the International Communist Committee.

CHAPTER X. THE CENTRAL PARTY COMMITTEE [5]

ARTICLE 38. The number of the Central Party Committee members shall be determined by the National Party Congress.

ARTICLE 39. While the National Party Congress is in session, the Central Party Committee is the supreme Party Organ. It represents the Party in contacts with the other political parties. Besides this its duties are: to establish various subordinate Party Organs; to supervise and control subordinate Party Organs; to edit the Party newspapers; to send special Party officers to different provinces; to form the Central Executive Bureau in order to encourage Party principles; to distribute the Party funds; to control the Central Accounting Department. The Central Party Committee shall be called at least three times a month.

ARTICLE 40. A Political Bureau shall be established in the Central Party Committee. It shall supervise the political affairs before and after the meeting of the Central Party Committee. A Standing Committee is to be elected to take charge of routine work.

ARTICLE 41. When necessary the Central Party Committee shall establish different subordinate departments or committees such as the Organization Department, Publicity Department, Laborers' Movement Committees, Women's Movement Committees and Farmers' Movement Committees. The functions of these Departments and Committees shall be guided by the Central Party Committee, which shall also appoint Department heads and Chairmen.

ARTICLE 42. The Central Party Committee shall determine the work and the scope of work of the District Party

[5] *Chung-yang Wei-yüan-hui.*

Organs with reference to their political and economic background. The distribution of Party Organs shall also be settled by the Central Party Committee.

Chapter XI. The Central Control Committee [6]

ARTICLE 43. For the control of the financial and accounting work of the subordinate Party Organs, Central or District Control Committees shall be elected by the National Party Congress, Central or District Party Committee.

Chapter XII. The Party Discipline

ARTICLE 44. Strict obedience to Party discipline is the highest duty of every Communist. Resolutions passed by the Communist International, Central Party Committee, or other superior Party Organs shall be carried out effectively and exactly by the Party members. Until resolutions have been passed, members are allowed to discuss them freely.

ARTICLE 45. Those who have failed to put into effect the orders or resolutions, or those who violate the Party discipline shall be punished by the Party Organs with reference to the Party regulations. The punishments for Organs are: reprimand, dissolution, and reregistration of its members. The punishments for the members are: reprimand, warning, deprivation of Party activities, expulsion from membership, or suspension from duties for stated periods. Cases involving punishment shall be studied and examined by the Party Members' Mass Meeting or by respective Party Organs. Special Committees may be formed with the approval of Party Organs to settle difficult cases. Expulsion from membership shall be carried out according to particulars stated in Item 6 of this Constitution.

Chapter XIII. Party Finance

ARTICLE 46. The sources of the Party revenue are: Party fees, special levies, income from printed materials, and the compensations from its superior Organs.

ARTICLE 47. The amount of the Party fee shall be determined by the Central Committee. Members without employment or those in poverty are allowed exemption from payment. Those who do not pay their fees for three months, without stating reasons, shall be recognized as released from

---

[6] The term here is *shên-ch'a wei-yüan-hui*, not *chien-ch'a*, which is the term used for "Control" as one of the five powers of Sun Yat-sen's plan.

membership, and their names shall be announced to the Mass Meeting.

Chapter XIV. Special Party Groups [Corps] [7]

Article 48. Special Party Groups are to be constituted by three or more Party members. The main function of these Party Groups is the encouragement of the Party principles among the non-Communist groups. The routine affairs of the Group shall be in charge of a Managing Board elected from the Party Group. Whenever a Party Committee and a Special Party Group conflict and then come to an agreement on certain points, these points shall be reconsidered and concurrently passed by the two Organs. Quick action must be taken. If agreement is not reached, a petition is required for submission to a superior Party Organ for final determination.

Article 49. Delegates of Party Groups shall attend the Party Committee Meeting whenever there is matter dealing with the Party Group.

Article 50. A Managing Board shall be formed in each Group with the approval of the Party Committee. The Committee can appoint its members to the Board and may also recall or remove those members when necessary. In such cases, however, the reasons for recall or removal require announcement to the Party Group.

Article 51. A list of names of the staff members of the Party Group shall be submitted to a Party Organ for approval. Removal of staff members from a group shall also require approval by the Party Organ.

Article 52. Resolutions to be carried out by the Party Group shall first be passed by the Group Meeting or Meeting of the Managing Board. In a Party Members' Mass Meeting all the Group members must support a resolution which is already passed by its own Group. If one fails to do so he may be punished according to the regulations.

Chapter XV. Relationship with the Communist Youth Corps [8]

Article 53. The District or Central Party Organs shall send Delegates to the Communist Youth Corps for exchanging ideas. At the same time the Communist Youth Corps can also send their members to attend the various meetings of the different Councils of the Party Delegates.

[7] *Tang-t'uan.*
[8] *Kung-ch'an Ch'ing-nien T'uan.*

APPENDIX III. MATERIALS ON POLICY

A. REPLY TO QUESTIONS (CHIANG K'AI-SHEK)[1]

Replies to the following questionnaire were very kindly supplied by Generalissimo Chiang K'ai-shek. The questions by the present author were submitted to him on July 23, 1940; the replies were transmitted through the Vice-Minister of Publicity, Mr. Hollington Tong, on November 26, 1940.

(*1*) Do you believe that the *San Min Chu I* are suited to China alone, or do you think it possible that they represent a golden mean between totalitarianism and democracy?
San Min Chu I is a type of democracy particularly suited to China. In its general features, I think, it is similar to Western democracies.

(*2*) Do you feel that a *San Min Chu I* China will have any positive proposals to make concerning the subject of world federation or confederation, if that subject is raised at the end of the current European war?
In as much as cosmopolitanism and world peace are two of the main aims of San Min Chu I, China will naturally be disposed to participate in any world federation or confederation based on the principle of equality of nations and for the good of mankind.

(*3*) Do you believe that the inauguration of the constitution and of a constitutional period will lead to the uncontrolled freedom of minor parties, including the Communist? Is there not a danger that the minor parties, because they do not share the responsibility for government, will be able to exploit formal democratic rights more unscrupulously than the Kuomintang?
No, because democracy in itself has the ability to work out the solutions for those problems if there are any.

(*4*) What do you regard as the clearest factual indication of the growth of democracy in Free China?

[1] Private communication by and to the present author, and in his possession.

The following are the clearest indications of the growth of democracy in China: *1*, the convocation of the People's Political Council; *2*, the convocation of the Provincial Political Councils; *3*, the growth of popular interest in both public and national affairs; *4*, the growth of the sentiment of national solidarity; *5*, the spontaneous response to the call for public services.

(5) *Within* the army, what democratic tendencies have you fostered or observed?
Since the army is now recruited from the different walks of life, it naturally shares the growing democratic sentiment. Within the army, however, the soldiers and officers are of course trained and disciplined in strict accordance with military regulations.

(6) When the war against Japan is successfully concluded, do you believe that the National Government will have any difficulty in re-establishing its full authority over the guerrilla-governed areas, which will have tasted autonomy?
No, because all these forces are fighting for the liberty and independence of China.

(7) Do you believe that the bogus Government at Nanking is intended by the enemy to deceive the Chinese, to fool the Japanese home public, or actually to govern China? Why do you think that a man as ambitious as Wang Ch'ing-wei put himself in such a humiliating and ridiculous position—before the world, and before history?
Whatever may be the intention of the Japanese in putting up Wang Ch'ing-wei as the head of the bogus government, they certainly have no idea of letting him or any other puppet govern China in reality. As to the latter part of the question, I prefer that you would ask Wang directly.

B. WHAT I MEAN BY ACTION, OR A PHILOSOPHY OF ACTION (CHIANG K'AI-SHEK) [1]

The following essay, delivered as a speech, represents the clearest formulation by Generalissimo Chiang of his own philosophy. To this must be joined his exegesis on the *San Min Chu I*, quoted in part above, p. 270.

The Truths We Must Endeavor to Grasp Anew

In 1932 I delivered a lecture on the subject "Stages in the Development of Revolutionary Philosophy." In it I dealt with two points of especial importance. Firstly, I tried to explain how the actual grasp of what we know comes only with positive action. I said: "The universe contains spirit in addition to matter. Spirit implies mind, and mind implies conscience. Conscience must find its expression in action, in the practice of what it urges. Otherwise the conscience would be a barren thing, and there would be no way of avoiding a futile idealism on the one hand or determinist materialism on the other." Secondly, I explained the importance of the philosophy of action in regard to the Revolution. I said: "Only the word 'action' covers the meaning of what has brought into being all things in space and time. Our philosophy therefore takes as the one central principle of human life and thought the maxim: 'From true knowledge action naturally proceeds.' In short, any philosophy of ours must be a philosophy of action. The consummation of the Republican revolution and the overthrow of Japanese Imperialist aggression depend upon our putting into practice Dr. Sun's principle of action as the natural product of knowledge."

Since I suggested this term *philosophy of action* and became the advocate of *positive action* as the course the revolutionary must follow, a considerable effect has been visible in our ranks. The spirit of positive action has been intensified among us. In the army and in schools, and in political and social life generally, a gradual transformation has taken place in the state of inert frustration, vagueness and depression formerly prevalent. There has been a general tendency to take the initiative, to express ourselves in positive action. Such indeed was my aim in promoting this

[1] Chiang K'ai-shek, *A Philosophy of Action, or What I Mean by Action*, Chungking, 1940; p. 7–20. The accompanying foreword and notes are here omitted. The translation is the work of Mr. Ma P'in-ho, a naturalized Chinese scholar but of European race and nativity.

philosophy of action. When I take note of the results achieved by our *action*, however, I remain unsatisfied on a number of points. For instance, there is sometimes mere action without clear realization of its why and wherefore, resulting in what the ancients called "unreal action." With others there is initial vigor and great positive effort, followed by impatience of checks and failure to persevere in the face of difficulties, leading some to throw the blame on circumstances and others upon their fellow-men. The irritable then proceed to arguing and quarrels; while the sweeter-tempered lose heart. In this way the real issue is lost to sight and obstacles unnecessarily multiplied; or the individual may be overcome with outright disgust and take on a completely negative attitude, the initial speed of his progress being in the end equalled by the speed of his subsequent retrogression. Another kind of failure comes with a man who impulsively imitates others; who when he sees others on the go feels any move on their part calls for some move on his; who spends all his time in acting on the spur of some transitory stimulus or exigency, forgetful of our broad revolutionary conceptions and far-reaching aims.

In seeking the reasons for such faulty conduct, I have been forced to the conclusion that it is due to imperfect knowledge of the essential meaning of *positive action,* and to imperfect realization of the significance and nature of *action,* that there is lack of determination, faith and perseverance among us.

Action Is Life Itself: the Tireless Pertinacity of Nature Our Example

According to my own individual experience, our first step must be to draw a clear distinction between *action* and *motion.* The monosyllabic structure of the Chinese language has occasioned the use of substantival phrases consisting of two words. One of these phrases is *hsing-tung* (action-motion), which in common parlance often has the meaning properly covered only by the word *hsing* alone, a word of far deeper and wider meaning than the word *tung.* In fact, we may say that action is *human life* itself. An antithesis is commonly implied between the words *action* and *thought,* and between *word* and *act.* In reality, however, thought and word are processes of action, and are properly to be considered as included within the scope of *action,* rather than as foreign to it. From birth to death, while he is subject to space and time, a man cannot withdraw himself from the sphere of action; he grows up in action and his character is formed and elevated by action. All saintly and heroic men, like the devoted revolutionary, attain their ends and achieve their nobility of character only through their planned and determined actions.

If we wish to realize the true nature of *action* we can do no better than take as the *point-de-départ* for our thinking the words of the *I-ching* or *Book of Changes:* "Let the superior man exert himself with the unfailing pertinacity of Nature." For the most obvious thing in the universe, the very principle animating all its phenomena, is the activity of the forces of Nature. The gloss reads: "Day by day the heavens revolve, with a constancy that only a supreme pertinacity could maintain. The superior man models himself upon it in the unceasing exertion of his energies." This *pertinacity* is something perennially unimpaired and ever changeless, greatest strength united to greatest durability, and moreover an absolute thoroughness and completeness. And we must model ourselves on the activity of nature, on its spontaneous and unremitting flow of energy. If there is this realization of the value and place of human life in the universe, action will appear to us something inevitable, and there will follow as a matter of course single-minded devotion to purpose, a completely natural attitude, and resolute advance with firm strides towards our ends—we shall have achieved, in the words of the *Chung-yung,* "the highest integrity, unfailing and enduring." Man's existence and progress depend entirely upon his perception of these truths.

Action, therefore, differs from *motion. Motion* is by no means necessarily *action,* though *action* may on occasion include some form of *motion.* Action is continuous, whereas motion is intermittent; action is essential, whereas motion is accidental; action is spontaneous, whereas motion is usually due to the application of external force. Action is in response to the supreme order of things and in harmony with the nature of man. Motion is impulsive response to some fortuitous external stimulus. Action we may describe as more natural and smoother intrinsically than motion; and extrinsically it is wholly good in its outcome, whereas motion may be good or may be evil. Action unfolds in uninterrupted continuity; motion proceeds by fits and starts. As an illustration, action may be compared to a ceaseless flow of water, in the words of Confucius, "racing on, unpausing day and night." The unremitting and insistent character of *positive action* may thus be figured forth. Motion on the other hand may be compared to the impact of a stone upon water into which it is thrown. The water is violently agitated and leaps high into the air; its movement is tumultuous while it lasts, but subsides when after a moment or so the extraneous force that caused it is expended. Such motion is, therefore, transitory, simply because its motive force comes from without.

Action Is Not Mere Motion

We cannot of course say that all *motion* is bad, but we can at least say that the value of *motion* is never comparable with that of *action*. What we commonly call *impulse* is a manifestation of the reflex action of some sense or faculty. When we speak of a man's motions as "blind," "wild," or "furious," it is always a case of response to external stimulus or of the application of external force. Such motions are not spontaneous and they therefore pursue no definite course; they have no basis in the consciousness of the individual and no precise direction or aim; the individual's concern with them is limited to the passing moment of their duration; he envisages nothing as to what may be their result. There may be great initial activity and force, but because there is no basis in reason, consciousness and spontaneity, momentary agitation is succeeded by relapse into quiescence. A man who lives by passion and impulse, who *moves* rather than *acts* is like a bell, which when struck vibrates and emits sound but unless struck is silent. All passive and transient activity, arising from mere impulse and sense-stimulation, is in opposition to the positive action required of us by our revolutionary philosophy, for such *motion* has no lasting effect and is powerless to transform the lives of men.

It is imperative therefore that there should be no confusion of what we mean by *action* with what is better termed *motion*. The action of which I have been speaking is the operation of man's innate faculties according to the true natural laws of his being; it is what I have called the expression of conscience in practice, the exercise of conscience. Although we colloquially speak of "violent actions" and "wrong-minded action" in describing men's conduct, such conduct, being that of men acting under the influence of impulse or illusion, should properly be classed as a form of *motion*. It is not what we mean by action.

Action Is Nature at Work in Man: the Whole Universe Is the Scene of Action

Genuine action is necessarily ordered, rhythmical, systematic and directed towards some aim. It arises from that fullness of consciousness described as the "calm of mature reflection." It is inevitably straightforward and continuous, undeviating and unhesitating. Such motion as that of the revolving globe we ought not to call mere motion; that ceaseless axial and orbital rotation is a phenomenon called in ancient times the *activity* of nature; and it may serve us as the best possible illustration of the qualities of action. We may proceed to a fuller description of the nature of action by saying it is always marked by a certain regularity and order in the course of its fulfilment. Human life in all its aspects of growth and development, in each transition from stage to stage, in the preparatory and supplementary acquisitions of substance and experience between phase and phase,—all this is action. The normal routine of daily life, —sleeping, resting, eating and working,—is all to be considered within the scope of action. For the meaning of action may apply equally well to what occurs both in states of repose and in states of movement. While work throughout the process of carrying out a given task may clearly be action, recreation may also be action. States of motion and repose are of course to a superficial view opposites. Moreover in the modern world *motion* is especially set up in opposition to *repose,* and emphasized almost to the exclusion of the latter. This has caused the importance of *stability* to be lost to view.

For the truth of the matter is: "stability allows of repose; repose allows of calm; calm allows of reflection, and reflection gives grasp." It should be realized that repose can have a positive function. And what I call the philosophy of action permits of no distinction between motion and repose, a distinction which is superficial. A course of action may involve intervals of both motion and of repose, just as the invisible working of living matter contributes to the visible growth of the body. We need only concern ourselves as to whether what is done is in harmony with the laws of man's innate character.

The natural processes of the universe and of human life go on unceasingly, and in trying to ameliorate human life by positive action we must realize that such action to be effectual must be similar to those processes in its continuity and tenacity. Positive action in its every phase, whether outwardly visible or impalpable, never ceases to be action, never really for a moment comes to a halt. The whole universe is the scene of such action, and man in so far as he truly acts participates in its immense activity. Let us therefore distinguish clearly between mere *motion* and the true *action* that works by a steady advance in an undeviating course, with the timeless inexhaustibility of flowing water towards its appointed aim.

And now I have something more to add in definition of the essential meaning of action and its relation to life. The ancients said "Man's innate character is given him at birth together with life itself." I consider *action* to be the expression of that innate character, and so as inseparable from life as it. Man in his earliest infancy can laugh and cry, eat and drink; as he grows up he learns to gaze and listen, speak and walk; and once grown up, no matter whether he be intelligent or stupid, he strives for existence, progress, and development. Or, in other words, he seeks to conform to the elementary needs of human life. All these phenomena are phenomena of *action,* the action of the faculties for discerning moral and material good, with which man is naturally endowed.

It is apparent to me that love of ease and dislike of exertion are no part of fundamental human nature, but that on the contrary mankind is naturally disposed to labor and work. If you compel a lively man accustomed to be always on his feet and busy with his hands to be idle and sedentary, depriving him of anything to do, he is certain to feel exceedingly unhappy. In the same way, the least intelligent or experienced of men has felt the satisfaction and content that come with work, the joy of contributing to the accomplishment of some undertaking. There is a colloquialism current in certain coastal districts of China which substitutes the word "life" for the word "work"; thus, you may be asked whether you have "lived your life" for the day, in the sense of "have you done your day's work?" Work is indeed life; unless a man be totally incapable he will inevitably require the means of expression for his abilities, and particularly such expression as will accrue to the benefit of somebody beyond himself. Even a little child is conscious of the intense satisfaction to be derived from doing one's best in the service of others. Though no praise be awarded the child it is aware of an extraordinary complaisance within itself.

The Broadest Sense of Life

All these little illustrations bear witness to the fact that action is the object of man's life; and we should, vice versa, make life the object of our action. We are born with faculties for the discernment of moral and material good; life, from childhood to old age, is the energetic, ceaseless, use of them, at first chiefly for the satisfaction of the needs of one's own existence, to secure one's own footing in life, but next, as one's mental perspective broadens, the family, the village, the community, the nation, and mankind become objects of the desire to express oneself and give of oneself. When we speak of *life* it should mean for us the life of mankind, the life and existence of people and nation, the livelihood of masses and citizenry. And when we speak of *action,* we should mean action performed in the service of *life* in such a broad sense.

The difference between man and the beasts of the field and the birds of the air consists just in this. We read in the classics of "a virtue of surpassing excellence, which is given to the people as a law of their being," and the virtue alluded to is this propensity to look after one's own welfare and at the same time the welfare of one's fellow-men. We are naturally endowed with the disposition to will the good of others and to act in their service. "Action," with the qualities I have sketched, is something primordially bound up with life.

The Revolution Demands Action of All Men at All Times

The essential meaning of action being once understood we may proceed to inquire into its spirit and wherein it finds its highest expression. How is it that men for all the apparent unity of their existence sometimes live lives of such devotion to the good of mankind and the world that they earn the admiration of posterity, while others live degenerate lives governed by the lowest desires, to the detriment of themselves and their neighbors? Education and environment are factors that play their part in this, but more important is what the ancient called "material desire"—the tendency to seek possession rather than creation, to enjoy rather than contribute. In the words of Dr. Sun, "making one's aim acquisition and not service" leads to degraded and uncontrolled conduct which is an obstacle to human progress and what we as comrades in Revolution must strive our utmost to avoid and eradicate.

Revolutionary motives are motives of service, of self-sacrifice for the good of others. The task the Revolution sets itself is the "practice of goodwill" in the broadest sense of those words,—action inspired by love for men to the exclusion of all that tends to their harm. In our revolutionary zeal to promote *positive action* throughout our world we aim to create an all-pervading moral attitude to life such as is rationally conformable to man's true nature; and we moreover seek to bring into full play the deep funds of humanity and benevolence in our own people. We push aside considerations of individual ability, of past education and environment, and of how far bad habits acquired may have become ingrained. We appeal to all as they are to take fresh stock of their lives and realize how from the very fact of their being alive they possess the ability to act,—to act in no less a sense than the great deliverers of mankind in their saintly and heroic deeds. The difference between such deeds and the actions of normal daily life is one of degree, not of kind. We are everyone men born of woman and passing our days between heaven and earth; not for us to vex ourselves with fear of failure; the only failure is in failing to act.

The Meaning of Ease

Let use take the three key-virtues of judgment, goodwill, and courage as our guides in the task of "playing the man." For the rest, let us follow the dictum of Sun Wên to the effect that "the very clever and able should strive to serve ten million fellow-men; a man of lesser ability may aspire to serve ten hundred men; while a man devoid of talent may content himself with doing the best he can for a single fellow-man." The highly talented may perform their duties with ease; the moderately gifted may make smooth progress with theirs; while the poorly gifted may do so with only a narrow margin of competence; but all that matters is our full use of our faculties in positive action for the good of others. If we advance without ever falling away from a pure and concentrated resolve to do our best, we shall certainly be able to realize the ideal of *action*. In a sense it will prove *easy*, though this does not of course mean that anything can be got without pains or anything managed in a facile and quiescent fashion. Nor does it mean that all will necessarily be plain sailing, fraught with no obstacles.

Our path through life is strewn with dangers, hindrances and obstructions. Revolutionary action is attended by many risks; it requires the will to make great sacrifices. Nevertheless, man's capacity for positive action has achieved many a colossal feat in the course of his history, the prodigious hydraulic engineering of the ancients, ascent into the air and penetration of the earth, and revolutionary deeds that have transformed the face of human affairs. The ultimate consideration is always whether we possess thorough determination and a spirit of unflinching zeal, for with these we may overcome towering obstacles as it were "in our stride," and "face dangers with imperturbable calm." A man worthy of his place in the ranks of the Revolution will regard as nothing extraordinary difficulties and dangers that would daunt others. His revolutionary spirit, which is the very spirit of action, gives him a sublime indifference to whatever may be the magnitude of the demands his duty makes upon him; whatever his principles, faith and responsibility involve is "all in the day's work" for him, though it be ordeal by fire and water or the abnegation of everything dearest to him. He takes no account of difficulty, and fear is a thing still stranger to him. It is in the sense that to a man with such an attitude action is *easy* that I use the word.

Action born of that innate character given us with life, conceived in absolute sincerity, and aimed at the good of others treats things as "all of a piece." From beginning to end of an appointed task it maintains a uniform consistency and integrity of purpose. The seeds of its final success are inherent in its first beginnings. Difficulty and failure as I understand them can have no part in such action.

Positive action with a complete integrity of purpose produces that honesty and trustworthiness which are distinctive marks of all true action. It penetrates to the core of matters, and deals only in realities. It is free from superficial trappings and fuss: permits of no slack approximation and evasion of the point, all of which comes from that shrinking from effort and hardship that is so incompatible with the spirit of positive action. Whereas I have called all true action *easy*, those who go about things without its spirit find themselves confronted with seemingly insurmountable difficulties everywhere. When the ancients said: "There is nothing either difficult or easy in the world," they had in mind this way of thinking, as I had too when I said that wartime and peacetime were one and the same.

Sincerity the Root of Action and Goodwill

The next thing to consider is what is to be the central aim of our action. I would answer if asked this with a single word: "Goodwill." Action is the *practice of goodwill* in its deepest sense.

Goodwill is grounded in the sense of justice and issues from complete sincerity. The sincere man is necessarily conscious of goodwill and he is necessarily possessed of the moral courage required to practice it. The ancients said "there is completeness in sincerity," and again, "where there is not sincerity there is a void." The place of sincerity in human life is indeed like that of energy in the atom, the structure of which would collapse without it. If a man's life lacks "ardent sincerity," he will likewise be powerless to form and manifest the three key-virtues of judgment, goodwill, and courage. And without the strength to be derived from those virtues, the Three Principles of the People can make no headway. Only by action inspired with perfect sincerity can the splendid truths of those Principles be asserted and translated into fact.

Sincerity is dependent upon the sense of justice. The keynote of our Republican Revolution has been the smashing of selfish individualism and the rescue of our people from their sufferings and of our nation from its peril. To achieve what yet remains to be done, to acquit ourselves well as a section of humanity, and to explore the full scope of possible human well-being, all we do and enact must be grounded in perfect sincerity. Then the pains we take and the plans we devise will prove creative, progressive, and constructive; we shall put flesh on the bones of the egalitarian philosophy of social justice; we shall be clear as to what we think and are aiming at; we shall be able to give full expression to our true nature and faculties, proceeding in all we do resolutely, frankly, and boldly.

Action attains its highest point of intensity in the giving of one's life in the cause of justice, when death in that cause is accepted as sweet and shorn of all its terrors. "One may die in the course of willing men good, but life is not to be purchased at the price of willing them ill" is a classical teaching we may take as a supreme ideal of positive action. Action that lives up to that ideal will inevitably be *revolutionary*, while, vice versa, it is only genuinely revolutionary conduct that possesses the true qualities of positive action. Sincerity is the primal motive force of action. With it, a man is aware only of the interests he has in common with his fellow-men, and of none that conflicts with those of his fellow-men. With sincerity, a man acts his will to good in perfect self-possession, pushing steadily onwards through difficulty and danger to success. This is the bearing of Dr. Sun's teaching on the revolutionary movement.

The Laws of Action

In what I have said so far I have sketched the outlines of our conception of action. Men differ in profession, rank and work; but there is not a single one of us but must be a *man of action* if our revolutionary aims are to be completely realized. Action, however, is subject to certain laws, which I now wish to go into. It must, firstly, have its *point-de-départ*, secondly its regular order of procedure (that is, a methodical and scientific plan), thirdly, its definite goal, and lastly it must possess the qualities of constancy and continuity.

One: The Starting Point

Firstly, by *point-de-départ* we mean the careful selection of whatever way of approach may be most appropriate, direct, and efficacious for the carrying out of our projects. The same is true of study, affairs, and revolutionary action. The ancients said: "Ascent must start from places low; remote objectives are attained from near beginnings." This was their way of expressing the nature of the *point-de-départ*. If any mistake is made about it we are bound to miss our objective and destination however sure we may be of the direction in which we want to go. Again, if we try to run before we can walk, or skip preliminaries, or gain the heights by some ill-considered short-cut, our work will inevitably prove abortive.

Two: Ordered Unfolding of Plans

Secondly, the necessity for what I have called "a regular order of procedure" means the uselessness of reliance upon mere verve and enthusiasm, and the futility of action taken on the spur of some transitory turn of thought, action which is bound to encounter unforeseen obstacles in its course, be disconcerted by them, and lose its character as action by becoming some irrational form of *motion*. Action must be preceded by the laying down of plans and choice of a mode of procedure whereby all possible contingencies may be allowed for and prepared for. The plans, moreover, must be precise in matters of time and space, and in quantitative and numerical considerations. They must, when decided upon, be carried out with due attention to detail, and with periodical stock-taking of the ground covered. A steady rate of advance will thus be maintained. When it is possible to make plans it is obviously also possible to foresee to a great extent the circumstances of time and place under which the plans will be carried out and the quantitative and numerical requirements that will have to be met. In scientific accordance with these foreseen circumstances and requirements the execution of the whole project should be apportioned among the persons involved so that each has work in all respects congenial to his qualities, while provision is also made for cooperation between all concerned. With order and method in procedure there will be no putting of the cart before the horse, no abrupt intrusion of irrelevancies, no slackening at moments of urgency, or precipitate speed where none is needed; day by day and step by step substantial progress will be made. In this way we shall have no abortive enterprises, nor the disappointment they engender.

Three: Unswerving Aim at the Target

Coming, thirdly, to the matter of *goal,* it should be like a conspicuous target at which one takes steady, unfaltering, aim. No matter whether the work we are engaged in be of vast or slight dimensions, its aim should be seen, as it were, through sights trained on the main target of an ideal goal. To every piece of work there must be a beginning and an end, a clearly-defined destination. Before the destination be reached there can be no pause in our concentrated effort.

Four: The Even Texture of a Life of Action

Lastly, with regard to the fourth and especially important point: perseverance and continuity, the very qualities that, as I said at the beginning, distinguish *action* from *motion.* I spoke of action as essentially regular, orderly, and purposeful, and said that such action would necessarily be revolutionary action and its influence revolutionary influence. In other words, revolutionary action unfolds in an unbroken uniformity of effort; it draws on the funds of moral vigor in our national genius, and provides a new channel for the expression of the great moral qualities of which that genius is composed, whereby it may rehabilitate the status to which it is properly entitled. It must be realized that our Revolutionary and the reconstructive activities pursue a broad and enlightened policy free from all manner of trickery and opportunism. We are actuated by a spirit of extraordinary power, but what we are doing is nothing abnormal as the word should be understood, and our methods are wholly realistic.

All unnatural and inhuman conduct, and illogical and unscientific methods, result in frustration and can have no place in revolutionary activity. The ancients spoke of "acts of routine virtue" in their emphasis upon the almost *humdrum,* stolid, qualities of true virtue. Our Revolution is likewise dependent upon the capacity to maintain a course of persevering and continuous effort; the behavior required is in no way peculiar or foreign to everyday life. For out of continuity comes perseverance and what we may call *ease.* Tsêng Kuo-fan said: "things should be done soundlessly and as it were 'odorlessly,' with both precision and economy of effort." By this he meant not wooden impassivity or dry-as-dust pedantry but directness, simplicity, and an absence of fuss, a straightforward and unassuming way of going about things. In working for the success of the Revolution we should cultivate the attitude of the nameless hero who braves dangers and endures hardships as matters of course. We shall thus keep in touch with the people and render the influence of what we do in the service of mankind broad and lasting.

Formation and Constancy of Purpose

Unremitting perseverance to the very end of our task, every day we live a day of positive action, and full employment of our powers in harmony with the laws of Nature and Man, are the conditions for our successful accomplishment of our revolutionary mission. Among Tsêng Kuo-fan's self-admonitory words on "Formation of Purpose" there are the following phrases: "To cast away the gifts of Heaven and live in sloth will bring upon me some evil catastrophe. . . . This I swear never to forget as long as I can still draw breath." That is to say, the formation of our purpose in life requires of us diligent and courageous devotion and the full exercise of our talents. The great writer and statesman also admonished himself on the subject of steadfastness of purpose, reproaching himself: "Again and again have you been delinquent in your duties and endeavors, and been swayed by material temptations; but no one has ever heard of your being unpunctual at mealtimes!" How is it, he meant, that if we can be regular in attending to our material wants we cannot be equally unfailing in the performance of our duties? The full accomplishment of any aim requires strong-minded formation and steadfastness of purpose. The true meaning of the words "let the superior man exert himself with the unfailing pertinacity of Nature" embraces this.

I have now completed my explanation of the fundamental principles involved in positive action. I wish to conclude by once again exhorting you all to firm faith in the Tsungli's teaching: "From true knowledge action naturally proceeds." The meaning of the Revolution is as bright and spacious as the skies; and the clearer our comprehension of it the more vigor we shall put into the practice of it. Moreover, the methods we are to adopt and the mode of procedure we are to follow have been laid down for us in detail by Dr. Sun Wên. We have only to obey his directions, each of us playing a part for which his temperament, calling and knowledge fits him, relying upon his faculties for the discernment of moral and material good at every step in his bold and resolute execution of his duty to nation and people.

Action Engenders Knowledge

I wish to say another word on the subject of the *knowledge* from which as we have seen action proceeds; and what I have to say is: that just as action proceeds from knowledge, action in its turn engenders knowledge. Dr. Sun said: "The ability to know implies the ability to act." I would add the words: "without action one cannot attain to knowledge." For knowledge comes with experience, and apart from the broad and fundamental truths of revolutionary thought our knowledge need not necessarily be in the first place very rich. Though, therefore, we must of course do all we can to acquire knowledge for its own sake, we must at the same time seek it as one of the fruits of positive action. Any knowledge acquired in the course of study, research, or experience which we do not proceed to put to the test of practice in the field of actuality is not to be considered with certainty as worthy of being called true knowledge. So it is that in all our undertakings practice will yield us true knowledge, and action alone will give us the ability to extend and enrich our knowledge. Chu Hsi in his commentary on the *Great Learning* wrote: "By long application of our powers we one day reach a point whence we see the whole scheme of things spread out before us, we perceive the realities underlying phenomena, the relation of accident to essence, and the structure and workings of the human mind." This attainment can come only as the fruit of positive action. If in the course of practice and experience knowledge we have acquired and methods we have based on it prove inefficacious we may take it that what we valued as knowledge was not true knowledge. In this way we shall be constantly broadening the scope and sifting the quality of our knowledge, which is the genuine process of gaining knowledge. "To be aware of ignorance brings knowledge" and "the open mind invites the entrance of information," are maxims than which none are better as guides in the search for knowledge.

Comrades in Revolution! Resolve Anew!

I am well aware of the magnitude of our revolutionary task of Resistance and Reconstruction, and I have been no less impressed with recent manifestations of my comrades' will to action. I have felt impelled by the one and encouraged by the other to present you today this exposition of positive action and of what is requisite for its success, in the hope that you will all keep in mind these indispensable principles, gathering fresh knowledge with experience, acting with deliberation, perspicacity, and conscientiousness, spurning all things that tend to distract you from your fixed purpose and involve you in the wild and motiveless conduct of those who possess no such fixed purpose. In the *Chung-Yung,* or *Doctrine of the Mean,* there is a passage emphasizing the importance of "conscientiousness" in action, by which it means the refusal to be satisfied with half-measures, the pursuit of ends to their logical conclusion. If you give earnest thought to what I have said you will realize that very much of what has long passed with us for action has not been true action, that is, not positive action, and that therefore we have failed in much that we have undertaken. It is only because our action has not been really positive that we have allowed our minds to enlarge on the difficulties and dangers of the Revolution. In fact, these difficulties exist only for those whose minds lack resolution, enthusiasm and faith. The ancient adage says: "There's nothing difficult in the world if there's a man of spirit to be found" (where there's a will there's a way). This is a piece of the age-old proverbial wisdom of the people, and it may well serve us as a salutary warning against the slack thinking and evil habits concealed beneath the airy phrase: "It's easy enough to know what should be done; it's acting accordingly that's hard."

We need, therefore, in the revolutionary nation-building we have before us only to assert our wills, inflame our hearts with a fresh sincerity and faith, and give ourselves up to positive action. If everyone of us does so, I have no hesitation in pronouncing it will mean the certainty of our success.

C. DEFINITION OF THE PROBLEMS CON-CERNING THE ORGANIZATION OF THE VARIOUS CLASSIFICATIONS OF *HSIEN* (CHIANG K'AI-SHEK) [1]

One of a series of lectures, each issued separately, entitled *The Conclusions of the Party Chief,* and originally delivered before the Party and Government Training Class of the Central Training Corps. Compare with Appendix I (G), p. 324.

The chart, opposite, is a translation of the chart appended to the original Chinese of the Generalissimo's booklet on *Hsien.* P.M.A.L.

At the fifth meeting of the Fourth Plenary Session of the Central Executive and Supervisory Committees of the Kuomintang on April 8, 1938, I made a speech on "The Reform of Party Affairs and Readjustments for Party and Political Organizations." Attached to that speech was a draft chart showing the interrelations among the Party and political organizations under the *hsien,* with illustrations and explanations. I pointed out then that the chart was only intended as an initial draft. As to promulgating the detailed formulae and laws for execution, I pointed out that the draft was only to serve as a basis and that the wording in which the draft was written should not prove too bind-

---

[1] [Chiang K'ai-shek], *Ch'üeh-ting Hsien Ko-chi Tsu-chih Wên-t'i* (Definition of the Problems Concerning the Organization of the Various Classifications of *Hsien*), [Chungking], 1939, p. 43 and chart.

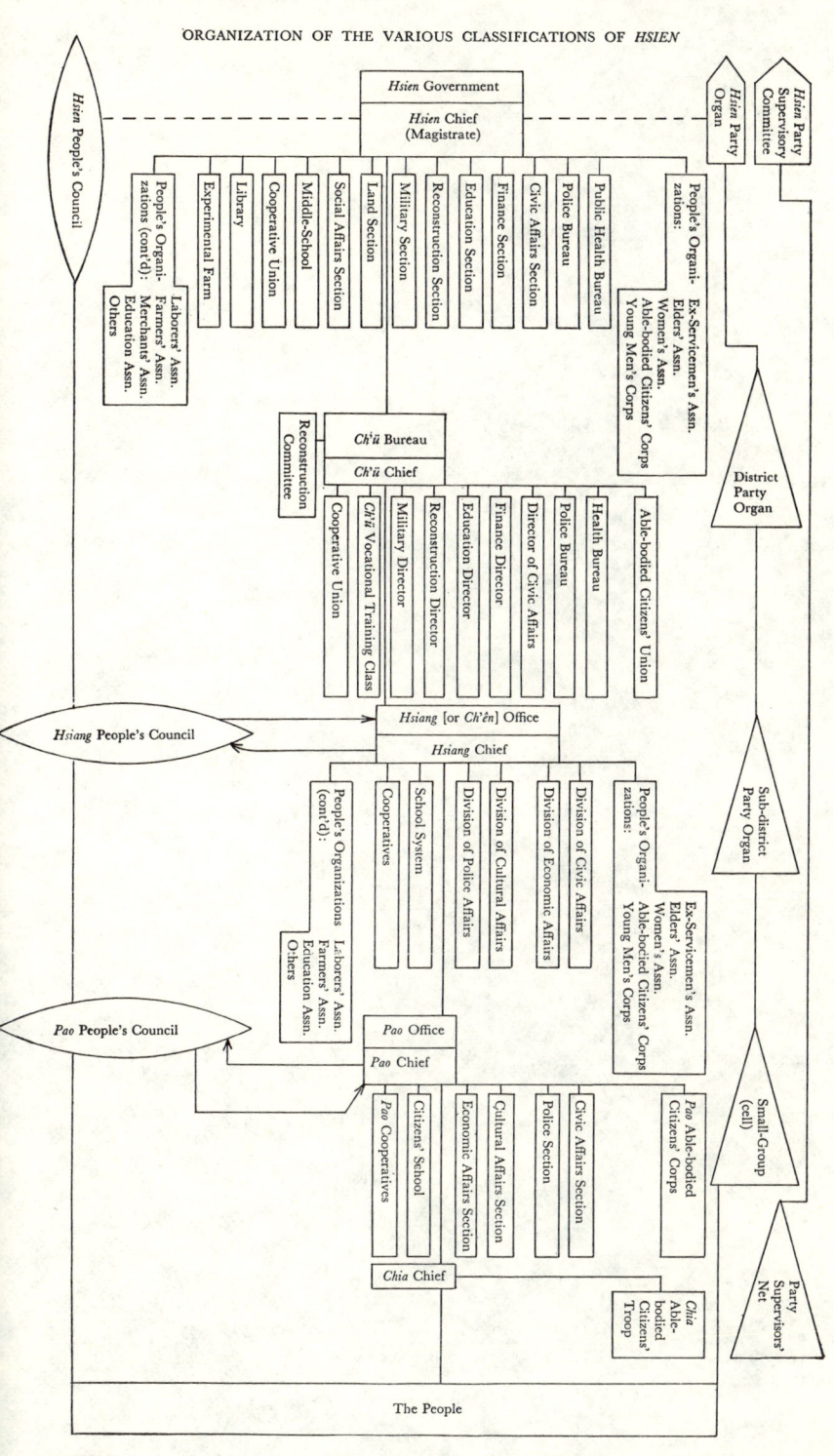

ORGANIZATION OF THE VARIOUS CLASSIFICATIONS OF *HSIEN*

ing. There should be plenty of room for further study and discussion so that perfection might be obtained. Furthermore, the draft chart was intended mainly as an exposition of the relations between Party and political organizations (hence it was also called "Party and Political Affairs Chart"). The various administrative organizations were attached as an appendix to it.

Since the publication of this draft chart, the serious attention of many of our comrades, scholars and specialists has been aroused. In many districts experiments have been carried on—a fact which is indeed very gratifying and which evidences the earnest desire on the part of various local administrations for reform.

The Party and Political Personnel Training Class was recently inaugurated by the Central Training Corps. In order to lecture on the problems covered in the draft chart and lay out the necessary formulae, I had instructed several of my associates to collect views and data from all possible sources and to make a thorough study of the question. Under my personal supervision, the original draft has been revised and supplemented. The main points contained therein may be summarized as follows:

1. In connection with Party organizations, the *ch'ü* [2] (township) office should be linked up with the *hsiang* (*chên*), while small units should be established under the *pao chia* system. Thus the Party organizations are brought to conformity with the political. The network of Party members' supervisory organizations should be placed directly under the Supervisory Committee of the *hsien* Party headquarters.

2. The *hsien* is the unit of local government autonomy. The *hsien* should be classified into three to six groups according to their area, population, economic resources, cultural and communication development. Below the *hsien*, the *hsiang* (*chên*) constitutes the basic lower unit, with *pao* or village and streets as their constituents. Elasticity may be allowed between the *hsien* and *hsiang* according to local requirements. When and where necessary, a *ch'ü* (township) office may be established to serve as the connecting link, but if this is not needed, the *hsiang* (*chên*) should be placed under the direct jurisdiction of the *hsien*. The same elasticity may exist between the *hsiang* (*chên*) and *pao*. In densely

---

[2] For explanation of such local government terms as *hsiang, pao, ch'ü*, see the text, p. 107.

populated areas, a village and a street may form one natural unit, inseparable from each other. In such cases, one unit may consist of two or three *pao* with one *pao chang* (chief of the *pao*) at the helm of affairs, so that unnecessary breaking-up of the village from the street may be avoided. To eliminate difficulties arising from finances and personnel, all the posts of secretaries (*kan shih*) of the *hsiang* (*chên*) and *pao* (or village and street) may be concurrently served by the teachers of primary schools, while the school principals of the *hsiang* (*chên*) and *pao* should concurrently serve as leader of the able-bodied citizens' corps (*Chuang ting tui*) in accordance with the principle of unity of administration, instruction, support and protection. In areas with better economic and educational development where affairs concerning local autonomy are multifarious, the principals of *hsiang* (*chên*) primary schools and *pao* citizens' [mass education] schools should preferably concentrate on their school jobs with a view to efficiency. The masses should be organized into different groups to undertake different works in order to meet the actual requirements.

3. In connection with organs for expressing the views and opinions of the people, there should be organized the *pao* people's assembly, the *hsiang* (*chên*) people's representative assembly, the *hsien* council, each vested with proper authority, with a view to increasing the people's interest in participating in government affairs. Thus the influence of the masses may be properly magnified and the goal of true democracy attained. With a view to greater alacrity, I wish to explain in further detail as follows:

A. Readjustments in the Relations among the Various Administrative Party and Political Organizations of the *Hsien*

(*This item, consisting of eleven articles, is not intended for publication.*)

A routine announcement of Party duties, of Party supervision of local morale, of seniorities as between Party and Government officers, etc. follows. It has been omitted in accordance with the statement in parentheses.

B. Political Organizations

1. The *hsien* is the unit of local autonomy. These units can be classified into from three to six groups according to the population, economic status, culture and communication. On the one hand, the *hsien* governments should

handle affairs concerning local autonomy of their respective district under the supervision of the provincial government and on the other hand should carry out the orders of the Central and provincial governments.

a. The area of the *hsien* under the present system should remain the same as before. The cancellation of the *hsien* and the change in its area are to be decided upon only with the authorization and approval of the Central Government. In the *hsien* there should be a magistrate, under whom there should be secretaries, section chiefs, directors, police officers, senior and junior staff members in the different sections, technicians and assistants and police patrol officers handling civic, financial, educational, construction, military, land, and social affairs. The number of sections to be provided under the *hsien* governments and their duties is to be decided by the provincial government which in making decisions is to take into consideration the local requirements of the *hsien* concerned. The number of staff members, and their ranks and salaries, is likewise to be decided upon by the provincial government.

b. In each *hsien* there should be held *hsien* political affairs meetings at which decisions concerning the *hsien* administration are to be reached and proposals made for submission to the *hsien* People's Council. The *hsien* political affairs meetings should be held irrespective of whether the *hsien* Council has been established or not.

c. The rules and regulations governing the organization of the *hsien* governments should be promulgated by the provincial governments and then submitted to the Central Government for approval.

2. The *ch'ü* (township) office is a subsidiary organization to the *hsien* government. Its duty is to supervise the affairs of the various *hsiang* (*chên*) on behalf of the *hsien* government in connection with the enforcement of local autonomy.

a. The scope of the *ch'ü* should consist of from six to fifteen *hsiang*. In those *hsien* in which the total number of *hsiang* is below fifteen, no *ch'ü* office should be established. The *hsiang* in such cases are to be placed under the direct jurisdiction of the *hsien* government. In frontier regions where special conditions obtain, specifications for the number of *hsiang* for the *ch'ü* office may be modified.

In *hsien* where no *ch'ü* office is established, the *hsien* government should appoint representatives to supervise the affairs of the different *hsiang*.

b. The *ch'ü* office is headed by a district chief under whom there should be two to five directors handling civic, financial, construction, education, and military affairs. All such personnel are by special appointment with pay, and they should be chosen by the superior organizations from those who have received appropriate training. The district chiefs should preferably be those who come from the districts to which they are designated, their qualifications and treatment to be fixed by law.

c. In the place where the *ch'ü* office is seated, there should be established a police bureau which is to be under the direction of the district chief dealing with the police administration of the place.

d. In the *ch'ü* there should be established the *hsiang* reconstruction committee comprising local leaders as members. This committee is to conduct research and map out the plans concerning rural reconstruction, the district chief acting concurrently as its chairman.

e. In order to increase the vocational ability of the people and develop local industries, there should be established in the *ch'ü* vocational training classes.

f. In addition to the number of policemen as specified, there should be organized in the *ch'ü* the joint able-bodied citizens' corps (*Chuang-ting lien tui-pu*) office which is to control and supervise the *Chuang-ting* of the various *hsiang* (*chên*). Whenever necessary, the *chuang-ting* may be summoned together for special training and organization.

g. The *ch'ü* office should unite together all the *hsiang* (*chên*) cooperative societies and organize them into cooperative unions. Each union is to consist of several departments dealing with different cooperative enterprises. The *ch'ü* office should appoint a supervisor to be stationed in the union.

3. The *hsiang* (*chên*) is to be defined as the basic administrative unit under the *hsien,* and its organization should be substantiated accordingly.

a. Each *hsiang* in principle comprises six to fifteen *pao.* In drawing such limits, however, consideration should be given to the historical background and natural conditions of the locality. The demarcation and the organization of the *pao chia* system are to be decided upon by the *hsien* government, subject to the approval of the provincial government. Reports must also be submitted to the **Central Government.**

b. The chief personnel of the *hsiang* guild (*kung so*) should include a director (*hsiang chang*) and one or two vice-directors. They are to be elected from qualified citizens at the *hsiang* people's representative meetings. In the guild there should be provided four departments, handling civic, police, economic and cultural affairs respectively, each to be headed by one man with several staff members. These posts should be held by the vice-directors and teachers of the *hsiang* primary schools. The date for the election of the director and vice-directors of the *hsiang* is to be fixed and announced in orders to be issued by the *hsien* government. The term of their office will be two years.

c. There should be established in each *hsiang* a central school composed of three divisions for children, women especially, and adults. There should be primary and higher primary classes. The posts of the school principal, leader of the able-bodied citizens' corps, and director of the *hsiang* are to be concurrently held by one man. The teachers are to undertake the extracurricular duties of training and supervising. They are also to help the *hsiang director* to handle affairs of the *hsiang*. In the higher primary class of the school stress should be laid on training the masses to enable them to undertake the work of census-taking, promotion of health and sanitation and cooperative affairs.

In places with better economic and educational development, the principals of the *hsiang* central schools should preferably concentrate on their own duties at school.

d. The cooperative societies also have the *hsiang* as the unit (with branch societies in the *pao*). There should also be established in the *hsiang* public safe-deposit agencies for the storage of articles. Separate granaries should be set up whenever necessary.

e. The leader of the *hsiang* able-bodied citizens' corps should from time to time summon chosen groups of the *chuang ting* of the *pao* to the *hsiang* to undergo advanced training. During the training period, they are to perform police duties and when the period expires they are to be sent back to take up the work as junior officers of the able-bodied citizens' corps of the *pao,* charged also with the duties of promoting local autonomy in the *pao*. Thus not only will the police force be strengthened, but various activities properly developed. The outposts established in the *hsiang* by the *hsien* police bureaus should also be placed under the direction of the *hsiang* director.

 f. The *hsiang* should convene *hsiang* affairs meetings with the director as chairman and all the department heads and senior members of the staff in attendance. The chiefs of the *pao* concerning whom proposals are submitted to the meeting should also be present.
 g. A hospital or clinic should be established for each *hsiang* or a number of *hsiang*. These hospitals or clinics should be staffed with Western-trained doctors. In case of lack of personnel and finance, [old-style] Chinese physicians may do on a temporary basis.
 4. The *pao* should be defined as a constituent of the *hsiang* and its organization be substantiated accordingly.
 a. Each *pao* is to consist of from six to fifteen *chia*, headed by a *pao chang* (chief of the *pao*) and an assistant *pao chang*. They are to be elected from qualified citizens at the *pao* people's meeting, and their names are to be submitted by the *hsiang* guild to the *hsien* government. Before the election, the *pao chang* and assistant *pao chang* may be nominated by the *hsiang* guild subject to official appointment by the *hsien* government. In the office of the *pao* there should be two to four secretaries (*kan shih*) handling civic, police, economic and cultural affairs. These posts may be concurrently held by the assistant *pao chang* and teachers of citizens' (mass education) schools. In *pao* with limited finances, one secretary may suffice.
 The term of office for the *pao chang* and assistant *pao chang* will be two years. They may be re-elected at the expiration of their term of office.
 b. All affairs of the *pao* should be discussed and transacted at *pao* affairs meeting in which as many capable citizens of the *pao* as possible are to be asked to participate, in order to hasten progress of the reconstruction of the *pao*.
 c. All the activities undertaken by the *pao* are to be under the supervision and direction of the *hsiang* guild, the *ch'ü* office and the *hsien* government. The latter superior organs should give constant help and advice so that the program of work may be carried out step by step as desired.
 d. Every *pao* is to have a mass education school, with the principal of the school concurrently serving as the *pao chang* and as the leader of the *pao* able-bodied citizens' corps. The school is to comprise three divisions for children, for women especially, and for adults, and its aim is to raise the level of education and vocational ability of the masses. Teachers are also to help the *pao chang* in dealing with various affairs of the *pao*.

In *pao* better-developed in economic resources and education, the principles of the mass education schools should preferably concentrate on their school duties.

e. Membership of the *pao* branches of the cooperative societies is composed of the families in the *pao*. The directors of the branch societies are to be elected by members. The *pao chang* can be elected and concurrently hold this office.

f. The *pao* office, the *pao* able-bodied citizens' corps and the *pao* mass education schools should be simultaneously established. They should have a joint office so that affairs of common interest may be pushed from the same center.

g. In densely populated areas where a village and a street seem each to be an integral part of the other, two or three *pao* may be amalgamated, the amalgamation not exceeding three *pao*. The mass education schools, branch cooperative societies and treasuries, likewise, may be amalgamated, with only the *pao* able-bodied citizens' corps remaining separate. One presiding *pao chang* is to be elected to take the helm of affairs, and a joint office is to be established.

h. The *pao* should be equipped with a medicine box, with one of the mass education school teachers trained in rudiments of the medical science, in charge. He is to give simple treatment for diseases and to give small-pox vaccination. If this should prove beyond the finances of one *pao*, several *pao* may join together.

i. The organization of the *chia* is to consist of from six to fifteen families, headed by a *chia chang*. There should be meetings of the heads of families, and general *chia* conferences, held from time to time.

The *chia chang* is to be elected at the meeting of heads of families. His name is to be submitted by the *pao* office to the *hsiang* guild.

j. The *pao* may retain its old name, such as *ts'un* (village), *chieh* (street) or *ch'ang* (market), but it is desired that they should gradually adopt the official name of *pao* with a view to uniformity.

C. People's Organs through Which Popular Political Opinions May Be Expressed

1. To increase the people's interest in participation in government affairs and to train their political insight and

ability in accordance with the principle of the inherent unity of teaching, learning and practicing, people's organs for discussion of government affairs for the various administrative units under the *hsien* should be established within specified time limits, and these organs should be vested with the appropriate authority.

2. In the *pao* should be established the *pao* people's meeting to elect the *pao chang;* the *hsiang*, the *hsiang* people's representative meeting to elect the *hsiang chang*.[3] (The qualifications and standards of both the *pao chang* and the *hsiang chang* are to be specified by law.) Thus it is hoped to attain the ideal standards of local government and to establish the system of the people's supervision of the government. No people's organ is needed for the *ch'ü* (district), while the *hsien* people's council will serve as the general organ for people of the entire *hsien*.

3. With a view to flexibility in the exercise of the people's privileges, members of the *hsien* people's council are to be brought forth at the *hsiang* people's representative meetings. Each *hsiang* is entitled to elect one representative as member of the council. The number of representatives of legitimate professional bodies may be increased in order to put representation of the districts and that of the professions on equal footing. Representatives to the *hsiang* people's meeting are to be produced at the *pao* people's meeting. Each *pao* is entitled to two representatives. The *pao* people's meeting should be attended by one person from each family whose qualifications and position in the family conforms to specifications in the law.

4. The *hsiang chang* and *pao chang* who are elected may both act as chairmen of their respective people's organs, namely the *hsiang* people's representative meeting and the *pao* people's meeting. The *hsien* people's council for the time being is not to elect the magistrate. It is to elect its own chairman.

5. Before the *hsien* people's council is organized, the budget and accounts of the *hsien* government should be studied and passed by the *hsien* Administrative Meeting and then submitted by the magistrate to the provincial government for approval.

After the *hsien* people's council is inaugurated, the budget and accounts of the *hsien* should be presented to the council for examination and then submitted to the pro-

---

[3] Heretofore translated as "director of the *hsiang*."

vincial government for approval. When necessary, the budget and accounts may first be sent to the provincial government for approval and then the council may be approached for confirmation and verification.

EXPLANATION

1. The basic spirit of this draft is to arouse and mobilize the masses, to strengthen local organization and hasten district autonomy enterprises so that the cornerstone of the revolution and national reconstruction may be laid. Some may be of the opinion that as education has not been popularized, it would be difficult to allow the masses participation in government affairs. But the political system stressing on people's privileges must be founded on the will of the masses. If participation in government affairs is allowed only after education has been developed on a nation-wide scale, the slogan "revolutionized people's privileges" will be of no meaning. The people need only be trained practically in the exercise of their political privileges, and the main task of the government during the political tutelage period lies in teaching the people how to exercise their four rights [election; recall; initiative; referendum]. Tutelary government [Party-dictatorship] and constitutional government are different only in degree but not in fundamentals. During the period of tutelage, therefore, the interest of the people in participation in government affairs must be gradually aroused and increased. Thus measures enforced with this purpose in view during the political tutelage period may not contravene the aims of constitutional government, and the progress from tutelage to constitutionalism may be attained smoothly. This explains the transitional process from the beginning to the complete realization of autonomous government and it was for such an explanation that this draft was prepared.

2. With a view to the solution of the personnel and financial problems confronting the various basic administrative units, the *hsiang* chief, *hsiang* central school principal, and the *hsiang* leader of the able-bodied citizens' corps, excepting in those areas more highly developed in education and economic resources, should be the same man. The same thing applies to the *pao*. All those charged with administrative duties should pay attention to education which should serve as the means to attain the objectives of the revolution and national reconstruction. Those with

educational responsibilities should give their time and energy also to the organization and training of the masses. They should consider the masses as their students, the society as a school and all existing circumstances and conditions as references of instruction. Emphasis should also be laid on instructing the people how to live properly, how to accomplish their duties. The basic principles governing the revolutionary movement and national reconstruction as laid down by our late Leader [Sun Yat-sen], measures on the control of rice and the control of land as stipulated in the ordinances and regulations governing district autonomy, together with the seven measures previously announced by the Central Government, should all be included in the scope of instruction. It was with these considerations in mind that this draft provides that teachers of the *hsiang* middle [secondary] and *pao* mass-education schools should concurrently act as secretaries of the *hsiang* guild and *pao* office. It would not do to maintain the old system when school teachers only taught in the classroom, with the result that in many places where schools have been conducted for many years people still refuse to be conscripted, to pay taxes, to observe the New Life principles. This could be attributed to the fact that teachers and others in charge of the schools failed to do their duties.

It is also provided in the ordinances and regulations governing the initial enforcement of district autonomy that "aside from enabling people to read and write, schools should also emphasize what has been known as the 'omnipotency of both hands' campaign." We should try to make all the tools or machines that can increase the productive ability of both hands, instead of relying on others. From now on, therefore, local schools should emphasize vocational training by which the students may be taught how to manufacture simple machines. This is not merely scientific education but also an important way of carrying out the doctrine of the people's livelihood. It is therefore provided in this draft that in the *ch'ü* (township) there should be established the district vocational training class so that education and living may be closely wedded.

In the past, educational organization has been too complicated. Besides primary schools, there have been mass education schools, short-term primary schools, rural schools. Now, since it is stipulated that the *pao* has *pao* mass education schools and the *hsiang* has *hsiang* middle schools, the children and adults should be taught in separate classes but at the same school so that all the former units of education may be absorbed. The tutor (*tao shêng*) system should be used as much as possible in the hope that the entire people of the nation may be given at least the minimum education for citizenship within a limited period of time. Thus all the personnel and finances may be concentrated; the teachers may conveniently do their duty in directing the masses into proper participation in various local enterprises. In this way, education and autonomy may be closely affiliated with each other.

3. The organization of the various local administrative units is roughly in accordance with the decimal system. In such provisions of this draft, allowances have been made whereby the difficulties in the way of enforcement of the system may be solved. Once the scope of the various local administrative units is fixed, all plans and programs such as establishing schools, training personnel, appropriation of funds and statistics may be mapped out according to definite standards. The conduct of a big nation with its variegated enterprises depends on strict organization in war-time as well as in peace-time. In the army, for instance, the number of units composing each army corps is definitely fixed. Scientific administration must be governed by rules and regulations.

For the convenience of execution, certain elasticity has been allowed in provisions concerning organization in this draft. The *hsiang*, for instance, is composed of from six to fifteen *pao*, and so on with other lower administrative units. In cases where the village and the street cannot be separated, joint organizations for the handling of affairs of common interest is allowed. All these provisions are arrived at in order to allow some flexibility whenever and wherever necessary. Within the bounds of these regulations, the various local district governments may exercise their discretion in disposing their respective affairs without consulting their superior governments. But they will not be permitted to trespass beyond the limits because disorderly organizations will make control and supervision hard.

After the scope of the various local administrative units is fixed, their respective spheres of education, health, cooperative movements and police must also be uniformly determined so that control, instruction, support, and protection may have an equal and well-balanced development.

4. Concerning the organization and training of the masses, it is indeed regrettable that no wholesome ac-

complishments have been achieved during the past many years. According to this new draft, the following explanations have to be made:

  a. Demarcation among people's groups and organizations: the former is determined by professions and the latter according to age and sex. From the standpoint of the requirements of the country, the latter should be organized first. Especially urgent is the demand for such organizations as the able-bodied citizens' corps and women's associations. From the standpoint of the needs of the people, the organization of the professional groups should be put on a sound basis as soon as possible, particularly the farmers, laborers, and merchants groups which are vitally concerned with the economic reconstruction movement of the country. Steps, therefore, should immediately be taken in the order of urgency. Next, for people's organizations, emphasis is to be laid on organization and training; for the groups, direction and supervision are to be stressed.

  b. The work of organizing the various people's groups should proceed from the bottom upwards because wholesome organizations can only be had when the foundation is soundly laid. In peace-time, this will help forward self-rule. In war-time, it will help meet military needs. In the past, the various people's groups (such as farmers' associations and women's associations) had only nominal existence, hanging their shingles in the *hsien* city, but few really worked. The reasons might be many, but the main one has been the failure on the part of those responsible to penetrate into the lower strata of activities and help develop them. It must be realized that the various people's groups are necessary to the various administrative units in the district autonomous government system just as parts to the main body of a machine. Without the parts, the machine would not be able to operate. From now on, therefore, efforts must be made to substantiate the people's bodies so that they may be enabled to function efficiently.

  c. The able-bodied citizens' corps are necessary in peace as well as in war-time. Attention should be paid both to training and to the supervision so that their usefulness may be fully developed. The constituents of the able-bodied citizens' corps are the pillars of society, and on them depends the successful realization of most enterprises concerning district autonomy. In this lies the importance of our late Leader's [Sun Yat-sen] teaching about "omnipotency of both hands." During the training, emphasis should not be on military alone but also on general and vocational ability, in order to turn corps members into useful members of society.

5. The people's organs for various local administrative units serve best the purpose of training the people in the exercise of their rights in government affairs. They constitute the prerequisites for democracy. In the past, it has proved difficult to secure *hsiang, pao* and *chia* chiefs; or, after they were elected to their respective offices, they failed to do their duties and some cf them even committed acts harmful to the people which slipped the notice of the superior government offices. All these shortcomings must be overcome by virtue of democratic measures. The higher supervisory organizations, limited in personnel, can hardly keep an eye on every small detail. The *hsiang* and *pao* chiefs and other staff members under them are most closely associated with the people. In order to prevent them from undermining the people's interest for their selfish gains, the democratic (*Min-chu*) control and supervision system should be enforced as the most efficient and effective method. That the *pao* people's meeting should be attended by the families as representative units is a preliminary step. This is so because China is an agricultural country, different from other industrialized nations where the individual citizens constitute the representative units. Representatives to the *hsiang* people's representative meetings are to be produced at the *pao* people's meeting. Councilors from the *hsiang* and higher administrative units for the *hsien* people's council are to be produced by indirect instead of direct election. Next comes the question of increasing the people's economic stability and developing local enterprises. It is specially provided that adequate representation to the various professional groups should be given in the *hsien* people's council. (This is limited to the professional groups and their representation is not to exceed thirty per cent.) In this way the district conception and the interests of professions are given equal consideration.

6. To prepare the personnel for the various local administrative government units, the various grades of schools should be adapted to the needs of the local organizations and enterprises. With such adaptation, the school training may not be in vain and young students upon graduation may find appropriate employment. A separate set of rules and regulations should be promulgated whereby these youths may be encouraged and their future welfare safe-

guarded. At present, the training of such personnel and their future disposal have not been systematically enough planned. Proper remedy must be provided so that definite standards may be fixed. Most important of all, persons properly trained should be assigned to places where are located their native home villages or towns. All such jobs concerning the development of district enterprises like insurance of treasuries or storehouses, transportation of rice and foodstuffs, farmland irrigation, fishing, grazing, and land reclamation, should all be filled by persons with special technical training. As the development of such district enterprises continues, the demand for appropriate personnel will grow as a foregone conclusion.

7. With regard to financial problems, the late Leader instructed that the district self-rule organizations should be founded on the basis of "political and economic cooperation." The sources of finance, therefore, should be derived from the people's public productive enterprises, instead of depending on new taxes. There are many public properties in various localities that should be utilized. Instead, these have mainly been exploited and monopolized by individuals who cared for nothing but their own selfish interests. Henceforth, these properties should be placed under public control. With efficient management, the proceeds from these enterprises should serve as finances for the entire *hsiang* or *pao*. In case such properties consist of land, they could be turned into experimental farms and be placed under the management of the schools for the improvement of agricultural products and for training the people in reformed farming methods. The joint property of a clan should be dealt with in a similar way so that their income may be increased and the results of agricultural improvement programs may be extended from one locality to another easily. In places where there are no such lands, steps should be taken to reclaim the mountainous or hilly regions or the streams and ponds. Free labor may be utilized with a view to increasing the income. Besides, surplus rice may be stored in the *hsiang* and the *pao,* under the management of the people of the respective districts. The various cooperative societies transporting agricultural products should also provide granaries and issue mortgage loans. Part of the profits thus derived should be devoted as funds for the development of local enterprises. Thus not only will the financial problem be solved but district autonomy development will follow local needs. Before the local pub-

lic enterprises (as described above) are so developed that income is sufficient to meet financial requirements, attention should be paid to the following measures:

a. Taxes which the *hsiang* guild may collect independent of the superior government offices.

b. The finances of the *hsien* should be demarcated from those of the province, and the quota of the former should be gradually increased if possible.

c In lean *hsien,* the *hsien* government should be subsidized by the provincial government.

8. Last of all, it should be pointed out that this draft was drawn up after repeated discussions and studies. Henceforth, all the *hsien* and lower district government units in the autonomy system should observe this draft as the basis. This is a time of national crisis when the destiny of our entire nation and race is hanging between life and death. It is hoped that all comrades of our Party and our fellow-countrymen should strive with strong determination for nation-wide enforcement of these district autonomy measures. Bold initiative should solve any unforeseen difficulties that may arise. Fear and hesitation should never be allowed to gain the upper hand. Only in this way, may we hope that the cornerstone for various political levels of true democracy is laid on a sound basis, and only in this way may we hope that the stupendous task of national reconstruction can be accomplished.

D. A DISCUSSION OF MAO TSÊ–TUNG'S COMMENTS ON THE PRESENT STATE OF INTERNATIONAL RELATIONS (CH'ÊN KUO–HSIN)[1]

The following article, expressing the general Kuomintang view, but written and published unofficially, illustrates debate on foreign policy, and the type of discussion between Nationalists and Communists. Written in the autumn of 1939, it was reprinted in 1940 as a part of a symposium, forming a critique of Chinese Communist views. Mao Tsê-tung (see above, p. 166) is the outstanding Chinese Communist leader.

I. The Question of Unexpected Political "Coups"

As the Central Government has already formulated correct principles of action, the recent German-Soviet Pact has

[1] Min-i Ts'ung-k'an (Popular Opinion Series), *Mao Tsê-tung Ch'ên Shao-yü Tsui-chin Yen-lun-ti Tsung Chien-t'ao* (A General Review of the Most Recent Utterances of Mao Tsê-tung and Ch'ên Shao-yü), Chungking, 1940; p. 1–17.

no influence upon our National policies. If we follow these policies, that Pact does not compel our attention. But it is not so with the Chinese Communists and their external organs. They are confounded and struck dumb by this unexpected blow so much that they can only keep their grief to themselves.

In all propaganda literature of the Communist Party, we can easily discern the great confusion resulting from this coup. For example, Hitler was the "Fascist Robber" or the "mad dog," but within these days, he becomes the Führer, with all due respects. The word "Fascist" is still being used, but whether they are planning to discard it altogether, we do not know. For instance, on the day previous to the announcement of the Pact, the Communists were saying, dreamily, that a clause prohibiting Germany's seizure of other countries was included in the Pact. Again, when Germany attacked Poland, the Communists cleverly said that this was caused by Great Britain's playing Judas against Poland, and they decisively said that Great Britain and France would not aid her, and some even said that the two antagonistic fronts were still there, though without giving any reason. When reports of these momentous international changes arrived in quick succession, they tried every means to make them appear unimportant. They did this perhaps to avoid the too much "heating up" of their followers on one side, and to avoid committing blunders before they could receive orders concerning their future policy. They were afraid of punishment, to be sure. Hence many ridiculed these poor people, saying that they were like a herd of sheep without a shepherd, for they showed their ignorance, their childishness, hesitation, and paradoxical thoughts and actions during this period.

Public opinion as a whole praises the policies we now adopt since they are independent of any outside element. On the other side, these praises show that while the principles of National Defense are still as sound as ever, the ten principles of the Communist Party are now just like ten big stones falling on Communist toes. The Communists are about to be killed by their own weapons. Had the Government of China been formed by the Communists, it would, in that event, have collapsed as easily as any Japanese cabinet since the War. What would become of the country, if under the present crisis foreign policy were to be the speculation of foreigners? These are exactly the ideas expressed by public gossip and in discussions in schools. It is true that the Chinese Communists cannot hold power because they lack political training and profound learning. This is their inner, incurable trouble. In fact, many young Communists have also spoken with me, and they show their sorrow when they feel the lack of a really efficient central organ.

But speaking with consideration, we can see their good qualities shown by censoring a great part of the news concerning Moscow's abolition of the Anti-Fascist movement, and on the other hand advertising in a special manner the news concerning the will of the French Communists to fight on the first line of defense, and to help the French Government to destroy Fascism. Perhaps this is a true revelation of the editor's faith in the principle "Country and Nation above all," so that unconsciously he showed it in his actions. This point is worthy of our praise and sympathy.

After about ten days of hesitation and aimless probing, Mr. Mao Tsê-tung, as the head of the Party, issued a lengthy talk entitled "On the Present International Situation and the War of National Resistance," in the form of a catechism in which the questions are asked by a news reporter. In the first section, he explained the German-Soviet Pact; in the second, he predicted the future development of international affairs, in the third he discussed the future of China. His aim in publishing this article is to pacify the agitated hearts of his fellow Communists. But since it is made public, we have the liberty of discussing it, especially so since the Communists themselves have the same habit and they also emphasize free speech. I hope they will not be irritated.

II. Is the German-Soviet Pact Casual?

Mr. Mao seems to take it for a treaty that has been signed "all of a sudden." Now this is quite untrue if we consider the facts.

Many periodicals and newspapers have published articles proving that the Pact was long-planned. We shall not consider them. We shall not even consider the original friendship between Germany and monarchic Russia. But we must remember how Germany brought Lenin back to Russia in a sealed train, how the formation of the Red Army was based upon German plans, and the fact that Germany established an aviation school in Russia. We see how Germany helped the Russian Soviet Revolution to succeed. I often think that if we trust the words of a country's foreign minister and the slogans the people shout to provide us an outline of the country's foreign policy, we end in the position of buying goods upon reading an advertisement. In the end we will find ourselves cheated. In fact shops which are "liquidating" their goods may sell their goods at an even higher price than in an ordinary sale. A more reliable way of observation is to judge the policy by studying the secret tendencies in the actions of high military and economic organs which are essential in national defense. If we believe in slogans alone, we might as well ask a salesman about the curative power of his patent medicine. In reality, the salesman is a mere hireling. What pharmacist discloses his real formula and method of combinations? Hence, to probe into the real relation between the two countries, we must ask the smaller nations between them; these make the closest observations.

For two years, these small states have been expecting this treaty. The question of "which to side with" gives them sharp suffering which has made them all the more sensitive. They know what the two countries have been planning when they see so many secret delegates coming and going very busily. Within the last two years, observers in Europe and America have also predicted cooperation between Germany and Soviet Russia. Even in China, did not Mr. Chiang Po-li write an essay to this effect, warning the Chinese people? According to them, the slogans shouted in both countries are strange diplomatic weapons; like the masques worn in a Greek play, they do not show the faces of the actors. When the Jewish Litvinoff went off the stage, it was the sign: "First Act Completed." Now the spectators who wear red glasses are still enchanted by the first act. Anyway, Mr. Mao's explanation that the Pact is a sudden one is unreasonable.

In China, many were doubting the National policy of independent struggle. Not until their "Soviet Help," "Single Alliance with Russia" essays had been erased by the recent coup, did the policy of independent struggle begin to shine in its brilliancy. At first our policy of independent foreign relations lost influence to the better-sounding slogan of "A united foreign front." After this lesson, we can perhaps see more clearly. Such a lesson to a political party not in power is a very wholesome admonition; had the party been in power, we know the damage which could have befallen the nation. Speaking with consideration, I also earnestly hoped for the success in the British-French-Soviet parleys because it would ensure safety in Europe by safeguarding all lesser states. Furthermore, it would help us also by checking Germany and Japan. But this was only a hope, and I seriously doubted its realization. The "united foreign policy front" advocated by the Communists is not too unreasonable; its error lies in stating with certainty the necessity of two international fronts. Some even acknowledged the existence of such a situation two years ago, and they forbade any doubt expressed to fellow-members concerning this point. Even a week prior to the signing of the Pact, they said with certainty that the rumor of such a Pact was a mere invention of Trotskyites and German spies. Such a ban on free speech is not only detrimental to the progress of a nation, but even to the Communists' own welfare. Their members will not only be made to look foolish, but they will even lose their faith by being called upon to change about. For the sake of our national intelligence, for the sake of the Communists themselves, I hope that in the future, such bans will be lifted, thus encouraging freer and more reasonable ideas. I hope this appeal will do some good, even to the editors of their newspapers.

III. Why the German-Soviet Pact?

Concerning this Pact, Mao Tsê-tung used words like "reactionary," "Capitalistic," "intrigue," etc., about Great Britain and France. On the other hand, he employed words like "great" (to be added "talented" if Ch'ên Shao-yü were to write it), "increasing the power," "more progressive," etc., about Soviet Russia. In the end, he even used the phrase "have laid the foundation for the world's oppressed people to seek for liberty and emancipation." All right! The term does not sound ugly, and to ensure better Sino-Soviet relations, we may leave it at that. But under the present state of affairs, too many attacks directed against Chamberlain and Daladier are certainly not good. As a matter of fact, all this is like sending congratulations to Soviet Russia, and a letter of condolence to those with whom Soviet Russia is dissatisfied. All these are but social affairs, the only point is that in both the ideas are not too logically expressed. That's all!

Now if you look at the Pact in the same way that you look into a kaleidoscope, you can see as many meanings as you want, while turning the thing around. Basically, Germany's only reason for wanting this Pact is, as she has stated, to avoid the British encircling policy. The economic cooperation talked of by politicians can also give further meaning to the Pact. Recently, in the occupation of Danzig and Warsaw, the sound of guns is the wordless explanation. As to the plan of partitioning Poland and absorbing the Eastern European States (enclosed in a secret clause), we do not know yet. Let us for the time being not discuss it.

As to Soviet Russia, her effort at bettering her friendly relationship with China can be no better revealed than in Molotov's own speech. He said: "We have always been trying to increase the amity between the peoples of Germany and Russia. This Pact is important because it means that the two big Powers in Europe have decided to be friends and to live peacefully." Thus we can see that the Pact is not a casual happening. Molotov again says: "There are some who want to take advantage of the strained relationship between Great Britain and Germany. . . . Such people aim at involving Soviet Russia in a war against Germany by taking sides with Great Britain. How foolish these political speculators for war are!" Hence we know that the Pact was signed according to Soviet Russia's own will, and, unlike what Mao said, it was planned long ago, and not at all after the failure of the British-French-Soviet parleys. Now we only want those who advocate "united foreign policy front" to think of the meaning of words like "foolish" and "war speculators." These words are new compared with "retrograde," "stubborn," "Trotskyites," etc.

Perhaps the greatest part of all in Molotov's speech is: "The Soviet Union will still continue to proceed in her own independent policy which is based upon the welfare of all Soviet Russian citizens." This corresponds exactly with our "Nation and country above all!" Sun Yat-sen also said that the success of the Soviet Russian October Revolution was based upon its ability to apply the laws concerning Nationalism. Leninism corrects Marxism by adding the idea of Nationalism. And Stalinism intensifies Leninism by an even greater emphasis laid on Nationalism. Hence we can say what the Soviet Revolution adopted was Leninism, and that what the Soviet Union is now adopting is Stalinism. The success of Lenin and Stalin is largely due to this reason. This Pact between Germany and Soviet Russia is but the fruit borne out of the principle "national welfare above all." The Soviets believe "The Soviet Government above all." Now what should we in China have?

As for Mr. Mao's reasons concerning the failure of the Three-Power Parley, the explanation he gives is just a reduced and "Chinafied" copy of the Soviet explanation concerning this problem. We can also say it is abridged. Mr. Mao always "Chinafies" things. I am sorry that this article has not been "Chinafied" (much to his distaste, I suppose) so its power must be weaker.

IV. A Discussion on the "New Front" as Made in a Chinese Story-Teller's Way

The manner in which Mr. Mao discussed the question resembles that of a Chinese story-teller, though his speech is less vivid. When he spoke of the "future development of the present international situation," it was like talking to a class of naive schoolboys who are always credulous.

He said that the present state of affairs in Europe was caused by the policy of non-intervention. The Second Imperialistic War has already entered the second stage. This is a war of plunder, not a rightful one. Concerning the East, he also made a vain distinction. He said the present state of affairs in China is also a new stage. No other explanation was given. We suppose he is always careful in expressing his ideas, so that if necessary he will have plenty of chances to make a shift. He divided the imperialistic nations into several camps: Germany and Italy belong to the Fascist [2] camp; Great Britain and France belong to the Fascistic [3] camp; the Americas under the U. S. are a capitalistic camp. As to Soviet Russia, she is presumably in another world. Mr. Mao said that she would cooperate with the U. S. to start the world's peace movement. Besides these, there were numerous tales as enchanting as the Arabian Nights. The most important ones: in Europe, a war on the entire front, and the movement planned by English and French Communists and Social Democrats to overthrow the Fascist regime; in the East, British policy was to partition China between herself and Japan. According to him, these are "present" situations, and if we take into consideration his manner of speaking, we can almost say that they meant the "actual" position at present.

His chess-board analysis of international situations resembles his former "front" theory—perhaps it is his new front theory. His aim, we believe, is to cheat his spectators.

[2] *Fa-hsi-ssŭ.*
[3] *Fa-hsi-ssŭ-hua-ti,* i.e., changing to Fascism.

Being ignorant of the real situation, he was at first dumbfounded. Now he tries to move our attention to other things, just like a magician at work, who needs a band to create enough noise to shift the audience's attention. We should be considerate, knowing his difficulties. But I suppose such a manner of doing things does not increase the reputation of the Chinese Communists, does it?

In fact, if any one of the following events occurs, his new front will immediately be shattered: 1. Soviet Russia also adopts a non-intervention policy; 2. Italy keeps herself aloof or joins the side of the Allies; 3. A sufficiently large number of European states remain neutral; 4. America cooperates with Great Britain; America or any country in America declares war against Germany; 5. Great Britain does not help Japan in dividing up China; 6. Soviet inclination to sign treaty with Japan is revealed; etc., etc. I believe anyone who has sufficient knowledge of international relations will know that the error in the old "front" theory lies in its presumption that countries of the same systems of government will tend to unite against those of another system. The new front theory is based upon the presumption that the central motivating ideas of different countries will form the basis of separating them between two hostile fronts. This is an even more mistaken conception than the first. It is built on sand. It is easy to teach such a rigidly formulated doctrine of "hostile fronts" but in case they meet with a really intelligent and well-informed member, they will be certainly at a loss. Hence as a matter of fact, such authoritative articles do more harm than good. Mr. Mao has written a great deal since the war for publication; if we now connect all these articles together for a thorough study, we can find numerous places where he is dropping a stone upon his own toe. In fact such a chessboard analysis of the international situation is based upon materials gotten from the G. P. U. plus some "judgment" derived accidentally. As a matter of fact, such G. P. U. reports are unreliable down to the last word. The work of the G. P. U. is to pay special attention in getting the past record of a man or organ important in a given country.

When required, some high-sounding or bad names are added to the personality so as to strengthen the mood of speech in propaganda literature. So somebody even said: "If you wish to follow the propaganda methods of the Communist Party, observe two dogs barking in the street. After due observation you should analyze their points of difference. You should be able to speak like this: This is a dog infused with British, French, American, German or Japanese imperialistic ideas. He is stubborn, retrograde, reactionary, capitalistic, Fascist, and in danger of being a Trotskyite traitor or a person like Wang Ch'ing-wei. Now the other is a Soviet Socialistic dog, talented, progressive, belonging to the world of light, a supporter of world peace, a dog who sides with the poor and oppressed."

In fact how can confused international situations be so simply analyzed by a mere figure drawn on a chess-board? Unless all their members are mechanical men deprived of the power of thinking, they will have their own doubts, especially when Mr. Mao has repeatedly dropped stones on his own toe. The more he shouts the correctness of his views, or the success of his work, the more he will be a laughing-stock to the people. He will be the Don Quixote of China, or Ah-Q,[4] to be ridiculed by all. Yet in fact, there is no necessity for him to make these comments, and such methods of talking without material basis are usually avoided by politicians, especially when they are in service or partly in service. For example, Molotov spoke very cleverly on the Pact: after giving a historical explanation of the necessities for signing the Pact, he concluded, almost carelessly, by saying: "When Germany showed her willingness to improve the friendship between the two countries, Soviet Russia certainly had no reason to refuse. Hence the Pact is made." Besides, he talked of the welfare of the nation, as if to give a further proof of the necessity in signing the Pact. How clever his manipulations are! But the same thing under Mr. Mao's pen becomes a series of hot-faced scoldings, now praising A, then cursing B. And concerning his doctrine that the German-Soviet Pact is caused by the failure of the British-French-Soviet parleys, he expounded and expounded his reasons and proof, only to lead himself into greater confusion, so that fewer will believe him. Now comparing these two events, this will be very detrimental to the Communists, who find it difficult to give a satisfactory explanation. Even from a rhetorical point of view, no matter how Mao curses the British non-intervention policy, no matter how he curses this policy as the reason for Japanese invasion of China, for German occupation of Austria, Czechoslovakia, no matter how he condemns the Munich

---

[4] The hero of a novella by Lu Hsün, China's outstanding modern writer, Ah-Q is a figure of profound pathos.

Meeting, any reader will correspondingly ask: Is Soviet Russia also adopting the policy of non-intervention? How about Poland? What is the difference between the Munich Meeting and the German-Soviet Pact? All these questions will produce the exactly opposite effect in the minds of the readers as that which was wished for by Mao. This is but one point. If we go on to have a closer analysis, we see that Mr. Mao's art of speaking needs more practice. As to his material proof in his article, up to date [September 15, 1939], the Soviet attitude is still the sit-and-look attitude condemned by him, as being the result of non-intervention policy; the countries proclaiming their neutrality are quite numerous; Italian attitude is yet uncertain; the British Communist Party is declaring that full confidence is placed in Chamberlain; the French Communists are on the front to fight for their motherland and the Third International has now no power over them. On the other hand, there are rumors concerning a *rapprochement* between Japan and Soviet Russia. All these only tend to disprove the sayings of Mr. Mao.

V. A Single Enemy? Or a Single Ally?

Everybody knows that our foreign policy during the period of the war is to spot one enemy only. We attack only Japan. We try to be friends with every country other than Japan. This spirit can be seen in the manifestoes and other proclamations of the Government. Hence although Germany and Italy are the allies of our enemy, we still have every wish to bind their friendship, and hope that they will help our enemy the less in her war of aggression, and contribute more materially to our success by selling us armaments. Such a "one-enemy" foreign policy is the basis of our future success. Otherwise, the Nation will easily be led into a path of thorns, if we adopt the policy of allying with one today and cutting another tomorrow. In Molotov's report, there are several sharp sentences: "In foreign policy, the aim is always not to make more enemies, but rather to lessen the number of enemies." This can be jotted down as a note to the "one-enemy" policy.

But what about Mao Tsê-tung's idea? In fact he preaches "one-ally" policy. He has condemned them all, except for the Soviet Union. Now he again places Soviet Russia in another almost intangible world. What does he mean, then? Does he mean that we can satisfy our hunger by looking at a cake? In fact, this was the same old question long before

disputed. We can all remember that the Communists were the advocates of a military alliance with Soviet Russia. Now it was Soviet Russia, not we, who declined. Those who were boasting of the alliance were Communists; and so were those who stopped it. Soviet Russia said that she alone was too weak and that she hoped China could find more allies. Because of this, the "one-ally" policy did not gain as much support as the British-American-French-Soviet union. When the British-French-Soviet parleys broke off, Mr. Mao found it difficult to give a good explanation, so that he could not but take up the old theory of "one-ally" to ward off attack.

The chief countries helping China in the war are Great Britain, the U. S. A., and Soviet Russia. In the past, at present, and in the future, their central powers of aiding China are economic power from Great Britain, political power from the U. S. A., and military power from Soviet Russia. It is a fact that even if Soviet Russia remains at peace, she can check Japan (unless Soviet Russia proclaims amity with Japan, and makes adequate assurances, in which case it will greatly influence our condition). But the economic power of Great Britain and the political power of the U. S. A. are also absolutely necessary. At present, we are still enjoying these advantages, and the breaking-up of the British-French-Soviet parleys does not influence this situation. We don't know why Mr. Mao is bent upon rejecting the friendly assistance of Great Britain and the U. S. Should we act like this if we believe that "the country and the nation are above all?" Now suppose we follow the Communists and throw ourselves into the bosom of Soviet Russia, are we sure that she will do everything for us? If she signs a treaty with our enemy, what then?

The most unreasonable point in Mao's discussion is his attitude toward Great Britain. He probably wants to please his superiors by guessing their ideas. Perhaps he thinks that the Third International is going back on the policy adopted years ago—the policy of "Anti-Britain" so much sung by Trotsky and his followers. Hence Mao starts this movement in China, and gathers false proofs that Japan and Great Britain will sooner or later be allies so that they can divide up China. Up to now, Mr. Mao's words have not yet become fact. Furthermore, Great Britain has reassured us that her policy towards China will not be changed. To us this is good news—but perhaps unhappy news for Mr. Mao.

Mr. Mao's opinion that we "may approach Germany" does not sound very safe or very natural. Mr. Mao does not adopt the foreign policy of "befriend those who help us and hate those who help our enemy," but rather of "befriend Soviet Russia's friend, attack Soviet Russia's enemies." This is flatly against the principles of independent foreign policy. The old German-Italian line advocated by Wang Ch'ing-wei is wrong because it makes us bend our knees. But we must also know what the new German line amounts to. Japan's *rapprochement* with Soviet Russia and Great Britain are rumors scattered out simultaneously, but are things that cannot be possible. According to foreign telegraphic reports, the German foreign minister is now trying to pull together Japan and Soviet Russia, with the hope of forming a future grand alliance among Germany, Italy, Japan, and Soviet Russia. As to the Japan-Soviet line, it is based upon the "double-south policy" of attacking Great Britain. Japan will move south from the Pacific and [Soviet] Russia will move south from Central Asia, so that British interest in all districts lying between the Near and the Far East will be equally divided up by [Soviet] Russia and Japan. Their method of procedure is like this: 1, A treaty will be signed by Soviet Russia, as the protector of Outer Mongolia, and Japan; Soviet Russia will stop enmity against "Manchukuo" and Japan, so that Japan may concentrate her attention on China. 2, A commercial treaty will be signed between them. 3, A final alliance promising mutual non-interference with appended clauses. Of course this is Germany's dream, or may be a flat rumor, since it is unbelievable that Soviet Russia should join Japan. Even from the point of material benefit, why should Soviet Russia act so as to hurt others but remain doubtful that she can derive real benefit? But to insure absolute safety, we must be careful of any German intrigue. We must warn her often. In the past we used to buy munitions from her, so we must have her goodwill. Now with the War, it is unlikely that Germany will still sell us munitions. Hence why must we still follow Germany and "approach her"? After all, what is the difference between this and the German-Italian line advocated by Wang Ch'ing-wei? Now, just a "warning": if [Soviet] Russia and Japan do join up to form an alliance, I must ask the Chinese Communist Party a question: Concerning the name, the Chinese Communist Party, are they going to throw away the word "Chinese" and adopt a Soviet Russian nationality, or, as said in the *Hsin Min Pao*, to be so base as to join Wang Ch'ing-wei's regime, or shall they stick to the word "Chinese" and cancel the word "Communist"? I hope they will reply to my question.

Concerning the theory of a Second Imperialistic War, Mao himself has for two years forbidden his followers to comment, on the charge of being a Rightist, a closed-door Rightest, a childish Rightest, or a Trotskyite who is plotting with Germany. Now we see that he himself has fully adopted a Trotskyite view. In that article he used the words "progressive" and "retrogressive" to suppress any upheaval within his party; but now what he means by "progressive" is exactly "retardation"; what he formerly advocated as "progress" is now a discarded fig. He is just making a circle, like a donkey fastened to turn a grind-stone, pressed onward by whipping and kicking, and when he has turned half a circle, he may be said to have retarded half a circle.

Now Mr. Mao condemns every country as imperialistic. But we must ask, in his opinion, does he think that Poland is imperialistic? Why is the war of national defense on the part of Poland not a rightful war? Under the exactly similar conditions, why did the Communists formerly show sympathy for Abyssinia and Spain, and are now cold toward Poland? He says that Communists always hate wars; then why did he advocate the Help-Abyssinia Movement? This is a paradox. Perhaps the saying that Communists hate war is invented by Mr. Mao himself. So far as we know, the Communists in Poland, Great Britain, and France are absolutely sympathizing with the Poles in their defensive war.

There is another ridiculous point: Mr. Mao also labelled Chamberlain and Daladier as Fascist Reactionaries. Before the German-Soviet Pact, they were hailed as saints, but now they are convicts, as it were. If Mr. Mao is not satisfied with them, then condemn them as he wishes. But why must he put such a "Fascist" hat upon the oldest democratic countries? This spring, one American politicial commentator predicted jokingly that in the near future Hitler will say that the headquarters of the Communists are located in London and Paris, hence anti-Communist will mean anti-French. Now the direction of this pseudo-prophecy is already established, though Hitler did not give the above reason. But we did not expect that the Chinese Communists would adopt such a belief by calling democratic countries Fascist and by advocating "that we may approach Germany." This is perhaps a conclusion by their special logic.

VI. A Reasonless Conclusion

Concerning the future of China, Mr. Mao made many surface talks, though in general there is no serious fault. But his theories and his conclusions are disjointed. For example, if he makes light of the Polish war, what will be the value of this Oriental war? Besides, is the policy of "single alliance with Soviet Russia" in unison with the principle: "We will befriend those who aid us, and attack those who aid our enemy"? If Soviet Russia aids Japan, what shall then be done? If he opposes the splitting movement, then why not advocate unity? These are but a few of the numerous contradictions that may be found in his article.

Especially strange is his idea that to ally with countries other than Soviet Russia, we should ally with their peoples and not with their governments. But the word "people" is not used in foreign affairs and its meaning is also most indistinct. According to him (I presume) he desires that China fan up revolutions in all countries while carrying on the War of National Resistance. True, the method may apply to Japan, but not to other countries. Otherwise, all world Powers will begin to hate China who is still fighting the War of National Resistance. What will we think of this? Now to speak frankly, the Communists in various countries have not succeeded in fanning up revolutions in their countries, and on the contrary, with their force weakening year after year, what shall we help them for? When we ourselves have not yet stood up firmly, we are already thinking of shouldering a weight of a thousand pounds. Is there a reason in such an attempt? In reality, we know the force of the Chinese proletarian classes. They amount to about two million people, mostly in Shanghai and Tientsin. Now the puppet regimes of Yin Ju-keng and Wang Ch'ing-wei are all formed in these districts. Ch'ên Shao-yü is the chief representative of the Shanghai section of the Communist Party. Has he gone there for an investigation? To whom do those who are performing Anti-Japanese and Anti-Traitor work belong—to the Communist Party, or what? It is better for Communists to moderate their tune and not boast of any more world revolution.

Concerning the present European war, Mr. Mao's attitude is that of a man expressing his joy on seeing others' loss and misfortune. This is not the way of the Chinese people. We always express our sorrow in a war. What General

Chiang has said concerning his hope for peace in Europe is the natural revelation of the Chinese moral character based upon love and compassion. What Mr. Mao expresses is something like the spirit of "kill-kill-kill" advocated by the notorious robber Chang Shen-chou. This is because Mr. Mao has not yet thoroughly imbibed the idea of "Chinafying" things. I express my sympathy for him in his policy of "Chinafication." This of course does not mean that I believe in the preachings of old-fashioned Chinese that the eight planets were first discovered by the Chinese because a line can be found in the *Book of Poetry:*[5] "Three and Five stars in the East." What I mean by sympathy is that I like the way he appreciates the Chinese national culture, and wants to be a one hundred per cent Chinese.[6] In this respect he is more worthy than Ch'ên Shao-yü, and hence deserving of greater achievement.

Lastly, I sincerely hope that Mr. Mao can find a better secretary, without considering the question of class. He must not follow the example of Mr. Lu, the Vice-President of the Anti-Japanese University, who never employs a secretary unless she is beautiful. Though he does not consider the question of class, such actions do not befit Mr. Mao. But speaking about this, we can have a comparison. The second wife of Mr. Mao, Miss Ho, is the heroine who marched with the Red Army for a distance of twenty-five thousand *li* to North Shensi. But why is it that Mr. Mao sends her to Soviet Russia, and lives together with film actress Miss Lan Pin? The reason is quite simple: considering the question of class, Miss Ho stands higher than Miss Lan; considering the question of sexual love, Miss Lan is much more beautiful than Miss Ho. Hence with similar reasoning, I should say that the standard set by Mr. Mao concerning the employment of a secretary will be whether she can write beautifully, and the question of class must not be considered. If so, I can predict that Mr. Mao's articles will be better written, not like his past ones which arouse a great deal of unnecessary argumentation. I hereby humbly present before him my personal ideas.[7]

[5] *Shih Ching,* one of the Confucian classics.
[6] The Americanism, *i-pai-fên chih pai-ti Chung-kuo-jen,* occurs in the original.
[7] The conclusion, couched in billingsgate, is less a violation of the unmentionable in China than it would be in America; but it does strike a note sharply discordant to the gently sardonic tone of the main line of debate. A secretary is germane to the point of

E. CHINA'S LONG-RANGE DIPLOMATIC ORIENTATION (WANG CH'UNG-HUI)[1]

This memorandum was graciously supplied by Dr. Wang Ch'ung-hui.

1. Outline of China's Foreign Policy

Since the establishment of the National Government, China's foreign policy has been elucidated from time to time. Following the outbreak of the war, the Extraordinary Session of the Kuomintang National Congress convened in 1938 laid down five principles:

"1. China is prepared to ally herself with all states and nations that sympathize with her and to wage a common struggle for peace and justice.

"2. China is prepared to safeguard and strengthen the machinery of peace as well as all treaties and conventions that have the maintenance of peace as their ultimate object.

"3. China is prepared to ally herself with all forces that are opposed to Japanese aggression and to safeguard peace in the Far East.

"4. China will endeavor not only to preserve but also to enhance the existing friendly relations with other countries.

"5. China repudiates all bogus organizations which Japan has created and declares all their actions null and void."

2. China's Stand Vis-à-Vis Japan

From the above outline it can be clearly seen that China's foreign policy aims at achieving independence internally and co-existence externally.

Shortly before the outbreak of the Lukouchiao Incident I told a group of Japanese newspapermen in Nanking that "China's diplomatic policy has always been consistent. It aims at self-existence and co-existence . . . It is important to harmonize the friendship between the two peoples; but such a task should not rest only upon the shoulders of one

---

literary style, however; ghost-writing is a rarely disturbed tradition of Chinese public life. Mao Tsê-tung, according to Western observers, is, with Chiang K'ai-shek, one of the few leaders to write his own speeches, so that the present charge, while familiar, is certainly unjust.

[1] Private communication transmitted from Chungking, September 10, 1940; in possession of the present author.

party . . . If any foreign country has any designs on China, the Chinese people are determined to resist . . . I hope Japan will respect China's territorial integrity and political sovereignty and will seek to readjust Sino-Japanese relations through diplomatic channels and in accordance with the spirit of reciprocity and equality."

Japan was bent on disturbing peace and order and launched her attack on North China on July 7, 1937. Not only had every effort at conciliation failed, but the hostilities were extended to Shanghai on August 13th. On the following day the Ministry of Foreign Affairs made China's position clear in an official statement, an extract of which follows:

"The Chinese Government now solemnly declares that China's territorial integrity and sovereign rights have been wantonly violated by Japan in glaring violation of such peace instruments as the Covenant of the League of Nations, the Nine-Power Treaty and the Paris Peace Pact. China is in duty bound to defend her territory and her national existence, as well as the sanctity of the abovementioned treaties. We will never surrender any part of our territory. When confronted with aggression, we cannot but exercise our natural right of self-defense. If Japan did not entertain territorial designs on China, she should use her efforts to seek a rational solution of Sino-Japanese problems and at the same time cease all her aggressions and military movements in China. In the event of such a happy change of heart, China would, in conformity with her traditional policy of peace, continue her efforts to avert a situation pregnant with dangerous possibilities both for East Asia and for the world at large.

"In this our supreme fight not only for a national but for a world cause, not only for the preservation of our own territory and sovereignty, but for the maintenance of international justice, we are confident that all friendly nations, while showing sympathy with us, will be conscious of their obligations under the international treaties to which they have solemnly subscribed."

3. Non-Recognition of Puppet Regimes

With regard to Japanese-sponsored puppet regimes in China, the Chinese Government has consistently denounced them as illegal. On December 20, 1937, following the appearance of the so-called "Provisional Government" in

Peiping, the National Government solemnly declared that "the establishment of any bogus regime in Peiping or other localities under Japanese military occupation constitutes a violation by Japan of China's sovereignty and administrative integrity. Any action taken by such puppet regimes, whether of an internal or external nature, shall *ipso facto* be null and void."

Following the installation by the Japanese of Wang Ch'ing-wei as the chief puppet of the bogus "National Government" in Nanking, the Foreign Minister reiterated this stand in his identic notes of March 30, 1940 to the various embassies and legations in China to the following effect:

"The Chinese Government desires to take this opportunity to repeat most emphatically the declaration already made on several occasions that any act done by such an unlawful organization as has just been set up in Nanking or any other puppet body that may exist elsewhere in China, is *ipso facto* null and void and shall never be recognized by the Chinese Government and people. The Chinese Government is convinced that all self-respecting States will uphold law and justice in the conduct of international relations and will never accord *de jure* or *de facto* recognition to Japan's puppet organization in China. Any manifestation of such recognition, in whatever form or manner, would be a violation of international law and treaties and would be considered as an act most unfriendly to the Chinese nation, for the consequences of which the recognizing party would have to bear full responsibility."

4. China's Foreign Relations Based on Nine-Power Treaty

China's foreign policy relating to the Sino-Japanese hostilities is based upon the Nine-Power Treaty, which provides that the contracting Powers, other than China, agreed to the following:

1. To respect the sovereignty, the independence and the territorial and administrative integrity of China;
2. To provide the fullest and most unembarrassed opportunity to China to develop and maintain for herself an effective and stable government;
3. To use their influence for the purpose of effectually establishing and maintaining the principle of equal opportunity for the commerce and industry of all nations throughout the territory of China.

4. To refrain from taking advantage of conditions in China in order to seek special rights or privileges which would abridge the rights of subjects or citizens of friendly States, and from countenancing action inimical to the security of such States.

Under present conditions, the aggressor is still reluctant to attend any international conference for seeking a just settlement. Therefore, the only alternative is for China to continue her war of resistance until Japan comes to her senses or reaches the point of exhaustion, which can be accomplished through the extension of greater assistance to China and the application of an embargo on military supplies to Japan.

There is no need to elaborate on the well-known fact that the role of the United States in the maintenance of peace in the Pacific area is an important one. We have great confidence in the sense of justice of America, our traditional friend, who realizes the full significance of the so-called "New Order in Greater East Asia," which Japanese spokesmen admit applies to the South Seas region.

World peace and peace between China and Japan are indivisible. An era of prosperity in this part of the world, which cannot but be of benefit to the world in general, can only be ushered in after a just and lasting solution to the Sino-Japanese conflict has been found.

GLOSSARY

[Chinese ideographs have been attached to the names of all the more important political terms, as given in the following list. Proper names may be found with their correct ideographs in *Who's Who in China* and the *Supplement* thereto, cited above. Place-names have been given in the Chinese Postal transliteration; all other names and terms are given in the Wade-Giles spelling, but with the tones omitted. In a few cases, the spelling of a name has been well established by long newspaper usage, by the caprice or decision of a man in re-spelling his own name, or by common practice which has become standard English. Examples are *tuchün*, Kuomintang (instead of *Kuo-min Tang* or *Kuo-min-tang*) and T. V. Soong. Capitalization and hyphenation follow, as closely as possible, the practices established by the *Quarterly Bulletin of Chinese Bibliography*, Peking and Kunming.]

Chan-ti Tang-chêng Wei-yüan-hui 戰地黨政委員會 the (Kuomintang) Party and (National) Government War Area Commission; the Chungking agency for the government of those parts of China technically occupied by the Japanese; under the Military Affairs Commission

chang 長 a chief, or head

Ch'ang-wu Wei-yüan 常務委員 a Standing Committee, or administrative committee

Ch'ang-wu Tz'ŭ-chang 常務次長 an Administrative Vice-Minister (of a *pu*)

chên 鎮 a unit of local government; "community"; the equivalent of a *hsiang*

Chên-chi Wei-yüan-hui 振濟委員會 the (National) Relief Commission

Chêng-chih-pu 政治部 the Political Department (of the Military Affairs Commission); the important and powerful agency which coordinates civilian aid to the war from Chungking, in propaganda, civilian mobilization, etc.; competitive with the Chinese Communists

Chêng-wu Ch'u 政務處 a Political Affairs Department; the political secretariat of a *Yüan*

Chêng-wu Tz'ŭ-chang 政務次長 a Political Vice-Minister (of a *pu*)

Ch'i Chün-tzŭ 七君子 the "Seven Gentlemen"; the leaders of the National Salvation movement

chia 甲 a group of households; a unit in the *pao-chia* system of local government

Chiao-t'ung Pu 交通部 Ministry of Communications

Ch'iao-wu Wei-yüan-hui 僑務委員會 Commission on Overseas Chinese Affairs (under the Executive *Yüan*)

Chiao-yü Pu 教育部 Ministry of Education (under the Executive *Yüan*)

chien-ch'a 監察 one of the five powers of government in the plans of Sun Yat-sen; a combination of impeachment, audit, supervisory investigation and other functions

Chien-ch'a Yüan 監察院 the Control (or Censoral) *Yüan;* one of the five major divisions of the government

Chien Kuo Ta Kang 建國大綱 the *Outline of National Reconstruction*, a manifesto by Sun Yat-sen which charted the subsequent formal policies of the Kuomintang

ch'ih 恥 self-respect; honor

Chin-ch'a-chi Pien-ch'ü Lin-shih Hsing-chêng Wei-yüan-hui 晉察冀邊區臨時行政委員會 "Provisional Executive Committee of the Shansi-Chahar-Hopei Border Region"; formal style of the Border Region, *q.v.*

Ching-chi Pu 經濟部 Ministry of Economic Affairs (under the Executive *Yüan*)

Chiu Kuo 救國 National Salvation; an anti-aggression movement organized outside the Kuomintang

Chu-hsi 主席 chairman; refers particularly to the *Kuo-min Chêng-fu Chu-hsi* (President of the National Government)

ch'ü 區 a unit of local government above the *pao, chia,* and *hsiang,* but below the *hsien* ("county"); a township; with reference to the Party organization of the Kuomintang, a district

GLOSSARY

ch'ü-fên 區分 sub-district; the lowest territorial unit in Kuomintang organization

ch'üan 權 "power," *i.e.*, of the people, as contrasted with the *nêng* (capacity) of the government; the distinction is Sun Yat-sen's, and applies to the political process

Ch'üan-hsü Pu 銓敘部 the Ministry of Personnel; under the Examination *Yüan*

Ch'üan-hsü T'ing 銓敘廳 Administration of Personnel (for the military); under the Military Affairs Commission

Ch'üan-kuo Hui-i 全國會議 the (Chinese Communist) National Party Convention

Ch'üan-kuo Ta-hui 全國大會 the (Chinese Communist) National Party Congress

Ch'üan-kuo Tai-piao Ta-hui 全國代表大會 the (Kuomintang) Party Congress

Chün-chêng-pu 軍政部 the Ministry of War; under the joint jurisdiction of the Executive *Yüan* and the Military Affairs Commission

Chün-fa Chih-hsing Tsung-chien-pu 軍法執行總監部 the Directorate-General of Courts Martial; under the Military Affairs Commission

Chün-hsün-pu 軍訓部 Department of Military Training; under the Military Affairs Commission

Chün-ling-pu 軍令部 Department of Military Operation; office of the Chinese high command; under the Military Affairs Commission

Chün-shih Ts'an-i-yüan 軍事參議院 Military Advisory Council; under the Military Affairs Commission

Chün-shih Wei-yüan-hui 軍事委員會 the Military Affairs Commission; the chief politico-military organ of the National Government

Chung-hua Min-kuo Kuo-min Chêng-fu 中華民國國民政府 literally: the Republic of China, National Government; the style of the National Government under the Kuomintang

Chung-hua Min-kuo Lin-shih Chêng-fu 中華民國臨時政府 the "Provisional Government of the Republic of China," Peking, 1937-1940; pro-Japanese

GLOSSARY

Chung-hua Min-kuo T'ê-ch'ü Chêng-fu 中華民國特區政府 "Special District Government of the Chinese Republic"; the first formal style of the Chinese Soviet area in the Northwest after the intra-national armistice

Chung-hua Min-kuo Hsiu-chêng Kuo-min Chêng fu 中華民國修正國民政府 the "Reorganized National Government of the Republic of China"; the National Government of Wang Ch'ing-wei at Nanking; pro-Japanese

Chung-hua Min-kuo Wei-hsin Chêng-fu 中華民國維新政府 the "Reformed Government of the Republic of China," Nanking, 1938–1940; pro-Japanese

Chung-hua Su-wei-ai Kung-ho-kuo 中華蘇維埃共和國 the Chinese Soviet Republic

Chung-kuo Kê-ming Tang 中國革命黨 the Chinese Revolutionary Party; style of the Kuomintang, 1914–1920; style of the Third Party, 1929–1930

Chung-kuo Kuo-min-tang Kê-ming Hsing-chêng Wei-yüan-hui 中國國民黨革命行政委員會 the Revolutionary Action Committee of the Chinese Kuomintang; first style of the Third Party

Chung-kuo Kung-yeh Ho-tso Hsieh-hui 中國工業合作協會 the Chinese Industrial Cooperatives

Chung-yang Chêng-chih Hsüeh-hsiao 中央政治學校 the Central Political Institute; under the Kuomintang

Chung-yang Chêng-chih Wei-yüan-hui 中央政治委員會 the Central Political Council; the agency whereby the Kuomintang exercised its power over the National Government until the Supreme National Defense Council was created

Chung-yang Chien-ch'a Wei-yüan-hui 中央監察委員會 the (Kuomintang) Central Control Committee

Chung-yang Chih-hsing Wei-yüan-hui 中央執行委員會 the (Kuomintang) Central Executive Committee

Chung-yang Hsüan-ch'uan Pu 中央宣傳部 the (Kuomintang) Party-Ministry of Publicity [or Central Publicity Board]

Chung-yang Wei-yüan-hui 中央委員會 the (Chinese Communist Party) Central Committee

fa-pi 法幣 (National Government) legal tender notes

fang 坊 a territorial unit of municipal government; roughly, a precinct

Fu-hsing Shê 復興社 the Regeneration Club; former center of the so-called Blue Shirts

Fu-hsüeh Wei-yüan-hui 撫邮委員會 the Pensions Commission; under the Military Affairs Commission

Fu I-chang 副議長 Deputy Speaker (of the People's Political Council)

Fu Mi-shu-chang 副秘書長 a Deputy Secretary-General

Fu-yüan-chang 副院長 the Vice-President of a *Yüan* (one of the five divisions of the government)

Hai-chün Tsung-ssŭ-ling-pu 海軍總司令部 Office of the Naval Commander-in-Chief, successor to the Ministry of the Navy which manages the up-river remnants of the Chinese fleet; under the Military Affairs Commission

Hang-k'ung Wei-yüan-hui 航空委員會 the (National) Aviation Commission; under the Military Affairs Commission

Hou-fang Ch'in-wu-pu 後方勤務部 the [Rear-Area] Service Department under the Military Affairs Commission

hsiang 鄉 a unit of local government, also termed *chên;* a village or community

hsiao-tsu 小組 the "small-group"; the lowest fraction of Kuomintang organization

Hsieh-ho-hui 協和會 the Concordia Society; the propaganda agency of Manchoukuo

hsien 縣 district; roughly comparable to the American county

Hsien-fa Ts'ao-an 憲法草案 the Draft Permanent Constitution; the official sponsored project for the new constitution, known most widely in the version of the Double Five Draft of May 5, 1936

Hsin-min-hui 新民會 a political "party" organized by pro-Japanese elements in North China

Hsin Min Chu I 新民主義 a pro-Japanese doctrine taught in occupied North China

Hsin Shêng-huo Yün-tung 新生活運動 the New Life Movement

Hsin-ssŭ-chün 新四軍 New Fourth Army; a guerrilla force under Communist influence; operating in the Yangtze lowlands, it clashed with Chinese National forces early in 1941, and was formally disbanded

Hsing-chêng Fa-yüan 行政法院 the Administrative Court; under the Judicial *Yüan*

Hsing-chêng Yüan 行政院 the Executive *Yüan*, greatest of the five divisions of the government

Hsün-lien T'uan 訓練團 the Training Corps (of the Kuomintang)

Hsün-lien Wei-yüan-hui 訓練委員會 the (Central) Training Committee (of the Kuomintang)

Huangpu 黃埔 the name of a military academy (in Cantonese, Whampoa), now applied to the Generalissimo's protégés as a political faction

hui 會 a meeting, guild, league, or society

Hui-i 會議 a deliberative body; particularly, a City Council (*Shih-chêng Hui-i*)

i 義 propriety; ethics; justice

I-chang 議長 Speaker (of the People's Political Council)

I Ho Ch'üan 義和拳 the "Boxers" of 1900

Kan Shih 幹事 the police executive in a *hsiang* or *chên*

K'ang-chan Chien-kuo Kang-ling 抗戰建國綱領 the Program of Resistance and Reconstruction; the formal declaration of government policy during the invasion; adopted at Hankow in March, 1938

K'ao-hsüan Wei-yüan-hui 考選委員會 the Examinations Commission; under the Examination *Yüan*

K'ao-shih Yüan 考試院 the Examination *Yüan;* one of the five major divisions of the government

Kung-ch'an Ch'ing-nien T'uan 共產青年團 the Communist Youth Corps

Kung-ch'an Tang 共產黨 the (Chinese) Communist Party

Kung-wu-yüan Ch'eng-chieh Wei-yüan-hui 公務員懲戒委員會 the Commission for the Disciplinary Punishment of Public Officers (under the Judicial *Yüan*), a lower agency than the Commission for the Disciplinary Punishment of Public Officials (attached to the Council of State)

Kuo-chia Chu-i P'ai 國家主義派 the "Nationalist Party"; Parti Républicain Nationaliste de la Jeune Chine

GLOSSARY

Kuo-chia Shê-hui Tang 國家社會黨 the (Chinese) National Social(ist) Party

Kuo-fang Tsui-kao Wei-yüan-hui 國防最高委員會 the Supreme National Defense Council; the quasi-governmental agency whereby the Kuomintang controls the National Government; established in 1938 as a war measure, it supersedes the *Chung-yang Chêng-chih Wei-yüan-hui* (Central Political Council)

Kuo-li Chung-yang Yen-chiu Yüan 國立中央研究院 the Academia Sinica; the national scientific and scholastic body, attached to the Council of State

Kuo-min Chêng-fu Wei-yüan-hui 國民政府委員會 "National Government Council"; commonly termed Council of State, this is the highest strictly governmental agency in China

Kuo-min Chêng-fu Chu-hsi 國民政府主席 "chairman of the National Government"; more formally, President of the National Government of China; *ex-officio* chairman of the Council of State, and ceremonial chief of the government

Kuo-min Ching-shên Tsung-tung-yüan 國民精神總動員 the National Spiritual Mobilization

Kuo-min Hui-i 國民會議 the National People's Convention of XX (1931), which adopted the Provisional Constitution

Kuo-min Ts'an-chêng Hui 國民參政會 the People's Political Council; advisory legislature inaugurated in Hankow

Kuo-min Ta-hui 國民大會 the National Congress or People's Congress; this term designates both the constituent body which shall adopt the projected Constitution, and a subsequent constitutional legislature meeting triennially

lao-pai-hsing 老百姓 old inhabitants; common people; archaically or etymologically, the Old Hundred Names

li 禮 rites; ceremonies; ideological conformity

Li-fa Wei-yüan 立法委員 members of the quasi-cameral plenary session of the Legislative *Yüan;* experts in legal matters, they combine the function of legislators with that of consultants in codification

Li-ja Yüan 立法院 the Legislative *Yüan;* one of the five divisions of the government

lien 廉 integrity

lü 旅 a brigade

Mêng-ku Lien-ho Tzŭ-chih Chêng-fu 蒙古聯合自治政府 the "Federated Autonomous Government of Mongolia"; pro-Japanese

Mêng Tsang Wei-yüan-hui 蒙藏委員會 Commission on Mongolian and Tibetan Affairs (under the Executive *Yüan*)

Mi-shu-chang 秘書長 a Secretary-General

Mi-shu Ch'u 秘書處 a Secretariat; particularly important in the case of the Executive *Yüan*

min ch'üan chu-i 民權主義 the "principle of democracy," by Sun Yat-sen; second of the *San Min Chu I*

min-shêng chu-i 民生主義 the "principle of the people's livelihood," by Sun Yat-sen; third of the *San Min Chu I*

Min-ts'u Chieh-fang Hsing-chêng Wei-yüan-hui 民族解放行政委員會 the Acting Commission for the National Emancipation of China; third, final, formal style of the Third Party

min ts'u chu-i 民族主義 the "principle of nationalism," by Sun Yat-sen; first of the *San Min Chu I*

Nei-chêng Pu 內政部 the Ministry of the Interior (or of home affairs); under the Executive *Yüan*

nêng 能 "capacity" (see *ch'üan*)

Nung Lin Pu 農林部 Ministry of Agriculture and Forestry (under the Executive *Yüan*)

Pa-lu-chün 八路軍 "Eighth Route Army"; the chief Chinese Communist force, formerly the Chinese Red Army and now the Eighteenth Army Corps

pao 保 a unit of local government; roughly, a neighborhood

pao-chia 保甲 a system of local government embodying principles of collective responsibility and mutual aid within interlocking groups of households and neighborhoods

Pien-ch'ü 邊區 Frontier Area or Border Region; the former translation is used for the Communist zone in the Northwest, and the latter for the guerrilla government in North China

Pu 部 a Ministry (under the *Yüan*), Department (under the Military Affairs Commission), or equivalent organ of government; the term is one of long standing in Chinese government

Pu Chang 部長 Minister; head of a *pu*

San Min Chu I 三民主義 the three principles of the people; Sun Yat-sen's political philosophy, now the official state dogma of China

San Min Chu I Ch'ing-nien T'uan 三民主義青年團 the *San Min Chu I* Youth Corps

Shan-kan-ning Pien-ch'ü Chêng-fu 陝甘寧邊區政府 the "Government of the Shensi-Kansu-Ninghsia Frontier Area"; second formal style of the Communist zone in the Northwest

Shan-pei Hsing-chêng-ch'ü 陝北行政區 the "Administrative Area of North Shensi"; third formal style of the Communist zone in the Northwest (Frontier Area)

Shê-hui Yün-tung Pu 社會運動部 the (Kuomintang) Party-Ministry of Social Movements

Shên-ch'a Wei-yüan-hui 審查委員會 the (Chinese Communist Party) Control Committee

Shêng 省 a province

Shêng-chang 省長 Governor; the civilian head of a province; now superseded by a Provincial Chairman

Shêng Chêng-fu 省政府 a Provincial Government

Shih 市 a Municipality

Shih-chang 市長 a Mayor

Sui-ching Chu-jên 綏靖主任 a Pacification Commissioner; the chief military officer of a province

Ssŭ-fa Hsing-chêng-pu 司法行政部 the Ministry of Justice, literally the "executive ministry of the judiciary"; under the Judicial *Yüan* in the National Government, but under the executive in the Reorganized Government of Wang Ch'ing-wei

Ssŭ-fa Yüan 司法院 the Judicial *Yüan*, one of the five divisions of the government

ssŭ p'ai 四派 the "four cliques" (in the People's Political Council)

ssŭ tang 四黨 the "four parties" (in the People's Political Council)

Ta-min-hui 大民會 a political "party" organized by pro-Japanese elements in Central China

tang chih 黨治 "party government"; the single-party tutelary dictatorship of the Kuomintang

Tai-piao Ta-hui 代表大會 the (Chinese Communist) "Council of Party Delegates"

Tangpu 黨部 (local) Party Headquarters of the Kuomintang

Ti-san Tang 第三黨 the Third Party; a popular name

Ts'ai-chêng Pu 財政部 Ministry of Finance

Ts'an-chêng-hui 參政會 a People's Political Council; preceded by a term indicating the level at which established, *e.g.*, *Shêng Ts'an-chêng-hui*, Provincial People's Political Council

Ts'an-chün Ch'u 參軍處 Office of Military Affairs; a military secretariat attached to the Council of State

Ts'an-i-hui 參議會 an Advisory Council, as in the Municipality

Tsui-kao Fa-yüan 最高埃院 the Supreme Court; under the Judicial *Yüan*

Tsung-li 總理 the [Party] Leader; the formal office held by Sun Yat-sen in the Kuomintang; his in perpetuity, the title is used as a respectful form of reference to Sun

Tsung-ts'ai 總裁 the [Party] Chief, or leader; title vested in Chiang K'ai-shek as formal head of the Kuomintang by the Emergency Party Congress, Hankow, March, 1938

t'uan 團 a regiment

tuchün 督軍 the military chief of a province, a war-lord

Wai-chiao Pu [also written *Waichiaopu*] 外交部 the Ministry of Foreign Affairs; under the Executive *Yüan*

Wang Tao 王道 "the kingly way," a cardinal concept of traditional Chinese political thought; now, reinterpreted, the state philosophy of Manchoukuo

Wei-shêng Shu 衛生署 National Health Administration (in the Ministry of the Interior)

Wei-yüan-chang 委員長 chairman (of a committee, commission, etc.); this title often refers to Generalissimo Chiang in his capacity of Chairman of the Military Affairs Commission

Wên-kuan Ch'u 文官處 Office of Civil Affairs; a civilian secretariat attached to the Council of State *wu-ch'üan hsien-fa* 五權憲法 the "five power constitution"; the five-fold separation of powers taught by Sun Yat-sen and applied by the National Government

Yüan 院 literally "board"; one of the five divisions of the National Government of China

Yüan-chang 院長 the President of a *Yüan*

Yüeh Fa 約法 the Provisional Constitution, adopted in 1931

INDEX

ABILITY (*nêng*), 253
Academia Sinica (*Kuo-li Chung-yang Yen-chiu Yüan*), 56
Act Governing the Elections of Representatives to the National Congress, 302
Acting Commission for the National Emancipation of China (*Min-ts'u Chieh-fang Hsing-chêng Wei-yüan-hui*), 178
Administration of Personnel (*Ch'uan-hsü T'ing*), 62
Administrative agencies, chart, 80
Administrative Area of North Shensi (*Shan-pei Hsing-chêng-ch'ü*), 112
Administrative Court (*Hsing-chêng Fa-yüan*), 67
Administrative:
 development, 96
 law, 65
 organs, 69
 pattern, 79
Administrative Vice-Minister (*Ch'ang-wu Tz'ŭ-chang*), 96
Adult education, 30
Agitation, 61
Agrarian problems, 104
Agriculture, 91
Agriculture and Forestry, Ministry of (*Nung Lin Pu*), 91
Air communications, 90
Alexander the Great, 239
Alley, Rewi, 224
Amendments to the Constitution (proposed constitutional provisions), 300
American Friends of the Chinese People, 234
American Lease-lend Bill, 217, 274
American loans, 19
Ao-yü-wan, 161
Appointment and discharge of officials, 59
Armistice, intra-national, 10

Army participation in rural reform, 221
Atatürk, Kemal, 272
Audit, Ministry of, 96, 320
Autonomous East Hopei Anti-Communist Government, 185

BANK OF CHINA, 87
Bank of Communications, 87
Basic patterns of modern Chinese politics, 8
Bibliographical notes, 20, 21, 160, 190, 221, 223, 242, 256
"Blue Shirts," 144
Border Region, 16, 35, 116
 chart of government, 118
Boxers (*I Ho Ch'üan*), 213, 237
Buddhism, 258
Budget, 59, 75
Bureaucracy:
 traditional ideal, 44
 at Chungking, 68
Burma, 189
Burma road, 93, 95, 279
Bukharin, 164
Bus services, 93

CABINET, 56
Canton, 18
Cantonese clique, 145
Capacity (*nêng*), 43
Capitalism, 30
Caribbean, 188
Carlson, Major Evans Fordyce, 116, 167
"C.C." clique, 142
Censor *Yüan* (*see* Control *Yüan*)
Censoral power, 27
Censorship of news, 138
Censure, motion of, 314
Central America, 188
Central Bank of China, 87
Central China clique (*Hua-chung P'ai*), 76
Central Executive Committee of the Kuomintang, 72

INDEX

Central government (proposed constitutional provisions), 287
Central Secretariat of the Kuomintang (*Chung-yang Mi-shu-ch'u*), 137
Central News Agency, 137
Central Political Council (*Chung-yang Chêng-chih Wei-yüan-hui*), 16, 46
Central Political Institute (*Chung-yang Chêng-chih Hsüeh-hsiao*), 134
Central Publicity Board (see Party-Ministry of Publicity)
Chamberlain, Neville, 15
Chang, Carson (Chang Chia-shêng), 179
Chang Ching-chiang, 261
Chang Hsüeh-liang, 9, 200
Chang Kuo-tao, 163, 167, 168
Chang Peh Chuen (Chang Pai-chün), 178
Charts (*see also* type of government)
   Control *Yüan*, 318
   Hsien classifications, 388
   Kuomintang organization, 331
   national governmental structure, 330
   provincial and urban government, 98
Chên (*see* Community)
Chen Ch'i-mei, 260
Chen Chi-tang, 91
Chen, Eugene, 178
Ch'ên brothers, 134
Ch'ên Ch'êng, 340
Ch'ên I, 102
Ch'ên Kung-po, 198
Ch'ên Kuo-fu, 84, 134, 142
Ch'ên Kuo-hsin, essay on Mao Tsê-tung, 403
Ch'ên Li-fu, 84, 142
Ch'ên Lo, 204
Ch'ên Shao-yu (Wang Ming), 163
Ch'ên Tu-hsiu, 163
Ch'ê-yeh Chiao-yü P'ai (*see* Vocational Educationists' Clique)
Chia, 107, 324, 395
Chiang Chieh-shih (*see* Chiang K'ai-shek)
Chiang Ching-kuo, 262
Chiang K'ai-shek:
   biography, 254

in Canton, 260
character, 255
childhood, 257
Chinese appraisals, 266
and Christianity, 257
on constitutionalism, 32
Definition of the Problems of Various Classifications of Hsien, 388
ethical theory, 150
governmental role, 48
historical role, 255
ideals, 257
kidnapped at Sian, 10
in the Kuomintang, 128
life, 256
marriage, 261
military rise, 263
military writings, 260
nature of his power, 268
and the New Life Movement, 149
political theory, 265, 269
present personality, 265
and President Lin, 53
relations with Wang Ch'ing-wei, 201
rise in the Kuomintang, 263
and Roosevelt, 278
secret police, 268
in Shanghai, 261
and the Shanghai Communists, 263
statement to the author, 371
Soviet training, 262
and Sun Yat-sen, 245
training in Japan, 259
What I Mean by Action (*Li-hsing Chê-hsiao*), 373
writings, 268
Chiao-shou P'ai (*see* Professors' Clique)
Chicherin, 164
Chief (*Tsung-ts'ai*), 239
Chien-ch'a power, 27
Chien Kuo Ta Kang, 6
Ch'ih, 150
China Branch of the International Peace Campaign, 234
China Defense League, 119
China Forum, The, 235
China Herald, The, 234
"China's Long-range Diplomatic Orientation," 418
China National Aviation Corporation, 93

INDEX 437

Chinese Central Asia (see Sinkiang)
Chinese Communist Party (see Communist Party)
Chinese ideals, 2
Chinese Industrial Cooperatives (see C.I.C.)
Chinese Mass Education Movement, 218
Chinese National Socialist Party (Kuo-chia Shê-hui Tang), 179
Chinese Red Army, 13, 161
Chinese Republic, 2
Chinese Revolutionary Party (Chung-kuo K'ê-ming Tang), 178
Chinese Soviet Republic (Chung-hua Su-wei-ai Kung-ho-kuo), 13, 112, 161
Chinese Turkestan (see also Sinkiang), 85
Chi, C.C., 139
Chin P'u-yi, 184, 256
Ch'in state and dynasty, 2, 107
Ch'in Po-k'u, 168
Chou En-lai, 64, 168
Chou Fu-hai, 198
Christian activities, 235
Chu Djang, 153
Chu-Mao, 166
Chung Fu Joint Mining Administration, 90
Chungking, 1, 15, 18, 56
Chung Shan (see also Sun Yatsen), 249
Chu Tê, 166, 261
Ch'ü, 107, 327, 391
Ch'üan (power), 253
Ch'üan-min K'ang-chan Shê (United Front Club), cited, 37
Ch'u Chia-hua, 136
C.I.C. (Chinese Industrial Cooperatives; Chung-kuo Kung-yeh Ho-tso Hsieh-hui):
 appraisal, 233
 distribution of profits, 230
 establishment, 224
 formation of cooperatives, 226
 the Model Constitution, 232
 regions, 226
 relation to government, 223
 social welfare work, 231
 the three zones, 224

Citizenship (proposed constitutional provisions), 284
City Council (Shih-chêng Hui-i), 104
Civil governor of a province (Shêng-chang), 99
Civil service reform, 66
Civil Service Training Corps, 134
Clark-Kerr, Sir Archibald, 224
Class politics in China, 146
Class war, 13
Coal and iron, 228
Coal mining, 90
Collection of revenue, 86
College students, 9
Commission for the Disciplinary Punishment of Public Officers (Kung-wu-yüan Ch'êng-chieh Wei-yüan-hui), 67
Commission on Mongolian and Tibetan Affairs (Mêng Tsang Wei-yüan-hui), 8
Commission on Overseas Chinese Affairs (Ch'iao-wu Wei-yüan-hui), 84
Committee Chairman (Wei-yüan-chang; see name of Committee)
Communications, Ministry of (Chiao-t'ung Pu), 92
Communications Southward, 95
Communications system, foreign personnel in, 95
Communism, 30, 270
Communist communes, 213
Communist Party (Kung-ch'an Tang), 13, 159, 263, 275
 and American aid to China, 172
 appraisal of, 173
 Branch Party Organs, 363
 Central Party Committee, 368
 chart of structure, 162
 and Chiang K'ai-shek, 175
 Constitution, 359
 Council of Party Delegates, 162, 364
 foundation, 160
 Hsien Organs, 364
 international policy, 403
 leaders, 166
 and Moscow, 163
 motives, 164
 National Party Congress, 367
 National Party Convention, 367
 organization, 361
 and peasants, 165, 213

INDEX

Communist Party (*Continued*)
  in perpetual revolution, 213
  policy toward the Kuomintang, 174
  potential treason, 172
  Provincial Party Organs, 366
  purges and schisms, 169
  Sun Yat-sen's alliance, 245
  Supreme Party Organs, 362
  views on Chaing K'ai-shek, 267
Communist Youth Corps (*Kung-ch'an Ch'ing-nien T'uan*), 132, 370
Communist zone (*see* Frontier Area)
Communists:
  compared with Kuomintang, 146
  and the five-power system, 45
  and the guerrillas, 162
  in the People's Political Council, 76
  policy of collaboration, 121
  and the proposed Constitution, 37
  rivalry with Kuomintang, 159
"Community" (*hsiang*), 107
Community life in China, 4
Complexity of government structure, 61
Concordia Society (*Hsieh-ho-hui*), 194
Conflict: the term, 11
Confucianism, 2, 3, 45, 189, 250
Confucius, 239
Constitution, Chiang's comment on, 32
Constitution of the Chinese Soviet Republic, 31
Constitution of the San Min Chu I *Youth Corps*, 331
Constitutional change, issues of, 31
Constitutionalism, 6, 177, 213, 371
Constitutions (*see also* Draft Constitution), 21
Constitutions, ineffectual, 39
Consultative organs, 39
Control (*chien-ch'a*) power, 27
Control Yüan (*Chien-ch'a Yüan*):
  appraisal, 66
  chart of functions, 318
  diagram of organization, 319
  proposed constitutional provisions, 292
  reorganization under the proposed Constitution, 29
  war work, 313, 318
Cooperatives (*see also* C.I.C.), 89, 393
Corruption, 38, 120
Cotton, 228
Council of State (*Kuo-min Chêng-fu Wei-yüan-hui*):
  administrative and constitutional status, 52
  agencies directly attached, 54
  functions, 47
  proposed constitutional role, 28
County (*see hsien*)
Courts of justice (proposed constitutional position), 292
Credit, national, 86
Currency, Japanese, 186
Currency rivalry, 87
Currents of documents in Chinese government, 55
Customs, 88

Declarations of war and peace, 59
Definition of the Problems Concerning the Organization of the Various Classifications of Hsien, 388
Delegates to the constituent People's Congress, 38
Democracy (*min chu;* Sun Yat-sen's term, *min ch'üan*), 270
Democracy in free China, 371
Democracy, inauguration of, 38
Democracy, prospects, 273
Democracy (*min ch'üan*), the theory of, 253
Democratic Centralism, 162
Democratic tendencies in the armies, 372
Democratic toleration, limits of, 40
Department of Military Operations (*Chün-ling-pu*), 62
Department of Military Training (*Chün-hsün-pu*), 62
Deputy Secretary-General (*Fu Mi-shu-chang*) of the People's Political Council, 73
Deputy Speaker (*Fu I-chang*) of the People's Political Council, 72
Dialectical materialism (*see* Communism, Communists)

INDEX 439

Diplomacy, 310
Diplomatic Orientation, China's Long-range, 418
Direct taxes, 87
Director of Political Affairs, 57
Directorate-General of Courts-Martial (*Chün-fa Chih-hsing Tsung-chien-pu*), 62
Discussion of Mao Tsê-tung's Comments on the Present State of International Relations (Ch'ên Kuo-hsin), 403
District (see hsien for government; *ch'ü* for parties)
Double Five Constitution (see Draft Permanent Constitution)
Draft Permanent Constitution (Hsien-fa Ts'ao-an), 25, 283
Duties and General Activities of the San Min Chu I *Youth Corps*, 340

EAST HOPEI AUTONOMOUS ANTI-COMMUNIST GOVERNMENT, 192
Eastern Inner Mongolia, 85
Economic affairs:
 advance in the West, 89
 industrial development, 90
 in *Program of Resistance and Reconstruction*, 311
 policy and administration, 85
 proposed constitutional provisions, 296
 war finance, 87
Economic Affairs, Ministry of (*Ching-chi Pu*), 88
Economic cycle in China, 106
Economic groups in politics, 236
Economic theory in the *San Min Chu I Youth Corps*, 351
Economics of old China, 3
Education, 30, 61, 83, 214, 312, 393
Education, Ministry of (*Chiao-yü Pu*), 83
Education: proposed constitutional provisions, 298
Eighteenth Army Corps, 168
Eighth Route Army, 13, 168
Election Committee for Representatives to the People's [Constituent] Congress, 38
Elections, Communist, 163
Elections of representatives to the National [People's] Congress, 302
Emergency Session of the Kuomintang Party Congress, 16
Empire, Chinese, 2
Erh Ch'ên group, 142
Espionage, 61
Establishment, period of, 5
Eurasia airlines, 93
Examination *Yüan*, 56, 66, 68, 134
 proposed constitutional provisions, 292
Examinations Commission (*K'ao-hsüan Wei-yüan-hui*), 68
Exclusive inspection, 316
Executive *Yüan* (*Hsing-chêng Yüan*):
 executive responsibility, 57
 functions, 59
 Meeting, 58
 proposed constitutional provisions, 29, 288
 structure, 58

Fa chih (government of laws), 33
Farmers, 218
Farmers' Bank of China, 87
Fêng Yü-hsiang, 104
Fenghua, Chekiang, 262
Farouk, 255
Fascism, 270
Finance, Ministry of (*Ts'ai-chêng Pu*), 86
Five-fold separation of powers, 27, 206, 264
Five-power constitution (*wu-ch'üan hsien-fa*), 42, 68
Five rights, 43
Five *yüan*, 253
Foo Shing Corporation, 88
Foochow insurrection, 179
Ford, Henry, 233
Foreign Affairs, Ministry of (*Waichiaopu*), 81
Foreign financial aid, 87
Foreign policy, 403, 418
Foreign trade, 88
Formosans, 187
Four Cliques (*Ssŭ P'ai*), 76
Four Parties (*Ssŭ Tang*), 76
Four powers, 43
France, 181
Frederick the Great, 255
Free China, extent of, 98
Free China, prosperity, 89, 222

440 INDEX

Freedoms under the proposed constitution:
  assembly and forming associations, 285
  domicile, 284
  religious belief, 284
  speech, writing, and publication, 284
French Indo-China, 19
Friends of the Wounded Society, 155
Frontier Area (for Chinese, see Administrative District of North Shensi), 13, 16, 111, 115, 162
Fu Hsiao-ên, 212
Fukien province, 102, 217
Function of auditing, 313
Fup'ing, 118
Future development of Chinese politics, 274

Gaimusho, 82
Galens, General (Vassili Blücher), 142
Gasoline, 91, 95
Gautama Buddha, 239
General inspection, 316
General Staff, 62
General strikes, 39
Generalissimo (*Tsung-ssŭ-ling*), 61
Genghis Khan, 239
Gentry in politics, 106
George, Henry, 30, 254
Germany, 273, 274
Glossary, 423–433
Gold-washing, 228
Government-owned corporations, 90
Government, nature of, 211
Government organization: chart, 330
Grants in aid to the provinces, 109
Grass cloth, 228
Great Revolution, 5, 60, 213
Green Gang, 261
Groups of households (*chia*), 107
Guerrillas:
  areas, 372
  governments, 116
  and the Military Affairs Commission, 62
  and the National Salvationists, 177
  schools, 84
  strategy, 12
  warfare, 310
  zones under Chungking, 64
Guilds, 10

HAN DYNASTY, 3
Han Fu-ch'u, 202
Hankow, 4, 15
Hanson, Haldore, 116
Hedin, Sven, 255
Highway system, 93
Hitler, Adolf, 239
Hong Kong, 4
Honolulu, Sun Yat-sen in, 243
Hopei-Chahar Political Council, 195
Hopei-Chahar-Shansi Border Region (*Chin-ch'a-ch'i Pien-ch'ü Lin-shih Hsing-chêng Wei-yüan-hui*), Provisional, Administrative Committee of, 116
Ho Ying-chin, 63
Hsiang (or *chên;* "community"), 107, 324, 391
Hsiang guild, 393
Hsiao-tsu ("small group") training program, 354
Hsien ("county" or district), 29, 107, 253, 311
  area, 391
  definition of problems by Chiang K'ai-shek, 388
  experimental, 219
  governments, 391
  organizations of the Communists, 364
  proposed constitutional provisions, 294
  regulations (text), 324
Hsin Min Chu I, 194
Hsin Min Hui, 208
Huang, J. L., 149
Huang Hsing, 245, 259, 262
Huangpu (Whampoa) Academy and political group, 142, 262
Huapeikuo, 194
Hu Han-min, 8, 142, 202, 262
Hui-i (a legislative "council"; *see* level of government concerned)
Hull, Cordell, 278
Hunan, 19
Hung Hsiu-ch'üan, 241

Hu Shih, 215
Hypo-colony, 190

I (ethics), 150
Ideological control, 251
I Ho Ch'üan (Boxers), 237
Impeachment, 313
Impeachment, proposed constitutional provisions, 293
"In accordance with law," 26
Incident, 11
Income taxes, 87
Indirect rule, 183
Indo-China, 183
Indusco (*see* C.I.C.)
Industrial cooperatives (*see* C.I.C.)
Inheritance, the Chinese political, 1
Inheritance taxes, 87
Inner Mongolia, Federated Autonomous Government of (*Mêng-ku Lien-ho Tzŭ-chih Chêng-fu*), 192
Inner Mongolia and Chungking, 85
Inspection systems, 108
Institute of National Culture, 179
Intellectual traditionalism, 251
Interior, Ministry of (*Nei-chêng Pu*), 82
Internal revenue, 88
International Development of China, The, 244
International relations (*see* diplomacy, foreign policy, etc.)
Interpretation of statutes and ordinances: proposed constitutional provisions, 291
Invasion, period of, 5
Italy, 274

JAPANESE:
aims in China, 184
army, 18, 276
army as a Chinese government, 185
attitudes to Chinese foreign policy, 82
Imperial Government in China, 183
prospects in China, 274
recognition of Wang Ch'ingwei, 209
role of the army, 183
subsidiary Chinese governments (*see* Pro-Japanese Groups)
training of Chiang K'ai-shek, 259
Japan's puppets or Japanophiles (*see* Pro-Japanese Groups)
Joint inspection, 316
Judicial Yüan (*Ssŭ-fa Yüan*), 65, 291
Justice, Ministry of (*Ssŭ-fa Hsing-chêng Pu*), 67, 96

K'AN NAI-KUANG, 137, 140
Kang Tê, Emperor of Manchoukuo, the (*see* Chin P'u-yi)
Kao Tsung-wu, 198
Kentwell, L. K., 205
Kialing river, 18
Kiang Kang-hu, 181
Kiangsi, 161
Korea, 189
Kung, H. H., 57, 86, 223
Kung, Mme. H. H. (Ai-ling Soong), 248
Kung so, 393
Kuo-chia Chu-i P'ai (*La Jeunesse* party), 181
Kuomintang:
appraisal of, 146
army connections, 143
attitude toward Communists, 144
Bolshevik pattern of organization, 131
bureaucracy, 7
central administrative structure, 72, 131, 137
Central Control Committee (*Chung-yang Chien-ch'a Wei-yüan-hui*), 127, 131
Central Executive Committee (*Chung-yang Chih-hsing Wei-yüan-hui*), 57, 126, 127, 131
Central Political Institute (*Chung-yang Chêng-chih Hsüeh-hsiao*), 134
Central Publicity Board (*see* Publicity, Party-Ministry of)
Central Training Committee (*Hsün-lien Wei-yüan-hui*), 133
chart of field organization, 139
chart of central organization, 131
chart of general structure, 331
and the Ch'ên brothers, 84
and the Communists, 159

INDEX

Kuomintang (*Continued*)
Congress (*Ch'üan-kuo Tai-piao Ta-hui*), 57
constitutional status, 124
democratic outlook, 143
and economic classes, 135
Emergency Session of the Party Congress, 69, 128
hsiao-tsu ("small-group"), 140, 354
intra-Party politics, 142
membership, 141
monopoly of government, 41
organization, 125, 129, 331
"Orthodox" fraction, 200
Party cell, 140
Party Chief (*Tsung-ts'ai*), 126, 128
Party Congress (see Congress)
Party Constitution, 125
Party democracy, 124
Party-Ministries, 136
Party purges, 141
in the People's Political Council, 76
policy toward Communist Party, 174
purposes, 125
"Reorganized" fraction, 200
rivalry with Communists in the Northwest, 135
"small-group" (*see hsiao-tsu*)
Supreme National Defense Council (*Kuo-fang Tsui-kao Wei-yüan-hui*), 132
Training Corps (*Hsün-lien T'uan*), 133
Wang Ch'ing-wei, 197
Youth Corps (*see San Min Chu I* Youth Corps)
Kwangsi province, 19, 102, 109, 217
Kwangtung province, 102

LABOR:
law, 39
proposed constitutional provisions, 297
La Jeunesse (Parti . . . de la jeune Chine; *Kuo-chia Chu-i P'ai*), 76, 181
Land problem:
proposed constitutional provisions, 296
reform, 106, 110, 218

Landlords, 4, 148, 221
Lao-pai-hsing (the common people), 236
Lattimore, Owen, 3
Law: the term, 299
Laws Governing the System of Organization of the National Government of the Republic of China (1925), 23
Laws Governing the System of Organization of the National Government (1931), 24
Leader (*Tsung-li*), 239
League of Nations Union, 234
Left Kuomintang, 264
Leftists and Leftism, 9, 101, 111, 248
Legal Adviser to the National Government (*Kuo-min Chêng-fu Fa-lü Ku-wên*), 54
Legal tender notes (*fa pi*), 87, 312
Legislative Yüan (*Li-fa Yüan*): function, 65
Members (*Li-fa Wei-yüan*), 66
proposed constitutional provisions, 29, 289
Li (ideological conformity), 150
Li chih (government by *li*), 33
Liang, Hubert, 224
Lien (integrity), 150
Li Hung-chang, 189
Li Li-san, 163
Linebarger, Paul M. W., 54, 105, 242, 246
Lin Pai-shêng, 198
Lin Shên (Lin Sen; Lim Sun), 53, 145
Li Shêng-wu, 206
Literacy, 214, 215
Liu, K. P., 224
Local finance, 402
Local government (*see also hsien*):
appraisals, 109
chart, 107
Chiang K'ai-shek's comment, 397
general role, 98
under the *Hsien Fa*, 29
proposed constitutional reforms, 294
in the recent past, 104
reform of, 311

INDEX

reform under the Kuomintang, 137
reform methods, 108
Long March of the Chinese Reds, 119, 161
Long-Range Diplomatic Orientation, China's, 418
Lung Yün, 101

MAHAYANA BUDDHISM, 259
Mail censorship, 95
Main Office of the Military Affairs Commission, 62
Malaysia, 183
Malraux, André, 161
Manchoukuo, 98, 183, 189, 256
Manchoukuo-Outer Mongol war, 19
Manchu Empire of China (Ch'ing dynasty), 5
Manchuria, 89
Manchus, 2, 241
Mao Tsê-tung, 166, 403–417
Marx, Karl, 241, 254
Marxism, 160, 234, 258, 263
Marxism and Chinese history, 165
Marxism-Leninism, 84
Marxist effect on the *San Min Chu I*, 252
Mass:
action, 10
education, 215
literacy movement, 84
marriages, 153
mobilization, 157
movements, 312
singing, 154
Material and Resources Control and Supervision Ministry, 91
Mayor (*Shih-chang*), 104
Mayors under the proposed constitution, 295
Mazzini, 241
Miao Ping, 194
Migration of schools, 83
Migrations, 88
Militarism in the provinces, 100
Military Advisory Council (*Chün-shih Ts'an-i-yüan*), 62
Military affairs, 310
Military Affairs Commission (*Chün-shih Wei-yüan-hui*), 13, 60, 162
Military governor (*tuchün*), 99
Military jurisdiction under the *Hsien Fa*, 284

Military policy, 61
Military service under the *Hsien Fa*, 285
Military unification, 6
Militia, 393
Min-ch'üan chu-i (see Democracy, Sun Yat-sen, and *San Min Chu I*)
Min shêng chu-i, 30, 223, 253
Min ts'u chu-i (see Nationalism, Sun Yat-sen, and *San Min Chu I*)
Ming Emperors, 249
Minister (*Pu Chang*), 96
Ministry of —— (see name of Ministry)
Ministries, 81
Minor parties:
and constitutionalism, 34
at Nanking, 208
in occupied China, 235
representation, 72
status, 160
Minority democracy, 41
Mobilization, economic, 86
Model *hsien*, 109
Modernization of West China, 89
Mohammed, 239
Monarchist legitimism, 184
Morale, governmental, 236
Moscow (see Communism)
Moslem rebellions, 213
Motor communications, 93
Motor fuel trade, 90
Municipal Advisory Assembly (*Shih Ts'an-i-hui*), 72, 104
Municipal food stores, 90
Municipal government, 103
Municipal People's Political Council (see Municipal Advisory Assembly)
Municipalities under the *Hsien Fa*, 295
Munitions, 90

NANKING, capture of, 14
Nanking regimes (see Reorganized Government; Reformed Government)
Napoleon, 239
"National" (see also "People's," "Chinese")
National Aviation Commission, 63
National capital in the *Hsien Fa*, 284

National [Constituent] Congress (*Kuo-min Ta-hui*), 25, 27, 300
National Congress: election of representatives, 302
National Congress: system of organization, 300
National Government (*Kuo-min Chêng-fu*): the term, 52
National Government Committee (*see* Council of State)
National Health Administration (*Wei-shêng Shu*), 83
National Institute of Rural Reconstruction, 220
National Military Council (*see* Military Affairs Commission)
National People's Convention (*Kuo-min Hui-i*), 7
National Relief Commission (*Chên-chi Wei-yüan-hui*), 92
National Salvation (*Chiu Kuo*) movement, 175
National Socialism (German), 252
National Socialist Party (*Kuo-chia Shê-hui Tang*), 75, 179
National Spiritual Mobilization (*Kuo-min Ching-shên Tsung-tung-yüan*), 157
National treasury, 88
Nationalism (*min ts'u*), theory of, 252
Negrin, 15
Neighborhood (*pao*), 107
Nêng (ability), 253
New Fourth Army (*Hsin-ssǔ-chün*), 119
New Life Movement (*Hsin Shêng-huo Yün-tung*), 149
New Life Secretaries' Camp, 155
New Life Students Rural Summer Service Corps, 154
New Order in East Asia, 184, 189
News services, 137
North China, 14
North Shensi (*see also* Frontier Area), 161
Northeastern Clique (*Tungpei P'ai*), 76

OCCUPIED CHINA:
Chungking control over, 64
missions, 235
poverty, 92

Office of Civil Affairs (*Wên-kuan Ch'u*), 54
Office of Military Affairs (*Tsan-chün Ch'u*), 54
Office of the Naval Commander-in-Chief (*Hai-chün Tsung-ssǔ-ling-pu*), 63
Office of Political Affairs (*Chêng-wu Ch'u*), 57
Officers' Moral Endeavor Corps, 63, 149
Old China:
economics, 3
government, 5
socio-economic structure, 211
in Sun Yat-sen's theory, 251
Old Hundred Names (*lao-pai-hsing*), 236
Opinion, public, 39
Organic Law of XVII (1928), 28
Organization of the Kuomintang, etc. (*see* relevant group or agency)
"Orthodox" Kuomintang, 200, 207
Outer Mongol People's Republic, 183, 188
Outline of National Reconstruction, 6
Outline of War-Time Control-ment, 313
Outlines of Political Tutelage, 24
Overseas Chinese, 84

PACIFICATION COMMISSIONER (*Sui-ching Chu-jên*), 100
Pai Chung-hsi, 102
pai-hua (written vernacular), 215
Pan American airlines, 93
Panchen Lama, 71
Pan Ch'ao, 81
Pao ("neighborhood"), 107, 324, 394
Pao schools, 216
Pao-chia system, 106
Paper money, 86
Parti Républicain Nationaliste de la Jeune Chine (*see* Kuo-chia Chu-i P'ai)
Party Affairs Committee of the Kuomintang (*Tang-wu Wei-yüan-hui*), 133
Party Chief (*Tsung-ts'ai*), 41
Party Constitution (*Tang-chang*):
Communist, 359
Kuomintang, 125

INDEX

Party dictatorship (*tang chih*), 6, 23
Party-government relations, 49
Party and Government War Area Commission (*Chan-ti Tang-chêng Wei-yüan-hui*), 64, 112
Party headquarters, 141
Party-politics, 158
Party-politics in the People's Political Council, 76
Party Supervisor's Net (*Tang-jên Chien-ch'a Wang*), 141
Party-Ministries of the Kuomintang, 136
Party's role in the constitutional system, 23
Peasant rebellions, 4
Pensions Commission (*Fu-hsüeh Wei-yüan-hui*), 62
People's Advisory Political Council (*see* People's Political Council)
People's Congress (*see* National Congress)
People's Foreign Relations Association, 234
People's Political Council (*Kuomin Ts'an-chêng Hui*):
competence, 73
election, 72
function of representation, 66
membership, 70
nominations, 71
practicality, 74
procedure, 74
in *Program of Resistance and Reconstruction*, 311
reorganization, 75
sessions, 70
Permanent Constitution, Draft (*Hsien-fa Ts'ao-an*), 5, 25, 283
Personnel, Ministry of (*Ch'üan-hsü Pu*), 68, 96
Philosophy of Action, A, 373
Pi Chiao Hsien Fa (*Comparative Constitutions*, by Wang Shihchieh), translated and quoted, 23, 49, 50, 52, 67, 125
Pilsudski, 272
Planning Committee for the Western Capital (*Hsi-ching Ch'ou-pei Wei-yüan-hui*), 56
Pluralism, 3, 211

Policy-making, 47, 74, 79
Political Affairs Department or Office (*Chêng-wu Ch'u*), 57
Political commissars in the army, 63
Political Department (*Chêng-chih-pu*) of the Military Affairs Commission, 64
Political laxity, 251
Political rights: proposed constitutional provisions, 285
Political Scientists' group (*Chêng-hüeh Hsi*), 145
Political Vice-Minister (*Chêng-wu Tz'u-chang*), 96
Politics of ideology, 8
Popular democracy, 39
Popular Front group, 78, 129
Popular government in the Border Region, 119
Population, 3
Poverty in occupied China, 222
Power (*ch'üan*), 43, 253
Pragmatic utilitarianism of Sun Yat-sen, 252
Presidency proposed under the *Hsien Fa*, 28, 287
President (*Yüan-chang*) of the Executive Yüan, 56
President (*Chu-hsi*) of the National Government, 52
Presidium of the People's Political Council, 73
Pressure politics, 234
Prime movers, 229
Principles of the Great People (*Ta Min Chu I*), 196
Private rights: proposed constitutional provisions, 284
Private property: proposed constitutional provisions, 285
Privy Council, 56
Problems of the *hsien:* comment of Chiang K'ai-shek, 388
Professors' Clique (*Chiao-shou P'ai*), 77
Program of Resistance and Reconstruction (*K'ang-chan Chien-kuo Kang-ling*), 17, 35, 309
Pro-Japanese elements, 186, 192, 212, 276, 310
Propaganda, 61, 137
Proposition, 314
Prosperity, 222
Protestant schools, 215

446 INDEX

Provincial Governments (Shêng Chêng-fu):
Chairman (Shêng Chêng-fu Chu-hsi), 100, 294
connection with central government, 82
councils, 72
current role, 98
proposed constitutional provisions, 293
Provincial People's Political Councils (Shêng Ts'an-chêng-hui), 103
structure, 102
Provincialism, 8, 99
Provisional Constitution (Yüeh Fa), 22, 24
Provisional Executive Committee of the Shansi-Chahar-Hopei Border Region (Chin-ch'a-chi Pien-ch'ü Lin-shih Hsing-chêng Wei-yüan-hui; see also Border Region), 16
Provisional Government of the Republic of China (Chung-hua Min-kuo Lin-shih Chêng-fu), 14, 192, 207
Pu (ministries or departments), 61
Public Administration, School of, 219
Public opinion, 214
Public service: proposed constitutional provisions, 285
Public utilities: proposed constitutional provisions, 296
Publicity, 79
Publicity, Party-Ministry of (Chung-yang Hsüan-ch'uan Pu), 137
Publicity of the San Min Chu I Youth Corps, 350
"Puppet states," 188
Purple Mountain, 249
P'u Yi (see Chin P'u-yi)

RACES: proposed constitutional provisions, 284
Radio, 94
Railways in Free China, 92
Resistance and Reconstruction, Program of, 309
Reformed Government of the Republic of China (Chung-hua Min-kuo Wei-hsin Chêng-fu), 17, 192, 195

Regeneration Club (Fu-hsing Shê), 144
Regional autonomy, 8
Regular troops, 8
Regulations Concerning the Organization of the Various Classifications of Hsien, 324
Relief, 61, 297
"Reorganized Kuomintang," 200
Reorganized National Government of China (Hsiu-chêng Kuo-min Chêng-fu):
affiliation with Japan, 183
creation and function, 197
personnel, 204
practical work, 205
significance to Chiang K'ai-shek, 372
status, 203
Representation, function of, 66
Republic: the term, 161
Republican revolution, 213
Republicans (Kung-ho Tang), 208
Resident Committee of the People's Political Council, 73
Resist-Japan University, 84
Resistance, 12, 213
Revolution by three stages, 6, 22, 35, 253
Revolutionary Action Commission of the Chinese Kuomintang (Chung-hua Kuo-min-tang K'ê-ming Hsing-chêng Wei-yüan-hui), 178
Rights, constitutional, 28
Roosevelt, Franklin D., 233, 278
Rosinger, Lawrence K., 81
Rural education, 218
Rural reconstruction, 218, 397
Rural Service Corps, 154
Russian Soviet Federal Socialist Republic, (R.S.F.S.R.), 188

SALAZAR, Antonio de O., 272
San Min Chu I:
and Chiang K'ai-shek, 270
explanation and comment, 8, 13, 34, 178, 245, 250, 371
and Hsin Min Chu I, 194
proposed constitutional provisons, 287
San Min Chu I Youth Corps (San Min Chu I Ch'ing-nien T'uan):
appraisal, 352

INDEX

chart of organization, 345
Constitution, 331
description by General Ch'ên Ch'êng, 340
history, 341
and the Kuomintang, 132
Leader, 342
Salt gabelle, 88
Scholars of old China, 3
Scholastic bureaucracy, 3, 250
School for the Border Provinces, 135
Schools (see education), 216
Scorched earth policy, 12
Second Revolution, 259
Secret societies, 10
Secretariat (Mi-shu-ch'u), 57, 73
Secretary-General (Mi-shu-chang), 57, 73
Service Department, military (Hou-fang Ch'in-wu-pu), 63
Seven Gentlemen (Ch'i Chün-tzu), 36, 76, 176
Shanghai, 13
Sharecropping, 91
Sheean, Vincent, 161
Shên Chun-lu, 176
Shêng Shih-ts'ai, 176
Shensi (see Frontier Area)
Shensi-Kansu-Ninghsia Frontier Area (Shan-kan-ning Pien-ch'ü Chêng-fu), 112
Shih (see municipality, q.v.)
Sian affair, 5, 10, 176
Sinkiang (Chinese Central Asia; Chinese Turkestan), 85, 101
Sino-American trade, 88
Sino-Siberian highway, 93, 95
Small-Group Training Program, 354
Smith, Joseph, 241
Snow, Edgar, 146, 160
Social Affairs, Ministry of, 96
Social Movements, Party-Ministry of (Shê-hui Yün-tung Pu; also translated Party-Ministry of Social Affairs, Board of Social Affairs), 96, 136
Social Democratic Party, 181
Social rigidity, 251
Social work, 61
Social work of the *San Min Chu I* Youth Corps, 351
Socialist Party, 181, 208
Soong, C. J., 247
Soong, T. V., 9, 86, 248

Soong Ching-ling, 245
Soong sisters, 248
Sovereignty: proposed constitutional provisions, 283
Soviet China, 275
Soviet form of government in China, 45
Soviet influence in Sinkiang, 101
Soviet-Japanese understanding, 275
Soviet policy in China, 171
Soviet training of Chiang K'ai-shek, 262
Soviet Union (see also Communists; Marxism), 188, 273, 275
Speaker (I-chang) of the People's Political Council, 72
Special Administrative District of the Chinese Republic (Chung-hua Min-kuo T'ê-ch'ü Chêng-fu), 112
Special-area governments, 98, 111, 120
Special inspection, 316
Special Regional Government . . . (see Special Administrative District . . .)
Specie, 86
Stalemate, 12
Stalin, Joseph, 263
Stalinism (see also Communist Party), 234
State Council (see Council of State)
State examinations: proposed constitutional provisions, 285
State socialism, 30, 89
Steamships, 93
Strategy of the Chinese, 12
Sub-district (ch'ü-fên) of the Kuomintang, 126, 139
Subterranean minerals: proposed constitutional provisions, 296
Sung Ai-ling (see Kung, Mme. H. H.)
Sung Ch'ing-ling (see Sun Yat-sen, Mme.)
Sung Mei-ling, 248, 261
Sung Tzu-wên (see Soong, T. V.)
Sun I-hsien (see Sun Yat-sen)
Sun K'ê (Sun Fo), 66, 145, 247
Sun Yat-sen:
biography, 240
doctrines (see also *San Min Chu I*), 6

448 INDEX

Sun Yat-sen: (*Continued*)
  family, 247
  historical role, 239
  on imperialism, 190
  on local government, 105
  Provisional President, 244
  revolutionary technique, 244
  sense of mission, 240
  state planning, 245
  Western training, 242
Sun Yat-sen, Mme., 145, 178, 247
Supreme Court (*Tsui-kao Fa-yüan*), 67
Supreme National Defense Council (*Tsui-kao Kuo-fang Wei-yüan-hui*), 16, 46
Symbolism of government, 45
System of organization of the National Congress, 300
Szechwan, 181

T'AI LI, 145
T'aip'ing Rebellion, 161, 213, 241
Taiwanese, 187
Ta Min Chu I, 196
Ta-min-hui, 196, 208
Tang Cheng Chien Chih T'u-piao, cited, 46, 54
T'ang Leang-li, 198
Tannu-Tuva, 189
Tao Hsi-shêng, 198
Tayler, J. B., 224
Taylor, George, 116
Taxation: proposed constitutional provisions, 285
Telecommunications, 93
Telegraph, 94
Telephone, 94
Têng Yen-ta, 178
Territory: proposed constitutional provisions, 283
Third International (*see also* Communist Party), 71, 161, 245
Third Party (*Ti-san Tang*), 178
Three-Power Pact, 274
Three-stage war, 12
Three stages of revolution (*see* Revolution by three stages)
"Three principles of the people" (*see San Min Chu I*)
Tibet, 85
Tientsin, 4
Tinghsien, 219
Tong, Hollington, 138, 255
Tongs (*tang*), 261

Township (ch'ü), 107
Training Committee (*Hsün-lien Wei-yüan-hui*) of the Kuomintang, 133
Training conferences, 109
Trans-Sinkiang highway, 93
Tridemism (*see San Min Chu I*)
Trotsky, Leon, 164, 263
Truck service, 93
Tseng Chi, 181
Tso Shen-sheng, 181
Tso Tao-fên, 36, 176
Tsung-ts'ai, 41
Tuchünism, 5, 244
Tungpei P'ai (*see* Northeastern Clique)
Turksib railroad, 101
Tutelage, period of, 7
Tutelary dictatorship (*tang chih*), 23
Types of government sponsorship, 89

UNEARNED INCREMENT, 30, 296
United Council of the pro-Japanese, 195
United Front, 70, 111, 113, 119, 129
United States of America, 273, 275, 277, 279
Universal Trading Corporation, 88
Urban pattern of local government, 104
Utterances on Reconstruction, The Party Chief's (*Tsung-ts'ai Chien-kuo Yen-lun Hsüan-chi*), quoted, 33

VAYO, Julio Alvarez del, 15
Vice-President of a *Yüan* (*Fu-yüan-chang*), 57
Vocational education, 217
Vocational Educationists' Clique (*Ch'ê-yeh Chiao-yü P'ai*), 77

WANG CH'ING-WEI, 20, 53, 56, 129, 142, 145, 192, 197, 239, 263, 372
  agreements with the Japanese, 203
  flight from Chungking, 203
  following, 197
  record of schism, 199
  significance, 208
Wang Ch'ung-hui, 82, 418

INDEX

Wang K'ê-min, 194
Wang Ming, 257
Wang Shih-chieh, 23, 73, 137
Wang Tao, 194
War Area Service Corps, 154
War finance, 87
War, Ministry of (*Chün-chêng-pu*), 60, 63, 96
War: the term, 11
War-time Controlment, Outline of, 313
Washington, George, 255
Water-conservancy regions, 4
Western imperialism, 4, 190
Western states, 3
Whampoa (*see Huangpu*)
What I Mean By Action, 373
William, Maurice, 254
Wireless, 94
Women's Advisory Council of the New Life Movement, 155
Wong Wen-hao, 91
Wool, 227
Workers' living conditions: proposed constitutional provisions, 296

World federation, 371
World government: comment of Chiang, 281
Wounded Soldiers' League, 155
Wu, Dr. John C. H., 26
Wu-han government, 15
Wu Pei-fu, 198

YANG KAN-TAO, 181
Yangtze, 18
Yeh Ch'u-tsang, 137
Yen, Dr. James Y. C., 84, 218
Yenan, 115
Yin Ju-kêng, 185, 192
Y. M. C. A., 149, 235
Young, Brigham, 241
Yüan, 24, 28
Yüan-chang, 28
Yüan Shih-k'ai, 244, 259
Yü Yu-jên, 145
Yünnan, 101

ZINOVIEV, G., 164

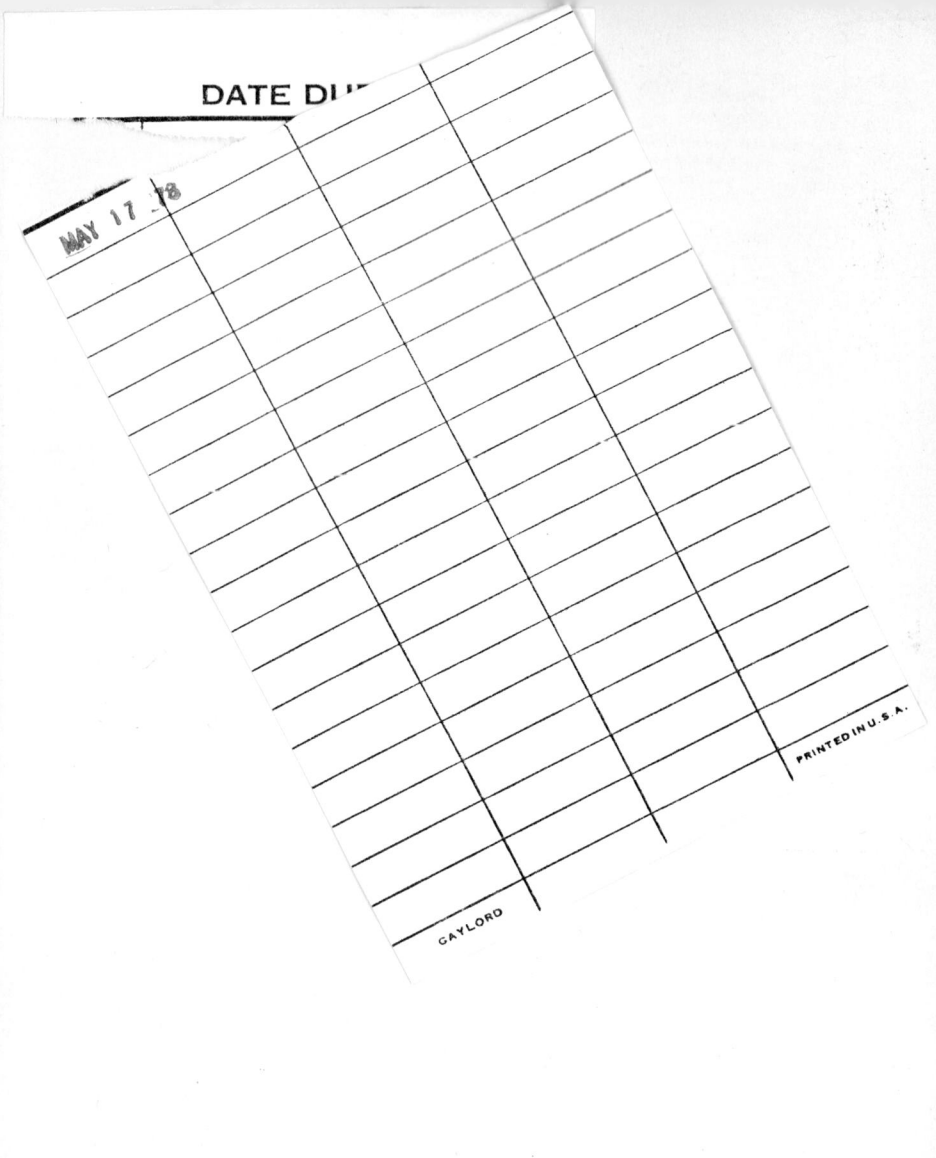